AELRED OF RIEVAULX'S
DE INSTITUTIONE INCLUSARUM

EARLY ENGLISH TEXT SOCIETY

Original Series 287

1984

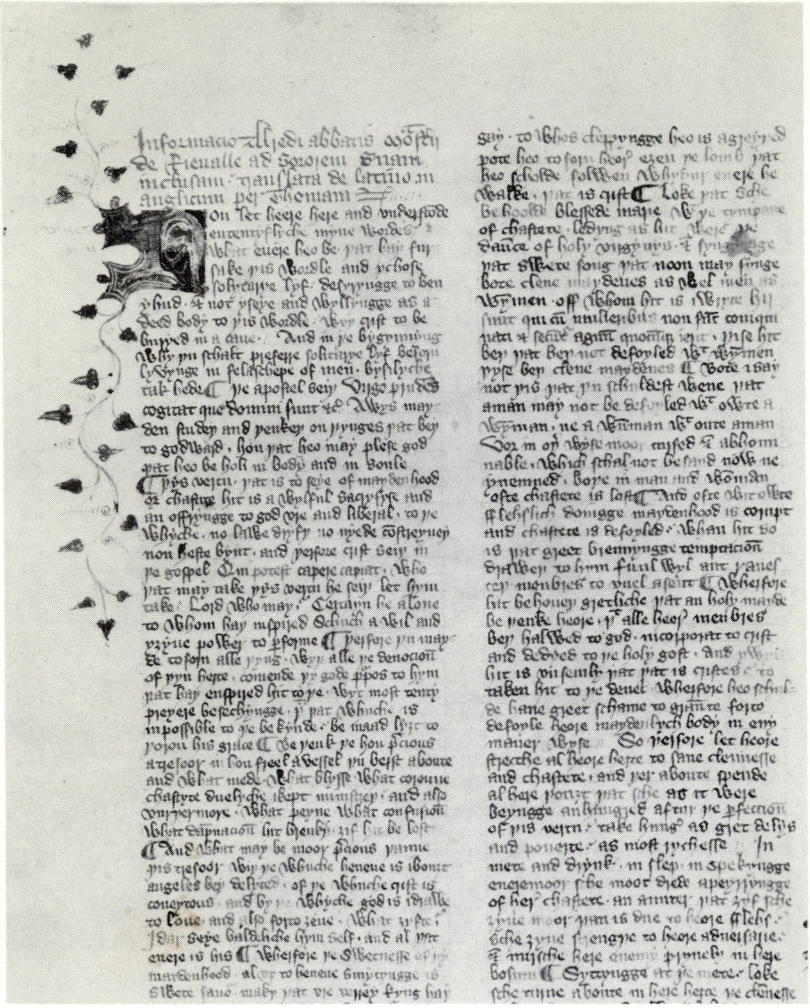

Plate I: MS Bodley Eng. poet. a. 1, f. iii^v (top)

AELRED OF RIEVAULX'S DE INSTITUTIONE INCLUSARUM

Two English Versions

EDITED BY

JOHN AYTO

AND

ALEXANDRA BARRATT

Published for
THE EARLY ENGLISH TEXT SOCIETY
by the
OXFORD UNIVERSITY PRESS
LONDON   NEW YORK   TORONTO
1984

Oxford University Press, Walton Street, Oxford OX2 6DP

London   Glasgow   New York   Toronto
Delhi   Bombay   Calcutta   Madras   Karachi
Kuala Lumpur   Singapore   Hong Kong   Tokyo
Nairobi   Dar es Salaam   Cape Town
Melbourne   Wellington

and associate companies in
Beirut   Berlin   Ibadan   Mexico

Published in the United States by
Oxford University Press, New York

British Library Cataloguing in Publication Data
Aelred, of Rievaulx
De institutione inclusarum.—(Early English Text
Society. Original series, 287)
1. Meditation
I. Title II. Ayto, John III. Barratt, Alexandra
IV. Series
248.3'4   BV4830
ISBN 0 19 722289 7

Phototypeset in Linotron 202 Imprint by
Western Printing Services Ltd, Bristol
Printed and bound at
The Pitman Press, Bath

CONTENTS

PREFACE   vii

ABBREVIATIONS   viii

INTRODUCTION

1. Aelred of Rievaulx   xi

2. Manuscripts   xiii

3. The Middle English translations and their relations with the textual tradition of the Latin   xxxii

4. The *De Institutione Inclusarum* and *Ancrene Wisse*   xxxviii

5. The language of the translations   xliii

SELECT BIBLIOGRAPHY   lvii

NOTE ON THE TEXTS   lix

THE TEXTS

MS Bodley 423   1

MS Bodley Eng. poet. a. 1 (Vernon MS)   26

NOTES   61

GLOSSARY   159

MS Bodley 423   161

Vernon MS   172

PLATES

I MS Bodley Eng. poet. a. 1, f. iii^v *frontispiece*

II MS Bodley 423, f. 178   *facing p. 1*

PREFACE

THE primary debt of the editors is to Dr A. George Rigg and Mr V. E. Watts, who supervised the theses on which this edition is based. We also wish to thank the Reverend Edmund Colledge, O.S.A., for assistance at an early stage of preparation, and Professor G. V. Smithers, Dr A. I. Doyle, the Reverend Leonard Boyle, O.P., Professor A. McIntosh, Mr Alan Thomson, Mr J. E. Fagg and Dr J. D. Thomas for help on particular aspects of our work. We are also grateful to the Bodleian Library for permission to reproduce pages from MS 423 and from the Vernon MS.

The Canada Council has throughout supported this edition by its Doctoral Fellowships and a Research Grant, while Miss Linda Clarke and Miss Catherine Keay provided invaluable assistance.

Our thanks are due finally to Dr Pamela Gradon for her help and encouragement in preparing this edition for the press.

ABBREVIATIONS

1. Languages and general

AF	Anglo-French	lME	late Middle English
AN	Anglo-Norman	lOE	late Old English
Du	Dutch	ME	Middle English
Eccl. L	Ecclesiastical Latin	ML	Medieval Latin
eME	early Middle English	NE	Modern English
F	French	OA	Anglian dialects of Old English
G	German		
Germ.	Germanic	OE	Old English
H.	C. Horstmann's edition of *De Institutione Inclusarum* in *Englische Studien*, VII (1884), 304–44	OF	Old French
		OK	Kentish dialect of Old English
		OM	Mercian dialect of Old English
L	Latin	ON	Old Norse
L.	The Latin text of *De Institutione Inclusarum*, ed. C. H. Talbot, *Aelredi Rievallensis Opera Omnia*, *CCCM I* (Turnholt, 1971), 637–82	ONF	Northern dialects of Old French
		prepl.	prepositional
		WS	West Saxon
		‡	hapax legomenon
*	(i) (before a word) hypothetical form; (ii) (before a line-reference) emended form		

2. *Sigla* of the Latin manuscripts of *De Institutione Inclusarum*

B	MS Bodley 36	N	BL MS Cotton Nero A III
D	MS Digby 218	R	BL MS Royal 8 D III
H	Hereford cath., MS P.I.XVII	T	MS Bodley Lat. theol. d.27
		U	MS Paris, Univ. 790

Ha   MS Hatton 101   V   MS Utrecht, Rijksuniv. 104
M   MS Mazarine 616

For full titles of works referred to by abbreviated titles or
by the author's surname, see Select Bibliography.

INTRODUCTION

I. AELRED OF RIEVAULX

Aelred of Rievaulx, one of the leading and most influential figures of early English Cistercianism, was born at Hexham in 1110 and died at Rievaulx Abbey, of which he had been abbot for some twenty years, on 12th January 1167. He left behind him, as well as a distinguished reputation as an active and compassionate churchman both within the confines of his own order and in a wider national context, a corpus of writings that is the finest literary and philosophical product of the Cistercian order in medieval England.[1]

His output falls into two main categories: historical works, such as a tract on the battle of the Standard, a life of Edward the Confessor and the *Genealogia regum Anglorum*; and religious and philosophical works. Of the latter, on which his reputation as a writer is largely based, the most important are the *Speculum Caritatis* (his first work), *De Spirituali Amicitia*, *De Anima* and *De Institutione Inclusarum*, a treatise on the ordering of the external and inner life of an anchoress, written in the form of a letter to his sister.

The influence of Aelred's writings continued to be felt throughout the Middle Ages, albeit often anonymously: his concept of the threefold meditation, for example, to be described below, found its widest audience through the medium of an English pseudo-Anselmian collection of meditations into which it was incorporated in the fourteenth century,[2] and *De Spirituali Amicitia* and *De Iesu Puero*, as well as *De Institutione Inclusarum*, were at various times attributed to other writers. Specific medieval references to Aelred and his works are limited

---

[1] His biography was written not long after his death by Walter Daniel (ed. F.M. Powicke, *The Life of Ailred of Rievaulx* (London, 1950)), a monk of Rievaulx and close companion of Aelred in his last years, which, although it is not free from some of the usual exaggerations of the hagiographer, is by and large a reliable work. The current standard study is A. Squire, *Aelred of Rievaulx* (London, 1969).

[2] See A. Wilmart, *Auteurs Spirituels et Textes Dévotes du Moyen Age Latin* (Paris, 1932, repr. 1971), p. 192.

to brief notices in *Upland's Rejoinder*[3] and the *Speculum Inclusorum*[4] and a well-known acknowledgment by the author of *Ancrene Wisse* of his debt to Aelred.[5] Somewhat surprisingly, extensive Middle English translations of only two of Aelred's Latin writings are known to have been made: one is the *Speculum Caritatis*, an extract from which is translated in the late fourteenth century *The Chastising of God's Children*;[6] the other is *De Institutione Inclusarum*, the two independent translations of which are edited in this volume.

De Institutione Inclusarum, which was probably written between about 1160 and 1162, is one of the two outstanding examples of the genre of the anchoritic rule produced in England in the Middle Ages, the other of course being *Ancrene Wisse*. Aelred's work shares with *Ancrene Wisse* the characteristic of being more than simply a set of peremptory injunctions concerning the recluse's external observances. The first fourteen sections of *De Institutione Inclusarum* are concerned with the non-spiritual aspects of the anchoritic life, such as the choice of diet and clothing that are proper to the anchoress, but the remaining and most substantial part of the work has as its subject the anchoress's inner life.

Aelred's treatment of this inner life falls into two sections. The first of these, which comprises §§ 14–28 of L. (chapters 9–13 of Bodley, chapters 1–13 of Vernon), is an ascetic guide – directives on personal morality, the virtues (especially that of chastity) and their preservation. The second, §§ 29–33 of L. (chapters 14–16 of Bodley, chapters 14–19 of Vernon), deals with private prayer and meditation, and is in many ways the most interesting and important part of *De Institutione Inclusarum*.

Aelred's technique of threefold meditation – meditation on things past, things present and things to come – which is here expounded, is undoubtedly his most appealing, and most original, contribution to the history of Latin spirituality. The practitioner of this meditative technique is enjoined successively to recreate imaginatively events from the life of Christ and

[3] ed. P. L. Heyworth, *Jack Upland, Friar Daw's Reply and Upland's Rejoinder* (Oxford, 1968), 'Upland's Rejoinder', ll. 341–3.
[4] ed. L. Oliger, *Lateranum*, Nova Series an. 4 no. 1, p. 140.
[5] See p. xxxix, note 1.
[6] ed. J. Bazire and E. Colledge (Oxford, 1957).

ponder on their implications for her (chapter 14 of Bodley, chapters 14–17 of Vernon), to meditate on her self and her present life, so that knowledge of self might lead to knowledge of God (chapter 15 of Bodley, chapter 18 of Vernon), and finally to contemplate the Four Last Things: death, judgment, hell and heaven (chapter 16 of Bodley, chapter 19 of Vernon). By such means the recluse attains to the rebirth of the soul through Christ that is the broad central theme of the work.

Although it is not the most unusual or original aspect of Aelred's meditative technique (according to a recent editor of his, parallels may be found in Origen and Jerome[7]), his exposition of meditation on things past was probably the most influential. This practice, which involves the imaginative reconstruction of Biblical or eschatological events at which the meditator is to imagine himself actually present as spectator or participant, achieved vast popularity during the Middle Ages, especially in vernacular writings, a popularity given a particular impetus by Aelred's work.

Of the two Middle English versions, the earlier, a late fourteenth-century translation, is contained in the Vernon MS, and the later, of the mid-fifteenth century, is contained in MS Bodley 423. The former translates only the last twenty sections of Aelred's work, which deal with the anchoress's spiritual welfare; it has been previously edited by C. Horstmann.[8] The latter translates the whole work and is here edited for the first time. The Vernon translation is as long as or longer than its original, owing largely to the translator's diffuse and expansive style; the Bodley version, however, is a far more drastic and thorough-going redaction of the Latin – abbreviation, conflation and omission are extensive.

2. MANUSCRIPTS

1. *The Vernon Manuscript*

MS Vernon (MS Bodley Eng. poet. a.l., *S.C.* 3938–42) is a membrane manuscript of viii + 342 ff., measuring about 520 mm × 400 mm and weighing just over 22 kg. Seventy-one folios

---

[7] *Quand Jésus eut douze ans*, ed. Dom A. Hoste, O.S.B. (Paris, 1958), pp. 7ff.
[8] *Englische Studien*, vii (1884), 304–44.

are now missing. It has the title *Salus anime* or *Sowlehele*, and, as is well known, contains a collection of religious pieces in prose and verse, including the works of Richard Rolle, the *Ancrene Riwle* and the A text of *Piers Plowman*. For a full list of the contents and a description of the main body of the manuscript, see *Summary Catalogue*, pp. 789–92 and also M. S. Serjeantson, 'The Index of the Vernon Manuscript', *MLR*, xxxii (1937), 222–61 and J. O. Halliwell, *Some Account of the Vernon Manuscript* (London, 1848).

Added on to the beginning of the main body of the manuscript is a preliminary quire of eight leaves, which contains:

1. ff. i–iii A table of the contents of the main manuscript.[1]
2. ff. iii^v–viii 'Informacio Alredi abbatis monasterij de Rieualle ad sororem suam inclusam.'[2]

The remainder of f. viii is ruled but blank.

The numbering of this quire does not match that of the rest of the manuscript. Whereas the latter is foliated at the top left-hand corner of each verso side by a contemporary hand in red roman numerals from 1 to 401 (the remaining leaves being numbered in a later hand), the former is not foliated at all, and bears only faint traces of original leaf-signatures – on the bottom left-hand corner of ff. iii^v and iv^v are written respectively, by a medieval hand, 'a III' and 'a IIII'. In the nineteenth century the portion of the quire containing *De Institutione Inclusarum* was paginated *a, b, c, d, e, f, g, h, j, k*, rectos in the top right-hand corners and versos in the top left-hand corners.

The ruled frame of the preliminary quire measures 413 mm × 287 mm. The text is contained in three columns of writing, each about 85–88 mm wide and comprising eighty lines. The lines have been ruled in ink. There is clear evidence of pricking on the inside of the leaves, and also on the top and bottom; no holes appear on the outside, however, and they must have been cut off (in contrast to the main body of the manuscript, where pricked holes occur also on the outside of the leaves throughout).

The title, chapter headings and sub-headings are rubricated, apparently by the scribe himself, and paraphs are done in red

---

[1] Printed by Serjeantson, *loc. cit.*

[2] Previously printed by C. Horstmann, *Englische Studien*, vii (1884), 304–44, and here re-edited.

and blue (some have been missed out, allowing the scribe's cue for a paraph to be seen). Initial letters are illuminated in gold, with blue and magenta decoration, but their quality is noticeably inferior to that of the majority in the main part of the manuscript. Decorations are of a conventional character, consisting of foliage, buds, tendrils etc. Visible beside the first large initial *N* on f. iii^v is the direction *vinet*, and below it *n*, both in red; and indications for the illuminator in black can be seen beside many of the other secondary initials. These initials normally occupy three lines, apart from *I*, which is written outside the lined space.

The two items in the preliminary quire were written by the same hand. The writing has by now faded to the extent that it appears a palish brown in colour. The hand is a distinctive one, of the general type characterized as *Anglicana Formata*. It is a round, neat hand, easily legible apart from a certain tendency to confuse *e* and *o*, *n* and *u* and, occasionally, *c* and *t*. Among the many characteristic letter forms are þ, ꝑ, two different but undifferentiated forms of *w*, two forms of capital *A*, '8'-shaped *s* and (sporadically) '2'-shaped *r*. From these and other such distinctive features it is possible to identify the hand as the first of Holkham Hall MS 668 and the first of Trinity College, Oxford, MS 16B, ff. 3–8^v l.6, 30^v l. 20–31, 53–78^v, 84–84^v l. 24 and 111^v–114 (both copies of a version of *The Prick of Conscience*).[3] It may be dated with reasonable certainty as belonging to the last decade of the fourteenth century or the early decades of the fifteenth century, and this accords well with the putative history of the manuscript as a whole.

The text of *De Institutione Inclusarum* shows some evidence of alterations by distinct hands, but their status is ambiguous. They fall into two categories, as follows:

1. 'Corrections' of original manuscript forms, made throughout the text in a contemporary hand. Some may be the work of the original scribe. It is clear that they do not represent a systematic attempt to correct all his mistakes, as a number of blatant errors remain unscathed.

2. On f. vi, a hand of the mid to late fifteenth century has made three minor additions to the text, using a finer pen and a paler ink. These appear to be rather in the nature of explana-

---

[3] For this information we are indebted to Dr A. I. Doyle.

tions than corrections, added by a later owner or reader of the manuscript as a sort of personal jotted gloss for his own amusement.

These alterations are noted in the textual apparatus where they appear.

The Vernon manuscript itself is dated between 1382[4] and *c*.1400. Recent scholarly opinion has tended to place it nearer the latter date,[5] and certainly a dating of the last decade of the fourteenth century would seem a reasonable assumption. It has been contended that the first quire is 'a very little later than the rest of the volume, being of the early fifteenth century,'[6] but there is strong evidence to suggest that this is not the case. Certainly f. 1 must have remained exposed for some considerable time, as its outside edge is so badly frayed as to require a repair about 50 mm across at its widest. Unless the manuscript was extraordinarily ill-used, this would seem to indicate that f. 1 remained the outside leaf for a period possibly extending into years. Furthermore, the hand of the preliminary quire is slightly later in style than that of the main manuscript. But two additional facts have to be taken into consideration. First, the hand of the preliminary quire supplies rubrics on ff. 89–92, 167–243, 288ff. and 307ff. of the main manuscript, and may have done some foliation; this is not conclusive, as it could, of course, have been done long after the completion of the texts. Secondly, the table of contents does not include the Aelred or many of the main items – it ignores some in the final quire of the third physical subdivision of the manuscript (ff. 314–18) – while the original foliator also missed out the folio numbers and other rubrication for ff. 311–18; the last item in the table is for f. 393 (*Piers Plowman*), and the last original folio number is on f. 401, the last leaf of the penultimate quire. The foliator and lister must have been working without the final quire of the third section and the end of the volume. All this would seem to indicate that when the preliminary quire was produced, the writing of the rest of the manuscript had not quite been com-

---

[4] The manuscript contains a poem which refers to a plague that occurred in 1382 (ed. R. H. Robbins, *Historical Poems of the XIVth and XVth Centuries* (New York, 1959), pp. 57–60), providing a *terminus a quo*.

[5] G. L. Kane, for example, in his edition of *Piers Plowman* (London, 1960), p. 17, argues for such a dating from the presence of the A text of that work.

[6] Serjeantson, *loc. cit.*, quoting the opinion of J. A. Herbert.

pleted, and that the quires had not all been gathered together, numbered and listed (though all had been allowed for); in view of the damage to f. 1 it is probable that the whole was still in quires, perhaps with limp covers. The apparent discrepancy between the dating of the two hands could be accounted for by postulating that the preliminary quire was written by a some-what younger scribe[7].

The localization of the manuscript, or rather, the homes of the two scribes, have been the subject of as much dispute as has the dating. Jordan places them in Staffordshire, 'wenn nicht in Shrops. oder Heref.,'[8] Serjeantson in south Staffordshire,[9] Pro-fessor McIntosh in Worcestershire. Sajavaara argues for north Worcestershire or Warwickshire, believing that it may have originated in a Cistercian house and suggesting Bordesley (near Redditch.)[10] The evidence of the language of *De Institutione Inclusarum* certainly tends to point to the more southerly of these localizations,[11] and indeed, Professor Samuels' mappings strongly suggest an area halfway between Worcester and Birmingham.[12] The argument for a Cistercian origin, however, is unconvincing, for it is based on the presence in the manu-script of a life of St. Bernard, interest in whom was hardly confined to Cistercians in the late fourteenth century, and also on the Aelred translation. But Aelred's treatise was never in any case aimed at a Cistercian audience. Furthermore, we know that his writings were not only to be found in Cistercian houses: manuscripts of *De Institutione Inclusarum* belonged to Au-gustinian Canons, Carthusians, Benedictines, Franciscans and Merton College, as well as to Cistercians.[13]

But whatever the origin of the Vernon manuscript as a whole,

[7] On the question of the assembly of the Vernon manuscript into its final form see A. I. Doyle, 'The Shaping of the Vernon and Simeon Manuscripts,' *Chaucer and Middle English Studies – in Honour of Rossell Hope Robbins*, ed. B. Rowland (London, 1974), p. 329 and K. Sajavaara, *Middle English Translations of Robert Grosseteste's Château d'Amour* (Helsinki, 1967), pp. 103–27.

[8] *Handbuch der Mittelenglischen Grammatik* (Breslau, 3rd. ed., repr. Heidelberg, 1968), p. 8.

[9] *loc. cit.*, p. 222.

[10] K. Sajavaara, 'The Relationship of the Vernon and Simeon Manuscripts,' *Neuphi-lologische Mitteilungen*, LXVIII (1967), 439. See also Mrs N. S. Baugh, *A Worcester-shire Miscellany* (Philadelphia, 1956), pp. 37–9.

[11] See pp. xliv–liv.

[12] In a private communication to Dr A. I. Doyle, to whom we are indebted for this information.

[13] See C. H. Talbot, *loc. cit.*, pp. 175–6.

it was clearly written primarily to be read aloud, possibly to a court or community.[14] Unfortunately this hardly narrows down the possible audience. Horstmann suggested that it belonged to a community of nuns;[15] if so, the field would be somewhat narrowed, as few English convents had the financial resources to possess such an opulent manuscript. It might equally well have belonged to a lay person, either a devout and aristocratic lay woman, or else a highly-placed secular ecclesiastic such as Thomas Arundel. The contents of the manuscript, in particular the presence of both Aelred's Rule and the *Ancrene Riwle*, suggest that the original audience was female, but in the absence of any hard evidence it is pointless to speculate any further.

Omitting, as it does, the first section of Aelred's treatise dealing with the external forms and practical aspects of an anchoress's life, and concentrating on the second and third sections, which are concerned strictly with the recluse's moral and spiritual life, this translation is self-evidently highly appropriate for inclusion in an anthology of works of a religious and devotional nature, concerned with *sowlehele*. Indeed, it is possible that it was planned from the outset to use it as a sort of preface to the whole volume. Alternatively, it may be that it was chosen only at a later stage, to use up the space left in the columns prepared for the contents table, whose extent might not have been certain when it was begun – its selection prompted, perhaps, by the presence of similar prose treatises in the fourth physical subdivision of the manuscript, such as the *Ancrene Riwle* and *A Talking of the Love of God*. Like the other texts in the Vernon manuscript, the translation was clearly not made specifically for inclusion here; the multiple layers of the language of the text show that it must have existed in earlier versions. The only question that remains, and must remain unanswered for lack of evidence, is, was it originally a translation of the whole of Aelred's treatise, or only of the last two parts? All that can be said is that even if the former was the case, the exigencies of both space and appropriateness would have influenced the scribe to produce the second and third sections to the exclusion of the first.

---

[14] See A. I. Doyle, *loc. cit.*, p. 331.
[15] *loc. cit.*, p. 304.

2. *Bodley 423*

MS Bodley 423 (*S.C.* 2322) consists of four separate manuscripts bound together, as follows:

1. ff. 1–127ᵛ *Section A*: a collection of Latin sermons: 12th
   century.
2. ff. 128–243ᵛ *Sections B and C*: see below.
3. ff. 244–345ᵛ *Section D*: the Middle English poem *Stimulus
   Conscientiae*: fifteenth century.[1]
4. ff. 346–416ᵛ *Section E*: John Capgrave, *The Solace of Pilgrims*: fifteenth century.[2]

The whole manuscript consists of i + 416 folios and measures
270 mm × 195 mm. Sections A, B, C and E are on vellum,
Section D on paper. There is one continuous foliation; in
addition another hand has foliated Section B as 1–97 and Section C ff. 228–233 only, as 1–6. According to the *Summary
Catalogue*, Sections A, B and C were donated to the library in
1605 by Dr W. Cotton, Bishop of Exeter. H. M. Bannister,
however, in his introduction to C. A. Mills's edition of *The
Solace of Pilgrims*, states that Sections A, B, C and D were all
donated together and were bound together with Section E on
the orders of Sir Thomas Bodley.[3] The binding appears to date
from the seventeenth century. As our concern is with Sections
B and C only, the rest of this composite manuscript will not be
further described.

The written area of Sections B and C measures between 214
and 224 mm by between 107 and 123 mm; the pages have been
trimmed slightly. There are regularly thirty-seven lines to the
page. The collation is: (Section B) 1⁸ (lacks 1–3); 2⁸ (lacks 2);
3–13⁸; (Section C) 1–2⁸.

The first gathering of Section B (ff. 128–32ᵛ) is decorated
with red reference letters, capitals and chapter headings and
blue initial letters for each chapter. Paraphs are alternately
red and blue; marginal glosses are underlined in red. The two
gatherings of Section C (ff. 228–43ᵛ) are similarly decorated;
in addition f. 228 has a large marginal decoration outlined, of
which parts have been filled in with red and blue and other areas

[1] On the authorship of this poem, and other surviving manuscripts, see H. E Allen,
Writings Ascribed to Richard Rolle (New York, 1927, repr. 1966), pp. 372–97.
[2] See *Ye Solace of Pilgrimes*, ed. C. A. Mills (Oxford, 1911).
[3] *Ibid.*, p. xi.

prepared with a beige undercoat which was probably intended to be covered with gold-leaf. The decorations of the remaining gatherings of Section B are unfinished, the red parts only having been supplied: the first letter of each chapter, which was to have been blue, has been provided in ink in minuscule as a guide to the illuminator. Gathering 4 has rubricated Latin quotations, but gathering 5 has no rubrication except for chapter headings. By the time one reaches gathering 11 the chapter headings and Latin quotations are simply in ink underlined in red. It is clear that the decorative scheme became progressively less ambitious in Section B.

Gathering 13 (ff. 220–27^v) is unfinished: there is a *lacuna* of nearly seven lines on f. 225; on f. 226 the first eighteen lines only have been written, the rest of the page being ruled but blank; f. 226^v, though ruled, is entirely blank; ff. 227 and 227^v are ruled but blank except for a note of ownership and a prayer in two later (sixteenth century) hands. Gathering 2 of Section C is also unfinished: on f. 242^v three lines only have been written (though these are the last lines of the text), the rest of the page being ruled but blank except for five lines in another later hand; ff. 243 and 243^v show traces of ruling and an erasure on f. 243^v. Both Sections B and C are written in the same clear, regular fifteenth-century hand.

Section B, though incomplete at the beginning, lacks only its first three folios. That this is the original first gathering is confirmed by the presence of quire letters and numbers in the lower right-hand corner of the first halves of Gatherings 3, 6, 9, 11, 12 (b, e, h, k, l). All the gatherings have accurate catchwords, sometimes underlined in red, which establish that there are at least no internal *lacunae*. Section B clearly existed in its incomplete state for some time before it was bound, as its first surviving page (f. 128) is dirty and much discoloured, as are ff. 243 and 243^v at the end of Section C. The first page of this section, however (f. 228), is not noticeably darker than any of the others which indicates that Section C, whatever the original intention of the compiler, never circulated separately from Section B.

The *Summary Catalogue* implies that Sections B and C are separate manuscripts. It does not mention that they were written by the same scribe and it dates Section B as 1420–30 but

Section C as about the middle of the fifteenth century. Both sections, however, are laid out identically and similarly decorated and appear to have circulated as a unit. It is therefore reasonable to assume that they were written, and left unfinished, at the same time and that their first gatherings were meant to be illuminated as the scribe finished with them. To all intents and purposes, then, Sections B and C make up a single manuscript and will from now on be treated as such.

The contents of Sections B and C are as follows:

1. ff. 128–50 *Fervor Amoris* (no title given; the opening is missing), *inc*. and ladies and husbonde men and her wyues; *expl*. these fewe wordes in helpynge of thy soule. Here endith þe tretyse that we clepen fferuor amoris.

This treatise (*inc*. In the begynnynge and endynge of all good works) is extant in more than sixteen manuscripts: see P. S. Jolliffe, *A Check-List of Middle English Prose Writings of Spiritual Guidance* (Toronto, 1974), Item H. 15. These include MSS BL Arundel 197 (an amended version) and C.U.L.Ii. 6. 40 (*v. infra*). In addition, Wynkyn de Worde published two printed editions, entitled *Contemplations of the Dread and Love of God* (STC 21259, 21260) in 1506 and ?1520, in which he attributed the work to Richard Rolle. This attribution has been rejected by C. Horstmann, who reprinted Wynkyn's 1506 edition[4] and by H. E. Allen.[5] A modernized version made from MS Harley 2409 has been edited by F. M. M. Comper.[6]

2. ff. 150–55 *These wordes and this matere whiche is folewynge is an Informacion of Contemplatif lyf and Actif, as it is drawe oute of the Reuelacion of seint Bride, inc*. I fynde as I rede by doctours; *expl*. that he folewith mary in contemplatif liuynge; ff. 155–56[v] *A short Informacyon of actif lyf, likned to þe liuyng of Martha, inc*. Actif lyf is ful meritory; *expl*. god graunte vs alle grace for his gret mercy Amen amen. Thus endith þis short tretys of actif lif and contemplatif.

These passages are a translation of the Revelations of St

---

[4] *Yorkshire Writers: Richard Rolle and His Followers*, ed. C. Horstmann (London, 1896), 2 vols., II, 72–105.

[5] *Op. cit.*, p. 357

[6] *Contemplations of the Dread and Love of God* (London, 1916). See also J. E. Krochalis, '"Contemplations . . .", two newly identified Pennsylvania Manuscripts', *The Library Chronicle* (University of Pennsylvania) xlii, pp. 3–22.

Bridget, Book 6, Chapter 65:[7] see Jolliffe, *op. cit.*, Items H. 13 and O. 23. The same translation of the same passages is found in four manuscripts including, again, MSS Arundel 197 and C.U.L. Ii. 6. 40. There is no indication in this latter manuscript that the passage is separate from *Fervor Amoris* and both the Cambridge cataloguer and the writer of the most recent description of the manuscript[8] have consequently assumed that these two passages were its last two chapters.

3. ff. 156^v–64 Two meditations: (i) *inc. Reliquie cogitacionis diem festum agent tibi* Mi good lord and merciful fader almighty; *expl.* (f. 161) þe grace of the holy goost Amen. Amen. (ii) *inc. Da nobis domine auxilium de tribulacione* Lord graunte vs helpe; *expl.* and say with herte and mouthe *Te deum Laudamus. Amen.*

These two meditations are also found in Arundel 197, ff. 64–73^v; *inc.* A devote meditacion to owre lorde Ihu. *Reliquie Cogitaciones*; *expl.* and sey wit herte and mouthe *Te deum laudamus*. Modernized versions have been printed by C. Kirchberger in *The Life of the Spirit*, August-September 1952, 106–10 and June 1950, 549–54.

4. ff. 164–64^v A verse translation of the *Salve regina* followed by a prayer, *inc. Salue* Heyl comely creature; *expl.* haue mynde on our preiere. See *Index of Middle English Verse* no. 1039. The poem has been printed from this, the unique manuscript, by C. Brown, *Religious Lyrics of the Fifteenth Century* (Oxford, 1939), pp. 45–7. Followed by a prayer, *inc.* Almighty euerlastyng god that hast ordeyned; *expl.* to euerlastyng ioye and blisse. Amen.

5. ff. 164^v–66 *The mirrour and the mede of sorow and of tribulacion, inc.* Oure lord ihu spekynge of sorow; *expl.* whiche for hem suffred here right gret and greuous turmentes. See Jolliffe, Item J.10; no other manuscripts apart from Bodley 423 are known.

6. ff. 166–67 *Ayenst the excusacion of lechery and othir dedly synnes, inc.* Seynt Austyn seith that ther may nooman be taken of the deuel; *expl.* thai that wiln mekely lyuen here saith seint

[7] *Revelationes Coelestes Seraphicae Matris S. Birgittae Suecae*, ed. C. Durantus (Monachii, 1680), pp. 534–8.
[8] *Þe Pater Noster of Richard Ermyte*, ed. F. G. A. M. Aarts (The Hague, 1967), pp. xvi–xvii.

Poule must nede suffre persecucion and sorwe. See Jolliffe, Item E.23. Again, no other manuscripts are known.

7. ff. 167–8ᵛ *Hov thou shalt be war and withstande temptacions bothe slepynge and wakynge, inc.* By the ordinaunce of god ther ben good aungels; *expl.* þe helthe of man is veyn and right nought. This is an abbreviated version of three chapters of *Fervor Amoris* (Chapters X–Z in Wynkyn's edition of 1506). See Jolliffe, Item K.2; no other manuscripts are known.

8. ff. 168ᵛ–70 *The counsaill of crist: inc.* Crist not compellynge; *expl.* and vnclennes of this werlde.

This is a treatise also found in the *Poor Caitiff* (see Jolliffe, Item B). Apart from manuscripts containing this compilation *in toto*, it is also found separately in MS C.U.L. Ff. 5. 45, ff. 59ᵛ–62.

9. ff. 170–71 *Of Pacience, inc.* But hoo that is verraily fedde; *expl.* Al this sentence seith a seynt in his boke.

This is also found as part of the *Poor Caitiff*, but it is ultimately a translation of Chapter 6 of the *Emendatio Vitae* of Richard Rolle. It is also found separately in C.U.L. Ff. 5. 45, ff. 62–63ᵛ.

10. ff. 171–71ᵛ *Of Temptacyon, inc.* Whan thou art tempted or troubled; *expl.* by odour of swetnes in the presence of god.

Again, this is part of the *Poor Caitiff* and also found separately in C.U.L. Ff. 5. 45, ff. 63ᵛ–64.

11. ff. 171ᵛ–74ᵛ *Chartre of Heuene, inc.* Euery wise man that claymeth his heritage; *expl.* Al this sentence saith seint Austyn in his boke to the erle.

This is also part of the *Poor Caitiff*: for other manuscripts, see M. C. Spalding, *The Middle English Charters of Christ* (Bryn Mawr, 1914) p. 99, and F. G. A. M. Aarts, *op. cit.*, p. xiii. It should be noted that among these manuscripts is C.U.L. Ii. 6. 40, ff. 191–8, where it is entitled *A charter of remissioun*.

12. ff. 174ᵛ–78 *Hors either armure of heuen, inc.* Almighty god seith by holy Iob; *expl.* hopynge to dwelle ther, worlde withouten ende.

This too is part of the *Poor Caitiff* and is also found separately in MS Douce 13, ff. 15ᵛ–33ᵛ. There are other manuscripts which contain an expanded version of this treatise, usually known as *A treatise of ghostly battle*.⁹

---

⁹ Printed by Horstmann, *op. cit.*, II, 420–36.

13. ff. 178–92 *A tretys that is a rule and a forme of lyuynge perteynyng to a Recluse, inc.* Suster thou hast ofte axed; *expl.* Here endith the Reule of a Recluse that seynt Alrede wrote to his suster. And here folewen the Chapiters of þe same.

This is a translation of Aelred's *De Institutione Inclusarum* followed by a list of the chapter headings and has not previously been printed.

14. ff. 192ᵛ–205 *A tretys to lerne to wepe, inc.* Now at my thought I wil begynne; *expl.* and withouten ende welcome to me. Thus endith an exhortacyon of oure lady to meue alle oþer to compassion of wepyng for cristes peyne and passyon.

A Middle English poem on the Passion; see *Index of Middle English Verse* no. 2347; it was printed from MS Harley 2274 by R. M. Garrett, *Anglia*, xxxii (1909), 270–94.

15. ff. 205–26 *The boke of Tribulacyon, inc.* Here begynneth the boke of Tribulacyon, sayeng thus; *expl.* wiþ good hert say to him. *Da nobis domine auxilium de tribulacione.*

This is a translation of the Old French prose text *Li douze services de tribulacion*, extant in at least twenty-four manuscripts.[10] It is also found in abbreviated form in MS Harley 1197; Jolliffe's Item J.3(a), in MS Arundel 286, is another, highly condensed, derivative of this Middle English version (see *The Book of Tribulation*, ed. Alexandra Barratt (Heidelberg, 1983), MET 15). Item J.3(d) is an independent version of the Old French, while Items J.3(b) and (c) are translations of the shorter Latin version, *De XII Vtilitatibus Tribulationum* (*PL* 207 cols. 989 ff.), which derives from the longer Latin version, as yet unpublished.

Section C

16. ff. 228–41ᵛ Here beginneth the boke of the crafte of dyeng *inc.* For asmuche as the passage of deeth; *expl.* mediatour bitwene god and man Amen. Explicit tractatus Vtilissimus de Arte moriendi.

This is the English translation of the *Ars Moriendi*; see Jolliffe, Item L.4(a). Jolliffe lists thirteen other manuscripts, among them C.U.L. Ff. 5.45. It has been published from MS

---

[10] See M. Chesney, 'Notes on some treatises of devotion intended for Margaret of York (MS Douce 365)', *Medium Aevum* XX (1951), 11–39, and A. Auer, *Leidenstheologie im Spätmittelalter* (St Ottilien, 1952).

Rawlinson C 894 by Horstmann[11] while a modernized version was edited by F. M. M. Comper.[12] It has been argued that the Latin treatise was written at the time of the Council of Constance (1418) and that the many vernacular versions were made after the various delegates had returned to their countries of origin.[13] If so, this would provide a valuable *terminus a quo* for Bodley 423, which is 'apparently the earliest of three English MSS in the Bodleian'.[14]

17. f. 241ᵛ *inc.* Haue in mynde, that thou hast oo god; *expl.* suffrynge gret passyon and deeth to saue the.

Again, this is an extract from *Fervor Amoris*, from Chapter AB in Wynkyn's edition. According to Horstmann, this chapter is also found as a separate piece in Harley 2398, ff. 186 seq.[15], but this is not recorded by Jolliffe (see Item I. 14).

18. ff. 241ᵛ–42ᵛ *inc.* Here folewen foure prophitable thynges to haue in mynde whiche ben had oute of the thridde Chapitre of a deuoute tretyse and a fourme of lyuynge that Rycharde Hampole wrote; *expl.* with hyse seruauntes that is euermore.

This is an extract from Chapter Four of Rolle's *Form of Living*[16]; it is also found as a separate piece in MSS Trinity College Dublin 154, Harley 1706 and in Wynkyn de Worde's editions of *The remedy ayenst the troubles of temptacyons* of 1508 and 1519 (STC 21262 and 21263)[17] which he ascribed to Rolle, though it is now known to be a translation of William Flete's *De Remediis contra Temptationes*.[18]

It is clear that this collection of devotional treatises in prose and verse belongs to a type common in the later middle ages. MSS Rawlinson C 894, Reg. 17 C XVIII and CCC Oxford 220, for instance, all contain two treatises on tribulation, *The Craft of Dying* and *A Treatise of Ghostly Battle* (related to *Hors*

[11] *Ibid.*, pp. 406–20.
[12] *The Book of the Craft of Dying* (London, 1917).
[13] M. C. O'Connor, *The Art of Dying Well* (New York, 1942) p. 54.
[14] *Ibid.*, p. 108
[15] *Yorkshire Writers*, II, 102.
[16] *English Writings of Richard Rolle*, ed. H. E. Allen (Oxford, 1931), p. 95/18 – p. 96/56; see also *note*, p. 155.
[17] See Horstmann, *op. cit.*, II, 106, and Allen, *Writings Ascribed to Richard Rolle*, pp. 359–60.
[18] See B. Hackett, E. Colledge, N. Chadwick, 'William Flete's *De Remediis . . .*', *Mediaeval Studies* xxvi (1964), 210–30, and B. Hackett, 'William Flete and the "De Remediis contra Temptaciones"', *Medieval Studies presented to Aubrey Gwynn, S. J.* (Dublin, 1961), pp. 330–48.

either Armure of Heuene), as do the two related manuscripts Douce 322 and Harley 1706; in addition Douce 322 has the *Charter of Heaven*. The combination of devotional and meditative interests, then, represented by MS Bodley 423 belongs to the mainstream of vernacular religious tradition; indeed, the only item in the collection that might possibly be considered as out-of-place or unusual is the translation of Aelred's Rule.

But MS Bodley 423 seems to enjoy a peculiarly close relationship with MS Arundel 197 and, to a lesser degree, with MS C.U.L. Ii.6.40. The scribal hands are completely different, but there is a strong and suggestive resemblance in the contents.

The contents of MS Arundel 197 are as follows:
Fervor Amoris, erroneously, at head of f. 1.

1. ff. 1–3ᵛ *inc.* Yf þou covete and desire to be made clene in soule; *expl.* bothe quicke and dede. þe whiche þou hast dure bowtte with þi precius blode. Amen. This meditation is edited by Horstmann.[19] According to Dr Jolliffe, Chapter AB of *Fervor Amoris* is interpolated on ff. 1ᵛ–3.

2. ff. 3ᵛ–6ᵛ. *S. Austine is seynge, inc.* Mi lyfe ferethe me sore; *expl.* y beseke þi grete mercy amen. Translation of St Anselm's Meditation I, *Terret me vita mea*; but in a private communication Dr Jolliffe says this is a partial version, followed by different meditational matter on ff. 5–6ᵛ. Printed by Horstmann.[20]

3. ff. 6ᵛ–7 *inc.* Here bethe nyne vertuis. þe whiche owre lorde iesu crist shewyd; *expl.* without any recouer. See Horstmann, *op. cit.*, I, 110–12, for others of the many versions, and H. E. Allen, *op. cit.*, pp. 317–19.

4. ff. 7–10 *Of þe day of dome a gode note, inc.* Who so wille haue in mynde þe dredeful day; *expl.* þat bought us with his precius blode. Amen. The *Meditation of the Three Arrows*.[21]

5. f. 10 *inc.* A þou sely sowle if þou wilte aske; *expl.* not aftur þi felyng but aftur my dome &c. According to Dr B. Hackett this is a derivative of the *Documento Spirituale* of St Catherine of Siena, found in several other MSS.

In a letter of 1966 to Dr A. I. Doyle, Dr Jolliffe said that few of these items are complete and nearly all vary considerably

---

[19] *Op. cit.* II, 441–3.
[20] *Ibid.*, 443–5.
[21] *Ibid.*, 446–8.

from their normal form. Items 1, 2, 4 and 5 are also found, in textually purer versions, as an addition to Trinity College Cambridge MS B. 14. 53. Dr. C. A. Martin has shown that the texts of 1 and 2 in Arundel 197 and the Trinity MS descend independently from a common source in each case.

6. ff. 10–38^v *Fervor Amoris, inc*. Ardeat in nobis diuini feruor amoris Amen. This short epistille þat folwith; *expl*. þes fewe wordis in helpynge of þi soule. Here endethe this tretise that we calle *ffervor amoris*.

7. ff. 38^v–47^v Three extracts from the Revelations of St Bridget: *inc*. Thes wordis and this mater whiche is folwynge is and [*sic*] infirmacion of contemplatife lyfe and actife and is drawynne out of þe reuelacion of sent Bryde. See above, p. xxi, for the first two (ff. 38^v–46^v). ff. 46^v–47^v *To sent Bryde, inc*. God almy3ti aperid to sent Bryde seynge to her on þis wise; *expl*. his owne spowse and derelynge. Also found in B.L. Add. 37790, f. 236^v.

8. ff. 47^v–48 *To the Sacramente, inc*. Hayle holy bodi; *expl*. y beseche þi mercy. Amen. Possibly translated from Suso's *Horologium Sapientie*, but these are not precisely the incipit or explicit of the prayer found in *The Seven Poyntes of Trewe Wisdom*,[22] nor of Nicholas Love's version.

9. ff. 48–64 *An abstracte owte of a boke þat is callid formula nouiciorum, inc*. Where for arte þou come to religion; *expl*. thou arte not worþi þat eny reuerence be do to the.

This is a translation of *De Exterioris et Interioris Hominis Compositione*, often attributed to the Dominican David of Augsburg; see Jolliffe, Item H. 2(b) for further information and his article, 'Middle English translations of *De exterioris et interioris hominis compositione*', *Mediaeval Studies* 36 (1974), 259–77. Another version, now MS C.U.L. Dd. 2. 33, belonged to Syon Abbey, written by Thomas Prestins who is known to have been a member of the Bridgettine community at the time of its dissolution in 1539.[23]

10. ff. 64–70 Two meditations on *Reliquie cogitacionis* and *Te deum laudamus*: see above, p. xxii.

---

[22] See C. Horstmann, 'Orologium Sapientiae or The Seven Poyntes of Trewe Wisdom', *Anglia* x (1888), 378.

[23] N. R. Ker, *Medieval Libraries of Great Britain* (London, 2nd ed. 1964) p. 309.

Arundel 197 seems to be relevant not just because it shares three items with Bodley 423 but more because the items which it does happen to have in common argue for a closeness beyond coincidence. Although the version found in Arundel 197 is different from that in all the other manuscripts, Arundel 197 and Bodley 423 both entitle the treatise we know by that name *Fervor amoris* while some other manuscripts call it simply 'thys shorte epistole'. The extracts from St Bridget, though not the exclusive property of the two manuscripts in question, in these two happen to share a very close association with *Fervor Amoris* and the two meditations on Latin texts are found in these two manuscripts and nowhere else.

Another manuscript which is clearly linked with Bodley 423, though less closely than Arundel 197, is C.U.L. Ii. 6. 40, which at one time belonged to Dame Joan Mouresleygh, recorded as a nun at Shaftesbury in 1441 and 1460.[24]

The contents are as follows:

1. ff. 2ᵛ–3ᵛ *inc*. domine ihu xpe qui uidens ierusalem; *expl*. ad celestem patriam Amen. A Latin prayer.

2. ff. 5–58ᵛ *An holy mater þe which is clepid xij Chapiters.* This is *Fervor Amoris*; see above, p. xxi; *cf*. below for the title, which is more appropriate for Rolle's *Emendatio Vitae*.

3. ff. 58ᵛ–74 The two extracts from St Bridget's Revelations on contemplative and active life; see above, p. xxi.

4. ff. 75–76ᵛ *A tretis of perfyt loue, inc*. Dere frendys ȝe wote wele; *expl*. þat to fore was gostly. See Jolliffe, Item K. 3; no other manuscripts are listed.

5. ff. 76ᵛ–95 *A tretis of tribulacion, inc*. Seynt poule techiþ vs; *expl*. graunt vs to fulfil þe holy trinite Amen.

This is not a translation of *De Duodecim Utilitatibus* or *Li douze services de tribulacion* nor is it the same as *The mirror and mede of sorrow* found in Bodley 423. See Jolliffe, Item J. 13, which lists two other manuscripts.

6. ff. 95–191 *A tretis of Pater Noster, inc*. To my dere suster in god; *expl*. in to oure last end. Amen. This treatise has been printed by Aarts, *op. cit*.

7. ff. 191–8 *A Charter of Remissioun*; that is, *Charter of Heaven*; see above, p. xxiii.

---

[24] We are indebted to Dr A. I. Doyle for this information.

8. ff. 198–207ᵛ In þis tretis we are tauȝt how we schul loue god on al wise *inc*. The comaundmente of god is þat we loue oure lord; *expl*. in þat hangiþ al þe law.

This is Rolle's *The Commandment* and has been printed by H. E. Allen, *op cit.*, pp. 73–81.

9. ff. 207ᵛ–220 *A deuout meditacion of Ric. Hampel, inc*. First þou schalt þinke how þis world is passing; *expl*. as we feble wrechis and frele auȝtyn for to do. Amen.

This is a partial translation of the Speculum of St Edmund; see Horstmann, *op. cit.* I, 219, Allen, *Writings*, p. 362 and H. W. Robbins, 'An English Version of St Edmund's *Speculum*', *PMLA* xl (1925), 240–51, where this text is printed. Also found in Longleat House MS 32, where Rolle's Commandment precedes it, and an English version of his *Emendatio Vitae* follows.

Again, this manuscript has three items in common with Bodley 423, though the *Charter of Heaven* is not a rare text by any means, and its presence may be merely a coincidence. Although the version of *Fervor Amoris* in this manuscript does not have the title given by Bodley 423 and Arundel 197, it is, as in those manuscripts, closely followed by the same extracts from the Revelations of St Bridget. So close, indeed, is the connection that their existence as separate pieces has been overlooked by at least two scholars; this suggests that the scribe of C.U.L. Ii. 6. 40 made his copy from a manuscript in which they were already closely associated.

As to the relationship of Bodley 423 and Arundel 197, Arundel 197 is probably not a direct descendent of Bodley 423 as it contains a third extract from St Bridget not found in Bodley 423 or C.U.L. Ii. 6. 40. It is not really possible, either, to date Bodley 423 quite as exactly as the *Summary Catalogue* does; we would not wish to suggest anything more definite than 'between 1430 and 1480'. Arundel 197 has kindly been dated for us by Fr Leonard Boyle, O.P., as 1450–1500 so it is not even possible to say definitely what is the temporal, let alone genetic, relationship between the two manuscripts.

Possibly the most interesting aspect of Bodley 423 is that it may be a Carthusian collection. Dr A. I. Doyle has kindly informed us that the scribe of Sections B and C of MS Bodley 423 was Stephen Dodesham, or (less probably), a scribe trained in the same school. He writes of Dodesham that 'from the variety of his production (including, for instance, Lydgate's *Siege of Thebes*) and the standard of his writing it seems most likely he was a professional scribe before becoming a Carthusian, working for diverse patrons, though it is not impossible he did some work for outsiders after entering the order. . . . From the evidence of date his career may have started in the 1420s, almost certainly by *c*.1430. The bulk of surviving so-far-identified work is not too much for one hand but in view of its well-drilled character the question whether it is all so or possibly some by others of the same school naturally arises: certain decorative mannerisms suggest not.'[25] In 1462 he was a monk at the Witham Charterhouse where he transcribed the Augustinian *Sermones Morales ad Fratres Suos in Heremo*. A flyleaf bears the inscription 'Liber domus beate Marie de Wytham ordinis Carthusiensis quem scripsit dominus Stephanus dodesham monachus eiusdem domus. Anno domini quadragintesimo sexagesimo secundo.' (This manuscript was the property of Sir Sydney Cockerell, was sold by Alan G. Thomas in 1957 for 300 guineas and stolen from Philip Duschnes in New York in 1962.)[26] In 1469 Dodesham wrote to the Carthusian authorities and 'was refused an answer for the time being because of the prolixity and irreverence of his letter', but a year or two later he was transferred to the Sheen Charterhouse as a result of his animosity towards the Witham prior.[27] In 1475 he transcribed what is now MS Glasgow University Library Hunterian 77, a copy of *The Mirror of the Blessed Life of Jesus Christ*, ascribed to him by a contemporary hand on an end-leaf: 'wrettyn be þe hand of dane stephene doddzam'.[28] He also transcribed a Latin psalter, now MS Trinity College Oxford 46, in a completely different, textura, script, as we know from

[25] Dr Doyle discussed the considerable number of manuscripts attributed to Dodesham in the 1967 Oxford Lyell lectures, and others have been found since. See also M. B. Parkes, *English Cursive Bookhands, 1250–1500* (Oxford, 1969), p. 6 and Plate 6; 2nd ed. (London, 1979), p. 25, lists other MSS including one, B.L. Add. 10053, which Dr Doyle does not think is by Dodesham.

[26] We are grateful to Alan G. Thomas, who provided us with a photocopy of his catalogue description, for this information.

[27] E. M. Thompson, *The Carthusian Order in England* (London, 1930), pp. 306–7.

[28] Ker, *op. cit.*, p. 305. See also J. Young and P. H. Aitken, *A Catalogue of the Manuscripts in the Library of the Hunterian Museum in the University of Glasgow* (Glasgow, 1908), p. 85.

the colophon written in his own hand on f. 167ᵛ: 'Orate pro anima domini Stephani Dodesham huius libri scriptoris dicendo deuote Anima eius et anime omnium fidelium defunctorum per misericordiam dei requiescant in pace.'[29] He died at Sheen in 1481–2.[30]

Dodesham also appears to have transcribed MS Bodley 549 (SC 2298) ff. 25–198, which is entirely in Latin except for a few pages of Middle English (ff. 77–89ʳ) in a different hand.[31] This compilation is quite clearly of Carthusian origin, as it includes tracts defending the Carthusian way of life, such as a *Declaratio optima Regule Cartusie* and a *Tractatus contra eos qui dicunt quod Carthusienses faciunt contra caritatem propter hoc quod non comedunt carnes, nec infirmis suis ministrant quoquo modo*. This manuscript is dated by the *Summary Catalogue* as early fifteenth century and according to S. P. Van Dijk's typescript catalogue of Bodleian liturgical manuscripts (II, 29) the list of holy kings it contains points to a Sheen origin, as Sheen was founded by Henry V.

Another manuscript written in the same hand and script as all the manuscripts mentioned so far except MS Trinity College Oxford 46, is MS Cambridge University Library Dd. 7. 7–11.[32] This is a very large four-volume copy of the biblical commentary of Nicholas of Lyra (1270–1349), consisting in all of over 1200 folios written in double columns. Vols. 1, 2 and 3 all have on the fly-leaf a copy of the same indenture, and the copies in Vols. 2 and 3 are written in a hand with similarities to Dodesham's, though it is probably not his hand. The indenture was made on 17 May 1457 between John Whethamstead, Abbot of St Alban's, Lady Alienora Hull and Roger Huswyff, clerk; Huswyff and Lady Alienora presented the volumes to the convent of St Alban's, the use of the volumes being granted to Roger Huswyff for life. Eleanor Hull was received into the honorary fraternity of St Alban's in February 1416/17, encouraged Henry V to found Syon, and knew Thomas Fishbourne who became the first Confessor-General of the Bridgettine

---

[29] See H. O. Coxe, *Catalogus Codicum manuscriptorum qui in collegiis aulisque Oxoniensibus hodie adservantur* (Oxford, 1852. 2 vols in 8 and 10 pts), 2, pt. 5, p. 18.
[30] Ker, *ibid*.
[31] See *Summary Catalogue* Vol. II Part 1, pp. 295–7.
[32] See *A Catalogue of the Manuscripts Preserved in the Library of the University of Cambridge* (Cambridge, 6 vols, 1856–67), 1, pp. 327–8.

foundation in 1420.[33] Huswyff was connected with St Alban's and was still alive in 1461.[34] Possibly the volumes were commissioned from a Carthusian scriptorium (other Carthusians, such as William Darker of Sheen, worked for Syon).[35] Possibly they were written at the Benedictine Abbey of St Alban's (and not necessarily as late as the date of the indenture) in which case Dodesham might at one stage have been a monk of that abbey. (It was perfectly acceptable under canon law for a religious to transfer to a more austere order.) Dr Doyle, however, considers that 'the illumination in his manuscripts is of a quality and type indicating close contact with the metropolitan book-trade', which favours his having originally been a layman. But it may be significant in this connection that the linguistic evidence places the scribal language of Bodley 423 in the Buckinghamshire-West Hertfordshire-Bedfordshire area, which would be consonant with Dodesham's being a native of St Alban's or the surrounding area. We have however found no mention of his name in the records of St Alban's under Whethamstead's abbacy of 1420–40.[36]

3. THE MIDDLE ENGLISH TRANSLATIONS AND THEIR RELATIONS WITH THE TEXTUAL TRADITION OF THE LATIN

Aelred's Latin text survives in six complete manuscript versions, three excerpted versions and one incomplete version. For a description of the manuscripts, see C. H. Talbot, *Analecta Sacri Ordinis Cisterciensis* vii (1959), 175–6. In the following discussion and throughout this edition Talbot's *sigla* are employed,[1] and line references are to this edition of the Latin text in the *CCCM* edition.

The Latin manuscripts were recollated in an attempt to

---

[33] This information is taken from Dr Doyle's Cambridge Ph.D. dissertation, *A Survey of the origins and circulation of theological writings in English in the 14th, 15th and early 16th centuries with special consideration of the part of the clergy therein.*

[34] See A. B. Emden, *A Biographical Register of the University of Oxford to A.D. 1500* (1957–9, 3 vols.), II, 990.

[35] Dr Doyle, in the communication quoted above.

[36] ed. H. T. Riley, *Annales de Monasterii S. Albani, a Johanne Ammundesham Monacho, ut videtur, conscripti, A.D. 1421–1440* (Rolls Series, 2 vols., 1870–1).

[1] See p. viii.

determine their stemmatic relation and the results are given in detail in *Revue d'histoire des textes* viii (1978), 195–211. To summarize, the tradition, though contaminated, falls into three families: β consisting of NTU and the excerpted versions RHa, which is an inferior family vitiated by numerous omissions caused by *homoioteleuton*; γ consisting of D and the unfinished but earlier H; and δ, made up of V, M and the very corrupt B.

The Vernon version is in general a very close, almost verbatim translation of the portion of the Latin it translates (that is, from Cap. 14 of the Latin onwards, *inc. Sed iam nunc audiat*) and it soon becomes clear that the Latin text from which the translator worked, to be called E, belonged to the β family. First, it omits to translate all the phrases the omission of which characterizes NTU. It also shows the following positive correspondences with the β family:

> 'he coueytede' (150) translates *appetebat* rather than D *expectaret*, HM *expeteret* or V *expetebat* (567)
>
> 'þu schuldest take good heede' (577) translates *diligenter attendas* (909) rather than γδ *diligas*
>
> 'let þy water-veynes of þyn heed altoberste and terys renne adoun' (1001–2) translates *rumpantur, eliciantur, trahantur* (1215–17) rather than the indicatives of γ and δ.

E was not, however, identical with any of the extant β manuscripts. It is possible to eliminate R and Ha straight away as they are incomplete; the Middle English contains parts of the text omitted by R and Ha. As to T, that too is soon eliminated, even apart from its late date (fifteenth century). T omits *in spelunca* (441); the Middle English translates 'in a caue' (6); T omits *in somno* (500); the Middle English translates 'in slep' (76). We can similarly demonstrate that E was not identical with N: in the phrase (1339) *quam iucunda facie . . . Christus occurrit* N omits *facie* but the Middle English translates 'wiþ how murye chiere' (1181); N, with T, reads *in initio suae conversationis* (562) for *conversionis*, but the Middle English has 'conversioun' (145); N reads *quid utilius pietate* for all other MSS, *quid humanius pietate*; the Middle English translates 'more ful of manhoode' (504); N reads *puritas conscientiae amauit* for *animauit* (1020) but the Middle English translates the verb as 'haad yquyked' (728). Finally, we can also rule out U; U omits the clauses *quam insuper poenam, quam confu-sionem . . . importet amissa* (457) but the Middle English has translated them as 'what peyne, what confusioun, what dampnacioun hit brenkþ ʒif hit be lost' (24–5).

In spite of this it remains true that E was a member of the β family. There are some significant correspondences with N against all other MSS: N reads *inimicior*, TURHa *immitior* (1229), the Middle English has 'straunge and mor enemy' (1021). But it is quite possible that E did have *immitior* and the translator simply misread it – it would be an easy mistake to make. E follows NU where N has *phantasma*, U *plasma vel fantasma*, DHVT *plasma* (601); the Middle English translates this as 'fantasies of fowl lust' (191). When NU read *nunquam ei remittentur peccata*, M *dimittentur*, all other MSS *remittuntur* (1028), E must have followed NU as the Middle English reads 'schulle neuere be forʒyue' (738), clearly rendering a future, not a present, verb. E probably read with NT where those MSS read *desiderata illa vestigia*, all others *desiderata vestigia illa tua* (1227); the Middle English translates 'þilke desiderable feet' (1018).

R and Ha probably derive from a common ancestor but it is unlikely that this was identical with E; it almost certainly included an interpolation in the meditation on the Day of Judgment found in R and Ha, of which the Middle English shows no trace. The Vernon translator did show some selectiv-ity and was capable of omitting sentences but there seems no reason why he should have failed to translate that passage, if it had been in his exemplar. There are nonetheless some interest-ing similarities between R and E. At 921 most MSS read *Hinc euntem in Bethleem . . . prosequere*, but N has *Hinc matrem*, R *hanc*. The Middle English here reads 'wayte whan Marie goþ to Bethleem, and ren after' (593). E could have had *hinc* however, and the translator could have misread it; or E could have read *hanc* with R (or could even have the reading of N). Or the translator could have made the change deliberately: he quite consistently increases the references to the Virgin Mary in his version. On the translation of 'his laste slep, þat he schulde be deed' (254–5) for all MSS *dormitionis* except for R, *dormita-cionis*, see note to the relevant lines. Again, where all other MSS read *Iesus rogatus sententiam*, R has *Iesus rogatus dare sententiam* (973) and the Middle English has 'whanne he was preyȝid to ȝyue þo doom' (667–8). Where all other MSS read *sic enim scriptum est*, R reads *sicut scriptum est* (1388), the Middle English has 'as þe book seyþ' (1252–3). But these are unimpressive compared with some of the correspondences between the Middle English and RHa. At 989–90 RHa read *laua lacrymis, terge capillis, demulce oculis*, a corrupt reading for *osculis* trustingly translated by the Middle English as 'whasch Cristes feet wit hote terys, wype hem wit þe herys of þyn heed, ley to softly þyn eȝen' (686–7). Where RHa read *tu curre* for all other MSS *tu currens* (1093), the Middle English concurs, translating 'ren þu, suster' (822). And where RHa read *liuor uulnerum* for all other MSS *liuor ulcerum* (1142) the Middle English translates this as 'þe wannesse of þe woundes' (890).

We have by no means exhausted the correspondences between the Middle English and R and/or Ha. The textual crux at 1018 where RHaU read *avaritia non contraxit* (see Note to ll. 725–6) is important for the Middle English as the translator, unfamiliar with the idiom, translated it literally as 'noon auarice haad wit-drawe' (726), which makes no sense but has the incidental virtue of betraying the reading of E. At 573 Ha alone of the β family reads *fricabat* for *fricat*; the Middle English adopts the past tense and translates this as 'he frotede' (159). At 620–1 where all other MSS read *quam pauci, quam pauci* R (with T) omits the repetition as does the Middle English (215). At 1272 all MSS except RHa read *quicumque inuenit me occidit me*, RHa have *occidet*. The Middle English follows this reading, quoting *Et quicumque inuenerit me, occidet me* (1085). (The reference is to Gen. 4:14.) Finally, we find an interesting reading at a point where one would hope for further evidence that E belonged to the β family. At 1271 where NTUHa have *in terra Naid*, probably the correct reading, the Middle English is obstinately silent, offering simply 'I made my dwellyngge vppon þe irþe, þat is to seyn, caste myn vnclene loue on irþely þyngges' (1083–4). But in R there is a blank after *in terra*; did E have a similar blank, or did E have the authentic reading which the translator could not understand, so he translated what he could and made a stab at a compensatory allegorical interpretation?

This consideration of E shows that it was connected with RHa and NTU. In fact E was probably derived from a common ancestor of RHaU, or one of its descendants. To be more specific, it is interesting that U does not carry the error *oculis* for *osculis*, so possibly E was intermediary between U and RHa, being made from the same exemplar as U (but without many of U's peculiar errors), and was the parent of the direct common ancestor of RHa.

One question to which the answer remains obscure is whether DH and VMB share a common ancestor other than the archetype. MS Bodley 423 helps answer this. It is not as useful for our purposes as the Vernon version, in that it is less communicative, but all the same one can intermittently perceive the Latin of its exemplar, which will be called O.

O clearly does not belong to the β family. The Middle English reads 'shaltow finde' (29) which translates *inuenies*, not, as NTU, *inuenias* (23); 'outake rogacion days and Whitsone Eue' (324) translates a phrase omitted by β at 419; 'couple myldenes to strengthe' (571–2) translates *Adde fortitudini modestiam* (707) but β omits *fortitudini*; 'solace and comfort of disperate' (610) translates *desperatorum erectio, peccatorum reconciliatio* (762), which β omits; 'in silence' (689) translates *in silentio* (882), omitted by β; the three verbs which occur as subjunctives in 1215–17 (*eliciantur, trahantur, rumpantur*) are translated as indicatives: 'alle the veynes of hir body dissolued and stilled oute teres of swete deuocyon' (882–3), 'the counceyle of his passyon' (820) is closer to γδ *secreta* than β *secretiora* (1101–2).

O, however, does not read consistently with γ or δ. As we shall see, O shows many positive correspondences with DH. At 101 all MSS except DH read *didicerint*; DH have *nouerint* and the Middle English 'whan they knowen' (101). At 453 all MSS except DH have *quod tibi impossible est per naturam*; DH omit *tibi* and the Middle English has 'the whiche is impossible by nature' (356); at 810 D (H is no longer running) reads *emulantur*, all others *emulentur*; the Middle English has 'thei . . . grucchen' (644–5); at 1234 D reads *redi*, all other MSS *redit*; the Middle English has 'and than come ayen' (898). At 392 where all other MSS read *certam . . . praescribere regulam tentabo* DH read *scribere*: the Middle English has 'I write . . . this forme of lyuynge' (302); at 494 all MSS except D have *Cogitet semper uirgo*, D omits *semper*: the Middle English reads

'A mayde shulde therfore thenke' (382). At 606 most MSS have *accipitris . . . superuolantis* but H has *superuenientis*; the Middle English conveys the idea of pursuit rather than flight with 'the ensaute and the pursute of hir enemy' (466); at 638 D has *in meditatione eius exardescit* for all other MSS *exarsit*; the Middle English does not have a direct translation but 'he waxe therby hugely ashamed and began with hymself a myghty batayl' (495–6) suggests that O had an inchoative verb.

But O was not identical with D, and probably not with the common ancestor of DH. At 540 where all other MSS read *illum . . . scito esse presentem*, and the Middle English 'haue mynde on oure Lorde' (423–4), D omits *scito*, H reads *cito* (homophonic with *scito* in Medieval Latin). The Middle English 'multiplieng of peny to peny' (51) did not translate D, *minimus . . . minimo* for all other MSS, *nummus . . . nummo* (58); 'then recluses' (52) did not translate D, *nam anachoritae*, all other MSS *non anachoritas* (55); the Middle English has 'wolde speke with the' (149), where D omits *loqui* (181); DH read corruptly *Qui potest capere ea* (448) but the Middle English quotes correctly *Qui potest capere, capiat* (350); 'he spak litel' (498) renders the phrase *loquacitati silentium* omitted by DH (641); and there are other less important discrepancies.

O sometimes reads with the δ family. At 212 both DH and V read *honeste honesta loqui*, a reading all too easily corrupted, as it is in the inferior δ manuscripts and by β into *honesta loqui*. The Middle English reads 'honestly to speke honest thinges'(166). O also has δ readings not shared by γ. 'Corrupcyon of nature' (592) is more likely to be a translation of MV *naturae . . . corruptione* than of all other MSS, *naturali . . . corruptione* (727); at 1083 V adds *absconditi* to *omnes thesauri . . . scientiae* and B has *sunt absconditi*. The Middle English has 'ther-yn is al the tresour . . . of wisdom and konnynge hyd' (805–6) although the translation could be influenced by a reminiscence of Col.2:3. At 1364, all MSS have *Ipse sit horreum tuum, ipse apotheca, ipse marsupium, ipse diuitiae tuae, ipse deliciae tuae*; BM add *ipse honor tuus*. V also has traces of this reading where one finds the meaningless *ipse hort=iuis* which is probably a corruption of *ipse hōr tuus*. The Middle English reads 'He wil be thy berne and thy richesse, thy whicche and thy purse, thy wurship and thy delytes' (928–9) where 'thy wurship' is accounted for by the γ reading. Another concurrence with a δ reading comes at 558 where DMV read *inter pueros et puellas*, all other MSS *inter puellas*. The Middle English has 'amongst conuersacion of children'(439). But O was not identical with M or V. Apart from those cases, already enumerated, where it reads with the unique D(H) reading, 'This were a gret vnkyndenes' (79) translates *Inhumanum hoc clamas* (80), which M omits; 'That this fastynge . . . excellith alle othir' (243–4) is the equivalent of the *excellentiae* omitted by MV (323); 'atte voys of a womman' (835–6) translates *ad uocem ancillae* (1126), which M omits; 'the rightwyse domesman mown they neither plete ne accuse' (961–2) translates *de iniquo . . . causatio* (1433–4), omitted by M. It is not worth proving that the translation was not made from B, an incomplete manuscript of such incredible corruptness that one would have the greatest trouble translating anything from it.

One is faced, then, with two possible conclusions. Perhaps DH and VMB do share a common ancestor, closer than the archetype, and it was from this common ancestor that the Middle English paraphrase was made. Or is it possible that O, which clearly had both γ and δ readings, was itself the archetype? It is unfortunate that all too often the Middle English is silent or evasive at a vital moment.

4. THE 'DE INSTITUTIONE INCLUSARUM' AND ANCRENE WISSE

There are obvious points of comparison between Aelred's *De Institutione Inclusarum* and *Ancrene Wisse*. Both are works of spiritual direction written by a man for a female audience and thus take their place in a long tradition which includes St Augustine's letter to the nuns of Hippo (the so-called Augustinian Rule), St Jerome's letter to Eustochium, Goscelin's to Eve, and Abelard's extensive correspondence with Heloise, Abbess of the Abbey of the Holy Paraclete. Furthermore, both Aelred and the author of *Ancrene Wisse* were writing to women not merely vowed to virginity, but more specifically those who had adopted a peculiar form of the religious life, that of the anchoress. Aelred's treatise exercised a considerable influence over the compiler of *Ancrene Wisse*, and the evidence for this has long been available.[1] Some passages, to summarize, are actually expanded translations from Aelred, while there are also general similarities of treatment which may be ascribed to the influence of a common subject and a common tradition, that of western asceticism, within which both writers worked. The most extensive borrowings are to be found in the sixth section of *Ancrene Wisse*, which is concerned with penance and bodily mortification. Here are four passages[2] taken from the Latin treatise and which were extensively discussed as long ago as 1929 by Miss H. E. Allen.[3] In general, the author of *Ancrene Wisse* follows Aelred closely but not slavishly, omitting passages from the Latin uncongenial to his own outlook and developing those aspects which appeal to him. His attitude towards mortification is throughout less extreme than Aelred's. For instance, while he expands Aelred's two ways of preserving chastity (*magna cordis contritione* and *carnis afflictione*) as 'pinsunge i flesch wið feasten, wið wecchen, wið disceplines, wið heard werunge, heard leohe, wið uuel, wið muchele swinkes' and 'heorte þeawes, deuotiun, reowfulnesse, riht luue, eadmodnesse, ant uertuz oþre swucche';[4] at the same time he has reversed the order and by implication exalted 'contrition of heart' above 'affliction of the body'. As the passage develops, *Ancrene Wisse* introduces the idea of the glad and willing, almost gay and chivalrous, acceptance of suffering, an attitude quite alien to Aelred; where the Latin has simply 'illos tamen

---

[1] H. E. Allen, 'The Origins of the Ancren Riwle', *PMLA* xliv (1929), 635–80. In spite of the author's explicit acknowledgement of his debt with the phrase 'as seint Ailred te abbat wrat to his suster', Miss Allen argued that this was a later scribal addition and that it was Aelred who was influenced by *Ancrene Wisse*. More recent scholars, however, have shown that her dating is impossibly early; far from pre-dating Aelred's treatise, the *Ancrene Riwle* is now dated as early thirteenth century and, more specifically by Professor Dobson, as written between 1215 and 1221. See E. J. Dobson, *The Origins of Ancrene Wisse* (Oxford, 1976), pp. 15–16.

[2] Morton 368, ff. These references to the *editio princeps, The Ancren Riwle*, ed. J. Morton, Camden Society LVII (1853), are conventionally given in *Ancrene Wisse* studies to facilitate comparison between the various recensions of the text; all the EETS editions are keyed periodically to Morton's original edition.

[3] *Art. cit.*, 655 ff.

[4] *Ancrene Wisse* f. 99^b/17–21 (M. 368). All quotations are taken from *The English Text of the Ancrene Riwle edited from MS Corpus Christi College Cambridge 402*, ed. J. R. R. Tolkien, EETS 249 (1962). This recension has been chosen on the grounds that it represents the author's final, revised version. Punctuation has been modernized and abbreviations expanded.

tanto dono indignos iudicat, qui aliquid laboris pro eo subire detrectant' the English reads, 'vngraciuse stondeð þer to3eines, ant makieð ham unwurðe to halden se heh þing, þe nulleð swinc þeruore bliðelice þolien'.[5]

The English writer contracts Aelred's lengthy enumeration of occasions of sin ('uolentes inter delicias casti esse, inter epulas continentes, inter puellas conuersari et non tentari, in commessationibus et ebrietatibus foedis distendi humoribus et non inquinari') to the concise 'bitweonen delices, ant eise, ant flesches este, hwa wes eauer chaste?'[6] And to the biblical image of the dangers of carrying fire in one's bosom, taken from Proverbs 6:27, he adds his own, more homely and colourful, example of a boiling pot to which one adds cold water to prevent it boiling over.[7] Further on, he follows Aelred in condemning those who seize on any trifling ailment as an excuse for avoiding mortification, but omits Aelred's impatient and exasperated conclusion that whether chastity is preserved by abstinence or sickness is a matter of indifference. Here *Ancrene Wisse* replaces the vague ailments of the Latin, 'ne incidant in languorem', by the more specific, and consequently more vivid, 'ofdred leste hare heaued ake, leste hare licome febli to swiðe, ant witeð swa hare heale',[8] but rejects Aelred's outburst against the shortcomings of contemporary ascetics. Instead we have a digression on the inferiority of physical to spiritual medicine, supported by two hagiographical anecdotes. And while Aelred's bald definition of true discretion is 'to put the soul before the body', for the author of *Ancrene Wisse* true wisdom lies in putting the health of the soul before that of the body and, only when a straight choice cannot be avoided, 'cheose ear licomes hurt, þen þurh to strong fondunge, sawle þrowunge'.

Apart from this section there are a few other direct textual parallels to be found. For instance, the description of the recluse as gossip, in the second part of *Ancrene Wisse*, 'an ald cwene to feden hire earen, a meaðelilt þe meaðeleð hire alle þe talen of þe lond, a rikelot þe cakeleð al þet ha sið ant hereð' translates Aelred's 'anus garrula uel rumigerula mulier . . . quae

[5] *CCCM*, ll. 555–7; *AW* f. 99ᵇ/23–5 (M. 368).
[6] *CCCM* ll. 557–60; *AW* f. 99ᵇ/25–6 (M. 368).
[7] *AW* f. 99ᵇ 27–100ᵃ/1.
[8] *CCCM* ll. 617–18, *AW* f. 100ᵃ, 4–5 (M. 368).
[9] *CCCM* 659–62; *AW* f. 100ᵇ, 14–15 (M. 372).

eam fabulis occupet, rumoribus ac detractionibus pascat'[10] (and provides evidence that the original reading was indeed *rikelot*, meaning 'chatterbox' and not *kikelot* (glossed with the OF *piot*) as found in MS Cotton Cleopatra C VI, f. 36/3[11]).

Ancrene Wisse also follows the central distinction which Aelred draws between the outer discipline of the body, which includes the practice of the virtues, *effectus operis*, and the inner discipline of the spirit and right disposition of heart, *affectus mentis*, in its treatment of penance and love (the sixth and seventh sections): 'Nu is al þis meast iseid of bitternesse *utewið*. Of bitternesse *inwið* segge we nu sumhweat, for of þes twa bitternesses awakeneð swetnesse her ȝet i þis world, nawt ane in heouene'.[12] We may also see a similar parallel in Aelred's distinction between 'corporales institutiones, quibus inclusa exterioris hominis mores componas' and 'formam praescriptam qua interiorem hominem uel purges a uitiis uel uirtutibus ornes' and the development in *Ancrene Wisse* of the idea of two rules, one the 'lady rule' of inner disposition (primarily love) and the other, outer, ancillary rule.[13] Other similarities of attitude may simply represent independent conclusions stimulated by similar problems. Both writers, for instance, consider it improper for an enclosed anchoress to give alms, as material charity can only too easily become an excuse for covetousness; in any case no recluse who is true to her vocation will have any money to spare.[14] But such remarks are not uncommon; Guigo, in his Carthusian Customs, says something very similar, and may well have influenced both writers independently.[15] Other works of mercy (such as keeping a school) are forbidden as emphatically by both writers, but here there may be another influence, that of the Cistercian Institutes.[16] Both writers use the story of the virtuous recluse who refused to admit even Martin, the saintly bishop of Tours; both use the image of gold tried in a

---

[10] *AW* f. 23ᵃ/15–17; *CCCM* ll. 24–6.

[11] On this, see B. Grattan Lee, *Linguistic Evidence for the Priority of the French Text of Ancrene Wisse* (The Hague, 1974), p. 20.

[12] *AW* f. 100ᵇ/25–8.

[13] *CCCM* ll. 1529–1532; *AW* f. 1ᵃ/15–1ᵇ/6.

[14] *CCCM* ll. 63–5; *AW* f. 112ᵃ/27–112ᵇ/9.

[15] On this, see A. Barratt, 'The *De Institutione Inclusarum* of Aelred of Rievaulx and the Carthusian Order', *Journal of Theological Studies* xxiii (1977), 531–2, and 'Anchoritic Aspects of *Ancrene Wisse*', *Medium Aevum* 49 (1980), 40–1.

[16] See n. to ll. 116–17 of the Bodley text, *infra*.

furnace as a metaphor for the trials of virginity; both urge the anchoress to be so continually recollected that she fall asleep at her book. But again common influences may be working independently – Sulpicius Severus, the bible and St Jerome in the examples cited – and they can hardly in themselves be used to demonstrate a relationship of dependence by the author of *Ancrene Wisse* on the English Cistercian. Even so, there is a considerable and undoubted debt on the part of the vernacular writer, whose treatment of the Latin is typical of his working methods: more and more he emerges as a remarkably creative synthesizer.[17]

It is interesting to observe, in this connection, that Aelred was a sufficiently unfamiliar authority in the early thirteenth century for the scribes of some of the *Ancrene Riwle* manuscripts to mangle his name without compunction. While the scribe of Cotton Cleopatra C VI represents him adequately as 'seint ailret' and the scribe of Cotton Titus D VIII as 'seint Ailreade', the scribe of Cotton Nero refers to a 'sein aldret' and the French version hazards an even wilder 'seint ailfred'. No wonder the author, in his own 'final and definitive version' as Professor Dobson characterizes *Ancrene Wisse*, was constrained to clarify his reference to 'seint ailred þe abbat'! (Some of the Latin MSS of *De Institutione* also have trouble with their author's name; Digby 218 refers to 'Aldredi abbatis' while Bodley Lat. theol. d.27 has 'Alveredum' and the very corrupt Bodley 36 'Eldredi abbatis'. But the Latin versions of *Ancrene Wisse* correctly describe him as 'sanctus Ailredus abbas'.)

By his own admission, then, the author of the *Ancrene Wisse* knew and used *De Institutione Inclusarum*. It only remains, in this connection, to dispose of a misconception. It has been asserted[18] that he also knew the meditative section of the treatise as part of the *corpus* of prayers and meditations erroneously ascribed to St Anselm.[19] The passage which is responsible for this reads as follows:

þear as seint Anselme seið þeos dredfule wordes. Hinc erunt

---

[17] As is shown by E. J. Dobson, *Moralities on the Gospels* (Oxford, 1975) *passim*.
[18] C. H. Talbot, 'The *De Institutis Inclusarum* of Aelred of Rievaulx', *Analecta Sacri Ordinis Cisterciensis* vii (1959), 170.
[19] See A. Wilmart, *op. cit.*, p. 192.

accusancia peccata. Illinc terens iusticia. Supra, iratus iudex. Subtra[20] patens horridum chaos inferni. Intus, urens consciencia. foris, ardens mundus. Peccator sic deprehensus in quam partem se premet?

Talbot asserts that this passage is from Chapter 33 of Aelred's treatise. Now it is true that there is a certain similarity; but the words here quoted are in fact from one of the few meditations which modern scholarship has left to Anselm.[21] (Two manuscripts of Aelred, however, compound the potential confusion by inserting parts of the Anselm text into the relevant passage (l. 1432 of the Latin text): MS BL Royal 8 D III, a thirteenth-century copy of parts of Aelred's treatise, adds to the sentence 'Si deponunt, infernalis putei eis ingeritur horror' the words 'uidebatur eis a dextris terrens iustitia, a sinistris peccata accusantia, intus conscientia urens, foris mundus ardens'; MS Oxford Hatton 101, another incomplete thirteenth-century manuscript, adds 'Sed si semetipsos respexerit interius apparebit conscientia torquens foris mundus ardens, a dextris terrens iustitia, a sinistris peccata accusantia.') The author of *Ancrene Wisse*, then, knew the work of both Anselm of Canterbury and Aelred of Rievaulx.

5. THE LANGUAGE OF THE TRANSLATIONS

1. *The Vernon Manuscript*

What follows is not an exhaustive linguistic description of the Vernon translation of *De Institutione Inclusarum*, but simply an attempt to highlight its most significant features, especially

---

[20] cf. *The English Text of the Ancrene Riwle edited from BM Cotton MS Cleopatra C VI*, EETS 267 (1972), p. 225 f.n.12.

[21] *AW* f. 83ª/1–5. (M.304). The *textus receptus* of Anselm at this point reads: Hinc erunt accusantia peccata, inde terrens iustitia; subtus patens horridum chaos inferni, desuper iratus iudex; intus urens conscientia, foris ardens mundus. 'Iustus vix salvabitur', peccator sic deprehensus in quam partem se premet? (*Anselmi Opera Omnia*, ed. F. S. Schmitt (Stuttgart, 1968) 6 vols. in 2, III, 83, ll. 72–4) This reading is followed by Cotton Nero (with the exception of 'Uix iustus salvabitur' (f. 82ᵛ, 16–20)). The variant readings of *AW*, however (*illinc* for *inde*, *supra* for *desuper*, *subtra* for *subtus*), the omission of 'vix iustus salvabitur' and the displacement of 'supra iratus iudex', are supported by MSS Cleopatra and Vitellius and Titus. It is of course possible that, with such a familiar passage, the *AW* author was quoting from memory; or he may have had access to a manuscript tradition no longer extant.

insofar as they can, without the benefit of rhyme evidence, be of use in considering the text's antecedents.

Bearing in mind the provenance of the Vernon manuscript[1] and the findings of Miss Serjeantson,[2] who located the language of the table of contents in the South Shropshire/South Staffordshire border area, one would expect the language of this text to exhibit strong West Midland characteristics.

And indeed it does. Numerous orthographic and grammatical forms point to a Western provenance, and many are specifically WMid:

Western

(i) Absence of unrounding of OE $\breve{y}$ is suggested by widespread *u*-spellings, e.g.: *dude* 157, 667, 824; *fulþe* 179, 1122, 1124; *gulty* 97; *(y)hud* 5, 1293; *hul* 580; *murye* 1181; *put* 'pit' 1275, 1315; *studefast* 1038; *sunne* 'sin' 183, 869; *vuel* 'evil' 67. In addition, the reflex of OE $\bar{y}$ is often represented by the AN grapheme *uy*, denoting $\bar{\ddot{u}}$, e.g.: *fuyr* 43, 45, 117, 119, etc.; *huyden* 1312; *pruyd(e* 277, 278, 279, 1300.

(ii) Absence of unrouding of OE $\bar{\breve{eo}}$ is suggested by several *eo*-spellings, e.g.: *deoreworthe* 1159; *eorþe* 1130; *freoly* 1157; *heo* 'she' 4, 11, 11, 51, etc.; *neode* 83, 96, 500; *neody* 433; *þeo* 454, 507 (on analogy with OE *hēo*, pron. pl.); *þeose* 255 (modelled on OE *þēos*, nom. sg. fem., or *þeossum*, dat. pl.). Occasional *ir*-spellings for OE *eor* + consonant may likewise point to the absence of eME unrounding, e.g.: *irnestly* 694; *irþe* 44, 348, 668, 784, etc.; *irþely* 669, 1084; *irþene* 342, 345; *irþi* 1111. Before *r*, the retained eME /ö/ often developed to /ü/ (cf., for example, the spellings *vrþe* (beside *erþe*), *vrþely* in *Pearl*), and this was later (much later than in the East or SE) unrounded to /i/.[3]

(iii) *here* 82, 87, 108, 108, etc., as the oblique case of the 3sg. fem. pron. is predominantly Western.

WMid

(i) There are sporadic occurrences of *o* for OE *a/o* before

---

[1] See p. xvii   [2] *loc. cit.*   [3] But see also p. li, III a (vi).

nasals (other than in lengthening combinations), e.g.: *from* 1294; *mon* 296, 432; *schome* 791; *þonke* 790.

(ii) The reflex of OM *ĕ* (OE *ǣ*) may be represented in *heþ* 1061, although in view of the lack of other corroborating forms in this text, and of the fact that this phenomenon is generally said to have disappeared by the end of the four-teenth century, the balance of probability is that *heþ* is simply a weakly stressed form.

(iii) The unvoicing of final *d* in *ant* 67, 83, 182, 541, etc., due to reduced stress, is characteristic of WMid texts.

(iv) The frequent use of *-ur*-graphies for secondarily stressed /-ər-/ (e.g. in *aftur*, *afturward*, *fadur*, *fadurles*, *modur*, *modurles*, etc., passim) is a WMid scribal characteristic.

The only major absentee among WMid forms is *a* as the product of *i*-mutation of OE *æ* before *l*-groups, of which there is no evidence in this text.

There is, therefore, ample linguistic evidence for a WMid provenance. But this is far from being the whole story. Beneath this top layer several other conflicting strata can be discerned. The extent to which the text is dialectally impure can be seen simply by reference to the confused pattern of forms of the past participle of verbs; for example, the following pairings occur in which it is possible to distinguish Southern, WMid and SE forms of strong verb past participles with final *-e* and (in verbs not otherwise prefixed) the prefix *y-* from EMid and Northern forms with final *-(e)n* and no prefix:

ybore, born; bynome, benomen; ido(o, doon; idrawe, drawen; yfalle, fallen; ifounde, founden; forʒite, forʒiten; forsake, forsaken; ygete, geten; yseye, yseyen (< OE *ge-sēon*); *ouercome, ouercomen; iwryte, wryten*

These dialectal strata can be conveniently discussed under three headings: WMid, Southerly, and Northern and EMid.

I WMid

In addition to the Western and more specifically WMid charac-teristics described above, there are numerous features of the accidence of the text which are Southern, SE or WMid and which, in view of the predominantly WMid overlay, might hesitantly be ascribed to this last region:

(i) The OE weak pl. ending of nouns is preserved, as -*(e)n*/ -*yn*, in *eʒen* 53, 123, 248, 326, etc.; *halwen* 1263; *heren* 'ears' 697; *lippen* 601, 970; *oxen* 476; *wrecchen*, -*yn* 394, 661, 1299, 1352.

(ii) Although the verbal inf. ending is overwhelmingly -*e*, many characteristic Southern and WMid -*(e)n* forms occur, in both native and OF loan words: *abyden* 1267; *adden* 329; *ben* 5, 45, 1287, 1291, etc.; *bern* 595; *cryen* 721; *doon* 258; *dwellen* 139; *eschewen* 199; *fynden* 203; *flen* 289, 1209; *folwen* 53; *gon, goon* 610, 740, 1088, 1301, etc.; *ʒyuen* 451; *han* 'have' 285; *handlen* 800; *hangen* 1214; *huyden* 1312; *knowen* 1318; *louen* 1046, 1319, 1396; *maken* 831, 1422; *ocupien* 491; *preyen* 721; *revyn* 928;[4] *sayn, seyn* 'say' 211, 259, 279, 410, etc.; *schewen* 230, 1396; *slen* 110, 167, 861; *sparen* 109; *taken* 70, 182; *wepen* 721; *wiþ-seyn* 732; *wryten* 1285.

(iii) The 1 and 3 pr. pl. endings of verbs is predominantly -*eþ*, with occasional -*yþ* spellings, e.g.: *byndeþ* 853; *benemyþ* 1176.

(iv) Sporadic examples occur of the pr.p. ending -*ynde*: *lykynde* 383; *stynkynde* 141, *179, 357, 478, etc.; *þenkynde* 204.

(v) There is a certain amount of evidence for the preservation of the -*i*- of OE Weak Class II verbs (*a*) with a short root syllable: *lotye* 'lurk' [OE *lotian*] 969, 1088, 1311; *styrye* 'incite' [OE *styrian*] 1412 (*b*) with a long root syllable: *revyn* 'forcibly deprive of' [OE *rēafian*] 928 (*c*) in the noun *louyere* 'lover' [f. OE *lufian*] 126.

(vi) Of the two more or less equally frequent forms of the 3sg. nom. fem. pron., *heo* is characteristic of this area (see further III c (iii) below).

II *Southerly*

There are numerous Southerly dialectal features in the text, ranging from broadly non-Northern, through Southern, to specifically SE or SW:

---

4 See further (v) below.

(a) Non-Northern

(i) The reflex of OE *a* + nasal in lengthening combination is frequently *o*: *hondes* 713; *lomb* 53, *876; *stond(e* 793, 919, 943, 949, etc.; *vnderstonde* 3; *wiþstonderes* 1265.[5]

(ii) *(o)o* is overwhelmingly predominant as the reflex of OE *ā*: *an(o)on* 103, 155, 484, 634, etc.; *g(o)on* 168, 610, 740, 1027, etc.; *h(o)ot(e* 571, 686, 968; etc.[6]

(iii) The widespread ME development of OE *e* + *nct* to *eynt*, as evidenced in *dreynt(e* 1069, 1119, 1132; *iqueynt* 118, is absent only from Northerly areas.

(iv) OE medial *c*, *cc* and final *c* are usually assibilated: *chirche*, *churche* 453, 454, 454, 458, etc.; *muche* 152, 189, 217, 236, etc.; *sechyþ* 309; *stench* 185, 299, 1099, 1278, etc.; *strecche* 73; etc.[7]

(v) The pr. 3sg. verbal ending *-(e)s* is entirely absent.

(vi) There are numerous unambiguous examples of *-(e)d* for *-(e)þ* as the pr. 3sg. and pl. verbal ending: *defoyled* 1300; *fayled* 531; *haad* 725, 725, 726, 727, etc.; *had* 927, 1055; *okepyed* 854; *seyd* 167, 420; *trauayled* 529; *turned* 594. It is not clear whether this phenomenon, which is not unexampled elsewhere in ME, reflects a genuine change, or whether it is merely scribal. There is some evidence to support the former view: cf., for example, (i) the forms *dan*, *dedyr*, *dis* of the *Paston Letters*; (ii) archaic NE *dem*, *den*, *dis* in the dialects of Kent, Sussex, etc.; (iii) the frequent appearance of *-d* in the pr. ind. 3sg. of verbs, and also in other words for final *-þ* (e.g. *moud* 'mouth', *wyd* 'with'), in *The Sayings of St Bernard* (ed. J. B. Monda, *Mediaeval Studies*, xxxii (1970), 299–307) the language of which is 'clearly Southeast Midland', and is localized by Prof. M. L. Samuels in SW Essex – although unfortunately there are no rhymes with etmyological *d* in this text

---

[5] The rather more frequent *a*-forms before *nd* (e.g. *fand* 615; *hand* 38, 39, 497, 724, etc.; *stand* 691, 842, 878, 899, etc.), although originating in the North, had a widespread southerly distribution by this time.

[6] But cf. III a (iii) below.

[7] The infinitival *k*-forms (*seke* 646; *þenke* 203, 386, 970; *werk* 358) are phonologically regular, arising from the reversion of palatalized /k^j/ to /k/ caused by the following back vowel; the other *k*-forms (*þenkeþ* 10; *þenkynde* 204) are on the analogy of the infinitive and the indicative pl. *sechyþ* (309) presumably exhibits levelling from the pr. 2 and 3sg. forms which were not syncopated in the OE period. Cf. also III a (x) below.

which would clarify the matter; and (iv) the abundant examples of *d* for *þ* in the Southern text of *Octavian* (ed. G. Sarrazin (Heilbronn, 1885)), which elicit the editor's comment (p. xii) that the confusion between *d* and *þ* arises from a Southern English dialectal change whereby the spirant /θ/ 'tönend geworden war, sowie aus dem Umstande, da inlaut. *d* in spätesten ME eine Neigung hat, zur Spirans zu werden (z.B. *faþyr* statt *fadyr*)'. Sarrazin probably approaches the heart of the matter here; that is to say, when the change, well evidenced, of late ME medial /d/ to /ð/ is matched by a more or less contemporary (Southern) voicing of /θ/ to /ð/ (and this latter phenomenon, which it would perhaps be more appropriate in this context to characterize as a change of consonant quality from fortis to lenis, is especially liable to happen in weakly stressed syllables, such as the verbal ending -*eþ*), the pattern /θ/>/ð/</d/ tends to be produced. This would naturally open the way (notably in a spelling system which had no distinct symbols for /θ/ and /ð/) to a back-spelling *d* for /ð/</θ/. Thus the *d*-graphy is in a sense both scribal, in that it is an erroneous back-spelling, and phonologically significant, in that it suggests that the weakly stressed verbal ending /-eθ/ was voiced to /-eð/.

(b) Southern

(i) There is evidence of Southern smoothing of OE *ea* to *e* before /χ/ and /χ/ + consonant: *(al)þey, þey3* 186, 202, 219, 221, etc. (OE *þēah* shortened to *þeah > þeh > þeih*); *flex* 342, 344, 347, 355, etc.; *sey3, say* 'saw' 242, 992; *were* 156, 549; *wext* 269 (on analogy with the inf. and pr. pl.) (cf. *Ayenbite ulexe, wexe*, etc.).

(ii) OE *f* in initial position is written usually *f*, but occasionally *v*: *av(i)er* 217, 793, 833, 943; *aviere* 572, 856; *ived* 781; *val* 589; *vattere* 722; *ved* 1043; *vedde* 1183; *veleþ* 182; *vieledest* 572; *vielþe* 352, 485, 552, 1102; *vier* 371, 572; *vylle* 1005; *vor* 62; *vorheed* 290; *vre* 'free' 13; *vrend* 33; *vurþermor(e* 24, 304, 355, 416, etc.

In view of the evidence of (c) and (d) it seems rather more

plausible to attribute these features to the SE rather than the SW area, although both are possible.

(c) South Eastern

(i)   There is ample evidence of OK *ē* for OE *ȳ*: (*a*) *e*-spellings, the reflex of OK *ē*: *ferst(e* 344, 424, 555; *fulfeld(e, -felþ* 473, 568, 570, 1286, etc.; *knet* 319, 1329; *lest* 734; *merþe* 587; *nel* 40, 168, 168, 169, etc.; *schette* 1207; *sennes* 677; *trest* 942; *mankende* 1065; *mende* 'mind' 205; *felþe* 891; *hediþ* 697; (*b*) *ie*-spellings, the reflex of OK *ē* and lengthened *ĕ*:[8] *aviere* 572, 856; *miende* 374, 511, 554, 622, etc.; *vielþe* 352, 485, 552, 1102; *vier* 371, 572.

(ii) The form *hiere* 'ear' (859) may indicate the characteristic SE development of a front glide before the reflex of OE *ēa*. The *ie*-graphy cannot, unless it is an error, have the same status as it has elsewhere in this text.[9] Possibly it is to be explained along the lines suggested by J. K. Wallenberg[10] to account for the graphies *ye, yea, ya* in the *Ayenbite of Inwyt*: that is, it represents /i̯ẹ̄/, showing the development (in speech) of a front glide *i̯* before slack *ē* (cf. the spelling *yeren* (× 2; = 'ears') in the *Ayenbite*). This glide is especially liable to develop before slack *ē* in initial position (and notably when the previous word ends in a front vowel, although that is not the case here).

(iii) There is sporadic evidence of OK *īo*: the 3sg. fem. pron. *hy* (49) is SE (OK *hī(o*; cf. *Ayenbite hi*); and *vylle, fil* 'fell' (1005, 1097) may represent OK *fīoll* (cf. *Ayenbite uille*), although it could alternatively show shortening and raising of /ẹ̄/ to /i/ in closed syllables before *l*, which phenomenon is recorded from over a very wide area, excluding only the South.[11]

(iv) The reflex of the *i*-mutation of OE *ea* + /χ/ + consonant is *eȝ*: *leȝȝe* 243. This form is Essex-London as well as SE (cf. *Ayenbite lheȝȝe, Kyng Alisaunder leighȝen*), but in

---

[8] The *ie*-graphy, which presumably represents /ẹ̄/, was adopted from AN; it originally represented the AN diphthong /ie/, which was monophthongized to /ẹ̄/ in the middle of the twelfth century.

[9] See footnote 8.

[10] *The Vocabulary of Dan Michel's* Ayenbite of Inwyt (Uppsala, 1923), pp. 305–9.

[11] See Jordan, §34.1.

view of the other SE forms it is probably to be ascribed to the latter area here.

(v) The *iew*-graphy of *fiewe* (879, 1404) indicates *ęu*, rather than the *ęu* one would normally expect in this word. General raising of ME *ęu* to *ęu* is not to be thought of at such an early date, so the graphy presumably represents specifically SE *ēaw>ęu* (*>iu*).[12]

(vi) The form *styngyn(g)ge* (107, 297) apparently reflects the voicing of /nk/ in medial position that is evidenced by numerous forms in ME texts from the SE and contiguous areas (e.g. in the *Ayenbite*: *þengþ* 'thinks', *dringþ* 'drinks'; in the *Lambeth Homilies*: *dringen* 'drink'), and is suggested by several back-spellings of *nc* for /ŋg/ in the OK Glosses.

(vii) The word 'world' and its derivatives are written *world(- : wordl(-* in the ratio 1:17 (e.g. *wordl(e* 4, 6, 282, 354, etc.; *wordliche* 106, 244, 432, 452, etc.). The *dl*-graphy probably represents a genuine metathesis of *ld*, which is well attested in this word in the SE (e.g. in the *Ayenbite* and the poems of William of Shoreham) and in contiguous areas (e.g. in the *Lambeth Homilies*).

(viii) The distribution of the conj. *al)what* 'until' (172, 974, 1286, 1415) is Southern and overwhelmingly SE, that of the ON loanword *agreyþeþ* (53, 926, 1351) markedly, though not exclusively, SE.

(d) South Western

One isolated form apparently indicates specifically SW provenance, namely *dire* 'dear' (548, 649), which seems to reflect earlier *dīere* with i-mutation of *īu* to WS *īe* (later *ī*).

It is, of course, tempting, in view of the large body of evidence for SE dialect forms in (c), to embrace the evidence of categories (a) and (b) as supportive material for theorizing about a major stage in the transmission of the text, when it was 'translated' by a SE redactor. In all prudence that temptation should probably be resisted, but on the basis of (c) alone, the possibility that such a stage existed can be admitted.

[12] See Luick, §399, 6.

III *Northern and EMid*

There is a significantly large body of evidence that at one stage in the transmission of the text it was written in a Northern dialect: several phonological and lexical features are specifically Northern, and although the majority of them are either somewhat dubious in validity or very small in comparative quantity of forms, or both, taken together with another body of phonological and inflectional features that are either Northern or EMid, their significance cannot be overlooked; the Northern features have the air of isolated survivors, indicating that they may represent a very early – perhaps even the earliest – stage of the text.

(a) *Northern*

(i) One example occurs of an *al*-graphy for OE *a* in open syllable: *walkyngge* 'keeping watch' 603. *OED* records *walk* as a fairly common Northern and Scottish form of *wake* from the fourteenth to the eighteenth century, where *l* is in effect a diacritic indicating the extreme back quality of the vowel in these dialects.

(ii) Seventeen examples occur of *a* for OE *a* before *ld*: *baldeliche* 28; *baldely* 600; *behald* 32, 507, 508, 779, etc.; *halde(þ* 216, 225, 1048, 1149.

(iii) There are isolated occurrences of *a* for OE *ā*: *gawe* 740; *wham* 111, 118 (with the vowel assimilated to that of the nom. masc. and fem. pron.).

(iv) The orthography of *poryngge* (794) may be Northern; the etymon of the verb is unclear, but the usual ME forms *pure, poure, powre* suggest an OE **pūrian*, and *o* was occasionally used in Northern dialects to represent /ū/.

(v) It seems likely that one example survives of the Northern *oy*-graphy for /ū/: *moynde* 'mind' 1408, although this depends upon an emendation.[13]

(vi) It is possible that the *ir*-graphies for OE *eor* + consonant in *irnestly* 694; *irþe* 44, 348, 668, 842, etc.; *irþely* 669, 1084; *irþene* 342, 345; *irþi* 1111; *wirschipe* 591 could evidence the retention of *ẹ̄* in Northern dialects, where

[13] See Commentary, p. 157.

lengthening in open syllables of *i* to *ę̄* took place, and thus *i* was a frequent back-spelling for *ę̄*.[14]

(vii) The form *teylys* 'tiles' 706 exhibits a development peculiar to districts north of the Humber, whereby OE *ĭ* + original /γ/ in open syllable >/iχ/>/ę̄χ/.[15]

(viii) The form *alþouʒt* 'although' 535, with unexplained final *-t*, is strictly Northern and Scottish in distribution.

(ix) The form *deed* 'death' 1225, 1225 is specifically Northern in distribution.

(x) It is possible that the *c*-graphy of *stenc* *552; *whic* 24, 145, 257, 268, etc.; *whyce* 178 may represent northerly /k/, rather than southerly /tʃ/.

(xi) It is not possible to tell without the evidence of rhymes whether the forms *ryg* 881; *ligge* 339; *liggynge* 615 exhibit northerly /g/ or southerly /dʒ/ as the reflex of OE *cg*. The *(g)g*-graphy suggests /g/ (cf. *leg(e* 859, 981 < ON *leggr*), but there is evidence to show that /g/ for /dʒ/ had extended into the language of the Midlands in the ME period, possibly as far south as Worcestershire, Warwickshire and Bedfordshire, so its value as a criterion of provenance is reduced.

(xii) The *v*-graphy of *yveue* 408 is probably just a scribal variant of *w* (cf. *driwe* 600, with *w* for *v*), but if it does represent a genuine phonetic change, it would point to a Northern provenance.

(b) Northern or EMid

(i) The *i*-graphy for OE *ē* in *hir* 582, 829, 889, 933; *hirυpon* 801 may represent lME raising of /ę̄/ to /ī/, an isolative change which took place in the fourteenth century chiefly before *r* (less often before *s*, *v* and perhaps *k*) and appears to have originated in the East and North, although it was

[14] More than one other explanation is, however, possible; cf. p. xliv, §ii, and, for *wirschipe*, p. liii, III c (i).

[15] If, however, the graphy *ey* indicates a diphthongal pronunciation, this would present a picture which is at variance with the later development of Northern *ę̄* + /χ/, in which the vowel remained undiphthongized, and would indicate rather the non-Northern development of /ę̄χ/ to /ēj/. A more likely explanation is that the *y* here is simply a diacritic of length (cf. the *uy*-graphy (p. xliv, §i) and the *oy*-graphy (p. li, III a (v))), and that *ey* represents /ę̄/, as elsewhere in this text (see p. xlix, footnote 8).

accepted early into London English (it is evidenced in Chaucer).

(ii) There is abundant evidence of unrounding of OE *ȳ*: *chirche* 454; *kyng(e* 31, 312, 312, 585, etc.; *kisse* 601, 619, 691, 698, etc.; *kitte* 858; *ryg* 881; *synne* 185, 259, 274, 346, etc.; *smyllyngge* 990; *þirlyd* 911; *kynde* 21, 419; *bisy* 438, 444; *ibyryed* 350, 443; *myrye* 828; *myryli* 638; *stire* 100, 102, 397, 635, etc.; *lyte* 128; *litul* 220, 226, 309, 485, etc.

(iii) There is abundant evidence of unrounding of OE *ēo*: *aver* 217, 833, 943; *derke* 86; *erþe* 568; *herte* 19, 73, 80, 122, etc.; *sterres* 35; *swerd* 857, 952; *alto-cleueþ* 918; *be(e* 6, 11, 21, 25, etc.; *breste(e* 95, 517, 807, 821, etc.; *depe* 693; *deuel* 43, 71, 191, 198, etc.; *fle(n* 289, 609, 660, 1121, etc.; *forbede* 714; *frely* 1063; *frend* 33, 591; *fresyngge* 158; *leem, lemes* 118, 616; *prestes* 455, 864; *þef* 613, 617, 624, 852; *see* 483, 494, 621, 656, etc.; *stee* 398, 580 (on analogy with OE *wrēon*); *trees* 308; and, with *ie*-graphy:[16] *avier* 793; *diere* 385, 442, 813; *lieue* 388; *ryed* 884; *þyef* 910, 958; *wieþ* 674.

(iv) Many past participial forms of verbs appear with final *-(e)n* and no *y*- prefix.[17]

(v) The distribution of *þe* as a weakly stressed variant of the 3pl. pron. is strictly EMid and Northern, according to M. L. Samuels' findings.[18]

(c) EMid

In addition to the above features that could be either EMid or Northern, there are a few that may be linked more specifically to the EMid area:

(i) It is possible that the form *wirschipe* (591) may be of EMid origin; generally speaking, lOE *weor-*, *wyr-* and *wur-* all fell together in eME *wur-*, but by contrast in EMid *wyr-* became *wir-*.[19]

(ii) The pr. 1 and 3pl. ending is predominantly *-eþ*, but a few *-en* and *-e* forms occur, which are, in non-preterite-present

[16] See p. xlix, footnote 8.
[17] See p. xlv above.
[18] 'Some Applications of Middle English Dialectology', *English Studies*, 44 (1963), 81–3.
[19] But cf. p. li, III a (vi).

verbs, specifically EMid: *coueyten* 1388; *ȝyuen* 927; *han* 464; *seyn* 181, 187, 530; *spare* 182; *take* 219.

(iii) The 3sg. nom. fem. pron. *sche(e, she* (54, 74, 77, 78, etc.), which is as frequent in the text as *heo*, appeared first in the EMid, although by the fourteenth century it was occurring with some frequency in London and in areas further west.[20]

The above data allow one to form the following hypothesis: before this text was written down in the form in which we now have it, with its overlaying of WMid characteristics, it existed in at least two other versions, the language of which had marked SE and Northern features (and possibly existed also in EMid and even SW versions). However, on the order in which these various strata came to be added, and thus on the area in which the translation was originally made, it is impossible to speculate with any profit.

2. *MS Bodley 423*

The language of the translation in MS Bodley 423 is remarkable mainly for its homogeneity and scribal consistency. It presents numerous features which enable one progressively to narrow down its possible area of provenance with some confidence:

I *Southerly*

(i) The reflex of OE *ā* and *ă* before a lengthening combination is (*o*)*o*: *stoon* 865; *honde* 145; *honycombe* 807.

(ii) The pr. 2 & 3sg. verbal ending -(*e*)*s* is entirely absent.

(iii) The pr.p. ends in -*ing(e* (or, if the verb stem ends in -*i*, in -*eng(e*).

II *Easterly*

(i) There is abundant evidence of unrounding of OE *ēo* (other than in the group *weor*-[21]): *erthe* 506; *herkne* 813; *brest* 402; *crepe* 863.

---

[20] See the map in M. W. Bloomfield and L. Newmark, *A Linguistic Introduction to the History of English* (New York, 1965), p. 221.

[21] E.g. *world* 948; *worthy* 149. *werld* 918 is due to Norse influence.

(ii) The reflex of OE *a/o* before nasals is *a*: *man* 141; *hamours* 595.

III *Easterly excluding South Eastern*

The reflex of OE *ȳ* is *i*: *byclippeth* 870; *kisse* 144; *shitte* 'shut' 653; *fyre* 370; *hyde* 864.

IV *EMid and London*

(i)   The 3sg. fem. pron. is *she*; *her*; and the 3pl. pron. *they*, *thei*, *thay*, *thai*; *her*; *hem*.

(ii) The 1 and 3pr. pl. ending of verbs is almost invariably *-en*, but some endingless forms are found, especially when the subject of the verb is inverted, and there are a very few *-eth* forms.

These features in a text of the mid-fifteenth century strongly suggest a dialect belonging to the East (probably South East) Midlands. Professor A. McIntosh has kindly informed us that the scribal dialect can be located in the Buckinghamshire–W.Hertfordshire–Bedfordshire area. It is interesting that there is some external evidence that the scribe may have been associated with St Alban's Abbey, which exactly fits the above geographical description.[22]

---

[22] See pp. xxxi–ii.

SELECT BIBLIOGRAPHY

The list given below is of works which for convenience are referred to in this edition by abbreviated titles or by the author's surname only.

DICTIONARIES, PERIODICALS, ETC.

ANTS: Anglo-Norman Text Society.
CCCM: Corpus Christianorum, Continuatio Mediaevalis.
DNB: The Dictionary of National Biography, ed. L. Stephen *et al.* (London, 1885–1900).
MED: Middle English Dictionary, ed. Hans Kurath, Sherman M. Kuhn, and John Reidy (Ann Arbor, 1952–).
MET: Middle English Texts.
MLR: Modern Language Review.
OED: The Oxford English Dictionary on Historical Principles, ed. J. A. H. Murray *et al.* (Oxford, 1884–1933).
OLD: Oxford Latin Dictionary, ed. A. Souter (Oxford, 1968–).
PL: Patrologia Latina.
PMLA: Publications of the Modern Language Association of America.
RMLWL: Revised Medieval Latin Word List, ed. R. E. Latham (London, 1965).
S.C.: Summary Catalogue.
TPS: Transactions of the Philological Society.

OTHER WORKS

AW: *The English Text of the Ancrene Riwle: Ancrene Wisse*, Corpus Christi College Cambridge MS 402, ed. J. R. R. Tolkien. EETS 249 (1962).
Ayenbite: Ayenbite of Inwyt, ed. R. Morris. EETS 23 (1866), rev. P. Gradon (1965).
Benedict, *Rule: Benedicti Regula*, ed. R. Hanslik (Vienna, 1960).
Brunner-Johnston: K. Brunner, *An Outline of Middle English Grammar*, trans. G. K. W. Johnston (Oxford, 1965).
CT: Canterbury Tales.
Jordan: R. Jordan, *Handbuch der mittelenglischen Grammatik*, 3rd edn. (Heidelberg, 1968).
Luick: K. Luick, *Historische Grammatik der englischen Sprache* (Leipzig, 1921–40, repr. Stuttgart, 1964).

Mustanoja: T. F. Mustanoja, *A Middle English Syntax*, Part 1 (Mémoires de la Société Néophilologique de Helsinki XXIII, Helsinki, 1960).

Spec. Car.: Aelred of Rievaulx, *Speculum Caritatis*, ed. C. H. Talbot, *Aelredi Rievallensis Opera Omnia, CCCM I* (Turnholt, 1971), 1–161.

Summary Catalogue: F. Madan *et al.*, *Summary Catalogue of Western Manuscripts in the Bodleian Library* (Oxford, 1895–1953).

NOTES ON THE TEXTS

The spelling of the manuscripts is reproduced, with the exception that in cases where a MS reading appears to be corrupt, we have emended it in an attempt to restore the original reading. In such cases the MS reading is given in the footnotes. Where, in the case of the Vernon text, the MS has been 'corrected' by a hand more or less contemporary with the scribe's[1] we have restored the scribe's original form; the alterations are given in the footnotes.

Punctuation and capitalization conform to modern practice, but single lexical units written as separate words have been hyphenated. However, where two lexical units are written as one word, this has been preserved.

Abbreviations are expanded conventionally unless this is contraindicated by the evidence of full forms in the MSS. Expansions used for such exceptions and for abbreviations of dubious significance are here noted:

(i) In both texts, *þ* is expanded as *per*, as there is no evidence for the lowering of *per* to *par*.

(ii) In Bodley 423, *Iħu*, which is nowhere written out in full, is expanded as *Iesu*, *Iħs* as *Iesus* and *Xm̄* as *C(h)ristum*; *on* and *ion* with varying forms of abbreviation marks are rendered as *ion*. A superscript *a* is usually expanded as *ra* except in *abrahm̆s*, *serŭnt* and *Adm̆*, which are rendered as *abrahams*, *seruant* and *Adam*. A suspension sign over a vowel is given its usual value, but a similar stroke through an ascender (e.g. *ħ,ƀ*) is not expanded unless it is next to a vowel. A suspension over a final consonant is not expanded.

(iii) In Vernon, *Iħu* and *Iħs* are expanded as *Ihesu* and *Ihesus*, on the basis of the uncontracted form *Ihesu* (871). *oū* is expanded as *oun*. The loop which conventionally indicates final *-es* is expanded accordingly where appropriate, but in cases where this is grammatically improbable or impossible it is

---

[1] See p. xv.

expanded as *-e*. A stroke through the ascender of final *h* (*ħ*) is expanded as *-e*.

In textual footnotes the abbreviation for nasals is indicated by a superscript dash (⁻) and final suspensions by an apostrophe (′).

purgith out al drede. and clensith the soule from filthe. & makith
it to se god. And often to fle by heuenly desire. hopynge to welle
ther. worlde withouten ende.

Here begynneth a tretys that is a rule and a forme of ly=
uyng suche solitary lyf. was &tuyuge. prepuyug to a recluse.
ordeyned of ffadirs in the olde tyme.

&fter thou hast ofte axed of me a forme of lyuyug. accordyg
to thyn estat. in asmuche as thou art enclose that thou
þou thou hauist axid it of suche con. as coude haue fulfilled thyn
desie. natheles after that simple felynge that god hath youen me
I shal write to the a forme. gadred out of holy fadirs doctrinis
afore tymes. ffirst the behoueth to knowe why that suche a so=
litary lyf was ordeyned. Some ther been. to whom it was
ful pilous to lyue among many. Ther were also some al though
it were not pilous to lyue amonge many. natheles it was ful
greuous. And many ther been whiche dradden noon of thes
two. but chosen this lyf. as a lyf moost fruytful to helthe of
soule. So that either thei fleen perel whiche might haue falle.
or muche harme whiche might betyde thurgh her presence. or ellis
that thei mighten by suche leyser. more fixly syghe and sobbe
after the loue of Ihu with longyng desie. many of these that
fledden fro perel and harm whiche might falle. haue her liflode
in wildirnes with gret labour. In that othir syde. thei that
fledden for fixdom of spirit. chosen to be closed in an house.
out of alle mennes sight. whose part hast thou chosen. and
auowed the to. But many ther ben. that knowe not. ne charge
not the profit of solitary liuyng. supposyng that it be ynogh.
only to shitte her body bitwene two walles. whan not
only the thoughte remeth aboute besynes of the worlde.
but also the tunge is occupied al day. either aboute tidynges
curiously enquering. and sechinge after hem. or elles of her
neighbores yuel name. by way of bakbityng. so that vnnethes
now a dayes shaltow finde a solitary recluse. that either tofore
the wyndowe shal sitte an olde woman fedynge hir with tales.
or elles a new iangeler. and teller of tidynges of that monke. or
of that clerke. or of twoes dissolucion. or of maidens wantoun
townes. of the whiche arisith laughyng. scornynge. and vnclene

DE INSTITUTIONE INCLUSARUM
MS BODLEY 423

Here begynneth a tretys that is a rule and a forme of lyuynge perteynyng to a recluse.

⌈*Capitulum primum*⌉

Why suche solitary lyf was ordeyned of fadirs in the olde tyme

Suster, thou hast ofte axed of me a forme of lyuyng accordyng to 5
thyn estat, inasmuche as thou art enclosed. That wolde Iesu thou
haddist axid it of suche oon as coude haue fulfilled thyn desire.
Natheles after that simple felynge that God hath youen me, I shal
write to the a forme gadert out of holy fadirs tradiciouns afore-tymes.

First the behoueth to knowe why that suche a solitary lyf was 10
ordeyned. Somme ther wern to whom it was ful perilous to lyue
among many. Ther were also somme [to whom], although it were not
perilous to lyue amonge many, natheles it was ful greuous. And many
ther wern whiche dradden noon of thes too but chosen this lyf as a lyf
moost fruytful to helthe of soule. So that either thei fledden perel 15
whiche might haue falle, or muche harme whiche might betyde
thurgh her presence, or ellis that thei mighten by suche leiser more
frely syghe and snobbe after the loue of Iesu with longyng desire.

Many of these that fledden fro perel and harm whiche might falle
wanne her liflode in wildirnes with gret laboure. In that othir syde, 20
thei that fledden for fredom of spirit chosen to be closed in an house
out of alle mennes sight, whiche part hast thou chosen and avowed the
to. But many ther ben that knowe not ne charge not the profit of
solitary liuyng, supposyng that it be ynow, oonly to shutte her body
bitwene too walles, whan not only the thoughte rennith aboute 25
besynes of the worlde, but also the tunge is occupied alday, either
aboute tidynges, curiously enquering and sechinge after hem, or elles
of her neighbores yuel name, by way of bakbityng, so that vnnethes
now-a-dayes shaltow finde a solitary recluse, that either tofore the
wyndowe shal sitte an olde womman fedynge hir with tales, or elles a 30
new iangeler and teller of tidynges of that monke, or of that clerke, or
of widowes dissolucion, or of maidens wantownes, of the whiche
arisith lawghyng, scornynge and vnclene / thoughtes slepynge or
wakynge, so that atte last the recluse is fulfilled with lust and likynge,
bakbitynge, sclaundre and hatrede and the tother with mete and 35
drinke.

12 to whom] *om.*

Alle thes causen gret lettyng to Goddes seruauntes bothe wakyng and slepynge, in meditacion and praier and contemplacion. What happith herof, trowist thou? Certeyn suche lusty tales gendren lecch-
40   erous ymaginatyf thou3tes, neuere cessynge vnto the tyme she consente to falle, sekynge by whom, where and whan she might fulfille in dede that the whiche hath so longe be vnclenly thoughte. This wrecchidnes hath often be seen of hem that han ben enclosed, by the whiche the wyndowe hath be maad moor, that euereyther might
45   come in or out to other, soo that atte last of a recluse or of an ancresse selle is maad a bordel hous.

⌜Capitulum ij⌝

That a recluse shal fle couetise and besynesse of getyng of worldly godes

50   Somme also ther ben which ben busy in gadrynge of worldly good, in bestaille, in wolle, in multipl[i]eng of peny to peny and shilyng, so þat thei oughten rather to be called housewyues than recluses. They ordeyne mete for her bestes, herdes for her catell and atte yeres ende they loke after the nomber or after the price. After this folewith
55   byinge and sellynge, of the whiche cometh couetise and auarice. Suche ben ofte deceyued by the fende counsailynge hem to gadre money forto departe it in almes, by releuynge of fadirles and modirles children, or for her frendes, or for gystnynge of poure religious men or wommen and suche othir; and al this is but a disceyt. Al this longith
60   not to the, but rathir to be poure and with pore peple to resceyue thy liflode.

It is a token of gret mistrust if a recluse care bisely for hir lyflode, sithen oure lord Iesu Crist seith: *Primum querite regnum dei et iusticiam eius et hec omnia adicientur vobis.* 'First,' he seith, 'sekith
65   the kyngdom of heuen and the rightwisnesse of him, and al that ye neden shal be cast to yow.' Therfore take good heed and be wel war that thou haue not to do with gret besynesse of worldly good but rather, if it may be, lyue with laboure and bysenesse of thin hondes with som honest trauail with-in thiself, for that is the moor syker way
70   to parfeccyon-warde.

Natheles, if thy compleccion be feblyd and might not trauaile, than
f. 179   er thou haddist ben / enclosed, thou shuldist haue enquered the suche frendes where thou mightist resceyue thy liflode with othir pore peple, that thou mightist haue noo cause to gadir worldly good. Ther
75   shuld no poure peple crye after worldly good aboute thy selle. Perauenture thou saist, 'Hoo might lette that?' I say not this for I wolde thou lettist it, bot I wolde that pitously thou sattist stil and

51 multiplieng] multipleng

suffredist it and yf they knewen that thei shuld no thinge resceyue,
thei wolden sone voide. Than saistow, 'This were a gret vnkyndenes';
yhe, and I say, 'If thou haue moor than mete and drinke and vesture,   80
thou art neither good mynchen ne recluse.' Natheles, what that thou
mightist gete with laboure of thyn hondes ouer that the nedith, I
wolde it were deled to pore peple by other menes than thiself.

Be wel war that no messanger, waiter of vnclennesse, bringer of
letters fro monke or from clerke rowne venym in thyn ere of veyn lust   85
or of likynge, for therof ariseth perels; therfore for no thynge resceyue
neither lettre ne rownyng without audience of hym that is thy gostly
fader, or som other honest persone.

⌐Capitulum iij⌐

That a recluse shuld not haue to do of hospitalyte anempst religiouse   90
gystes, for it longith not to hir

Firthermore I wolde thou were war of resceiuynge of yistes by way
of hospitalite anempst wommen of deuocyon, religious or other, for
ofte-sithes amonge gode ben medled badde; al-though her communicacion atte begynnynge be of sadnes and vertuous lyuynge, er than   95
thei departe worldly daliaunce shal be shewed furthe, and otherwhile
wordes of flesshly loue. Of suche be war, lest thou be compelled to
here that thow shuldist not and to speke that thou woldist not. By this
perauenture thou dredist shame, that neither thou maist comforte
pore folke in yeuynge of almes ne resceyue religious gystes: yhe, and I   100
say, drede not this, for whan they knowen thy naked purpos, thanne
haue thei no cause to repreue the, neither for pore folke ne for noo
religious gystes.

I nolde thou were a mony-maker: sithen than I nolde, as I seyde
before, that thou were a mony-maker for noo suche causes, muche   105
moor than for noo gret meyne in housholde. Se now what meyne
thou shuldist haue. First chese an honest anxient womman in
lyuynge, no iangler ne royler-aboute, noo chider, noo tidynges-teller,
but such oon that may haue witnesse of hir good conuersacyon, and
honest. Hir charge / shal be to kepe thyn houshold and thy lyflod, to   f. 179ᵛ
close thy dores and to resceyue that shuld be resceyued and to voide
that shuld be auoided. Vnder hir gouernaile shuld she haue a yonger
womman of age to bere gretter charges, in fettynge of wode and water
and sethynge and greithynge of mete and drynke. And that she be
ouerloked vnder gret awe, lest thurgh hir wantownes and dissolucyon   115
thyn holy temple be defouled and sclaundred. Be war also that thou be
not occupyed in techynge of children. For somme recluses ther ben
that thorugh techinge of children turnen her celle in-to a scole-house:

doo not so, but holde the apayde, bothe to thy communicacyon and
120   thy seruice, of these too wommen afore-saide.

⌐Capitulum 4⌐

Hou a recluse shulde kepe hir in sylence

I shal now telle the of sylence, for there-in lyeth moor reste and
muche fruyt: do as the prophete saith: *Dixi, custodiam vias meas, vt*
125   *non delinquam in lingua mea.* 'I haue saide,' seith the prophete, 'I
shal kepe my waies, that I offende not in my tonge.'

A recluse shuld euere drede hir lest she offended by hir tonge, for as
Seint Iame saith, 'It is a membre that no man may tame'; therfore
kepe wel thy tunge by silence and sitte alone from worldly noyce and
130   be styl, that thou may deserue to speke with him whiche list not to
speke but with suche that ben allone. And yf thou shalt speke, speke
selde, as certeyn tymes and houres in the day; and that thou speke
suche as is needful to body and to soule and that mekely and esily with
noon hye voice, ne sharply ne glosyngly ne with noon hye chere. And
135   sith this longith to eche honest recluse, gode sustir, and thou wilt be
Goddys owne derlynge, fle the homly communicacyoun of alle men
but if it be suche that ben assigned to the.

Me semith she was a blessed womman and wel sette, that dradde hir
to speke with Seint Martyn and alle other neither wolde she se ne
140   speke with. But for-asmuche as thou maist not kepe this straight
liuynge to speke with no man, se now with whom thou shuldist speke.
Chese the a confessour, the whiche is an auncyant man of gode fame
and of gode oppinyon, of whom thou shalt resceyue comfort in al
manere doutes and sorwes. And in eny wyse bewar that thou kisse not
f. 180   hys honde ne he thyne, as it were for / deuocyon, for that makith deed
folke, be thei neuere so olde, prone and redy to synne. Al this say I not
oonly for the but for other that in tyme comynge mowe atteyne to
suche a forme of lyuynge.

If eny worthy persone, abbot or priour, wolde speke with the, in
150   presence of som honest persone thou sholdist speke with hem. In noo
wyse be not to famulier in suche visitacions, for bothe thy good name
and thy conscience shulden so be blemysshed, were thei neuere so
good. For as ofte as thou seest him and herist him, so ofte in his
absence his ymage shal be enpressed in thy mynde and lette the fro
155   many gode meritory occupacions that thou art bounde to. Therfor
shuldest thou speke with no man but with a veyl afore thy visage, that
neuer neither of you might se other. For I doute it not, it is ful
dredful and right perylous ofte-sithes to admitte the voyce of a man.
Fle in eny wise the communicacyoun of yonge folke and suspecte
160   persones and speke not with hem but in presence of hym that is thy

gostly fader, and yhit loke that gret nede cause it. Suche silence makith muche rest in conscience.

Gete by grace the vertu of shamfastnesse, for that arayeth a clene soule in vertuous maners and vertuous speche; it gouernith the tonge, it swagith wratthe and auoidith chidynge. For if a chaste soule be 165 a-shamed honestly to speke honest thinges, hou shamfast shuld she be to speke vnshamful thynges or forto grucche with wronges or forto speke with a spiryt of ire. A recluse shuld not aunswere to a chider ne edwite hir bakbiter, but mekely to suffre alle wronges, bothe pryue and apert, ne charge it not as for hirself, seieng as Seint Poule seith: 170 *Michi autem pro minimo est vt a vobis iudicer.* That is to saye, 'It is to me but litel charge al-though I be demed of you.'

Trauaile therfor to gete reste and pees in herte and bisely kepe it and foryete suche outwarde thynges, hauynge hym in mynde that is l[i]uyer euerlastynge, of whom the prophete seieth thus: *In pace* 175 *factus est locus eius.* 'His dwellynge-place is in reste and pees of conscience.' Oure lorde Iesu spekith by the prophete and seieth: *Super quem requiescit spiritus meus nisi super humilem et quietem et contritum spiritu et timentem sermones meos?* 'Vpon whom shal my spirit reste, but vpon the quiet and meke and contrite of spirit and 180 dredynge my wordes?' Al / this I saye for that I wolde thou louedist f. 180ᵛ silence and litel speche.

⌐Capitulum v⌐

Also hou a recluse shuld speke and whanne

Now sith I haue tolde the of silence, I shal also shewe the of 185 speche, whan thou shalt speke. From Exaltacyon of the Crosse vnto Estern, after tyme complyn is seyde vnto pryme be do a-morwe, to speke with noon saaf after pryme with the mynistres that seruen the, yit vnder fewe wordes of suche thynges as the nedith; and fro that tyme tyl thou haue ete, kepe the in silence, in deuoute praiers and holy 190 meditacions. And than vse communicacioun tyl euensonge-tyme and be wel war of dissolute speche, lest oure Lorde blame the and seie: *Sedit populus manducare et bibere et surrexerunt ludere:* 'After the peple had ete and dronke, they rysen and pleyden.' After euensonge is do, to speke with thy mynistres of thynges that the bihoueth, til tyme 195 of collacioun, and so kepe silence for al that nyght.

From Estern til the Exaltacion of the Crosse come ayen, after tyme that complyn is seide til the sonne arise a-morwe, to kepe silence and than to speke with thy mynistres. After tyme pryme is seide tyl the thridde houre, to comune with othir that comen, honestly and vnder 200 fewe wordes. In the saam wise shalt thou do bitwene the houre of

175 liuyer] louyer

noon, after thou hast ete, tyl euensonge-tyme; and after euensong is
doon, than to speke with thy mynistres tyl the tyme of collacyon. But
in Lente kepe silence that thou speke with noon saaf with thy confes-
205   sour and thy mynistres, or ellys but it be som body that cometh from
fer contre.

⌜*Capitulum vj*⌝

Hou a recluse shuld be occupyed
         For-asmuche as ydelnesse is a deedly enemy to mannys soule,
210   whiche may be cleped moder of alle vices, wurcher of alle lustes,
norsher of veyn thoughtes, former of vnclene affeccions, sturer of
vnclene desires, greither of heuynesse, I wolde thou were not vnoccupyed, but with dyuerse honeste occupacions to voide this foule vice
of ydelnesse.
215   After tyme thou hast saide diuyne seruice, thow shalt occupie the
with som honest labour of thyn hondes and than shalt thow renne to
f. 181   som pryuat prayer, as for a gret refute and / helpe of thyn holy purpos
that thou stondist inne, and vse it now lenger, now shorter, after that
thou art stured by grace: be wel war of multitude of psalmes in thy
220   pryuat prayer; put it in noo certeyn, but as longe as thou delitist
ther-inne, so longe vse hem. And whan thou begynnest to waxe heuy
of hem or wery, than take a boke and rede, or do som labour with thyn
hondes, soo that thorugh suche diuersite of besinesse thou might
putte away slouthe and ydelnesse.
225   Thus shalt thou be occupied bitwene euery diuyne houre of the
nyght and of the day, from the kalendes of Nouembre vnto Lente; so
that a litel tofore complyn thou be occupied with redynge of holy
faders priuely by thiself in stede of thy collacyon, that thou mightest
by grace gete the som compunccyon of teres and feruour of deuocion
230   in saienge of thy complyn.
         And whan thou art thus replet and fedde with deuocion, reste the
and go to to thy bed, restynge the there vnto the tyme that it be passed
mydnyght; here than thou begynne thy matyns, for thou shalt slepe
no more of al day. This same rule shalt thou kepe from Estern vnto the
235   kalendes of Nouember, saaf that thou shalt slepe after mete afore the
houre of noon. Loke also that thou be in bed after complyn, by than
the sonne goo to reste. Take heed of oo thynge, that thou slepe not
whan thou shuldest wake.

211 norsher] norcher *corr. to* norsher

⌜Capitulum vij⌝

Hou deuoutly a recluse shulde behaue hyr in Lent-tyme   240

Amonge al the fastynge in the yere, the fastyng in Lente excelleth and passith al othir in dignite, the whiche not oonly religiouse peple but also euery cristen man is bounde to kepe. That this fastynge in Lente excellith alle othir we han witnes bothe of the lawe, of   245 prophetes and of the euangelistes. Moyses fasted fourty daies and fourty nyghtes, that he might deserue to resceyue the lawe; Helye the prophete fastid fourty daies and fourty nyght, that he might deserue to here the voyce of God; oure lorde and oure sauyour Iesu Crist, whan he had faste fourty daies and fourty nyght, he ouercome the fende and anoon aungels mynistred to him.   250

By this myght thou se that fastynge is ayenst al temptacion a   f. 181ᵛ myghty / shelde and in al tribulacion a profitable refute and to deuoute praier a souereyn fode. The vertu of fastynge oure Lord Iesu taughte his disciples whan he saide that ther was o kynde of deuels might not be caste oute but by praier and fastynge; al-though fastynge   255 be the duke and the leder of al religion, without whom chastite may not sikerly be kepte, yit the fastinge of Lente mightily passeth al other.

Here now why: the first place of oure duellynge was paradise. The seconde is this worlde ful of wrecchednes. The thridde shal be in   260 heuen with blessed spirites and aungels, if we wel do. Al the tyme that we lyue in this lyf betokeneth no more than fourty days, for fro the tyme that Adam was put oute of paradyse vnto the last day that we shul be delyuered oute of this worlde we lyuen in laboure, sorwe and drede, cast out of the sight of God, excluded from the ioye of paradyse   265 and fastynge from heuenly swetnes.

Thys shuldest thou euere considre and beholde in al thy werkes, thorugh weilynge of thy wrecchednesse, that thou art but a straunger and a pilgrime in this wrecched worlde; but for we ben freel and mowe not contynuely with-oute cessynge vse this weilynge and wepynge,   270 holichirche by worchinge of the Holigost hath ordeyned a certayn tyme of contynuel wailynge, the whiche is called the tyme of Lente, for to reduce to oure mynde that we ben putte away out of paradyse. In the begynnynge of Lente it is saide thus: *Memento quod cinis es et in cinerem reuerteris*. That is, 'Haue mynde that thou art asshes and   275 in-to asshes thou shalt be turned.'

To reduce to oure mynde that we ben letted from heuenly desire, ther is hanged bitwene vs and Crist, his flesshe and his blood, the sacrament of the autere, a veyl. To reduce to oure mynde that we ben fer fro that holy companye, the whiche dwellen in blisse for euere, we   280 leuen vnsongen in Lente a songe and a worde of melodye that is called

Alleluia. To reduce to oure mynde that we be not fulfilled of heuenly
suetnesse, we coarte oure flesshe with fastynge in tyme of Lente, moor
than a-nothir tyme.

285   In that tyme shuld euery cristen man adde somwhat moor to his
fastynge, as in besy keping his hert from veyn thoughtes, his mouthe
from veyn speche, moor than in a-nother tyme; muche moor thou,

f. 182 that / art a recluse and shuldest passe alle othir in lyuynge, oughtist to
plese hym passingly, [v]owynge thiself to his seruice, despisyng lustes

290   and likinges, fleynge communicacion and daliaunce, holdynge these
days weddynge days, sighynge and sorwyng, wepyng and wailyng,
knelyng and praienge after thy lorde, thy maker, thyn ayenbier, thy
loue and thy louyer, thy spouse and thy domesman, Iesu Crist.

The manere of þi slepynge in this tyme a-fore mydnyght shal be
295   lasse than in a-nothir tyme, so that thou may night and day for þe
moor partie deuoutly be occupied with praier, meditacion and
redyng.

⌜Capitulum viij⌝

Hou she shuld be dyeted and what shuld be hir array

300   Now shal I shewe the, suster, a certeyn forme and rule of etynge
and dr[ynk]ynge and also what shal be thyn array and vesture of thy
body. I write not this forme of lyuynge of etynge and drynkyng only to
the, that hast euir holde thiself lowe thorugh scarsete of liflode, but to
othir whiche konnen not rule hem, that outher wiln take to muche,

305   either to litel. Fro al manere of mete and drynke that the semeth
shulde enflaume thy compleccyon and make the prone and redy to
synne, ⌜abstyne the⌝, but if thou be syke or feble. Abstyne the also
from mete and drinke, as thou woldist vse a medicyn. Al-though Seint
Benet in his reule ordeyned to monkes a certeyn weight of brede and a

310   certeyn mesure of drynke in the day, yit natheles to yonge folke and
mighty of complexion, it is alday denyed; to feble, to syke, to tendir
folke of complexion, it is suffred. Fle delicat metes and doucet drinkes
al the while thou art not syke; fle hem as venym and poyson, contrary
to thy clene and chast purpose. Serue so thy nede by etynge and

315   drinkynge, that hunger be put away and thyn appetyt be not fulfilled,
with oo manere of potage, of wortes or of peses or of benys, or elles of
form[ente pot]age medled with mylke or with oyle, to put away or
a-voyde the bitternes; and with o kynde of fysshe, with apples or with
herbes. And vpon the Wednesday, Friday and Saturday, to vse but

320   Lent metes.

285 cristen man] man cristen (*marked for reversal*)
289 vowynge] bowynge
301 drynkynge] dredynge   317 formente potage] formage

In Lente o manere of potage euery day, but siknesse it make; euery
Friday brede and water. And the tyme of thy meles shal be euery day
at / hye none and in Lente-tyme after euensonge. From Estern to
Whitsontyde, outake rogacion days and W[hit]sone Eue, thou shalt
ete at mydday and sithen at euen. This rule shaltow kepe al the
somer-tyme, outake Wednesday and Friday and othir solempne
vigils. Also thou maist, and thou wilt, euery fastynge day in the somer
ceson, by cause thou hast noo meridyan after noon, to slepe bitwene
matyns and pryme.

Thy vesture that thou shalt vse ben these: a warme pylche for
wynter and oo kirtel and oo cote for somer, with a blak habite aboue
hem; and euereither tyme ij stamyns. Also loke the veyle of thyn heed
be of noo precyouse clothe but of a mene blak, lest preciosite or
dyuersite of array and of precious coloure defoule thy soule with-
ynne. Be also wel war that thou haue no moor than the nedeth to
hos[e]n and to shoon and of other thynge that longeth to thy feet, but
rather desire pouerte and kepe it.

Loo, sustir, now I haue write the a forme of lyuynge touchinge thy
conuersacion after thin outwarde lyuinge. Now shal I write the a
forme of lyuynge touchinge thin ynner conuersacion, bi the helpe of
Iesu and thy deuoute prayers.

⌜*Capitulum ix*⌝

A short commendacyon of maydenhood and of chastite
First take heed why thou shalt preferre solitary lyuynge aboue the
conuersacion of the worlde. *Virgo, inquit apostolus, cogitat que dei
sunt, quomodo placeat deo vt sit sancta corpore et spiritu.* ⌜1ª Cor. 7. f.⌝
That is, 'A mayde,' saith the apostel, 'remembrith tho thinges that
ben of God and in what wise she might plese him, by the whiche she
might be holy in body and soule.' This is a wilful sacrifice and a fre
oblacyon, of whiche oure Lord saith: *Qui potest capere, capiat.* That
is, 'Whos may take, take he': as ho saith, hoo may atteyne to come to
the vertu of chastite, take he it and forsake it not. Hoo is he that may?
Certys, he that oure Lorde enspirith with good wille: therfore
comaunde thyn holy purpos with al the deuocion of thin hert to him
that hath thus enspired it and biseche him in thy praier that thou may
fele, by grace, the whiche is impossible by nature. Thinke what mede,
what ioye maydenhood shal resceyue if it be contynued; also what
confusion fallith to / hem that losen it. What is a moor preciouse
tresoure than thilk that heuen is bought with, aungels deliten in, the
whiche Crist coueitith to loue and to yeue – what, trowist thou?

f. 182ᵛ

325

330

335

340

345

350

355

f. 183

360

324 Whitsone] Withsone   336 hosen] hoson
359 deliten in, the whiche] deliten . in the whiche.

Certeyn, I dar wel say, him-self and hise, for the sweet odoure of maydenhood sauoreth mightily in the blys of heuen.

Se now what spouse thou hast chose to the, what frende thou hast take to the: he passith in semlynesse the shap of eny man moor firther

365 than the sonne, excedynge the brightnes of the sterres, swetter than hony. He it is that desireth thi bewte. In his righthonde lengthe of days, in his lifte honde riches and ioye; he it is that hath chose the to his loue and wil crowne noon but such as ben preued, for he that is not tempted is not proued. Thy maydenhood is golde, thy selle is an ouen,

370 the fyre of this ouen is temptacyon, the vessel that thou berist is a vessel of cley, in the whiche thy maydenhood is hid to be preued inne. If the fyre of temptacyon haue the maistrie, than is thy golden maydenhood lost and thy vessel may neuere be reparailed ayen in-to the same estat.

375 These thinges shuld a mayde bisely kepe with gret drede and besinesse, that so lightly may be lost and so profitably be kept. She shuld thenke on that blessed lombe, whider-so-euere he goo; and on oure blessed Lady goynge afore the queer of maydens, syngynge a songe that noon othir may synge but suche as ben vndefouled.

380 Trowist thou not that thou maist lese thy maydenhod but thorugh felouship of man: yhis certeyn, ful foule and abhomy[na]bly; be war of that. A mayde shulde therfore thenke that alle hyr lymes ben halowed, incorporat to the Holy Gost; God forbede than that suche holy lymes shuld be youe to the fende.

385 Strecche out therfor al thy wille in kepynge this maydenhode and atteyne, if thou maist come to that vertu, that thou may holde honger, delices; pouerte, rychesse; dredful of mete and drynke, of sleep, of worde, lest thou excede and passe the bondes of nede, wenynge that thou susteynest thy flesshe and thou norshist thyn enemy and thyn

390 aduersary. Whan thow sittist at thy mete, than shuldest thou chewe vpon chastite and clennes, desirynge that Iesu Crist thy spouse shuld

f. 183ᵛ make it parfyt in the, with syghinge and snobbynge, wepynge and / wailynge; and if thou do thus, than shaltow litel lust haue of mete or of drynke but as nede axith, and vnnethes that.

395 ⌈*Capitulum x*⌉

Hou a recluse or an ankeras shuld comende hir chastite to God.

Therfore, suster, whan thou gost to reste atte euen, commende thy clennes in-to his hondes that loueth clene and chaste soules, remem-brynge the hou thou hast mysspended the day, in thought, in worde

400 and in dede, by lightnes, ydelnes and negligence passynge the bondes of honest gladnes and by dissolucyon of chere. If eny of these comen

381 abhomynably] abho=mybly

to thy mynde, wayle hem and wepe hem and smyte the on the brest, that thou might the sonner by grace be reconcyled to thy lord Iesu Crist.

If thy body be stured with an vnclene heet of flesshly lust thorugh entysynge of the fende, slepynge or wakynge, anoon remembre the of these holy maydens, as Agnes, Cecile, Lucye and other moo, the whiche ouercomen her enemyes and hadden the victory in tendir age, for they yaf no more, forsothe, of gold and siluer, riche array and precyous stones, than they wolden by the foulist fen in the felde. They chargeden no more the flaterynge of the domesman than the thret-nynge, but rather dredynge the sparynge of him than his punys-shynge. And somme ther were, as Seint Agnes, the whiche thorugh her prayer turned a bordel hous in-to an oratory; and the aungel of God was nyhe to auenge hir of hir enemy. So if thou praye with teres of contricion whan thou art traueiled with vnchastite, trust right wel that an aungel, keper of thy chastite, shal be ful nye.

We rede also of othir maydens, whan thei were put in the fyre to be brent, the fire vanysshed and did hem no harme. Why? Certeyn for the leyt of flesshly lust was quenched in hem; and also for the fyre of charite, the whiche brenned with-inne, ouercame the fire that brent with-oute.

As ofte, therfore, as thou art stured to vnclennes, haue mynde on oure Lorde that beholdith the and what thou thenkest, he wote. Also yelde reuerence to the aungel the [whiche] cheris[shith t]he day and nyght, and say to thyn enemy, 'I haue an aungel to my loue, that bisely kepith me day and nyght.' If it need be, adde therto abstynence and other manere turmentynge of thy flesshe, for truste it wel, where moche turmentynge is by affliccyon in flesshe, there is / litel flesshly delectacyon or noon. For if I shulde not flatere the but say the sothe, chastite may not wel be kepte in yonge folke withoute gret affliccion of the body, sith it so is that in olde folke and syke it stondith in gret perel.

Natheles, though chastite be a yifte of God and may not be gote ne had with-out him, be we yit neuere so vertuous, whan we han it we shulden kepe it as vertuously as we konne with affliccyon of oure flesshe, or by othir vertuouse menes. It is ful harde to be amonge occasyon and not to be stured either by etynge of deliciouse metes, or drinkynge of deliciouse drinkes, or amongst conuersacion of children.

I knewe a man that passingly was traueiled in the begynnynge of his conuersion with many vnclene thoughtes, by the whiche he dredde hym to falle. Atte last sodenly he roos ayen himself, no thinge hatynge so moche as himself, vnto the tyme that he had brought hym so lowe

405

410

415

420

425

f. 184
430

435

440

420 lust was] was lust (*marked for reversal*)
425 the whiche cherisshith the] the cherisliche

by turmentynge of his flesshe that almost he failed for defaute. After
445 that he say himself feble and wayke, needfully he began to strengthe
himself ayen litel and litel. Thanne eftesone the saam temptacyon was
as breem vpon hym after as it was before, or moor: he praide, he
wepte, he snobbed, he wailed, he bathed him in colde watir and
rubbed his body with netlys, that the tone hete shuld ouercome the
450 tother; not-withstondynge al this, the spirit of vnclennes lefte him
not, but trauailed him mightily. Than he fel down atte fete of oure
lord Iesu, besechinge him either to delyuere hym out of this present
lyf, if it plesed him, either hele him of these vnclene thoughtes. And
euere he saide with stedfaste abidynge, 'Lord, I shal not cesse
455 cryenge, I shal not go fro the, I shal not leeue the tyl thou graunte me
that I aske.' Sone after this he fonde rest for a tyme, but sikernesse
might he noon gete and this passion lefte him neuere, yonge ne olde,
but euere in sondry tymes began vpon him fresshe and fresshe.

Sithen oure Lord suffred thus a chosen soule be traueiled that
460 mightily withstood it, what shulden we say of hem that holden hem so
seker that, though they hadden oportunyte, leyser, tyme or space,
thei witen wel thei shold not falle? Certeyn I dar wel seie, thay ben
f. 184ᵛ deceyued, / for though the hete be quenched in somme, the wille and
the desire is not so. Therfor, suster, haue noo sikernesse of thiself but
465 alway be dredful, hauynge thiself suspect, and doo as the culuer doth,
that seeth in ryuers al a-fer the ensaute and the pursute of hir enemy.
So do thou: beholde in the ryuers of holy wryt hou besy thyn enemy is
to ouercome the and fle hym, for ther is no thinge that ouercometh so
sone the fende as doth redynge of deuoute thinge and prayer and
470 meditacyon of Cristys passyon. A mayde shuld so be occupied vpon
oon of these thre, prayer, meditacion, or redynge, that though she
were stured to do vnlauful thinges, she shuld not be suffred for remors
of conscience. Vse wel this remedye, that whether thou slepe or wake,
thy mynde be euere vpon som sentence of holy writ or vpon som
475 seyntes lyf, for it is a souerayne remedy ayenst temptacyon.

⌈*Capitulum xj*⌉

How somme dreden hem to doo wilful bodily penaunce for drede of
infirmyte.

Somme ther ben that wil not vse bodily affliccion by wakynge, by
480 abstinence, by liggynge, by weryng and such othir, for drede of bodily
infirmyte, lest thei shulde herby be chargeous to her frendes. This is
an excusacion of synne, for fewe ther ben the whiche han this feruour
to chastise her body so.

Alle men ben witty and wyse and discret now-a-days, for for the
485 drede of bodily siknes thei ben negligent aboute the helthe of her

soule, as though thei myghten bettir suffre, and were moor tolerable,
temptacion than honger of the wombe: treuly thei ben to fauorable to
hemself. Be war of that wyle, that for encheson of bodily infirmyte
thou falle in-to vnleeful thoughtes of flesshly lustes. For certeyn if it
happe thou be syke or weyke, or thy stomak waxe drye for abstynence,   490
than shal al maner likynges and flesshly delectacions be to the rather
peynful than delitable or lustful.

I knewe a man whiche might not kepe hym chaste, for cause he was
custum[a]bly vsed to vnclennes in tendir age. Atte last he turned to
himself and byhelde hou he had mysspended his lyf; he waxe therby   495
hugely ashamed and began with hymself a myghty batayl / of ab-   f. 185
stinence, that vnnethes wolde he suffre the body to resceyue that it
neded, but ofte withdrowe it; he waxe sad, he spak litel, ther was noo
creature after that tyme sawe him iape ne lawghe ne herde him speke an
ydel worde; he auoyded so al manere comforte of bodily thinges, that   500
neither he fonde eese in etynge ne drinkynge ne slepinge; he was euere
so scrupulous in conscience of mysspendynge of his thoughtes, that
he had euere ynow to do in amendynge of his lyf by confession. Stood
he, sate he, wente he, wroughte he and what-so-euere he dide, him
thoughte he stood and was presented afore the dredful doom; he was   505
so aferde that he dorst neuere lifte vp his eyen from the erthe.

Trowist thou not that alle these thinges dide him not gret eese? Yhis
certeyn, he wanne herby the victory of his enemy: after this he fel in
gret passyng siknesse by an entishynge of his stomak and yit not-
withstondinge whan he shuld take his rest and ese of his body for   510
febilnes and wolde slepe, than wolde he say thus to himself, 'Abyde
now a litel while, for Iesu Crist cometh anoon to the doom.'

I say not this for that I wolde destroie thy discrecyon, but for I
wolde thou fleddist the matier of vices, as of glotonye, slouthe,
lechery, rest of body, familiarite and suche other; for often-tymes   515
vnder colour of false discrecyon we hyden flesshly lust. If it be
discrecyon to put the soule aboue the body in reuerence, than is it
discrecion to put the body bynethe the soule by subieccyon and that
may not be if thou suffre the body haue his wille. Alle this I say for
thou shuldest knowe what besynesse is in the kepynge of the vertu of   520
chastite.

⌜Capitulum xij⌝

Hou chastite with-oute mekenes is as a drye floure.

Al-though chastite be the flour of alle vertues, yit with-oute
mekenesse she waxith drye and fadith his colour. Therfor I shal telle   525
the somwhat of mekenes: ther is noon so syker a grounde and stable

487 than] than were   494 custumably] custumbly.

foundement anemst alle vertues as is mekenesse, with-oute whom alle
gostly begynnynges ben ful ruynous. Right as mekenesse is the

grounde of alle vertues, as I / haue saide bifore, so is pride the grounde

and the moder of alle vices, the whiche caste Lucifer out of heuen and
Adam oute of paradys. Of this wrecched rote springen many b[ra]un-
ches: natheles alle mown be diuyded in-to too spices, that is in-to
bodily pride and gostly pride. Bodily pride stondith in bostynge and
veyn-glory of outwarde bodily thinges. Gostly pride stondith in bost-

535   ynge and veyn-glory of inwarde gostly thynges.

Than if thou that shuldist be Cristys mayde haue eny veyn-glory
with-in thiself of eny array, of nobleye, of ty[r]e, of beute, of shap of
body, of semelyheed or of dyuerse ornamentes of thy selle, of clothes,
of peyntures or of ymages and suche othir, thou offendist thy lorde

540   and thy special louyer in pride of outward thinges. If thou haue eny
veyn-glory of thy poure array for Goddis sake, of deuocyons, of gostly
felynges, of diuerse preseruacions day or nyght, not thonkynge Iesu
Crist therfore bot wenynge that it cometh of thiself, than thou offendist thy lord and thy special louyer in pride of inward thinges. Oure

545   Lord whom thou louest so specialy, whan he cam in-to this worlde, he
made hym poure to make the riche and he chees a poure moder, a pore
house, a poure meyne and a cracche to lye inne, in stede of a ryal
bedde.

Loue him therfor wel and thanke him that he hath so enspired the to

550   chese rather chastite and clennes than flesshly lust and likynge, for
certeyn thou hast chosen the best part; kepe it if thou may and if thou
be ioyful, be thou ioyful in God with-in-forthe, for þe prophete saith
thus: *Omnis gloria filie regis abintus in fimbreis aureis circumamicta
varietatibus*. 'Al the ioye of the kinges doughter', he saith, 'he shuld

555   be with-in-forthe, in golden hemmes vmbigon with diuersitees of vertues,' and there may she here hir fader speke to hir and say, as the
prophete saith: *Audi filia et vide et inclina aurem tuam et obliuiscere
populum tuum et domum patris tui quia concupiscet rex decorem
tuum*. That is to say, 'Here, doughter, and se and bowe down thyn

560   eere.' Why? To listne what he saith. 'Foryete the peple of veyn
thoughtes and thy fadirs hous, that is to say of worldly vanitees, for
the kynge my sone hath desired thy beute.' This is a blessed wower,

that wowith / for his sone. Here therfore and se, al this shuld be thyn
in ioye; this ioye shuld be witnes of thy conscience, this ioye shuld be

565   thy gardeyn, thyn orcharde and thy disport.

Ther maist thow beholde and se hou dyuerse vertues swetely
semblen hem togidir: euery of hem encressith other vertues and
fairnes, for she that is fair ynowgh in hir owen kynde, is fairir for hir

felowe. Se now how: couple mekenes to chastite and ther is no thynge
brighter; couple mercy to rightwesnes and ther is noo thynge swetter; 570
couple symplenes to prudence and ther is no thynge lighter; couple
myldenes to strengthe and ther is no thynge profitabler. In this
dyuersite of vertues occupie thy gostly eye in thy disport and forme
hem in thiself; and if thou annexe hem to the gilden hemmes, than art
thou rialy arrayed with a mottely cote, the whiche thy lord Iesu hath 575
ordeyned for þe.

An hemme is the lower partie and, as were, the ende of a cote. By
this hemme I vnderstonde charite, whiche is the ende and the hemme
of al the lawe, in a clene herte, a good conscience and a trewe feith. In
these thinges sette al thy ioye inwardly, and not in outwarde thinges. 580

⌐Capitulum xiij ⌐

How the awtier of a recluse oratorye shuld be arrayed

Now shal I shewe the how thou shalt arraye thyn oratory. Arraye
thyn autier with white lynnen clothe, the whiche bitokeneth bothe
chastite and symplenesse. Thenke first hou flexe cometh oute of the 585
erthe and with gret labour is maad white, as with dyuerse wasshinges
and purginges, and than dryed and atte last, to make it moor whyte, it
nedeth to haue both fire and water. By this flexe I vnderstonde al
mankynde that cam oute of the erthe, the whiche mankynde is by
grace maad white by baptem, where that wickednes is put a-way, but 590
not infirmyte, for in partie we resceyue clennes in baptem but not
fully, for cause of corrupcyon of nature that aboundith in vs.

After this baptem mankynde nedeth to be dryed by abstinence and
other bodely affliccyons from vnclene and vnleeful humours and than
nedith mankynde to be brused with yren hamours, that is with 595
dyuerse temptacions / and so be rent with dyuerse hokes of discip- f. 186ᵛ
lynes and confessions to auoyde the foule rust of synne of quotidyan
defautes the whiche thei beren aboute. And firthermore, if thei wil
ascende to an hyer grace of moor clennes, that is chastite, than mosten
þei passe by fire of tribulacion and water of compunccyon. Thus shalt 600
thou arraye thyn autier of thyn oratorye.

In this autere sette an ymage of Cristis passion, that thou may haue
mynde and se hou he sette and spredde his armes a-brood to resceyue
the and al mankynde to mercy, if thai wil axe it. And if it plese the,
sette on that oo syde an ymage of oure Lady and a-nother on that other 605
syde of Seint Iohn, for commendacyon of moor chastite, in token that
oure Lord is wel plesed with chastite, bothe of man and of womman,
the whiche he [halow]ed in oure Lady and Seint Iohn. Beholde the
ymage of oure Lady and thenke that she is helper of mankynde, ioye of

608 halowed] ended

610 heuen, refute of wrecches, solace and comfort of disperate, lady of the
worlde, queen of heuen.

And than renne to Cristys passyon, sekynge therin oo thynge,
that is oure Lorde himself, for who-so cleueth to him, he is oo spiryt
with hym, passynge in-to hym, the whiche is alway the same, whos
615 yeres faylen neuere. This cleuynge to Iesu is no thynge elles but
charite, whiche is the hemme and the ende of al the lawe, as I haue
saide before.

Now haue I shewed the a motley cote, a weddynge cote, a cote with
golden hemmes, the whiche shuld be a maydens cote, vmbigoon with
620 diuersitees of vertues, annexed to the [whiche] the hemme of charite,
the whiche charite is dyuyded in-to tweyne, loue of God and loue of
thy neighboure; the loue of thy neighbore stondith in good wille and
in innocence. Good wille wolde that al that thou woldist men diden to
the, thou shuldest do to hem. Innocence wolde that thou sholdest not
625 do to a-noþer, the whiche thou woldist not were doon to the.

The first the semeth is harde, sith thy profession wolde that thou
sholdist noo temperal good haue; nay, is it not so. The seconde the
semeth is light ynowgh, for thou maist hurte no man but with thy
tonge. Certeyn the first is as light as thys, for ther may no matere be of
630 yuel wille wher no couetise is; therfore wilne wel to alle folke and do
f. 187 the profyt that / thou maist. Perauenture thou saist, 'What profyt shal I
doo, sith I may be suffred to haue no thynge forto yeue to pore folke?'
Thou seist wel, good suster; knowe what staat thou standist in.

Ther wern too sustirs: that one Martha and that oþir Maria, as the
635 gospel tellith; that oon labored, and that other was as she were ydel;
that one yaf, the tothir asked; the tone serued, the tothir norisshed hir
affeccyon, not rennynge aboute hyder and tyder in resceyuynge of
pore gestes ne distrayt of gouernayl of housholde, but she saat at Iesus
feet, herynge deuoutly what he saide. This is thy part, suster, in this
640 stondist thou, dere sustir, for thou art deed and buryed to the worlde.
Martha was commended as for good occupacion, but Marye was
commended of oure Lorde as for the better partye. Trowist thow that
Marye grucched of Martha? Nay, but rather Martha of Marye. In the
saam wise thei the whiche ben holden good comoun lyuers of the
645 worlde grucchen of thy lyuynge, not thov of hers.

Therfore almes that shuld be youen longeth to hem whiche han
worldly godes or holy chirche godes to dispende. For the godes
whiche cristen peple yeuen to holy chirche, the mynistres that han it
to kepe shulde departe it either to wydowes, fadirles children, pil-
650 grimes, or to other pore folke and also to hem that seruen in holy

615 yeres] eres *corrected to* yeres.
620 the whiche the] the . the.
638 of housholde] of housholde of gouernayl *marked for reversal*

chirche. Also the godes whiche are youen to abbeys or to othir houses of religyon it is committed to certeyne persones of the saam house to dispende as it nedeth and þe ouer-pluys shuld be shitte in hucches to be deled to poure folke, as I saide before. Alle this peple representen þe staat of Martha. 655

Cloistrers han not to do with this, but þei shulden norisshe her affeccions with blessed idelnes and feden her soule with gostly de-lytes. Than sithen to cloistrers it is not suffred to ben occupyed with the lyf of Martha, muche moor to the that vtterly hast forsake al worldly besynesse and art called a recluse. If it so be that thou haue 660 eny thynge in stoor thorugh thyn owen labore, dele it to pore folke. Yhe and though thou haue no thynge for-to yeue, yhit in the sight of God a gode wille is moor to be commen/ded than eny bodily yifte: f. 187ᵛ yeue that therfore. What is better than praier? Yeue that. What is kynder than pyte? Yeue þat. And al the worlde attones biclippe and 665 gripe in the bosom of loue and charite. And for hem whiche thou fyndest good lyuers, thanke oure Lorde, and for hem that thou fyndest yuel lyuers, by wailyng and wepynge praie oure Lorde for hem; with pyte biholde hem the whiche ben in dissese, as pore peple, destitucion of widowes, desperat soules, nedes of pilgrymes, perels of 670 shipmen, vowe of maydens, temptacion of monkes, besynes of pre-lates and laboures of tilyenge peple. To alle these shaltow open thy bosom of loue and charite, for this almes is moost accordynge to thy professyon and to our Lord most acceptable and to hem that it is youen to, most spedful and profitable. Alle these thynges helpen 675 gretly thyn holy purpos for truly, as Seynt Gregory seith, holy faders afore these days studieden with al her besynes to refuse al worldly good as nye as they mighten, that thei mighten therby the lightlyer loue God and her neighbore.

⌜Capitulum xiiij⌝ 680

Hou a recleuse shuld encresse the loue of Iesu in hir soule by medita-cion of þinges whiche ben passed. Also of the meditacion of þinges that ben present. Also by meditacion of thinges whiche ben to come

Thus moche haue I seyde of the loue of neighbore; now shal I telle the of the loue of God, hou thou shalt loue him. To the loue of God 685 longeth too thinges, desire of the soule and worchinge of the body. Desire of the soule lyethe in þe swetnes of gostly loue; vertuous worchinge of the body stondith in a maner of lyuynge, the whiche is in fastinge, in wakynge, in laboure, in prayenge, in redynge, in silence, in pouert and suche other. The desire of thy soule is norsshed with 690 holy meditacions. Than if the loue of Iesu shuld growe and encresse in thy desire, thre thinges the nedeth to haue in mynde. That is, thinges

the whiche ben passed, thinges that ben present and thinges whiche
ben to come.

695   As touchinge to the first, whan thy soule is purged clerly from alle
vnclene thoughtes, than entre in-to that pryue chambre where oure
blessed Lady praide deuoutly vnto the tyme the aungel grette hir,
beholdyng bisely hou she was occupied with redynge of suche prophe-
f. 188   cies in the whiche weren profecyed / Cristis comynge thorugh a
700   maydens birthe. Abyde there awhile and thou shalt se hou the aungel
cometh and gretith hir, seieng thus: *Aue Maria gracia plena, dominus
tecum.* Al-though thow be astonyed of this seconde comynge,
natheles dresse the vpward and grete oure Lady with the aungel and
saye, *Aue Maria gracia etcetera;* reherse and efte reherse the saam,
705   merueilynge what fulnes of grace this might be, of the whiche al the
worlde is fulfilled. Also beholde and meruaile the with deuocyon,
what lord this myght be, the whiche vouchith-saaf to ben enclosed in a
maydens wombe; than speke to hir and say, 'O blessed lady, what
swetnesse myght that be that thou were fulfilled with? What fire might
710   that be, that thou were enflaumed with, whan a blessed lord chees a
bodily substaunce, verray blode and flesshe of thy body, and whan
thou felist the presence of his gostly maieste in thy blessed wombe?'.
This shuld be a maydens meditacion. Than goo furth with hir in-to the
mountaynes and beholde the gretynge bitwene hir and Elizabeth,
715   where also the seruaunt knewe his lorde and with passynge ioye dide
him reuerence, enclosed yit in the moder wombe. Mayde, what dost
thou now? I praie þe, renne furth and annexe the to that ioye; falle
dovn to euereither feet and in the maydens wombe wurshipe thy lorde
and thyn husbonde and in the wombe of the tother beholde louely thy
720   frende.

Yit the nedeth to folewe hir firther in-to Bethleem with gret deuocyon and whan thou comest there, be to hir obsequyous atte birthe of
hir childe and than breke oute and say with the prophete: *Paruulus
natus est nobis et filius datus est nobis.* That is to say, 'A litel blessed
725   childe is born to vs and a graciouse sone is youen to vs.' Leeue not for
no shame, but that thou kisse the cracche the whiche he lay in; putte
a-way drede with affeccyon and shame with loue; after this occupye
thy mynde vpon þe shepherdes wakyng wacche and vpon the songe of
aungels; to that blessed melody put the boldely in prees, bothe with
730   hert and mouthe syngynge: *Gloria in excelsis deo et in terra pax
hominibus bone voluntatis.* Foryete not in thy meditacion the
offrynge of thre kinges, ne forsake not his company whan he fledde
in-to Egipte, but folewe him with as gret deuocyon as he can yeue the.

699 *catchword* cristis comyng, *in lower margin.*
729 to] go *corrected to* to.
733 as] a *corrected to* as.

Were it not, trowist thou, a faire meditacyon to beholde / hym, hou
he obeyed to his moder, helpyng his norisshe Ioseph? What and thou   735
soughtist him in Ierusalem with his moder, sittynge in the temple
amonge doctours, techynge and axinge questions? O what abundaunce of teres shuldist thou than haue, whan thou herdist the moder
mekely rebuke the childe, seyeng thus: *Fili, quid fecisti nobis sic?*
Pater tuus et ego dolentes querebamus te. That is to say, 'Sone, why   740
hastow do to vs so? Thy fader and I with gret sorwe haue sought the.'
Wilt thov yit se pryuyer thynges? Go furthe to the place wher he was
baptised and there shalt thou here the Fader in a voyce, the Sone in
the flesshe, the Holy Gost in liknes of a culuer.

Folewe yit this mayde vnto the feste of Architriclyne and there   745
beholde a gostly weddynge and water turned in-to wyne; preye than
thy gostly spouse Iesu that thy water of teres mown be turned in-to
delicyous wyne of brennynge loue.

Yit passe further and beholde what Iesu saide to the womman the
whiche was accused of auoutrye; ymagyne here hou mercifully, hou   750
pitously, hou louely, how graciously he lyfte vp his eyen and hou
swetly he assoiled hir whan he had a-shamed hir accusours and seyde:
Nemo condempnauit te, mulier, nec ego te condempnabo. Vade et
iam amplius noli peccare. That is to say, 'Womman, noo body hath
condempned the ne I condempne the not; go now and be in wille to   755
synne no more.' Praye him here that thou mowe disserue to here his
blessed voys, though thou be vnworthy. Who is he, trowist thou, wil
condempne, if he say, 'I wil not condempne'? Certeyn noon.

Wilt thou se moor? Go forthe in-to the pharisees hous and se hou
thy lorde is sette atte mete. Seest thou not hov Mary Magdalen, that   760
blessed synner, wassh Iesus feet with teres and dried hem with her
heres and swetly kissed hem? At last she anoynted hem with an holy
oynement; go furthe and do the saam and if he wil denye it the, lette
not therfore, but go, procede furth contynuely with besy praier;
beholdynge hym with thy soor wepynge and weylinge, axe hym that   765
thou desirest. Wrastle with him as Iacob dide, that he may be ioyful to
be ouercome of the. It semeth other-while that Iesu turneth away
from the and, as it were, hydeth hys feet from the, yit natheles praye
and crye to hym with an vnpacyent loue. Certeyn, if thou crye so, he
wil not / denye his feet fro the to be moysted with thy teres, that
vouched-saaf to suffre hem be kyssed of a synner.

Bythenke the firthermoor and se now hov a man that had the
palseye was leyde at Iesus feet, axinge help of body and no thynge
elles, and yit our Lorde by his merueilous mekenes and vnspecable
mercy graunted hym that he axed and yaf him therto helthe of soule,   775
sayinge thus: *Remittuntur tibi, fili, peccata tua;* that is, 'Sone, thy

761 wassh] wasshith

synnes ben foryeue; ryse and goo.' Now lyfte vp thin [hondes] and
pray to hym with snobbynge teres, that he vouche-saaf to foryeue the
thy synnes.

780 And thou wolt do wel, yit go further in-to Bethanye, where the
blessed bondes of loue and frendship were knytte for euere bitwene
oure Lorde and Mary Magdalen and Martha and Lazarus. Truste
right wel, he loued wel Lazar, wytnes of the blessed teres that he
wepte for hym. Beholde now what was doon to oure Lord when he
785 was sette atte soper: Martha serued, Lazarus saat with him atte soper
and Mary anoynted hym. Art thou not wel apayde to se thys? Truste
right wel, this last office longith to the. Therfore breke the harde
alebastir boxe of thyn hert and that that is with-in of deuocyon, of
loue, of desire or of affeccyon, helde it on Iesu thy spouses heed,
790 wurshipynge God in man and man in God. Though the pharise
grucche with the as he dyde with Mary, charge it not, for Iesu will
excuse the.

Leeue not this blessed idelnes for Marthays besynesse, for treuly
thou hast chose the best partye. Arise now and lete vs go hens;
795 whider, trowist thou? Certayn to folowe hym in-to Ierusalem, beholdynge hym hou he rideth on an asse towarde hys passyon. Leeue hym
not now but go with him in-to the hous where he made a soper to his
disciples. Be not ashamed, al-though thou be a womman, to come
amonge men; let loue put away shame, or elles stonde a-fer as a pore
800 womman and axe som almes with wepyng teres.

Loke vp now, I praye the, seest thou not who is he that leieth his
heed so homly in Cristys lappe? He is a blessed man, what-so-euere he
be. I praye the, what hatte he? Certes his name is Iohn. O Iohn, what
grace, what swetnes, what deuocion foundist thou there, I praye þe
f. 189ᵛ telle me? Certeyn ther-yn is al the tresour, / I trowe, of wisdom and
konnynge hyd, for it is a welle of mercy, an hous of pyte and an
honycombe of euerlastynge swetnes. Blessed Iohn, hou disseruedist
thou to come to this grace? Whethir thou be hyer than Petir and holyer
than Andrew, worthier than Iames? This, woot I wel, is a specyal
810 priuilege, certeyn, I trowe, for thou art a mayde chosen of oure Lord;
go to the mayde now and axe hym som part of this swetnesse to
norisshe with thy deuocion.

Herkne now, herkne, herist thow not what oure Lord saith to his
Fader for his disciples? *Pater, serua eos in nomine meo;* that is,
815 'Fader, kepe my disciples in my name, for I wil that where I am, they
ben with me.' Bowe down thyn heed, that thou be oon of thoo. O here
is good abidynge, ho-so myght tarye, bot thou must yit go ferther and
folewe hym, as it were al a-fer, vnto the Mounte of Olyuete and forsake
him not. Al-though he toke with hym Petir and Iohn and Iames to

777 thin hondes] thin.

trete wiþ hem of the counceyle of his passyon, yit he forbiddith the 820
not, and thou wilt come.

Seest thou not now hov he fallith dovn and praieth and how he
swetith blood for anguisshe of his passyon? Why stondist thou stille?
Go furthe and gadere vp clene these swete dropes, for certeyn they
ben ful preciouse; slepe not now as Petir dide. 825

Beholde where Iudas that traytour cometh with a companye of
peple to take oure Lord: he kisseth; they bynden his blessed hondes
togiders and streyned hem ful soor. Maist thou suffre this? I trowe,
nay. I woot now hov it stondeth with the: thyn hert is fulfilled with
pyte. I holde it no wonder, yit suffir a while and thou shalt se moor. 830
Folewe him in-to the paleys and beholde hou vnkyndely they ferden
with him. Se now how pitously, hou mercifully, hov graciously he
beholdeth Petir that thryes denyed hym atte voys of a womman,
wepynge bitterly for sorwe, and pray him that he vouche-saaf to
beholde the with his merciful eye, that so ofte hast forsake him atte 835
voys of a womman, the whiche is thyn owne flesh, with wicked werkes
and vnleful affeccyons.

Beholde now and se hou he stondeth as a meke lombe before the
iuge, bowynge down his heed and his eyen, spekynge fewe, redy to
suffre repreues and betynge. Se than hou his face is buffeted, his heed 840
is crowned with thornes and his hondes despitously bounden with
bondes. I woot wel thou maist not suffre this, natheles yit loke
vp / with thyn wepynge eyen and beholde hou he berith his cros to his f. 190
passyon with a clothe of purpure arrayed, cleuynge ful sore to his
forbeten woundes. 845

Now is he nayled to the cros and youen eysel medled with galle to
drynke, hangynge bytwene too theues. Heuen and erthe han
meruaile; hast thov no meruaile? I trowe, yhis, for if heuen and erthe
ben sory, thou must nedes be sory. If stones breke, thyn hert must
nedys breke. If wommen wepten beside his passyon, thou must nedes 850
wepe. And amonge alle thinges, haue mynde on his blessed pacience,
hov he shewed pyte for wronge: he heled hem that wounded him, he
gate hem lyf that slowe him; with what swetnes, what charite, trowist
thou, he saide þese wordes: *Pater, ignosce illis quia nesciunt quid
faciunt*. That is to say, 'Fader, foryeue hem for they wyte not what 855
they doon.' Falle down to his feet and beseche him that his blessed
passyon mote commende the to his Fader, seyenge thus, 'Fader,
foryeue hem her trespas.'

Seest thou not how oure Lady wepith? What eyleth the that thou
maist not wepe? Why ben thyn eyen so drye, and thorugh the soule of 860
oure Lady wente a swerde of sorwe? Hou maistow here him speke to
his moder, 'Womman, lo thy sone', wiþ-oute snobbynge? An harde

856 beseche] before seche

hert is that, þe whiche may not wepe now. Crepe in-to that blessed
syde where that blood and water cam forthe, and hyde the ther as a
865 culuer in the stoon, wel likynge the dropes of his blood, til that thy
lippes be maad like to a reed scarlet hood.

Abyde a-while; seest thou not al a-fer, wher an auncyent man
cometh, Ioseph of Armathye? Stonde styl and se what that blessed
man wil do. Als sone as he cometh, he vndoth the nayles of his hondes
870 and feet and byclippeth that swete body with his blessed armes for-to
burye it; certeyn he myght wel say than, as I fynde in a boke of loue:
Fasciculus mirre dilectus meus mihi, that is to say, 'My welbeloued
Iesu is to me a boundel of myrre.' Folewe this precious tresoure and
helpe to bere vp eyther feet or hondes or elles go behynde and gadre vp
875 the smale dropes of blood that fallen by the way. Se nov hou softly,
hou swetly, thay anoynteden that blessed body with bawme and
wyndeth it in se[nd]e[l] and so burieth it.

Wiltow now do wel? Go nowe furthe with Mary Magdalen and
f. 190ᵛ ordeyne for oynementes / ayenst the day of his resurreccyon and than
880 shalt thou se and here hou oure Lord spekith to Mary, clepynge hir by
hir name, 'Mary.' O this was a swete voyce, a softe voyce and a
iocunde; at thys voyce alle the veynes of hir body dissolued and stilled
oute teres of swete deuocyon.

O blessed Mary, what deuocion, what affeccyon, what desire, what
885 brennynge of loue was ther, whan thou aunswerdist, 'Raby,' that is to
say, 'Maister.' Treuly I trowe thy plenteuous wepynge wolde suffre
the say no moor, for thou were stopped with desire of loue. Bot that
was an harde worde and an vntolerable whan he seyde to the: *Noli me
tangere;* that is, 'Mary, touche me not.' Certys yit woldist thou not
890 leeue therfore, for treuly I trowe thyn herte wold brest for wepynge
but if thou haddist touched hym. Gode suster, do thou the saam,
al-though the seme that he withdraweth and wil not suffre the, that
thou touche him by swetnes of deuocyon; lette not therfore but abide
awhile and it shal be right wel.

895 Here now hou he comforted Mary ayen, after that he had seyde þis
worde, 'Touche me not'. 'Mary, drede the not, for though I deferre
hem now, I wil not withdrawe hem fro the; go now first and telle my
brethren that I am rysen and than come ayen.'

Now renne thov fast with Mary, if thou wilt sone come ayen; hir
900 erande was sone doo. Than cam she not alone but with other wommen
and oure Lorde of his curtesy mette hem in the way and grette hem.
What moor? Than he yaf hem leeue to touche his feet: *Accesserunt et
tenuerunt eum*. 'And thay nyeden nye and touched him.' Gode sustir,
abide here as longe as thou maist and fede thy soule with these
905 delicious meditacions.

868 of] ab *expunged, corrected to* of *above*.   877 sendel] selden

⌐*Capitulum xv*⌐

The seconde meditacion the whiche the nedith to haue is of thynges that ben present, as to se how oure Lord hath suffred somme ben forshape or deed in the moder wombe; the and suche other that ben clene and hool in lymes, he hath kepte and reserued from alle suche meschefs. Whethir this be not a gret matere to loue God?

910

Another that he voucheth-saaf to haue vs bore in suche place and amonge suche, where we ben fed alday with the sacramentes of holy chirche. Many ther ben whiche haue not this grace: why, trowist thou? Certeyn for thai ben forsake by rightwesnes and we ben take and called by grace and mercy.

915

Se yit what oure Lord hath do moor. After tyme / we were brought in-to this werld, he kepith vs from dyuerse perels in-to this day, norshyng vs in good wille and feith of holy chirche. And ouer this paciently suffrith oure wickednes vnto the tyme we wil amende vs.

f. 191

920

Thenke ofte her-vpon and than shal al affeccyon of flesshe and worldly loue stynke vpon the; sette thyn hert ther wher thy tresoure is and not in a bagge of golde and seluer, for thou maist not fle to heuen with a bagge of money.

Thynke also euery day that thou shalt dye or eue; than litel shal thy thought be, hov thou shalt fare on the morwe. Be not aferde ne care for honger ne colde, but caste al thy trust in hym whiche fedith birdes and clotheth lilyes. He wil be thy berne and thy richesse, thy whicche and thy purse, thy wurship and thy delytes and al that thou nedyst.

925

930

⌐*Capitulum xvj*⌐

The thridde meditacion the whiche þe nedith to thenke vpon, is of thinges whiche ben to come: that is of thy deth, hou thou shalt dye. For a blessed deth is the begynnyng of lyf, rest and ende of al trauayl and deth of al vices.

935

Beati mortui qui in domino moriuntur, amodo iam dicit spiritus vt requiesca[n]t a laboribus suis; that is to say, 'Tho ben blessed folke the whiche dyen in God, for fro this tyme forwarde, saith oure Lorde, thei shuln reste from al her trauaile.' This I say, disseuerynge the deeth of chosen soules fro the deeth of repreued soules, for chosen soules dyen in [ioye] of conscience. Why, trowist thou? For the deeth of holy peple is precious in the sight of God. They dyen also in ioye of conscience, at whos departyng aungels ben nye. Rightwyse men ben obsequyous by prayer vnto the tyme the soule be in Abrahams bosom. Certeyn þer can no tonge telle the ioye and the reste whiche is in

940

945

937 requiescant] requiescat.   941 ioye] deth

Abrahams boso[m], for ther shul chosen soules abide, tyl the nombre
of other chosen soules be fulfilled. Wiche folke dyen not thus, but in
[f]oule fleshly luste and passynge couetise of the world and suche
other abhominable synnes, by the whiche thei deseruen place of
950   derknes for her mede.

    Considre now the dredful day of doom, in whiche day shal appere
euery thynge naked as it is in his owne kynd; he is a blessed man that
in that day is founde cleer to appere in the sight of God.

f. 191ᵛ   Ymagyne now in thyself hov thou apperist / and stondist in the
955   doom bitwene chosen soules and repreued soules, not yit departed to
the toon syde ne to that othir.

    Beholde stondynge on the lift syde a wrecched companye with gret
stenche, gret drede and gret sorwe, gnastyng with her teeth, horrible
in sight; hyde hem they wolden and thai note whider. If they loke vp,
960   they seen a dredful iuge; if thy loke dovn, thei seen the horrible place
of euerlastynge derknes gapynge after hem; the rightwyse domesman
mown they neither plete ne accuse, for he is rightwys in his domes.

    Now turne we thens and beholde hem the whiche stonden on the
rightsyde, to the whiche company and feloushep Crist Iesu, thy loue
965   and thy spouse, as thou hopist hath chosen the to, for ther maist thou
se som sittyng in doom, somme crouned with a diademe of martirdom, somme white with virginite and chastite, somme rewarded
passyngly for almes-dede, somme for her trewe doctrine and techynge
and alle these ben annexed to oo bonde of chastite and charite and
970   oure Lorde beholdeth eche of hem ful amyable.

    Stonde now stylle, as it were in an vncerteyn whethir thou shalt be
sette to that oo syde or to that other. O that shal be an harde abidynge.
If he sette the on the lyfte syde, what drede shaltow than haue? If he
sette the on the right syde, what ioye shaltow than haue?

975   When the sentence is youen vpon the dampned soules, lyfte vp than
thy gostly eye and se what a fair processyon of chosen soules goon to
the blessed court of heuen, euery in her degre, after her meryt
resceyuynge her heritage, the whiche was ordeyned for hem atte
begynnynge of the worlde, whiche ioye may no tonge telle ne hert
980   thenke.

    But this knowe wel, ther shal no thynge lak that thou woldest were
there present, ne no thynge be present that thou woldist were absent;
and in specyal ther shal be and is oo thinge whiche passith al good,
that is sight and knoulache and loue of oure Lord Iesu.

985   He shal be seen, in hymself and in alle creatures, gouernynge al thyng
without besynes, susteynyng alle thynge without trauail, yeuyng
himself to euery chosen soule as they neden with-oute diuysion and

---

946 bosom] boson   947 Wiche] whiche
948 foule] soule   971 shal] shalt

departyng; he shal than be seen, not as it were in a myrrour, but as he
is, face to face. And than shal he fulfille hys promys whiche he
behighte: *Qui diligit me, diligetur a patre meo et ego manifestabo*   990
ei /meipsum. That is to say, 'He that loueth me shal be loued of my   f. 192
fadir and I shal loue him and shewe him myself as I am.' Of this loue
springeth out an excellent knowlache, of whiche knoulache þus I
fynde write: *Hec est vita eterna vt cognoscant te vnum deum et quem*
misisti, Iesum Christum. That is to say, 'This is lyf euerlastyng, that   995
thy chosen soules mowe knowe the o God and hym that thou sentyst
in-to the erthe, Iesu Crist.'

Of thes too thinges, knouleche and loue, riseth suche swetnes and
charite and suche abundaunce in vsynge therof, that neither plente
lesith the desire ne the desire lesith plente. What this might be, can   1000
noon hert thenke ne tonge telle. To the whiche ioye brynge vs he that
boughte vs vpon the rode tre, amen.

Here endith the Reule of a Recluse that Seynt Alrede wrote to his
suster. And here folewen the chapiters of þe same.

Why suche solitary lyf was ordeyned of fadirs in the olde tyme   1005
                                                    Cap. primum
That a recluse shulde fle couetyse and besynesse of getynge of worldly
godes   Cap. ij
That a recluse shulde not haue to do of hospitalyte anempst religious
gestes, for it longeth not to hir   Cap. iij   1010
How a recluse shulde kepe hir in sylence   Cap. iiij
Also hov a recluse shulde speke and whanne   Cap. v
How a recluse shulde be occupyed   Cap. vj
Hou deuoutly a recluse shulde be-haue hir in Lente tyme   Cap. vij
How she sholde be dyeted and what shuld be hir array   Cap. viij   1015
A short commendacyon of maydenhode and of chastite   Cap. ix
Hou a recluse or an ankeras shulde commende hir chastite to God
                                                     Cap. x
Hov somme dreden hem to do wilful bodely penaunce for drede of
infirmyte   Cap. xj   1020
Hou chastite with-oute mekenesse is as a drye floure   Cap. xij
How the awtier of a reclusys oratorye shold be arrayed   Cap. xiij
Hov a recluse shulde encresse the loue of Iesu in hir soule by medita-
cyon of thynges that ben passed.   Cap. xiiij
Also of meditacyon of thynges that ben present   Cap. xv   1025
Also by meditacyon of thynges whiche ben to come   Cap. xvj

1025 present] prٖeresent

DE INSTITUTIONE INCLUSARUM
THE VERNON MANUSCRIPT

Informacio Alredi, abbatis monasterij de Rieualle, ad sororem suam inclusam, translata de latino in anglicum per Thomam N.

Nou let heere here and vnderstonde ententyflyche myne wordes, what euere heo be þat haþ fursake þis wordle and ychose solytarye lyf,
5 desyryngge to ben yhud and not yseye, and wyllyngge, as a deed body to þis wordle, wyþ Crist to be buryed in a caue. And in þe bygynnyng, why þu schalt preferre solitarye lyf beforn lyvynge in felaschepe of men, bysilyche tak hede.

Þe apostel seiþ: *Virgo prudens cogitat que domini sunt, etcetera –*
10 'A wys mayden studeþ and þenkeþ on þynges þat beþ to Godward, hou þat heo may plese God, þat heo be holi in body and in soule.' Þys vertu, þat is to seye of maydenhood or chastite, hit is a wylful sacryfyse and an offryngge to God vre and liberal, to þe whyche no lawe dryfþ, no nyede constreyneþ, non heste bynt; and þerfore Crist
15 seiþ in þe gospel: *Qui potest capere, capiat –* 'Who þat may take þys vertu', he seiþ, 'let hym take.' Lord, who may? Certayn, he alone to whom [he] haþ inspired schuch a wil and y3yue power to performe.

Þerfore þu, mayde, toforn alle þyng wyþ alle þe deuocioun of þyn herte comende þy gode purpos to hym þat haþ enspired hit to þe, wyt
20 most tenty preyere besechyngge þat þat whuche is inpossible to þe be kynde, be maad ly3t to [þe] þorou his grace. Be-þenk þe hou precious a tresoor in hou freel a vessel þu berst aboute, and what mede, what blysse, what coroune chastyte, duelyche ikept, ministreþ; and also vurþermore, what peyne, what confusioun, what dampnacioun hit
25 brenkþ 3if hit be lost. And what may be moor precious þanne þis tresoor, wiþ þe whuche heuene is ibou3t, angeles beþ delyted, of þe whuche Crist is coueytous, and by þe whyche God is idrawe to loue – and also forto 3eue: what 3yfte? I dar seye baldeliche: hym-self, and al þat euere is his.

30 Wherfore þe swetnesse of þy maydenhood, al vp to heuene smytyngge is swete sauour, makþ þat vre verrey kyng haþ coueytise of þy fayrnesse: and þat is þyn owne Lord, almyti God. Behold now whuche a spouse þu hast ychose, whyche a vrend þu hast ygete. Iwys, he is fair in schap before alle þat euere were born, fayrere þen þe
35 sunne, and passyngge wit-outen mesure al fayrnesse of þe sterres. His breþ is swettere þan eny hony, and his heritage is aboue hony and al swetnesse. *Longitudo dierum in dextera eius, et in sinistra eius diuicie*

17 he] *om.*   21 þe] *om.*

et gloria – 'Lengþe of euere-lastyngge dayes in his ry3t hand, and in
his left hand al rychesse and blisse.' He haþ ichose þe to his wyf, but
he nel not corounne þe er þu be asaid.   40

Þe boc seyþ: *Qui non est temptatus, non est probatus* – 'He þat is
not itempted, he nys not asaid.' Now maydenhood is gold, þy celle is a
furnays, þe blowere to melte þys gold is þe deuel, fuyr is temptacioun;
a maydenes flesche is as hit where a vessel off irþe, wherin gold is iput
to ben asayd; wherfore, 3if þis vessel to-berste þorou gret fuyr of   45
temptacioun, þe gold is ischad out, and schal neuere þis vessel of no
crafty man be maad a3eyn as hit was.

Capitulum secundum

Þyse beþenkyngge, an holy womman loke hy kepe wit al diligence
and drede þilke precious tresour of maydenhood, which so profitable   50
is ihad, and ilost wit-oute recouerer. Be-þenke heo heore continuelly
to whos chaumbre heo is imaad / gay, to whos cleppyngge heo is   f. iii^vb
agreyþed; pote heo toforn heore e3en þe lomb þat heo scholde folwen
whydur euere he walke – þat is Crist. Loke þat sche be-hoolde
blessede Marie wit þe tympane of chastete, ledyng as hit were þe   55
daunce of holy virgynys, and syngyngge þat swete song þat noon may
synge bote clene maydenes, as wel men as wymmen, off whom hit is
iwryte: *Hii sunt qui cum mulieribus non sunt coinquinati, et secuntur
agnum quocumque ierit* – 'Þise hit beþ þat beþ not defoyled wit
wymmen; þyse beþ clene maydenes.'   60

Bote I say not þis þat þu schuldest wene þat a man may not be
defoyled wit-owte a wymman, ne a wumman wit-oute a man; vor in
oþer wyse, moor cursed and abhominable, which schal not be sayd
now ne ynemned, boþe in man and woman ofte chastete is lost. And
ofte witowte flehslich doingge maydenhood is corupt, and chastete is   65
defoyled, whan hit so is þat greet brennyngge temptacioun draweþ to
hym fuul wyl, ant rauesceþ menbres to vuel asent. Wherfore hit
behoueþ gretliche þat an holy mayde be-þenke heore þat alle heore
menbres beþ halwed to God, incorporat to Crist and dedyed to þe
Holy Gost. And ywys, hit is vnsemly, þat þat is Cristes, to taken hit to   70
þe deuel; wherfore heo schulde haue greet schame to graunte forto
defoyle heore maydenlych body in eny maner wyse. So þerfore let
heore strecche al heore herte to saue clennesse and chastete, and
þer-aboute spende al here þou3t, þat sche, as it were beyngge anhungred aftur þe parfeccioun of þis vertu, take hunger as gret delys, and   75
pouerte as most rychesse. In mete and drynk, in slep, in spekyngge,
eueremoor sche moot drede apeyrryngge of here chastete, an-aunter
þat 3yf sche 3yue moor þan is due to heore flehs, sche 3yue strengþe to
heore aduersarie, and nursche here enemy pryuely in here bosum.

80 Syttyngge at þe mete, loke sche turne aboute in here herte þe
clennesse of here chastete, and inwardliche siȝȝyngge to þe parfeccioun of þat vertu, let here saade here mete, and oþur-while haue
scorn of here drynke; ant þat þat neode dryfþ forto take, loke sche take
hit now wit sorwe, now wit schame, and oþer-wyle wit bitter terys.

85 In caas sche schulle speke wit eny man, þat sche be alwey in drede to
here eny-þing or to speke þat myȝte make derke þe brytnesse of
here clennesse. For sche may drede þat here may be benomen
special grace, ȝif sche put forþ a word þat be aȝens clennesse and
honestete.

90   *Capitulum tercium*

Whan þu lyst doun in þy bed, commende and bytak þy clennesse to
þy God, and þanne, y-armed wit þe signe of þe cros, beþenk þe
hertyliche how þu hast ileued þat day. And ȝif in word or dede or
þouȝt þu hast offended þe siȝte of þy God, cry mercy, siȝȝe and smyt

95 þy brest. Ȝif þu hast be moor idel, mor necligent þan þu shuldest be,
ȝif also in mete or drynke þu hast ipassed þe boundes of due neode: ȝif
þu art gulty in eny of þis, þu most preye mercy of þy God; and soo wit
þis euen-sacrifise let slep fynde þe reconsiled to þy spouse. And in caas
þat whan þu wakest sodeynliche, wheþur it be of to muche slep, or
100 elles of queyntyse of þe temptour, þe hete of þy flehs be styred, and
f. iiiᵛᶜ þyn cruel enemy / wolde drawe þe in-to nyce fantacye, to asayle þe
reste of þy chastete and clennesse; ȝif he styre þe to delites, and wolde
make þe agast of hardere lyf: anon let come in-to þy þouȝt þe blessede
vyrgines þat sum-tyme where.

105 Þenk how þilke blessede Agnete gold and seluer, precious closes
and vertuous stones, and al þe pompe off wordliche blisse despysede
as styngynge dunge. Whan sche was cleped to doom, sche voydede
not; þe tyraunt glosede here, sche defyede hit; he þretnede here, sche
low hym to skorn, more dredyngge þat he wolde sparen here, þan þat
110 he wolde slen here for here loues sake. A blessed mayden, þat turnde
an hoore-hows in-to an oratorie, wit wham an angel, entryngge in-to
prysoun, turnede derknesse in-to liȝt, and slow wit sodeyn deþ here
pursuour of here maydenhood.

And þerfore, and þu wyl preye and lefte vp þe armes of bitere terys
115 aȝens þe temptour of lecherie, wit-owte doute holy angeles nole nouȝt
be fer fro þy chaste bed, which þat entrede wit Agnete in-to an
hoore-hows. And for-soþe, it was ful skylful þat material fuir myȝte
not brenne þis holy mayde, in wham þe leem of lecherie was iqueynt,
and þe fuir of charite hadde iset afuyre. As ofte as eny brennyngge
120 temptacioun comeþ vp-on þe, as ofte as þe wyckede spyryt put to þe
vnlifful lustes, wite it wel þat he is present þat aschercheþ entrayles of

þyn herte, and what so euere þu do or þenke, hit is open biforn his
eʒen.

Haue also reuerence of þe gode angel, whic þu schalt not doute þat
is iput to þe, and to þy temptour answere in þis wyse: 'I haue to my   125
louyere þe angel of God, þat wit gret ielouste kept my body.' And ʒif
such temptacioun dure, let helpe þy partye streytere abstinence; for
þer þat is muche abstinence idoo to þe flehs, noon or lyte may be
flehsliche delectacioun.

Capitulum quartum   130

Noman glose hym-selfe, no man ne womman chape hym-self ne
by-gyle hym-self; for trewely, wit-oute gret contricioun of herte and
penaunce bodily ne may not chastete be gete ne kept, and namely in
ʒungge, which þat ofte in syke and oolde is greuously iperisched. For
alþouʒ castete be a special ʒift of God, and no-body may be continent   135
of his owne merytis, bote onlyche of þe liberal ʒyft of þe grace of God,
naþeles almyty God halt hem vnworþy þis ʒifte þat nulle not by-
sylyche trauayle to come þer-to, willyngge and wenyngge forto be
chast among delices, continent among delauey festes, to dwellen
among nyce wommen and nouʒt be tempted, in glotonye and drunke-   140
schipe be ful of stynkynde humours and nouʒt be defoyled, to bere
leyt of fuir in here bosum and nouʒt be brend. Suster, þis is ryth hard;
whoþer it be inpossible or noon, avise þe!

Narracio valde deuota contra te[m]ptacionem

I knew sum-tyme a monke, whic in þe bygynnyngge of his conuer-   145
sioun, what þorouʒ steryngge of naturel complexioun, what for
violence of vicious vs and custum, what also þorouʒ suggestioun of þe
wyckede temptour, he, dredyngge his clennesse be persced and spild,
areysede hym-self aʒens hym-self, and, co[nc]ey[u]yngge a wondur
gret hate aʒens his owne flehs, he coueytede no-þyng more þan þat þat   150
myʒte do his body turment and disese. And þerfore wit mysese he
made his body lene, in so muche þat forto refreyne vnlyfful mociouns
of / flehs, swyche þynges as were ryʒtful and lyfful to þe body,   f. iv
oþer-wyle he witdrow hem. But afterward, whan gret feblenesse
compellede hym to take more hede of his body, anoon þe flehs gan   155
wexe proud, and gan to fiʒte aʒens þe reste þat he hadde had a whyle
in clannesse. And what dude he þanne bote sum-tyme caste hym-self
in cold fresyngge water, and so cheueryngge he cryde and preyde
aʒens his temptaciouns; and oþerwyle he frotede his nakede body
wit brymme brennyngge netlys, for þat he wolde wit on maner bren-   160

144 *temptacionem*] teptacionem   149 conceyuyngge] coueytyngge

nyngge haue ouer-come þe brennyngge off flehslich mocioun to
vnclennesse.

But whan al þis no suffiscede not, and neuere þe lattere þe spirit of
lecherie asaylede hym – certes, þo cowde he noon oþur refut, bote ful
165 doun longstreiȝt by-fore þe feet of Ihesu Crist, preyingge, wepyngge,
syȝȝyngge, coniuryngge, besechyngge þat he wolde hele hym, or elles
slen hym. Pitously and ofte he cryde, as þe booc seyd: *Non te
dimittam nisi benedixeris michi* – 'I nel neuere go hennys, I nel
neuere haue reste, I nel neuere lete þe er þu haue iȝeue me þy
170 b[l]essyngge.' And þanne oþer-wyle as for a tyme he hadde lysse; bote
soerte was deveyed hym. A, swete God, what sorwe suffrede þylke
wrecche, what turment hadde he, alwhat þer was igraunted hym so
gret delytyngge in chastete þat alle þe lustes þat mowe be þouȝt or
spoken ne scholde not haue moved hym. Bote ȝit whanne þys wrecche
175 hadde so gret temptacioun, he was boþe syk and hoold; and naþeles he
was vynsyker.

Capitulum sextum

Þerfore hit is gret schame of manye mannes woodschype, why[c]e
þat whanne þey haue lyued al here lyf in sty[n]kynde fulþe, ȝit in here
180 oolde age þey nulleþ not wit-drawe hem fro þe companye of suspekt
persones, bote seyn þat þey ben siker ynow of hem-self, for þat þey
veleþ here body sumdel akeled; ant þerfore þey spare not to taken hem
nyȝt and day to occasiones of sunne. Bote among alle resonable
creatures þise beþ foles and acursed wrecches, in þe whyche, alþouȝ
185 þat myȝt lacke, ȝit wyl and lust dureþ in hem of stench of synne; and
so fowl desir ne resteþ not in hem, þey feblenesse of age denye power
of dede, as þey seyn. Bote auyse hem, what so þey euere be, wheþer
þey seye sooþ, or elles here falsnesse lye openly in here face. For
trywely oþerwyle, þo þat beþ ycome in-to here laste age, in so muche
190 þat here bodyes beþ half ded and half alyue, ȝit swhiche men sum-
tyme beþ yskorned in here slep of þe deuel by fantasies of fowl lust,
and bodyly disesed.

And þerfore, suster, I nel neuere be no wey þat þu be to siker of
þy-self, bote euere be in drede, and hold þy freelte suspekt, and, as a
195 dredful douve, haunte ryueres of cler water, wher þu miȝt isee þe
ymage of þe raueynous hauke þat flikt aboue þe, and be war. Þyse
ryueres beþ holy scriptures, þat welleþ out fro þe welle of wysdom,
þat is Crist, þe whyche wyl schewe þe þe schadue of þe deueles
suggestioun, and wyt and consayl to eschewen hem. For þer is noþyng
200 þat so put awey wyckede and vnclene þouȝtes as dooþ good ocupa-

170 blessyngge] bessyngge
178 whyce] whyte   179 stynkynde] stykynde

cioun in holy scripture, to þe whyche a good womman, and specially a
mayde, schulde so vse al here herte and wit þat, þei3 sche wolde, sche
mowe / not þenke bote on Godes lawe. Let slep fynden here
þenkynde on holi scripture; whan sche awakeþ of here slep, let renne
to here mende sum clause of holy techyngge; and whil þe slep is on
here, let cleue to here ribbes sum sentence of holy wrytyngges, þat
mowe moor surliche kepe here menbrys, and also boþe body and soule
in here slep.

f. iv^b

205

Capitulum vij

Bote þe more sorwe is, þer beþ manye þat beþ refreyned fro gostly
ocupacioun bi a maner fals drede – þat is to seyn, þat þey falle not in-to
gret syknesse for gret wakyngge in Godes seruise, or for gret abstinence; for þanne þey dredeþ þat þey scholde be in charge to oþere
men, and hem-self in sorwe. Bote certes, þis is oure synful excusacioun; for Lord, how fewe beþ þer now-aday þat habbeþ þo gret
feruour of holynesse. We haldeþ vs alle wyse, alle discret, alle auyse;
we smelleþ aver a faynt batayle, and certes, we dredeþ so muche
syknesse of body þat we dredeþ to-comyngge, þat siknesse of soule þat
we feleþ present we take noon hede of; as þey it were more bettere to
suffre brennyngge of lecherie þan a litul grucchynge of stomac; as
þey3 it nere not bettere be syknesse of þe body eschewe vnclene
wildenesse of þe flehs, þan be hool in body, and ouercome, as a þral, of
flehsliche lustes.

210

215

220

Lord, what fors is it whoþer be abstinence oþer be syknesse þe
proude carayne be halde a-doun and chastete be kept? Bote vp-an ap
þu seist þat a man mot be war þat he take not to litel hede of his body,
an-aunter þat after chier and delicat kepyngge in syknesse which he
my3te falle into of to muche abstinence, he be take wit foule lustes. I
answere þat certeynly, 3if þe flesh be mornyngge, syk and feble, 3if þe
stomac be vnsauery and drye, alle þe delites þat þu my3t schewen hym
beþ raþere to heuynesse of hym þan to fowl lustes.

225

230

Narracio bona Capitulum viij

I saw ones a man which þat by euel roted custum ibounde[n] and
ouercomen in his 3ouþe, myte not conteyne and be chaast; naþeles at
þe laste he took hede of his owne perilous stat, and wax al rebuked and
aschamed of hym-self, in so muche þat in þenkyngge of his foule
synful lyf, his herte gan brenne wyt-ynne hym as eny fuyr. And
aftur-ward, beyngge ynlyche wroþ wit hym-self, he ful on to smyte
most greuous batayl a3ens his owne body; so greuous þat þe þyng þat

235

233 ibounden] iboundem

240 semede necessarie to þe body, he witdrow hem. Þer þat he hadde be
toforhand ly3t and nyce, he wax sad; þer he hadde ibe blaberynge and
chaterynge, he took hym to silence. Noman say hym after chape ne
le33e, no-man saw hym pleye, noman herde eny ydel or nyce word of
his mouþ; of alle wordliche solaces and delites in sleep, in mete, in
245 drynke, þat my3te seme swete to þe flehs, he hadde skorn and dispyt.
Of þe þou3tes of his herte, to refreyne hem, he was so busy and so
curious þat it wolde haue semed to manye þat he hadde ipassed
mesure. Wyþ so euy chiere, wiþ þe e3en icast adoun, he saat, he wente
and stood, þat tremlyngge and quakyngge hit semede þat he stood
250 to-forn his dredful domesman at þe day of dome.

f. iv^c   And what? Certes, wit swyche armes he gat hym glorious victorie of
his enemys gostliche, and of his wickede tiraunt, his flehs. For wit-
inne a while he ful in a gret and greuous siknesse of his stomac, and
after long siknesse, whan þe houre cam of his laste slep, þat he schulde
255 be deed, wit gret spirit he sayde þeose wordes: 'Suffre a while, suffre;
loo wher Ihesus comeþ' – *Sine, inquid, ecce Ihesus venit.*

Naþeles, I say not þis to wit-seie good discrecioun, whic is moder
and nursche of vertus, bote þat we schulde resteyne or elles doon awey
þe matyres of synne; þat is to seyn, glotonye, slep, to muche reste, to
260 muche communyngge wit wommen or nyce men of here body; for wel
ofte by a fals name of discrecioun we coloureþ to excuse owre foule
lustes. Hit is a noble and a verrey discrecioun to putte þe soule tofore
þe body; and þer þat þey beþ boþe in peril, and wit-oute greuaunce of
þat on, þat oþer may not be saued, hit is ful skilful þat for profit of þe
265 soule, þe body be put by-hynde.

Þyse þynges I sey to þe, suster, þat þu schuldest take ententyly
heede how gret bysynesse þu most haue to kepe þe chast and clene; þe
whic vertu of chastete maydenly, alþou3 it be ornament and flour of
vertues, 3it witowte meknesse it wext al faad.

270   *Capitulum nonum*

Þis vertu of meknesse is a sur fundement of alle maner vertues,
whit-oute which fundement, what so euere þu wylt gostly reyse vp,
hit falleþ doun. *Inicium omnis peccati superbia*: 'Bygynnyngge of alle
synne is proude', which cast owt an angel out of heuene, and man out
275 of paradys. And of þis cursede rote, alþou3 þer spryngge out manye
venenous braunches, alle naþeles ben departed in-to two spices: in-to
gostly, and bodyly. Bodyly pruyde is to be proud of bodyly 3ynges;
gostly pruyde is to be pruyd of gostly 3yftes. And furþermor, bodyly
pruyde is departed in tweyen; þat is to sayn, in-to bost, and vanite.
280 Vanite is as ofte as þe hand-mayden of Crist haþ a veyn-glorie in here
herte þat sche is ycomen of gret blood and noble, and þerwit haþ a

flehsly delytyngge þat sche haþ forsake richesse of þe wordle and
nobleye and take here to pouerte, or elles þat sche holde here-self
wondurliche holy and to be commendeþ þat sche haþ forsake grete
and ryche mariages off worþy mennes sones þat sche my3te han be   285
maried to – al þis is vanite. Also hit is a spice of vanite 3if þu coueyte to
muche bodyly fairnesse, or þat þu delite þe to muche in gaynesse of þy
celle, in diuerse peyntyngges or celures, or swyche oþere tryfles; alle
þyse iapes þu most flen as contrarie to þy professioun.

Whit what vorheed my3t þu haue veyn-glorie of rychesse or of   290
noble blood, þat coueytest to be iseye his spouse þat for vs was mad
ri3t pouere, alþou3 he were verreyly ryche – þat is Crist. A pore
moder, a pouere may[n]e, a pouere hows he chees hym; þe streytnesse of an oxe-stalle. And Lord, wheþer it seme a gret woundour to
þe, in þe whiche þu schuldest haue a veyn-glorie, þat þu hast forsake   295
to wedde a monnes sone for þe loue þat þu hast to be Cristes spouse? Is
hit a gret woundour þat þu hast forsake styngyngge / lust of body for   f. iv^v
þe swete sauour of maydenhood? Semeþ hit a wundur þat þu hast
ychaunged matere of stench and of corupcioun for euer-lastynge
delices and rychesse of heuene? Schuldest þu haue a veyn-glorie,   300
al-þey þu haue idoo þus?

Holy scripture seyt: *Si gloriaris, in domino glorieris* – Suster, 3if þu
be glad for þise þyngges, loke þy ioye be in God, and serue hym in
parfit drede. And vurþermor, I nel not be no wey þat, as it where
vndur colour of deuocioun and holynesse, þ[u] delite þe in veyne   305
peyntyngges, kyttyngges and in grauyngges in þy celle, noþer in
cloþys gaylyche yweue, ne steyned wit bryddes or bestes, or diuerse
trees or floures, or oþer babounrye. Let hem haue swych aray þat,
noon or litul ioye hauyngge wit-ynne, sechyþ al here ioye wit-oute.

Capitulum decimum   310

Omnis gloria filie Regis abintus. As holy wryt seiþ, alle þe ioie of a
kynges douter schulde be wit-ynne. Perfore, 3if þu be þe kynges
douter of heuene, for as muche as þu hast ywedded his sone Criste,
loke þu hiere þe veys of þy Fader, which seiþ to þe þat al þy ioye
schulde be wyt-ynne þe.   315

Loke þerfore þat al þy gladnesse come of clene wytnesse of a good
conscience wit-ynne. Let þer be fair peynture and grauyngge of
diuerse vertues; let þer fressche coloures of goode þewes wit curious
knottes be knet to-gydere, þat þe fayrnesse of o vertu, an-oþer wel
icoupled to hym, mowe make þe mor brit in schynyngge. Let mek-   320
nesse be ioyned to chastete, and noþyng schal be bry3tere; let also
simplenesse be associod to good inward wysdom, and noþyng schal be

293 mayne] mayde   305 þu] *the* u *in Vernon is preceded by the first stroke of* e

clierere; let mercy be coupled wit ry3twisnesse, and noþyng is mor
swete; and to alle þyse þanne put good temprure and good dis-
325 crecioun, and mor profitable peynture schalt þu noon fynde.

In swich curiosite ocupye þyn e3en of þyn herte, swich vertuous
diuersete fourme in þy soule wit al þy wit, and þerwit let enbroude þy
spiritual cloþynge. *In fimbrijs aureis etcetera.* 3if þu wylt, as þe book
seiþ, adden goldene hemmys, certes, þenne þu hast a garnement wel
330 iweue adoun to þi foot, in whiche þyn husbounde Crist wil haue gret
lykyngge to fynde þe icloþed in. An hemme, as þu wost wel, is þe laste
ende of a cloþ; and þe ende wherto draweþ al þe parfeccioun of Godes
lawe is charyte, as þe apostel seiþ: *Finis precepti est caritas.* Þis
charyte most þu nyede haue, louyngge God and þyn euene-cristene of
335 clene herte, wit good conscience, and wit fey not feyned ne fayllynge.

Capitulum xj

In swich ray, suster, haue likyngge and gladnesse, wit-ynne, and
not wit-oute; in verrey vertus and in verrey peyntures put þy lust.

Let faire lynnene towayles ligge vppon þyn awter, 3if þu hast eny;
340 þe whiche for here whitnesse and clennesse mowe signefie and schewe
to þe þe whitnesse of chastete and simplenesse. Beþenk þe wit ow
muche trauayl and betyngge lynne or flex is ibrou3t out of þe irþene
colour þat it grew in, er hit were so wyth as hit is whan it makeþ fair
þyn awter, and Cristes body is wrapped þer-in. Ferst flex is brou3t
345 forþ wit irþene colour; and so be [we] ybrout forþ wit wickednesse
and synne: *Quoniam ego in iniquitatibus conceptus sum, et in peccatis
concepit me mater mea.* Afterward, whan flex is itake out of þe
irþe, hit is icast in-to water; and ry3t so, whan we ben take out of owre
f. iv^vb   oune moder wombe, we beþ icast in-to þe water of bapteme, and / þer
350 we beþ ibyryed wit Crist. And þer, alþou3 synne be put awey, 3it
syknesse of synne dureþ. Þer we takeþ sumwhat off whitnesse in þe
wasschyngge awey of þe vielþe of synne, bote, certes, al parfytly clene
and whith be we not imaad, for þe enclinaunce þat we habbeþ, as
longe as we beþ in þis wordle, to synne and to wrecchednesse.

355 Vurþermor flex, after water, it is dryed; and so we, after þat we beþ
icristned, it be-houeþ þat oure body by abstinence be ymaad drye fro
stynkynde humores of vnclennesse. And ri3t as after-ward flex is ibete
wit a betyl, to be þe mor suple to werk; rith so oure flehs is ibete and
bouyd wit temptacioun many and diuers, to be þe more obedient to þe
360 spirit. 3it ouermor, þat lynne or flex is ipurged wit grete yrene
kombes, to putte awey þe grete superfluites; and so mote we wit þe
scharpe 3erd of discipline putte awey alle superfluites, and holde þat is
streyt nyede to vs. And ry3t as afterward þis is iput to flex: a comb of

345 we] *om.*

smallere pryckes, to clense it more curiously – ry3t so we, whan we
haue ouercome, wit gret trauayle, grete and wickede temptaciouns   365
and passiouns of þe flehs, we schul be aboute to make vs clene of
cotidian defautes by meke schryfte and due satisfaccioun. Ouermor,
after þis flex is ispunne a-long; and so we by long perseueraunce
mote dure in oure goode purpos. And at þe laste, schortly, ri3t as to
lynnene, er it be parfytly fair and whit, is iput boþe water and fuir;   370
ri3t so we mote þorou3 vier of tribulacioun and water of scharp
contricioun, er we come fully to þe refreschyngge of chastete and
clennesse.

Swyche þynges let brynge to þyn myende þe ornamentes of þyn
oratorye, and not fulfylle þyn e3en wit vnlyfsum iaperyes a[n]d   375
vanites.

De ymaginibus.

And as touchyngge holy ymages, haue in þyn awter þe ymage of þe
crucifix hangynge on þe cros, which represente to þe þe passioun of
Crist, which þu schalt folwe. Al-to-gydere he is ysprad abrood to   380
bykleppe þe in his armes, in which þu schalt haue gret delectacioun;
and hys tetys beþ al naked ischewd to þe to 3yue þe melk of spiritual
delectacioun and confortacioun. And, 3if it be lykynde to þe, to
commende þe grete excellence of virginite, let þilke blessede mayden
and moder in o syde, and þilke diere deciple Ihon, a mayde also, in þat   385
oþer syde of þe cros be ihad in here ymages, þat þu mowe þenke
her-by hou plesaunt to God is chastete boþe of man and womman,
which he halewode so preciously in his moder and his lieue deciple,
seynt Ihon; and þerfore he couplede hem so tendrely to-gydere,
hangynge on þe roode, whan he bytook to his moder þe deciple to   390
kepe, and a3enward þe maydenly deciple to haue warde of þe moder
and mayde. And a blessed testament was þis to seynt Ihon, to whom
þe fayrnesse of alle mankynde, hope of al þe wordle, ioye of heuene,
refut of wrecchen, solas of þo þat beþ in sorwe, cumfort of pouere,
and at þe laste, lady of al þe wordle, queen of heuene wit so gret   395
auctorite was take to kepe.

Suster, let þyse þynges styre þe to feruour of parfit charite, and to
noo spectacle of vanite; for þorou3 þyse alle it is necessarie þat þu stee
vp oon, alone – for þilke on is only necessarie: *Porro vnum est
necessarium.* Þis is þilke on þat is not yfounde bote in oon, / at oon   f. iv^{vc}
and wit oon, in whom is noon vnstabilite ne chaungyngge; and þat
cleueþ to þylke oon, he is oon in spirit wit hym, alwey goynge in-to
þilke oon þat is eueremoore oon wit-outen eny mutacioun, and whos
3eres ne tyme neuere ne fayleþ – *Tu semper idem ipse es, et anni non
deficient.* Þis cleuyngge to þis oon is charite, whic, as I seyde, is as it   405
were a goldene hem, finally to make fair þy weddyng-coote.

375 and] ad

De caritate. Capitulum duodecimum

Þis weddyng-garnement, suttylly yveue wit diuers vertus, it bihoueþ þat it be be-goon aboute wit swiche goldene hemmes, þat is to 410 seyn wit þe briȝtnesse of charite, þe wyche mowen conteyne and bynde alle vertus in oon and make oon of manye, departyngge to alle here clernesse, and so cleuyngge to alle vertus þat as it were þey alle bete not manye, bote oon.

Diuisio caritatis.

415 Þis charite is departyd in two: in-to þe loue of God, and in-to þe loue of þyn emcristene. And vurþermor, þe loue of þyn emcristene is departyd in two: in-to innocence and beneficience. Pat is to seyn, þat þu greue ne harme noman, bote do good and profyt to as manye as þu myȝt – for þis is lawe of kynde. *Quod tibi non vis fieri, alij ne feceris –* 420 and þis is innocence. And God seyd in þe gospel: *Omnia quecumque vultis vt faciant vobis etcetera* – alle þynges þat ȝe woolde þat men dede to ȝouȝ, do ȝe to hem aȝenward: and þis is benificience.

Now tak good heede, suster, how þise two parteyneþ to þe. Þe ferste is þat þu schost greue no-man; and certayn, þat howte be liȝt 425 inouȝ to þe, for þu myȝt greue no-body, þey þe woldest, bote ȝif þu smyte hym wit þy tounge. And for-soþe, þe secunde scal be liȝt inouȝ to þe, ȝif þu take good heede to þi purpos, and loue þe nakede and bare pouerte þat þu hast take þe to. For þer may be no matere of euel wil aȝens no-man wher reigneþ no coueytyse, ne noþyng is iloued þat may 430 be doon awey. Þerfore wylne wel to alle men, and do good to as manye as þu miȝt. Bote hier þu askest of me in what þyng þu miȝt do good to eny mon, soþþe þu hast forsake alle wordliche godys, and hast no maner þynge to ȝyue to þe neody.

Capitulum xiij

435 Suster, know wel þe condicioun of þy lyf. Þer were two sustren, Marthe and Marye: þat oon trauaylede, þat oþer restyde; þat oon ȝaf, þat oþer askede and baad; Marthe ȝaf outward seruise, Marie nurschede ynward loue. Marie ne ran not hyder and þyder, bisy to vnderfonge gystes; Marie was not distracte aboute husbondrye; 440 Maria was not entendaunt to pore mennes cryyngge; bote sche saat meekely at Ihesu feet and herde deuoutly his word and his lore.

My diere sister, þis is þy party: þu þat art deed to þe wordle and ybyried, þu schalt be deef to hiere eny-þyng of þe wordle, and dump forto speke it; ne þu schalt not be bysy ne distract aboute wordly 445 ocupaciouns. Let Marthe alone wit þat partye, whos partye, alþouȝ it be nouȝt deneyed good, Maries partye naþeles is yseyd þe bettere.

Lord, wheþer Marie hadde eny enuye of Marthe? Nay, dredeles;

bote raþer Marthe hadde enuye as it were of Maryes deel. And in þe
same manere let hem þat beþ beste wommen i þe wordle, let hem, I
seie, haue a spiritual enuye to folwe þy lyuyngge; bote not so þu to 450
hemward. To hem þat beþ in þe wordle longeþ to 3yuen almesse,
wiche þat haueþ wordliche possessioun, and also to men of holy
churche to whom is itake þe dispensacioun of þe godys of holy
churche. / For þeo þynges þat beþ y3iue to holy chirche bysschopes, f. v
prestes and clerkes, after þat þey haue itake þrof here nyede þey 455
scholde parte to þe pore; for here godys beþ pouere menne godys, and
wydue godes, and faderles and moderles children godes, and also
minystres of holy churche goodis – for þey þat ministreþ þe awter, it is
skyleful þat þey lyue of þe awter. To þyse, þoo þat beþ benefysed in
holi churche schulde in tyme of nyede dele here godes, and not 460
coueytously close hem v[p] in here cofres. And also þoo goodes þat
beþ y3yue to holy monasteries in-to þe vs of Cristes seruauns, hit is
resoun þat þey [be] ministred by certayn persones þat beþ y-ordeyned
þer-to, so þat þat þat is more þan here breþryn han nyede to, be
goodly y3iue to gystes, to pilgrymes and pore men, and not auarously 465
iput vp in here purses. Bote suster, þis partyneþ to hem to whom is
itake Marthes office, not to hem þat resteþ hem in holynesse of
contemplacioun, as þu art.

For þoo þat beþ in cloystre schulde not bysi hem to vnderfonge
gystes, ne þey schulde not be distract to ministre to þe pouere men; 470
for þey beþ þilke þat schulde make no purvyaunce fro o day to anoþer,
ne haue no þou3t ne care of mete ne of drynke; certayn, þey schulle be
okepied in swettere þyngges, and be fulfeld more profitably of spiritual delices. Let hem þat beþ more contemptible and rude to spiritualte, let hem bysie hem wit þe wordle, let hem cleppe to hem 475
carayne and dung; for þey beþ þilke oxen þat þe book spekeþ of:
Quorum piger stercoribus lapidetur – Among þe whiche he þat is slow
schal be stened to deþe wit stynkynde dung.

Bote þer beþ manye þat beþ slow and vnlusty aboute spiritual
þyngges, as were þilke slow3 and synneful poeple in desert þat hadde 480
skorn and abhominacioun of angeles mete: *Anima nostra nauseat
super cibo etcetera*. For swyche nyce foolys, whan þey beþ ydulled in
here life, and þey see oþere y-ocupied in þe wordle aboute temperal
godys, anoon þey haueþ envye, and gruccheþ, and bagbyteþ here
breþeryn; and so for a lytul stynkynde vielþe, in þe whiche oþre beþ 485
defoyled in þe wordle, þey hem-self beþ ismyte wit pryckes of enuye
and biternesse; of þe whiche, in caas þey falle a3en to þe wordle, to
antermete of wordly þyngges, certes, it may be sayd: *Qui nutriebantur in croceis, amplexati sunt stercora.*

And þerfor, suster, seþþe þat þey þat beþ in holy monasteries ne 490

455 þat] þat þat   461 vp] vt   463 be] *om.*

schulle not ocupien hem wit þe wordle, bote þilke þat beþ assigned
þer-to, and to whom is itaken Marthes bisynesse, muche more þu, þat
hast forsake þe wordle, neþer schalt haue worldly goodes in dispensacioun, neþer see ne hiere matires of þe wordle. Þu þat hast al forsake,
495   wher-of schuldest þu ȝyue almesse? Napeles, ȝif þu hast a wyȝt of þyn
owne trauayle more þan þu dispendist þy-self, ȝif almesse a Godes alf,
and ȝit not by þyn owne hand, bote by sum oþer. Soþþe þy lifnoode
comeþ bote of oþere folk, wherto schalt þu care to ȝyue almesse of
oþere menne godes, a namely seþþe þu schalt not vsurpe to þe bote þy
500   neode?

What þanne almesse or good schalt þu doo to þyn emcristen, as I
sayde byforn, whan I spake of beneficience? Suster, an holy seynt
seiþ: 'Þer is noþynge rychere þan a good wyl' – þat ȝif! What is more
profitable þan deuout preyere? Þat ȝif! What is more ful of manhoode
505   þan pite? Þat spreed aboute! And in þis wise, suster, bynd al þis
wordle to-gydere in þy bosum wit o bond of pyte and of loue; and þer
f. vᵇ   by-hald alle þeo þat ben goode, / and þanke God þer-of and be glaad;
behald o þat oþer side alle þoo þat ben wickede and in dedly synne,
and wyep vp-on hem and be sory! Þer tak heede of hem þat beþ
510   oppressed þoruȝ greet meschyef, and haue conpassioun of hem; let
renne þer in þy myende þe misese of þe pouere, þe whepyngge of
fadurles and modurles children, þe desolacions of wydues, þe bitere
siȝȝyngge and weylyngge of [þo] þat beþ ouercome by greet sorwe, þe
niede of pilgrymes, þe periles of hem þat beþ in þe see, þe heȝe vowes
515   of holy virgynes, þe temptacions of holy men, þe bysynesse of prela-
tys, þe trauayle of hem þat beþ in wherre, oþer in oþer maner ryȝtful
trauayle. To alle þyse opene þy brest, to þyse ȝif þyn almesse, to þyse
departe þy bitere terys, for þyse sched out þy clene preyeres.

For-soþe, suster, þis almesse is more plesaunt to God, more accep-
520   tyd of Crist, more competent to þy professioun, more fructuous to
hem þat þu ȝifst hit to, þan eny oþer bodyly ȝifte. Swych maner ȝifte,
þat is to seye gostly almesse, spiritual beneficience, helpeþ þy purpoos
and not hyndreþ it, also hit encreseþ þe loue of þyn emcristene and
not amenuseþ it. Hit kept þe quite of þyn herte, and let hit nouth. And
525   what schal I say more? Certayn, as seynt Gregory sayȝt: 'Summe-
tyme holy men, for þe more parfeccioun, for þe loue of God and of
here emcristene þe wolde no-þyng of wordly richesse haue in þe
wordle, ne noþyng coueyte forte haue.' Bote manye and to manye þer
beþ þat doþ euen þe contrarie, for þey trauayled nyȝt and day to haue
530   wordly good; and þey seyn to doo charite and almesse, for þey wolde

507 þanke God þer-of and be glaad]   þanke God þer of and alle þoo þat beþ
goode and be glaad   509 vp-on hem] vp hem on (*marked for reversal*)
513 þo] *om.*
514 heȝe vowes] heȝe of vowes   521 ȝifst] ȝifst'

haue what for-to 3yue. Bote certayn, þyse wel ofte fayled of þe he3e
parfeccioun off charite.

Capitulum quartumdecimum

After þat I haue itold sumwhat of þe loue of þyn emcristene, now
schortly I wyl telle þe sum party of þe loue of G[od]. For alþou3t þoo   535
sustren þat I haue spoken of louede, boþe hem, God and here emcristene, 3it more specially Marthe was okepyed aboute þe seruyse of here
emcristene þan Marie, which þat halyde to here continually holy
affeccioun of þe euerlastyngge welle of loue. To þyse loue of God
parteyneþ two þyngges: clene affeccioun of herte, and effecte of good   540
deede. Þe affeccioun moot be in taste of gostly swetnesse, ant þe
effecte of good deede moot be in excercise of vertus – þe which
excercise of vertus is in a certayn god maner of lyuyngge, in fastyngge,
in wakyngge, in trauayl, in redyngge, in preyeris, in pouerte, and
swych oþere. And as to speken of affeccioun, gostly and bodyly, þu   545
most nursche hit wit holy and hoolsum meditacioun.
De meditacione.

Wherfore, dire suster, þat þe swete affeccioun of loue of swete
Ihesu mowe wexe in þyn herte, þu most haue þre maner meditacioun:
þat is to seyn of þyngges þat ben apassed, of þingges þat beþ present,   550
of þyngges þat beþ comyngge. And þerfore, suster, when þyn herte is
iclensed fro al vielþe and sten[c] of foule 3ou3tes by þe excercise of
holy vertus, cast þi cliere e3en abake to þyngges þat beþ apassyd, of þe
whiche is imaad miende in þe trewe gospel.

And ferst goo in-to þy pryue chaumbre wit oure lady Marie,   555
wher schee abood þe angel message, and þer, suster, abyd þe angel
comyngge, þat þu mowe isee whanne he comeþ in, and hou graciously
he grette þilke gracious mayde; and soo þu, as it were irauesched of al
þy wittes, whanne þe angel begynþ is salutacioun [t]o þilke blessede
mayde and modur, cry þu as lowde / as þu my3t grede to þy lady and   f. v^c
sey: *Aue maria, gratia plena, dominus tecum; benedicta tu in
mulieribus et benedictus fructus ventris tui Ihesus, amen.* And þis
rehersyngge ofte and many tyme be-þenke þe how muche was þilke
fulsumnesse of grace in Marie, of whom al þis wordle borwede and
beggede grace, whanne Godys sone was maad man, ful of grace and   565
sooþfastnesse.

Þanne, suster, wundre gretly in þyn herte how þilke lord, þat
fulfelþ boþe euene and erþe, was iclosed wit-ynne þe bowelys of a smal
gentil mayden, whom God þe Fader halwede, God þe Sone brou3te
wit childe, God þe Holy Gost fulfelde of grace. A, swete blessyd lady,   570

535 God] good   552 stenc] stent
552 3ou3tes] *corrected to* þou3tes   559 to] þo

wit how muche swetnesse were þu ivisited, wit how hoot brennyngge
vier of loue were þu iset aviere, whanne þu vieledest in þyn herte and
in þy wombe þe presence of so greet a maieste, whanne þat Crist took
flehs of þy flehs, whanne of þy clene maydenly blood he made hym
575 blood, whanne of þy menbres he made hym menbres, in þe whyche
was þe fulle godhede bodyly. And certayn, suster, al þis for þe, þat art
a mayde, be-cause þat þu schuldest take good heede of þis mayde þat
þu scholdest folwe, and of þis maydenes sone Crist, to whom þu art
iweddid.

580   Now after þis stee vp wit þy lady to þe hul wher þat Eliȝabeth and
blessede Marye wit sw[e]te kleppyngge and kissyngge mette to-
gydere; and hir take heede, suster, of þe maner of gretyngge in þe
whiche Ihon Baptiste in his moder wombe, hoppyngge for ioye, knew
and saluede as a seruaunt his lord, as a criour his verray iustyse, as a
585 kniȝt is verrey kynge. And blessyd were and beþ þoo wombes to-fore
alle oþre, of þe wiche sprang oute hele of alle þe wordle, and was
iprofecyed merþe and ioye, aȝens derknesse of wo and sorwe þat longe
to-fore hadde reygned. What dost þu, suster? I prey þe, ren forth wit
alle hast, and among so muche ioye antermete þe sumwhat, val adoun
590 by-foore þe feet of þyse blessyd wymmen, and in þat onys wombe
honoure þyn husbonde Criste, and in þat oþrys wirschipe his frend,
sein Ihon.

    And after þis, wayte whan Marie goþ to Bethleem, and ren after wit
meek deuocioun; and whan sche turned in-to þilke pouere ostage to
595 bern here child, pote þe forþ and doo what seruise þat þu canst; and
whanne þilke faire baby is ilappyd in an oxe-stalle, berst out in-to a
voys of gladnesse wit Ysaie and sey: *Paruulus natus est nobis, filius
datus est nobis.* And þanne wit alle reuerence beklep sum party of
þilke swete stalle þer þy ȝunge husbonde lyþ in, and after let loue
600 ouercome schame and driwe awey drede, and baldely go forþ and
þrast þi lippen to þilke tendre feet of Crist, kissyngge hem wit al þyn
herte ofte-tyme er þu reste.

    And whan þis is doon, taak heede enterly in þy sowle þe walkyngge
of þe scherperdys, behold þe oostes of angeles syngynge and wur-
605 schepynge, and to here melodye auntre þe to pote forþ þi voys and sey:
Gloria in excelsis Deo, et in terra pax hominibus bone voluntatis.

Capitulum quintumdecimum

    And in þy meditacioun þu schalt nouȝt forȝite þe offryngge of þre
kynges; and also whan vre lady for drede of Herowd fleþ in-to Egypte

581 swete] swte
595 to bern here child] *repeated and cancelled*
595 canst] canst'

wit here child in here lappe, let here not goon alone, bot go forþ wit 610
here, and haue on opinion þat þis is soþ þat I schal now telle to þe.
Narracio bona. /

Whanne hure lady wente to Egiptewarde, she was [itake] of þeues. f. vᵛ
And among hem þe maister-þef hadde a sone, whic sterte to vre lady
and vndyde here lappe, and þer he fand here swete child liggynge. 615
And þer come swhiche lemes of liȝt and britnesse out of his blessede
fas, þat þis þef wyste wel in his herte þat þis child was of grettere
mageste þan an-oþur pur man; and for greet loue he kleppede hym in
his armes and kyst hym, seyinge deuoutly in þis wyse: 'O þu most
blessede babe among alle þat euere were; heraftur whanne þu cumst 620
to þy grete lordschipe, in caas þu see me euere at eny myscheef, help
me and haue myende of þis tyme, for I wyl kepe þe and þy moder
harmles.'

Suster, it is iseyd þat þis was þilke þef þat hynge on Cristes riȝt
syde, wiche vndernam þat oþer þat hynge on his left syde, seyingge to 625
hym, as it is iwryten in þe gospel, in þis wyse: *Neque tu times Deum,*
quod in eadem dampnacione es? Et nos quidem iuste, nam digna
factis recepimus; hic vero nichil mali gessit etcetera. And þoo wit gret
meknesse and contricioun he turn[y]de hym to Criste, and seingge þe
same schynyngge and briȝtnesse þat he hadde longe by-fore iseye in 630
his face in his moder lappe, wit alle þe veynes of his herte he cryede:
Memento mei, Domine, dum veneris in regnum tuum – þat is to seyn:
'Lord, haue myende of me whan þu comest in-to þy kyndom!' And
for-soþe, Crist forȝat not is couenaunt, for he answerede anoon and
seyde: *Amen dico tibi, hodie mecum eris in paradyso.* Suster, to stire 635
þe to more tendrenesse of loue, haue an opinioun þat þis tale is soþ.
And hit schal be non harm to þe alþouȝ þu be-þenke þe how þy ȝunge
husbonde Crist, while he was child, childly and myryli pleyde hym
among oþer children at Nazareth, and oþer-whyle hou seruisable he
was to his moder, and anoþer tyme how swete and gracious he was to 640
his nursche.

Capitulum sextumdecimum

And, suster, wanne after þat he is twelf ȝer old, and goþ to Ierusalem in-to þe temple wit his fadur and his moder and, hem vnwyt-
yngge, leueþ in þe citee þre dayes be-hynde, as þe gospel seyþ; ȝif þu 645
wilt bysyly seke hym þyse þre dayes, gode suster, what sorwe schalt
þu haue? How manye bitere teres schulle renne out of þyn eȝen,
whanne þu byȝenkeste of þe sorwe of his moder Marie, whanne sche
hadde iloste so dire a child? And after, whan she hadde ifounde hym
syttyngge among þe doctoures in þe temple, how pytously sche smot 650

613 itake] *om.* 629 turnyde] turnþde

hym, as hit were, wit þis mornful vndernymyngge: *Fili, quid fecisti nobis sic? Ecce pater tuus et ego dolentes querebamus te.*

And vu[r]þermore, ʒif þu folwe þis blessed mayde whider þat euer sche goþ, þu miʒth ascherche mor heyʒere priuitees; and þanne in flem Iordan þu miʒt hiere þe Fadur in voys, þe Sone in verray flehs, and see þe Holy Goste in liknesse of a douve. And þer, suster, at þylke gostly breedale þu miʒt vnderfo[ng]e þyn husbounde iʒyue of þe Fader, purgacioun of þe Sone, and receyue þe bond of loue of þe Holy Goste. Aftur þis many day þy spouse Crist goþ in-to desert, ʒyuyngge þe ensaumple to fle blast and bost of þe wordle; þer he fastyde fourty dayes, and was tempted of þe deuel, techyngge vs wrecchen what conflit we mote haue and batayle aʒens vre gostly enemy. How þat þyse þyngges were ido to þe and for þe I prey þe tak good heede, þat þu mowe do þer-after.

Let renne also to þy myende þilke wrecchede wymm[a]n þat was itake in avoutrye, as þe gospel telleþ, and beþenk þe / entierly what Ihesus dude and wat he seyde whanne he was preyʒid to ʒyue þo doom aʒens here. Furst he wroot in þe irþe – and in þat he schewede þat þey where irþely þat hadde acused heore; and þanne he seyde: *Qui sine peccato est vestrum, primus in illam lapidem mittat.* Whan þis sentence hadde agast hem alle, and dryuen hem out of þe temple, beþenke þe how pytous and how godly eʒen Crist cast vpon here, wit how softe and swete voys he asoylede here. Trowst þu not þat he siʒʒyde, trowst þu not þat he wiep wit is blessede eʒen whan he seyde: *Nemo te condempnauit, mulier? Nec ego te condempnabo.* And ʒif I schal seye hit, iblessyd was þis wumman þat was þus founden in swhich avoutrye, þe which was asoyled of Crist of sennes þat where apassed, and ymaad syker of tyme to-comyngge.

Gode Ihesu, whanne þu seyst 'I nel not dampne', ho is it þat may dampne? Whan God iustefyeþ, ho may acuse? Bote naþeles, þat noman be to bold herfore, let þe voys of Crist be herd, þat comeþ after – what is þat? *Vade, et iam amplius noli peccare* – 'Go, and loke þu neuere haue wyl to doo no synne.'

Þanne after þis go forþ in-to Symons hows þe pharise, and auyse þe wel how godly Crist syt þer ate mete; and pryuely stele forþ wit þilke blessede synnere, Marie Magdeleyn, and whasch Cristes feet wit hote terys, wype hem wit þe herys of þyn heed, ley to softly þyn eʒen, and at þe laste anoynte hem wit spiritual oynement. Lord, suster, whoþer þu haue no gostly smel in þy sowle of þis precious liquour? Bote in caas for þyn vnwurþynesse þyn husbonde Crist trawþ awey his feet, and foucheþ not saaf þat þu kysse hem; stand stille, naþeles, stede-fastly and pray mekly, sete þyn eʒen on hym al for-smoteryd wyt

655

660

665
f. vᵛᵇ

670

675

680

685

690

653 vurþermore] vuþermore
657 vnderfonge] vnderfoûde   665 wymman] wymmen

terys, and wit depe siȝȝyngges and pytous cryingge cacche of hym
þat þu coueytest. Wrastle irnestly wit þy God as Iacob dede, for
feyþfully he wil be glaad þat þu ouercome hym. For happyly it schal   695
seme þe at sum tyme þat he cast awey is eȝen fro þe, þat he closeþ is
heren and wil not hiere þe, þat he hediþ his feet for þu schuldest not
kysse hem; bote for al þis loke þu abyde stille, and gredyly cry to hym
wit-owte cessyngge: *Vsquequo auertis faciem tuam a me? Vsquequo*
clamabo, et non exaudies? Redde michi, bone Ihesu, leticiam salutaris   700
tui, quia tibi dixit cor meum: Quesiui faciem tuam, faciem tuam,
Domine, requiram. And hardely I dar boldely seyn þat he wyl not
denye his feet to þe, þat art a mayde, wan he grauntede hem to be kyst
of a synful womman.

Loke also þat þu forȝyte not þilke hows þer þilke man ysmete wit þe   705
palsye was lete adoun þorouȝ þe teylys to-fore þe feet of Ihesu, where
pyte and power mette to-gydere. *Fili, inquid, remittuntur tibi pec-*
cata. 'Sone', seyþ Crist, 'þy synnes beþ forȝyue þe.' A, Ihesu, þy
wundurful pyte, þy mercy þat may not be told! Þis synful wrecche
hadde remissioun of his synnes, þe whiche outwardly he ne askede   710
nouȝt, ne duely ne hadde not deseruyd; he askede hele of body, and
mercyful Criste grauntede hym hele boþe of body and sowle. Now
iwis, good God, lyf a[n]d deþ is in þy hondes; ȝif þy wil be to saue
me, may no-man forbede hit; ȝif þu wilt fynally dampne me, no-man
may be so bold to aske þe: 'Why dost þu so?' Ȝif þe envyous pharyse   715
gruccheþ þat Crist is so merciable to forȝyue a synful man his
synnes, / anoon Crist hym-self smyt hym in þe face and seyþ: *An*   f. vᵛᶜ
oculus tuus nequam est, quia ego bonus sum? For certes, Crist wyl
haue mercy of whom þat is wille is, maugre þe pharises face. And
þerfore, þat Cristes wyl be forto save vs and haue mercy vppon vs, let   720
vs wepen, cryen and preyen. And þat oure preyere mowe be þe
vattere, let it be vnderset wyþ gode dedys, and in þat wyse let oure
deuocioun be acresyd, and brennyngge loue isteryd to Godwarde.

In oure preyeres let vs lefte vp vre clene handys, þe wyche no blood
of synne haad defoyled, noon vnclene touchyngge haad a-steynt, noon   725
auarice haad wit-drawe. Let also vre herte be left vp wit-oute wraþþe,
wit-oute stryf, þat tranquillite haþ put in reste, pees haad imaad fair,
clennesse of conscience haad yquyked. Bote noon of alle þyse rede we
þat þis man hadde þat was in þe palsye, þat I spak of byfore; and
neuere þe lattere he gaat pleyn remissioun of his synnes. And certes,   730
þis is þe wondurful vertu of þe grete mercy of God; to þe whiche
mercy, as it is a biter blasphemye to wiþ-seyn, so it is a woodschipe to
haue to gret [hope] þerof. For it is no doute, God may seye to whom
hym euere lest þe same þat he seyde to þis paltyk man: 'Sone, þy
synnes beþ forȝyue þe.' Bote who þat euere abydeþ þat þis be iseyd to   735

713 and] ad   717 synnes] synnes'   733 hope] *om.*

hym, wit-outen his grete trauayle, wit-oute verrey contricioun, wit-
oute open confessioun and clene preyere – wit-oute fayle his synnes
schulle neuere be for3yue hym.

Capitulum xvij

740 Bote, suster, let vs now gon hennys and gawe to Bethanye, to þilke
blessyde feste of Ihesu and Marthe, Marie and La3ar, wher blessyde
bondes of loue and frendschipe be þe auctorite of Crist were ysacryd.
Þe gospel seyþ: *Diligebat Ihesus Martham, etcetera* – 'Ihesus louede
Marthe, Marie and La3ar'; and þat þis ne was iseyd for a greet
745 priuilegie of special loue, noman is þat douteþ. For ywis, Ihesu louede
hem feruently; þat witnessede wel þilke swete and tendre terys þat he
wepte wit hem for La3ar, whanne þat he was deed – þe wyche terys al
þe poeple vnderstood wel þat it was a gret signe of gret loue, whanne
þey seyde: *Ecce quomodo amabat eum, etcetera*. Bote now, forto
750 speke of þis feste þat þyse þre, as þe gospel seiþ, made to Ihesu:
Marthe seruyde, La3ar was oon of hem þat saat, Marie Magdeleyne
tooke an alabaustre box of precious oynement and alto-barst þe box
and helde þe oynement on Ihesu heed. Suster, be glad wit al þyn herte
to be at þis feste, and tak good hied, I preye þe, of euery mannes offys;
755 for Marthe ministreþ, La3ar syt, Marie anoynteþ. Suster, þis laste is
þyn offys; and þerfore brek þe alabastre box of þyn herte, and al þat
euere þu hast or my3t haue of deuocioun, of loue, off affeccioun, of
gostly desir, of eny maner spiritual swetnesse, al-to-gydere scheed hit
on þy spouses heed, wurschepyngge verrey man in God, and verrey
760 God in man.
    And þey3 Iudas þe treytour grynte wit his teþ and alþou3 he
grucche, þou3 he be enuyous and skorne þe and seye þat þis oynement
of spiritual deuocioun is not bote ilost, haue þu neuere fors. *Vt quid,*
ait Iudas, perdicio hec? Posset hoc vnguentum venumdari multo, et
765 *dari pauperibus*. And þis is þe voys of manye men now-aday. Bote
what? Þe pharyse grucchede, hauynge enuye of Marye, verrey
f. vi penaunt; Iudas gruccheþ, / hauyngge enuye of þe precious oynement; naþeles, trewely, he þat was ry3tful and mercyful iugge, he
acceptede not þis accusacioun; bote here þat was accused, þat was
770 Marie Magdeleyne, he asoylede and excusyde. *Sine, inquit, illam;*
opus enim bonum operata est in me – 'Suffre here doo', seyþ Crist, 'for
sche had ydoo a good dede in me'.
    Let Marthe þerfore trauayle owtwardly and mynystre in owtward
ocupacioun, let here receuye pilgrymes, 3yue þe hungry meete, þe
775 þursty drynke, cloþyngge to þe nakede, and so forþ of oþre; bote let
Maryes partye suffise to me, and I wil be entendaunt to here. Whoþer

736 wit-oute (1)] wit oute wit oute   771 seyþ] 'seythe'

eny man woolde conseyle me forsake þilke feet of Ihesu, þat Marie so
swetly kyssede; or þat I schulde turne awey myn eȝen fro þat blessyde
face so fair and frehs, þat Marye so entierly be-haldeþ; or elles þat I
schulde turne awey myn erys fro þylke sauery talkyngge of Criste, of   780
þe whiche so fulsumly Marie is ived? I suppose, nay.

Bote now, suster, let vs aryse and walke ennys. 'Whidur?', seyst þu?
Certes, þat þu mowe folwe þy meke husbonde, hym þat is Lord of
heuene and irþe, sittyngge so homly vp an asse; and beyngge as hit
were astonyed of þe grete honour and reuerence þat is idoo to hym in   785
which aray, amang þe worschipyngge of þilke deuoute children of
Ebru pote forþ þat þu canst doo, and cry: *Osanna filio Dauid,*
benedictus qui venit in nomine Domini. And þanne walke forþ in-to
þat faire large halle fr[eh]sly istrowed and adiȝt for Cristes soper a
Schereþursday, ant þonke þy God þat þu mowe come to swych a   790
feste. Let loue ouercome schome, let stedefast affeccioun exclude al
drede and preye þat þu mowe sum almesse of þoo crummes þat ben o
þat blessyde boord. Or elles, suster, stond avier, and as a pore
wrecche poryngge on a gret lord, pote forþ þyn hand, þat þu mowe
sumwhat gete, and let biter terys move þilke pytous lord to haue pyte   795
of þyn hungur.

And whanne Crist aryst fro þe soper, gurdyngge hymself aboute
wit a lynnene cloþ, and put water into a basyn, beþenk how wondurful
was þat mageste of God, þat wyste and also wypede so entierly
synneful mennes feet, and how gret a benignyte it was to handlen wit   800
his holy handys þe feet of Iudas, his cursede traytour. Abid hirvpon,
suster, and beþenk þe wel, and ate laste of alle pote forþ deuoutly þyn
oune feet, to be whasschen as oþre ben – for, certes, he þat is not
iwhasschen and ymaad clene of hym, he schal haue no partye wit hym
in blisse. Suster, hast þu eny haste to hye hens-ward? Abid a while, I   805
prey þe, and taak good kep ho it is þat leneþ hym so boldely to Cristes
brest and slepþ so sauerly in his lappe. I blessyd is þat man, what euere he
bee. A, now I haue aspyed; certayn and wit-owte doute, Ihon is is name.

Now, goode seynt Ihon, what swetnesse, what grace, what liȝt,
what deuocion, what goodnesse þu drawst vp of þat euere-wellyngge   810
welle Criste, I prey þe tel me, ȝif hit be þy wylle. Certayn, þer beþ alle
þe tresores off whit and of wysdom, þer is welle of mercy, hows of
pyte, hony of euere-lastyngge swetnesse. A, a, swete and diere disciple, wher hast þu geten al þis? Art þu heȝȝere þan Petre; holiere þan
Andrew; more accepted þan alle þe apostles? Trewely, þe grete   815
pryuylegie of þy chastete haþ / igete al þis dignite, for þu were ichose   f. vi^b
a mayde of God, and þerfore among alle oþre þu art most iloued.
Now, suster, þu art clene mayde, be glad and reuerently go nyer and
chalange sum partye of alle þis swete wurþynesse. And ȝif þu darst

789 frehsly] frhesly   810 drawst] drawst'

820 auntre þe no furþere, let þilke pryue disciple Ihon slepe stille at
Cristes brest, and let hym drynke þe precious wyn of ioye in
knowyngge of þe grete godheede; and ren þu, suster, to þe pappys of
his manhede, and þerof suk out melke, þat þu mowe gostly be fed in
þenkyngge what he dude for vs in vre flehs.

825   And amang al þis, whan Crist by-fore his passioun commendede his
disciples to þe fader in þat holy orisoun, whan he seyþ: *Pater, serua
eos in nomine tuo;* mekely enclyne þyn heed, þat þu mowe hiere þe
same oryson yseyd to þe fader for þe. I trowe hit were ryth myrye for
þe to abyde hir stille; bote certayn, suster, ȝith þu most forþere. And
830 þerfore, whan Crist goþ to-fore to þe mount of Olyuet in blody
anguyssche, to maken his preyere, folwe after, and þouȝ he take no
mo wit hym bote Petre, Iames and Ihon, and wit hem goþ in-to a
pryue place, ȝit at þe hardeste behald aver how goode God took vp-on
hym vre wrecchidnesse; tak heede how he þat is Lord of alle bygynþ,
835 after þe manhoode, to be agast, and seyþ: *Tristis est anima mea vsque
ad mortem.*
    My goode lord God, what is þis? Hit semeþ þat þu hast so greet
conpassioun of me, þat þu louest me so muche, by-comyngge man for
me, þat as hit were þu hast forȝyte þat þu art verrey God. Þu falst
840 adoun long-streyt in þy face and preyest for me, and also for anguyssche þu swast so grevously þat it semeþ dropes of blood rennyngge
doun on þe irþe. Wher-aboute standest þu, suster? Ren to, for Godys
sake, and suk of þe swete blessyde dropes, þat þey be not spild, and
wyþ þy tounge likke awey þe dust of hijs feet. Ȝif þu canst do nomore,
845 loke þu slepe not, as Petre dede, anaunter þat þu hiere þilke mornful
vndernymyngge þat Crist putte to Petre: *Sic non potuisti vna hora
vigilare mecum?* – 'Miȝtest þu not wake on houre wit me?', seiþ
Criste.
    And anoon after þis behald how Iudas þe traytour geþ before, and
850 which acursyd compaynye of Iewes comeþ after; and þer at þe gylous
cus of þis treccherous traytour tak heede how þey setteþ handes on þy
Lord, and how fersly þey to-teryþ hym and drawyþ hym forþ as a þef,
how cruelly þey streyneþ and byndeþ wit coordes þoo swete tendre
handes. Alas, ho may suffre þis? Suster, I whot wel þat pyte okepyed
855 now al þyn herte, sorwe and conpassioun haþ set alle þy boweles
aviere. Bote naþeles, suster, ȝit suffre a while, and let hym deyȝe for
þe, þat þus wyl deye. Draw neþer staf ne swerd, haue noon vnwys
indignacioun. For alþouȝ þu woldest, as Petre dede, kitte of eny
mannes hiere, þouȝ þu smyte of arm or lege, certes, Crist wil restore al
860 þise, as he dede Malkes were; ȝe, and þouȝ þu woldest, forto avenge
þyn husbonde, slen eny man, wit-oute douȝte he wil areyse hym fro
deþ to lyf.

831 folwe] 'folowe'; þouȝ] 'thovgh'

Let be al þis þerfore, suster, and folwe hym forþ to þe prince of
prestys halle þat he was ydemed in; and þat fayrest face þat euere was,
þe whiche þe cursede Iewes defoyleþ wit here foule spatelyngge, þu   865
whash hit wit terys of þyn eȝen. Be-þenk þe wit how pytous eȝen and
how goodly, how mercyfully he lokede vp-on / Petre whanne he   f. vi^c
hadde forsaken hym; and anon turnede aȝen to hym-self and wepte
biterly for his sunne.
    Oracio conpilatoris.   870
    Gode Ihesu, fowche saaf þat þy swete eȝe moote ones loke mercifully
on me, þat ofte in a maner haue forsake þe þorouȝ my cursyde þowtys
and wickede dedys ate cryingge of þe wickede seruaunt, my flehs.
    Bote now, suster, forþermore on þe morwe þy spouse Crist is itake
tretourusly to Pilat. Þer he is accuseed, and he halt his pees, and as a   875
schep þat is ilad to his deþ, or as a [l]omb þat is on scheryngge, riȝt so
he ne openede not is mouþ. Avyse þe inwardly and tak tent how
bonerly he stant by-fore þe jugge, wit is heed enclined, wit his eȝen
icast adoun, wit good chiere and fiewe wurdes, al redy for þi sake to
dispysyngge, al redy to harde betyngge. I am siker, suster, þu miȝt   880
not longe suffre þis, þu miȝt not suffre his comely ryg be so to-torn wit
schurges, his gracious face to be bouyd wit bofattes, his wurschipful
heed to be corouned wit scharpe thornes to þe brayn, his riȝt hand,
þat made heuen and irþe, be dishonest[ed] wit a ryed; I wot wel þu
miȝt not longe dure to see þis wit þyn eȝen.   885
    Bote ȝit naþeles behald, after al þis he is ibrout out al forbled and
beten, beryngge a coroune of þornes on his heed, and a purpre
garnement on his body; and þanne seyt Pilat to þe Iewes: *Ecce homo –*
'Lo, hir is þe man.' Iwis, wrecche, a man he is; who douteþ hit? Þe
harde betyngge of ȝouȝre scharpe ȝerdes, þe wannesse of þe woundes,   890
þe felþe of ȝouȝre stynkynde spatelynge witnesseþ wel þat he is a man.
Bote par caas þu seist to me: 'I am syker he is a man; how may it be,
naþeles, þat in alle his iniuries he nis not wroþ as a man, he takþ not
vengaunce of his turmentours as a man?' Wit-oute fayle, he is more
þanne a man; he is iproued now a man, suffryngge fals dom of curside   895
schrewes, bote whanne he schal come hym-self to ȝyue riȝtful dom ate
day of dome, þanne he schal be knowe a verrey myȝtful God.
    Now, naþeles, þe false iugge Pilat sit sollennely in þe jugge-sege,
Ihesu stant pouerly to-fore hym, and þe sentence of deþ is ȝyue aȝens
hym; and so, beryngge pitously his owne galewes, he is ilad to þe deþ.   900
A wundurful spectacle! Sykst þu not? By-hold, suster, wat a signe of
princehood and wurschipe þyn husbounde Crist berþ vp his schuldre
– as þe book seyt: *Ecce principatus super humerum eius.* And certeyn, þat was þe ȝerd off þy riȝtwisnesse and þe sceptre of his

905 kyngdom, as holy scripture also spekeþ of: *Virga equitatis, virga regni tui.*

Þey casteþ hym out of his garnemens, and among knytes þey beþ departyd, saue his precious cote þat vre lady hadde iwrouȝt wit-oute seem – þat was nouȝt to-kit, bote by lot it fel to oon al hool. Þanne
910 among þieves he was sprad abrood on þe cros, and his swete handes and feet were þirlyd þouȝr wit nayles; þer profriþ hym drynke corrupt wyn ymedlyd wit galle, and manye oþre dispiteȝ doþ hym.

And so he, þat mediatour bytwyxe God and man, hyng in þe myddul bytwene heuene and irþe, bryngyngge as hit were heuene and
915 irþe to-gydere. Heuene is agast, þe irþe wundryþ – and what þu,
f. vi⁽ᵛ⁾ suster? Certayn, it is no wunder ȝif þu be sory, seþþe / þe sunne þat is vnresonable is sory. Ȝif þe irþe tremble and quake, what wundur þey þu tremble? Ȝyf harde flyntes alto-cleueþ, wat woundur þouȝ þyn herte to-burste? Seþþe straunge wummen stondeþ bysyde þe cros and
920 wepeþ, what merueyl þey þu wepe for sorwe of so pytous deþ? Bote among alle þyse þyngges haue good consideracioun of þilke mylde herte of Crist – what pacience, what benignite, what pyte it kepte alwey in his torment. He takþ non heede of his iniurie, he makþ no fors of his bitere peynes, he ne chargeþ not þe vilanyes and þe dispyt
925 þat beþ doo to hym. He takþ no reward of al þis, bote he haþ pite and conpassioun of hem þat doþ hym to hys passioun, he agreyþeþ salue for hem þat ȝyuen hym smarte woundes, and had procured hem lyfe þat beþ abouȝte to revyn hym þe lyf and putte hym to þe deþ.

Wit how swetnesse of herte, trowest þu, wyþ wat mildenesse of alle
930 his spirit, wit how gret fulsumnesse of charyte crieþ he to þe fadur and seiþ: *Pater, ignosce illis* – 'Fader, forȝif hem.'

Oratio conpilatoris.

Benigne Ihesu, lo me hir, a symple and deuout wurschipere of þy maieste and not sleere of þy body, adorour of þi spytous deþ and not
935 skornere of þy passioun, a stedefast knowelechere of þy grete mercy and not despisere of þyn infirmite þat þu hast itake of mankynde; and þerfore I prey þe þat þy swete blessyd manhoode mote preye for me, and þat þy wunderful pite mote commende me to þy fader. Swete Ihesu, sey for me, þat wyþ mek herte wurschipe þy passioun and þy
940 deþ, þat þu seydest for hem þat putte þe to þy deþ. Merciful Lord, sey ones for me to þy fader: *Pater, ignosce illi.*

And þu, mayde, þat schuldest haue mor ful trest on þis maydenes sone Crist, wyþdraw þe fro þoo wummen þat stondeþ aver, as þe gospel sayþ, and wit Marie, moder and mayde, and seynt Jhon, also a
945 clene mayde, so sadlyche to Cristes cros and byhold avysily how þilke face, þat angeles haueþ delyt to loke in, is bycome al dym and paal. Cast also þyn eȝe asyde to Maries cher, and loke how here fresche

929 of alle his spirit] of alle his of al spirit

maydenly visage is al to-bollen and forsmoteryd wit terys. Lord, suster, whoþer þu schulle stonde by-syde wit drie eȝen, whanne þu sikst so manye salte teris lassche adoun so vnmesurably ouer here rodye chekes? Miȝt þu be wit-owte sobbyngge and whepyngge, whanne þu sikst a swerd of so scharp sorwe renne þorouȝ here tendre herte? Miȝt þu heere wit-oute gret pite how straungely Crist [seiþ] of seynt Jhon to his moder: 'Wumman, lo þer þy sone' – *Mulier, ecce filius tuus;* as hoo seyt: 'Tak to þe anoþer sone, for I go fro þe'? And þanne he seyde to seynt Jhon: *Ecce mater tua.* Was not þis a mornful þyng to Marie, whan he bitooke so passauntly here þat was his moder to þe disciple, and beheet a þyef þe blisse of paradys, þat he schulde be wit hym þryn þe same day.

After al þis, oon of þe knytes wit a spere persyde his syde to his tendre herte; and þanne, as þe gospel seyþ, þer cam out blood and water. Hye þe, suster, hye þe and tarye þe not, foonde forto gete þe sum of þyse precious liquours, for blood is yturned to þe in-to wyn, to do þe confort, and water in-to melke, to nursche þe gostly. Þer beþ ymaad to þe fayre fressche rennyngge ryueres in a stoon, and þat beþ Cristes reede woundes in his bodyly menbris; and riȝt as in cul-verhows beþ ymaad holys in þe wal forto warsche þe culvren in, ryȝt so in þe wal of Cristes flehs beþ ymaad nestes al hoot of blood, þat þu schuldest lotye in and bryngge forþ gostly bryddes. / Of þis blood, suster, þu scholdest þenke and speke so muche þat þy lippen schulde be as blood reed, as hit were a reed liste, and þanne schulde þy talkyngge be sauery and swete to euery man þat spake wit þe, as þe book seyþ: *Eloquium tuum dulce.*

Bote now abid what þilke noble knyȝt come, Ioseph ab-Arimathie, and vnlaceþ Cristes handes and feet, softly drawyngge out þe nayles. Byhald hou he byklippeþ wiþ his blessyde armes þe swete body of Crist, and hou faste he streyneþ it to is breste. For-soþe, þo miȝte þis blessid man wel seye þat þat is iwryte in holy wryt: *Fasciculus mirre dilectus mea michi inter vbera mea commorabitur.* Go forþ after þis holy man, suster, and folewe þilke precious tresour of heuene and irþe, and ber vp hand, leg or foot, þat þey hange not doun so pitously, or elles gadere to-gydere wit al suttilte þilke holsum dropys of blood þat droppeþ doun of his wondes, and suke þe dust of his blessyd feet. Behald furþeremor how swetly and diligently þilke holy man Nichodeme tretiþ wit his gentil fyngres þe sacrede menbres of Crist and anoynteþ hem wit swete oynemens, and wit holy Ioseph how he lappeþ Cristes body in a clene cloþ and leiþ hit in þe sepulcre.

And after þis, loke þu forsake not þe felaschipe of Marie Magdeleyn, bote whan sche goþ to Cristes sepulcre wit here swete smyllyngge baaumes to anoynte Cristes menbrys, loke þu go after. A

953 seiþ] *om.*

Lord, suster, ȝif þu myȝtest be wurþy to see wit þy gostly eȝe þat
Marie seyȝ wyȝ here bodyly – now þe stoon yturned awey fro þe dore
of þat blessyd sepulcre, and þer-vppon an angel sittyngge; now
wiþ-inne þe sepulcre oon angel at þe heed, anoþer ate feet, syngyngge

995 and wurschippyngge þe joye and blisse of Cristes resurrexioun; now
Ihesu lokyngge wit a gladly eȝe vp-on Marye Magdeleyn, þat was sory
and wepyngge for Cristes deþ, and how swete a uoys it was to Marie
Magdeleyne whanne he clepede here wit here name, as þe gospel seyt,
and seyde to here: 'Maria.'

1000 A, what was swettere þan þis voys? What was mor ioyeful or mor
blisful? 'Maria.' Now, Marie, let þy water-veynes of þyn heed alto-
berste and terys renne a-doun, drawȝ vp sobbyngge and siȝȝyngge fro
þe deppeste ende of þy bowelys, whanne Crist clepiþ: 'Maria.' O
blessyde Marie, what herte haddest þu, what spirit, what strenkþe,

1005 whanne þu vylle adoun longstreit to-fore Crist and grettest hym
wepynggely and seydest: 'Raby!' I pray þe, wit wat affeccioun, wit
what desir, wit what brennyngge of þyn herte, wit hou gret deuocioun
of al þi soule crydest þu whan þu answeredest þy Lord, and seydest:
'Rabi, Maister!' For mor myȝtest þu not speke for sobbyngge and for

1010 wepyngge; þy grete loue þat þu haddest to Ihesu hadde raueschid alle
þy wittes, boþe of body and of soule.

Bote þu, derewurthe lord, why puttest þu awey fro þe swh[i]ch on
as louede þe so muche and so brennyngly, þat sche most not come so
neyȝ þe to kisse þyn holy and blisful feet? *Noli, inquit, me tangere* –

1015 'Touche me not, com not neiȝ me!', seiþ Crist. A, an hard word, an
vnsuffrable word, a word þat wolde to-breke þey it were a stony herte:
Noli me tangere – 'Touche not!' Why so, blisful lord? Whi schal I not
neyȝȝe þe? Why may I not touche þilke desiderable feet þat where
iþirled for me wit nayles on þe cros, þat where al by-schad for me wit

1020 blood? Why mot I not handle hem, whi mot I not kysse hem? Gode
Ihesu, art þu bycome straunge and mor enemy, for þi body is mor

f. vi^vc glorious? Now for-soþe, I nel not lete þe, I nel not /go fro þe, I schal
neuere cesse fro wepyngge, my brest and herte schulle alto-breke for
sobbyngge and sikyngge, bote I mote onys touche þy swete feet. And

1025 þanne seyþ merciful Ihesu: *Noli timere* – 'Ne be þu not agast ne
disconforte þe nouȝt, for þat þat þu askest is not bynome þe, bote it is
iput in delay. Only doo as I say þe: goo and tel my breþryn þat I ham
ryse fro deþ to lyve.'

Þanne renþ Marie forþ, and certeyn, sche renþ wel þe fastere for þat

1030 sche wolde sone come aȝeyn. And whanne sche comeþ aȝen, sche
comþ not alone, bote wyþ oþre wummen, aȝens þe whyche Ihesus
hym-self geþ and wit benigne and glad gretyngge he conforteþ hem,
þat where ouercome wiþ so biter sorwe of his deeþ. Suster, I pray þe

1012 swhich] swhch   1029 þe] ? þo

tak good heede; for þoo it was fully igraunted to Marie Magdeleyn and
here felawes þat arst was put in delacioun. *Accesserunt namque et* 1035
tenuerunt pedes eius. As þe gospel seyþ, þo þey wente to and klepte
Ihesu aboute his feet.

In þyse and swyche oþere, suster, abid, and of þyse haue studefast
meditacioun; in swyche þyngges haue þy delyt, þe whyche no sleep
ne smyte of noon outward boostes ne ocupacioun lette. Bote for as 1040
muche as in þis wrecchede lyf is noþyng stable, noþyng certaynly is
abydyngge, and a man dwelleþ not ne dureþ noon whyle in oon stat;
þerfore it is nyedful þat oure soule be ved wit a maner diuersyte of
chaungyngge. Wherfore we schulle goo fro þyngges þat beþ apassed,
to beþenke vs on þyngges þat beþ present, of þe whiche we mowe be 1045
steryd þe mor parfytly to louen vre God.

De presencium meditacione. Capitulum xviij

I ne halde it not a litel ʒyfte of God ʒif þu vse wel and take good
consideracioun of men þat haueþ ibe tofore vs, and hou we beþ ikept
of manye myscheues þat þey were in; how God made vs of þe same 1050
matere þat he maade hem, and ʒit he haþ departid vs fro hem; somme
þat were ycast out of here moder wombe al deed, and somme þat in
here moder wombe were astrangled, þe whiche, as it semeþ, were
raþer ybore to peyne þanne to lyf.

And what ʒif we beþenke vs hou God had ymad vs hole menbres 1055
and sounde, and not ysuffred vs be bore in meselrye or palsye or elles
croked or lame, or so forþ of oþre, þat we schulde haue ibe in sorwe to
vs-self, and to oþre to dispyt and schame. Bote of hou gret goodnesse
of God was it, and is, þat he ordeynede so for vs þat we beþ ibore
among swyche folk, be þe whiche we mowe come to þe knowyngge of 1060
God and to vre byleue. For þis ʒifte to many a þousand heþ be
denyed, which þat rytfully beþ ydampned for euere; and þis ʒifte is
frely yʒeue to vs, þat only of his goodnesse beþ ichose þorouʒ his
grace; and ʒit naþeles alle we were of on condicioun and of on
mankende. 1065

Gowe furþere, and let vs behoolde what a benefys it is of God þat
we were ynursched, whanne whe cowde no mor good þan a best, of
oure fader and moder, and ikept so þat whe nere not ybrend in þe
fuyr, as many anoþer haþ ibe, not idreynt in water, not wood and
trauayled of þe deuel, not ysmyte ne venymed of no foul wurm, not 1070
yfalle and broke vre necke; þat we beþ to couenable age itauʒt in hool
fey, and in sacramens of holy churche. Suster, of þyse let vs beþenke
vs ryʒt wel, for in alle þis benefys we beþ parteners ilyke, as we beþ of
oon condicioun, of oon fader begete and oon moder wombe cast out

1035 delacioun] desolacioun

1075 in-to þis wordle; and þyse benefis God haþ doo to vs as to þe
body. /

f. vii   Bote auyse þe inwardly what God haþ ido to þe graciously to þy
soule – for in þat partye haþ departyd betwixe þe and me as muche as
is bytwyxe liȝt and derknesse; þe haþ ikept to hym euere in clennesse,

1080 bote me haþ ilete alone to my-self. My mercyful God, wher am I
bycome? Whider am I went? Whider was I aschaped? Wyder was I
runne awey fro þy face? I was icast out fro þy blessede chiere as Caym
was; I made my dwellyngge vppon þe irþe, þat is to seyn, caste myn
vnclene loue on irþely þyngges; I was wandryngge aboute wit Caym

1085 acursed: *Et quicumque inuenerit me, occidet me* – And who þat euere
mete wit me, haad power to sle me. And no wonder; for what scholde
a wrecche creature doo, forsaken of his creatour? Whedur schulde an
erraunt scheep gon, or were scholde he lotye, whan he is destitut of his
scheperde? A, suster, haue pite of me, for: *Fera pessima deuorauit*

1090 *fratrem tuum* – þe most wickede best of alle þat is þe deuel haþ
deuoured þy broþer.

And þerfore, suster, in me behald how muche þy God haþ do for
þe, þat haþ kept and saued þe fro þat wickede best. How wrecched
was I þoo, whanne I foylede me-self and loste my clennesse! How

1095 blessyd were þu, whos clennesse and chastete only þe grace of God
defendede and kepte! How ofte asayled, itempted and steryd was þy
maydenhood and clennesse kept and saued of God, whan I wilfully fil
in-to many and greuous synnes, and gadryde to me on an heep matere
of fuyr [by] þe whiche I scholde be brend, matyre of stench þorouȝ þe

1100 wyche I scholde be deed, matere of wormes of þe wyche I scholde be
g[n]awen in helle, nere þe mercy of God.

Gode suster, byþenk þe of þe vielþys for þe [whiche þu] weptest
vppon me sumtyme and vndernome me whan þu were bote a ȝung
mayde; bote certes, holy wryt fayleþ not þat seyt: *Nemo potest*

1105 *corrigere quem Deus despexit* – No-man may amend[e] þat God haþ
despised – þat is to seye, wit-owte gret repentaunce of man and special
grace of God. A, how muche outest þu loue þy gode God, þe wyche,
whan he despisede me, a-drow þe to hym; and aȝens we were of on
fader and moder ybore, ȝit me he hatede and þe he louede.

1110   Be-þenk þe, as I seyde, of my foule corupcions, whanne þe cloudes
of vnclennesse smokede vp in me of þe irþi and stynkynde concupiscence of flehs and of owtrage styrynge of childhood, and no-man was
to defende me ne saue me of suche myscheues. Spekyngge and
styryngge of wycked companye hadde hard ywrout vppon me, þe

1115 wyche in swete drynke of flehsly loue ȝaue me puysoun of fowl
vnclennesse; and so metyngge to-gydere biter swetnesse of charnel

1099 by] *om.*   1101 gnawen] gwawen   1102 whiche þu] *om.*
1105 amende] amendo   1106 repentaunce] repentaūnce

affeccioun and vnclennesse of flehsly concupiscence, þey rauysschede me syke and feble age of childhood in-to manye foule vices, and dreynte my wrecchede soule in þe stynkynde flood of synne.

My mercyable God, þyn indignacioun and þy wraþþe was fallen vppon me and I felyd it nouȝt; I was flowe fer awey fro þe and al þu suffredest; I was cast and possyd in-to alle maner fulþe, ant þu lete me alone. Lo, suster, lo, diligently I prey þe tak heede; for in-to alle suche fulþes and a[b]hominaciouns þat my cursede wyl caste me in, wite it wel þat þu miȝtest haue falle in þe same, nadde þe mercy of Crist ikepte. Bote I seye nat þis grucchynge aȝens God, as þey he nadde do me nd gret goodnesse – for wit-oute alle þe benefis þat I rehersede beforn whiche were iȝeue to vs in commune, as wel to me as to þe, þe pacience and þe benignite of God / was wundurfully yschewed to me in þat, þat whil I was in dedly synnes, þe eorþe openede not and swolewode me in. I am bound[e] hugely to my God þat þe heuene smot me not adoun wit þounder or wit lytnyngge, þat I was not dreynt in þe water, or deed sodeynly on oþer orrible deeþ; for ow scholde eny creature suffre þe hydouse wrong þat I hadde doon to here creatour, bote he hadde refreyned hem þat made hem alle of nouȝt, þe wyche whyle ne coueytyþ not þe deeþ or dampnacioun of a synneful wrecche, bote þat he turne hym fro his wickednesse and liue in lyf of grace.

And of ow gret grace, mercy and goodnesse of my God was it þat wan I ran awey fro hym, he pursuede after to drawe me aȝen; þer þat I was agast of euere-lastyng dampnacioun, he confortede me and byheet me lyf; whan I was cast adoun in-to dispeyr, he areysede me vp aȝen in-to parfyt hoope; whanne I was most vnkynde, he auaunsede me wit his gret benefys to styre me to turne aȝen to hym; and þer I was custummablely alto-gydere y-vsed to vnclennesse, he drow me awey þens þorouȝ sauour and tast of inwarde gostly swetnesse, and to-barst þe harde chaynes and bondes of cursede custum. And also after, whan I was drawen out of þe wordl, benignely he receyuede me to his grace.

I halde my pees of many wundurful and grete benefys of his mercy, an-aunter þat eny partye of wurschipe þat is alto-gydere his, I were yseye take to me-ward. For after mannes estimacioun ful ofte þe grace and þe goodnesse of þe ȝyvere and þe prosperite of þe receyuour cleueþ so neyȝ to-gydere, þat he is not only worschiped þat only ouȝte to be worschiped and preysed, not only to hym þat ȝift al is iȝoue blisse and þank, bote to hym þat receyueþ; and þat is wronge. What haþ eny wrecche of eny goodnesse bote þat þat he haþ receyued of God? Ȝif he haþ freoly, he haþ it of Godes ȝifte; why þanne scholde he be wurschiped as þeiȝ it were of his owne merytes? And þerfore, my

1120

1125

f. vii[b]
1130

1135

1140

1145

1150

1155

deoreworthe lord, my blisful lord, to þe alone be blisse, to þe be ioye,
1160 to þe be worschipe, to þe be þankyngge of al oure herte; to me, synful
wrecche, noþyng bote confusioun of my face, which þat haue idoo
wyckenesses, and so manye goodnesses haue receyued.

Bote þu askest me, par caas, what I haue lasse þan þu of Godes
ȝiftes. A, suster, where is he mor fortunat þat wit esy and softe wedur
1165 brynkt his schip saaf and sound to þe hauene, ful of marchaundise and
of richesse, or elles he þat in wylde wawes and in greet tempest
alto-breket his vessel, and vnneþe naked and quakynge asschapeþ to
lond alyue? Suster, þu myȝt be glad and bliþe for þe grete gostly
rychesses þat þe grace of God haþ ikept to þe wyþ-oute tempest of
1170 dedly temptacioun; bote certes, to me byhoueþ gret bysynesse and
eke trauayle forto make hool þat was to-broke, forto gete aȝen þat I
hadde ilost, forto cloute aȝen þat was in tempest of temptacioun
al-to-rend. And naþeles, sooþly, suster, wite it wel þat hit ouȝte be a
maner schame to þe ȝif þat I, after so manye abhominable vnclen-
1175 nesses, be yfounde euene wit þe in lyf þat is to comen!

And ȝit wel ofte hit falleþ so þat manye diuerse vices benemyþ þe
meryt and þe blysse of maydenhood; and on þat oþer syde, þat
chaungynge of euele maneres, and vertues comyngge in after vices,
wipeþ awey þe vilanows schame of oold vnclene conuersacioun. Bote
1180 now, suster, behald entierly þe grete ȝyftes of þe goodnesse of God,
þat þu wost wel þu hast receyued; wiþ how murye chiere he ȝyde
f. viiᶜ aȝens þe, as it were, whanne þu forsoke þe wordl and / come to hym;
wit how delices he vedde þe whanne þu were anhungred aftur hym;
what richesse of his mercy he profrede, what holy desires he in-
1185 spirede, of how swete drynke of charyte he ȝaf þe drynke. For ȝif
God, only of his gret mercyful benignite, haþ not ylete me al wyþ-
outen experience of his wundurful and gostly confortes, wych ne am
bote a fugitif and a rebel wrecche, what swetnesse may [I] trowe þat
he ȝyue to þe þat art and euere were a clene mayde. For ȝif þu hast be
1190 in temptacioun, he haþ defended þe; ȝif þu hast be in peryl, he haþ
kept [þe] saaf; ȝif þu hast be in sorwe, he haþ conforted þe; ȝif þu
were dowtyngge or flecchyngge, he haþ confermed þe in good purpos.
How ofte, suster, whan þu hast be asadded and dul or wery of þy lyfe,
haþ he be a pytous confortour to þe; ȝif þu [were] longynge in
1195 brennyngge loue after hym, haþ ilept in-to þyn herte; ȝif þu hast yrad
or ystotid on holy scripture, haþ yliȝted þy soule wit liȝt of spiritual
vnderstondynge? How ofte, whanne þu hast be in þy preyeres, haþ he
yrauyssched þe in-to so heiȝ desir þat þu canst not telle hit? How ofte
haþ he wit-drawe þyn herte fro wordly þynges to delices of heuene and
1200 to þe murþes of paradys? Alle þyse beþenk þe of inwardly in þyn

1165 brynkt] brynkt'   1188 I] om.   1191 þe] om.
1194 were] om.

herte, þat al þyn affeccioun and al þy loue mowe be turned to hym
alone.

Haue bote skorn of al þe wordl, let al flehsly loue seme sty[n]kynde
to þe; and þu þat hast iset al þy purpos on God and on þoo þat beþ in
euene and lyueþ þere wit God, þenk as þei3 þu nere not in þe wordle.   1205
Vbi est thesaurus tuus, ibi et cor tuum erit – 'Þer þat is þy tresour, let
þer be þyn herte'. And loke þat þu schette not þy soule in no fowl
bagge or purs ful of seluer or gold or wordliche rychesse, for trewely
þy soule may neuere, wiþ þe heuy peys of þe peny, flen vp li3t to þe
blisse of heuene. Suppose euery day þat þu scholdest be deed, and   1210
certayn, þu schalt not care ne bysye þe for þe morwen.

Let no wordly aduersite of tyme þat is to comene make þe agast; let
no drede of hungour þat is to comene disese þyn herte, bote on hym let
al þy trust and al þy stedefaste hope hangen, þat fedeþ þe bryddes on
þe eyr and cloþeþ þe lylyes and floures in þe feld fayrere þan euere was   1215
Salomon in al his blisse. Let hym be þy stoorhous, let hym be þy
tresour-hows, let hym be þy gold purs, let hym b[e] þy rychesse and al
þy delys, let hym be to þe alle þyng in alle maner nyede, *qui sit
benedictus in secula seculorum. Amen. Et hec de meditacione
presencium ad presens sufficiant.*   1220

De meditacione futurorum. Capitulum xix

He þat graunteþ so gret benefys to his seruauns in wordle þat now
is, hou grete 3iftes kepþ he for hem in lyf þat is to comene. Þe
principle and þe bykynnyng of þynges þat beþ to comene, and þe final
ende of þynges þat now beþ present, þat is deed. Of þe whyche deed,   1225
wat nature is hit þat haþ not horrour þrof? What herte is hit þat dredeþ
hit nou3t? For bestes and bryddes wit rennyngge and lotyngge and
many an-oþer þousand maner slekþe escheweþ deeþ and defendeþ
here lyf.

Bote 3it, suster, ententyfly auyse þe in þyn owne herte wat þyn   1230
owne conscience answerþ to þe in þis matere; what þy feyt is bold on,
and what þy parfyt hope byhoot þe and þy desyr coueyteþ. For
certayn, and þy lyf be to heuynesse; and þu be saad and haue despyt of
þe wordle; and þyn owne flehs be to þe to sorwe – certes, þanne
coueytest þu deeþ wit gret desyr. / For deeþ put awey heuynesse of   f. vii^v
þys lyf, and makeþ an ende of saadnesse of þis wordle, and deliuereþ
þe body out of muche sorwe.

And feyþfully, I schal sey þe on þyng þat is mor worthy þan alle þe
delis, al þe rychesse and al þo wurschipe of þis wordle – and þat þyng
is, 3if þat þu for gret clennesse of conscience, for parfyt stedefastnesse   1240
of feyt and for clier sourtee of verrey hope, ne drede not bodyly deeþ.

1203 stynkynde] stykynde   1205 euene] `h´euene   1217 be] by

And þis poynt þorow þe ȝiftes of God he may at sum tyme haue
experience of, þat after sykyngge and mornynge for wrecched
seruitute of þis wordle, is so ileft vp in-to heiȝ clennesse of conscience
1245   and holy contemplacioun þat he haþ in a maner forȝyten al þis
wordle. And iwis, suster, þise beþ þe holsum erris and þe ioyeful
begynnyngges of euerelastynge blisse þat is to comene, whanne at þe
comyngge and at þe asaylyngge of deeþ, parfyt feyt ouercome his
natural horrour, hope tempre hit, and surtee of clene conscience put
1250   awey al drede.

Loke now, suster, how deeþ is bygynnyngge of reste and of blisse,
ende of trauayl, and sleere of vices and of wrecchidnesse; as þe book
seyþ: *Beati mortui qui in domino moriuntur; amodo iam dicit spiritus
ut requiescant a laboribus suis.* Wherfore þe prophete, discryvyngge
1255   þe deeþ of Godes derlyngges fro þe deeþ of þoo þat beþ acursed and
schulle be dampned, seiþ on þis wyse: *Omnes reges dormierunt in
gloria* – 'Alle', he seyþ, 'gloriouse kyngges haueþ be deed in ioye.' For
þey deyeþ in gret ioye and gladnesse, whos deeþ commendeþ parfyt
and clene conscience; þe whiche deeþ is ful precious i þe siȝte of God,
1260   as þe book seyþ: *Preciosa est in conspectu domini mors sanctorum
eius.* And certes, he is a glorious kyng and deyeþ in ioye, what so euere
he be, to whos deeþ beþ angeles present, to whos laste slep holy
halwen hiȝetþ to and, ȝyvyngge help as to here cyteseyn of heuene and
mynystryngge hertly confort, fiȝteþ for hym aȝens his enemys, casteþ
1265   adoun his wiþstonderes and scharply conuicteþ his accousours, bryngyngge his soule euene to Abrahames bosum and to þe siȝt of God,
þer þat he schal abyden in reste, pees and liȝt.

Bote *non sic impij, non sic* – Noþyng so of Godys curslynges; for of
ech of hem seiþ þe same prophete in þe same place þat I seyde nekst:
1270   *Tu autem proiectus es de sepulcro tuo quasi stirps inutilis pollutus,
etcetera* – 'Þu', he seiþ, 'art icast out of þy sepulcre – þat is þy foule
body – þu art icast out, I seye, as a foul and vnþryfty drye stycke þat is
not wurþ bote to þe fuyr.' Fur iwis, Godys curslyngges in heere deeþ
beeþ idrawe of wickede spirites out of here body as out of a stynkynde
1275   put, al defoyled wit lecherye, al iwrapped aboute wyþ cursede coueytise, and so wiþ instrumens of helle þey beþ idrawe to be brend in
fuyr, itake to be gnawe of wurmes and iput to be astrangled of
euerlastyngge stench.

Now soþly and trewely it is seyd: *Expectacio iustorum leticia, spes
1280   autem impiorum peribit* – 'Þe abydynge and þe hope of rytful men is
ioye and blisse, þe hope of wickede men schal perysche and fayle.'

Bote for-soþe, what reste, what pees, what murþe and liȝt is
be-hoote and is abide of þe blessede spirites þat now resteþ in Abrahames bosum, for experience haþ not ȝit itauȝt vs, þerfore noon of

1272 vnþryfty] vnþrysty

vre penne or poyntel may owtly wryten it as it is. Bote þey abideþ in   1285
blisse, alwhat þe noumbre of here breþryn be fulfeld; and þat schal
ben at þe day of þe laste resurrexioun, at þe day of dome, whanne /
þey beþ cloþed in duble stole, þat is to seyn in ioye of body and soule   f. vii^{vb}
to-gydere in euere-lastyng blisse.

Of þis day of dome, suster, I preye þe þat þu byholde þe horrour   1290
and þe drede, whanne þe angelles of heuene schulle ben as it were
a-stonyed, þe elemens schul ben dissolued for heete of fuyr, helle-
ȝates schulle ben al open, and al þat is now priue and hud schal ben
openly knowen. From aboue schal come þe jugge fers and wroþ; his
wraþþe schal brenne as eny fuyr, his chaar þat be terrible as eny   1295
tempest forto take veniaunce in gret ire, and to destruye his enemys in
leytyngge fuyr. Now certes, *Beatus qui paratus est occurrere illi* –
'Yblessed is he þat is redy to meete wit hym at þat our.'

What sorwe schal be þanne to cursede wrecchen whom now
lecherye defoyled, cursede coueytise al disturbeþ, Luciferes pruyde   1300
areyseþ an heiȝ. Angeles schulle gon and departe þe wickede fro þe
goode, puttyngge riȝtful men on Godes riȝt syde, and on his left syde
þoo þat schulle be dampned. Suster, byþenk þe now in þyn owne
herte as þey þu were euene by-twyx þyse tweye companyes to-fore þe
jugge-sege of God, and not iputte outerly to on party no to oþer; cast   1305
þanne þyn eȝen asyde to þe left syde of þis riȝtful jugge Crist, and
byhald þat cursed, wrecchid and weepful companye. A, suster, wat
stench is t[e]r þer, what horrour, what drede, what sorwe! A-cursede
coniones standeþ þer gryntyngge wit teeþ, al naked to here bare brest,
orrible in siȝt, deformed in face, al irebuked in confusioun and   1310
schame for nakednesse and fowlnesse of here body. Þey wolde fayn
lotye and huyden hem, bote þey schul not mowe; þey wolde renne
a-wey, bote þey schulle not be suffred. Ȝif þey lyfte vp here eȝen, þe
wraþþe of here domesman is above here heed; ȝif þey lokeþ doun-
ward, þe orrour of þe put of helle is aȝens here face. Þey schulle fynde   1315
noon excusacioun of her synne, ne þey schulle not apele fro eny
vnrytful dom; for what euere schal þanne be demyd, here owne
conscience schal knowen it and deme it soþ.

Beþenk þe now, suster, how muche þu owest to louen hym of al þy
myȝt, þat haþ departyd þe fro þilke grete vnsauery multitude þat   1320
schal be dampned, and yclepyd þe to his grace and ipurgyd þe and
iustefyed þe to his blisse. And þerfore cast þyn eȝen to þe ryȝt syde,
and byhold to how blisful a cumpanye [he] haþ coupled þe. A, Ihesu,
what fayrnesse is in hem, what honour, what felicite, what ioye, what
surtee! Summe beþ put an heiȝ to be domesmen wit Crist, summe   1325
beþ al briȝt schynynge wit coroune of martirdom, summe beþ whyt
as þe lylye of virginite, summe ben fructuous þorouȝ ȝyuyngge of

1304 to-fore] *corrected to* be fore   1308 ter] tir   1323 he] *om.*

almesse, summe ben clier and excellent þorou3 holsum doctrine of
Godes lawe; and alle þyse beþ knet and coupled to-gydere in o bond
1330   of blisful loue and euere-lastyngge charyte. Þe swete face of Ihesu
schyneþ to hem, not terrible and gastly as it doþ to Cristes curslynges,
but ful amyable and blisful, not biter bote ful swete, not gastyngge
bote gladyngge and confortyngge.

Now, suster, 3if þu woldest stonde in þe myddul of þyse two
1335   companyes, not wetyngge as it were to wyche partye þe sentence of þe
domesman wyle put þe too, lord, how hard schulde þis abydyng be to
þe! Þanne forsoþe my3test þu wel say: *Timor et tremor venerunt
super me et contexerunt me tenebre.* For 3yf he putte þe on þe lyft
f. vii^{vc}   syde, þu schalt not mowe / seye þat he is vnri3tful; 3if he ha ordeyneþ
1340   þe o þe ri3t syde, it is only of his grace, and not to be put to þyn owne
merytes. Now iwis, lord God, lif and deeþ is in þy wyl and in þy
power alone. Sykst þu now, suster, how muche al þyn herte and þy
soule schulde be set only in his loue, þe wyche, alþou3 ha my3te
ry3tfully turne þe same sentence of deeþ to þe þat he smyt on hem þat
1345   schulle be dampned, 3i[t] of his goodnesse haþ leuere to putte þe on
his ri3t syde and associe þe to his blisful derlyng.

And þerfore now a Godes half ymagyne as þey þu were ioyned to
þat ioyful and holy felauschip, heryngge þilke precious decree of his
swete voys: *Venite benedicti patris mei, percipite regnum quod vobis*
1350   *paratum est ab origine mundi* – 'Comeþ 3e, iblessid of my fadur,
receyueþ þe kyngdoom þat was agreyþed to 3ow er þe bygynnyngge of
þe world.' And þanne schulle þilke wyepful wrecchyn heere þilke
harde and vnsuffrable word ful of wraþþe, ful of sorwe, ful of indignacioun: *Discedite a me, maledicti, in ignem eternum* – 'Departeþ fro
1355   me, 3e curslyngges, in-to euerlastyngge fuyr.' And þanne schul þe
goon into perpetuel turment, and ri3twyse men into blisse wiþ-
oute[n] eende. A, a, an hard departyngge, a wrecchyd and wiepful
condicioun to þilke acursede caytyfs!

And whan þey beþ itake awey and departid otterlyche fro þe blisse
1360   of God, and ri3twyse men after heere degree and heere meryt beþ iput
in among þe ordres of holy angeles; þanne þannys let þilke gloriouse
processioun go forþ in-to þe he3e Ierusalem, þe cite euerlastyngge of
heuene, Crist hym-self as oure verrey heed goynge to-fore, and alle his
blisful menbres folwynge after. Þanne schal þilke glorious kyng regne
1365   in hem, and þey in hym, vndurfonggyngge to here heritage þilke real
kyngdom of blisse þat was ordeyned for hem er þe wordle were.

Þe staat of þat realme may not hiere be fully þou3t, and muche more
noþer seyd ne wryten in book. Bote þis wot I wel, and daar booldely
sayn, þat þu schalt lakke noþynge þat þu woldest haue, ne þu schalt

1343 ha] *corrected to* he   1345 3it] 3if   1356 wiþ-outen] wiþ outem
1363 to-fore] *corrected to* be fore

haue noþyng þat þu woldest lacke. Þer schal be no wepynge ne   1370
weylyngge, no sorwe, no drede, no discord, noon envye, no tribulacioun ne temptacioun, no chaungynge of þe eyr, no corrupcioun ne
wicked suspecioun, non ambicioun, non adulacioun, no detraccioun,
no siknesse of old age, no deþ, no pouerte, no derknesse, noon hungur
ne þurste, no nyede ne werynesse ne no maner faylyngge. Þer þat   1375
noon of alle þyse þynges beþ, what may þer be bote parfyt ioye, parfit
murþe, parfit tranquillite, parfit surtee, most parfit loue and charite,
parfit rychesse, parfit fayrnesse, parfit reste, parfit strencthe, parfit
hele, and parfit siȝt of þe face of God; and in þyse, euere-lastyngge,
abydyngge and euere-durynge lyf.   1380

What wolde ȝe more, whanne oure creatour God [schal] be clierly
yseyen, iknowen and iloued? He schal be seyen in hym-self blisful, he
schal be seyen in his creatures, gouernyngge alle þyng wit-oute
trauayl or bisynesse, susteynyngge alle þyng wit-oute[n] eny
werynesse, ȝyuynge hym-self to alle creatures after here capacite   1385
wit-oute eny laskyngge or diuisioun of his godhede. Þanne schal be
seyn þilke swete, amyable and desiderable face of God þat angeles
coueyten to loke in; of whos fayrnasse, of whos cliernesse, of whos
swetnesse hoo may auȝt seyn worthyly? Þer schal be seye þanne þe
Fader in þe Sone, þe Sone in þe Fader, and þe Holy Gost in hem   1390
boþe. Þer God vre creatour schal be seye not in a myrour or in
derknesse, bote face to face, as þe / gospel seyþ. Þer God schal be seye   f. viii
as he is, whanne þat byheste schal be fulfeld þat hym-self saiþ in þe
gospel: *Qui diligit me, diligetur a patre meo, et ego diligam eum, et*
manifestabo ei meipsum – 'Who þat loueþ me', seiþ Crist, 'he schal be   1395
loued of my Fader, and I schal louen hym and schewen hym myn
owne self.' Of þis cliere siȝt comeþ þat blisful knowynge þat Crist
hym-self spekþ of in þe gospel: *Hec est vita eterna vt cognoscant te*
vnum et verum Deum, et quem misisti Ihesum Cristum. Of þyse
sprynkt out so muche loue, is igendred so greet feruour of blisful   1400
desir, so muche plentevousnesse of lykyngge, so muche swetnesse of
charite þat non oþer fulsumnesse of blisse bynemeþ þe blisful desir
and appetit, noþer þat blisful desir fayleþ of parfit and plentevous
fulsumnesse. And wat is al þis, forto seyn hit in fiewe wordes? Certes,
suster: *Quod oculus non vidit, nec auris audiuit, que preparauit Deus*   1405
diligentibus se.

    Recapitulacio.

    Now, suster, I haue wryte to þe in schorte wordes of þe mo[y]nde
of Cristes benefices þat ben apassed, of þe experience of þo þat beþ

1370 ne] *corrected to* no   1373 non] noñ; non] noñ
1381 schal] þat   1384 wit-outen] wit outem   1389 seye] *corrected to*
seȳe   1391 seye] *corrected to* seȳe   1402 non] noñ
1408 moynde] moþñde

1410 present, and of þe abydyngge hope of þ[o] þat beþ to comene – of þe
whiche mor plentevous fruyt of þe loue of God mowe sprynge out of
þyn herte – so þat þis þre maner meditacioun mowe styrye þy gostly
affeccioun, and þyn affeccioun mowe gendre brennyngge desir, and
þy desir mowe brynge þe in-to mornyngge and eke in-to wepyngge
1415 after þe loue of þi husbounde Crist, alwhat þu be brouȝt in-to his
owne siȝt and be iklept in his blessede armes; so þat þu mowe seye to þy
singuler loue, þat þu hast ichose byfore alle oþre, þat þat is iwryte in
þe book of loue in holy wryt: *Dilectus meus michi et ego illi.*

And now hast þu, suster, þat þu coueytist and þat þu askedist; for
1420 þu hast bodyly informaciouns, after þe whiche þu schalt rule and
gouerne þe owtward man; and also I haue itake þe a maner forme by
þe whiche þu miȝt purge þe inward man fro vices, and maken hym
fayr in vertu. Þu hast in þre maner of meditacioun how þu schalt
nursche þe, and feruently excite þe in-to þe loue of God. And in caas
1425 þat eny deuout creature profite in þe redynge of þis litul booke in eny
gostly profit, I preye hym þat he wyl ȝyue me þis to my meede: þat to
my savyour þat I abide, and to my domesman þat I drede, he wylle
deuoutly preye for my mysdedes, þat he and I mowe come to þat
blisse þat I vnworþyly haue spoken of. *Quod nobis misericorditer*
1430 *concedat, qui viuit et regnat in secula seculorum. Amen.*

NOTES

5   *ofte: pluribus annis* (Prologue, 4).

5–6   *a forme of lyuyng accordyng to thyn estat: secundum modum uiuendi quem arripuisti pro Christo, certam . . . formulam* (ibid., 5–6).

6–7   *That wolde Iesu thou haddist axid it: utinam . . . id peteres* (ibid., 7); this construction has clearly been formed by analogy with the more common 'that would God' followed by a past subjunctive verb, used to express an exclamation of desire which is unlikely to be fulfilled (see *OED* THAT *conj.* II. 3. c). Here however the verb is in the indicative.

7   *suche oon as coude haue fulfilled thyn desire: sapientiore . . . qui non coniectura qualibet sed experientia didicisset, quod alios doceret* (ibid., 7–9).

8   *after that simple felynge that God hath youen me*: not in L., but replacing *quoniam non possum negare quidquid iniungis* (ibid., 10–11). *Felynge* clearly has the sense here of 'mental awareness, skill, understanding' (see *MED feling(e*, 6) and 'simple' presumably that of 'humble, unpretentious' or even 'weak, feeble'; the phrase might be rendered 'rudimentary understanding'.

1: L. adds *qui tibi et carne et spiritu frater sum* (ibid., 9–10).

9   *a forme:* a succinct translation of *aliqua quae tibi necessaria uidentur . . . ad componendum exterioris hominis statum, certam tibi regulam tradere curabo, pro loco et tempore quaedam adiciens, et spiritualia corporalibus, ubi utile uisum fuerit, interserens* (ibid., 12–16).

10–11   *why that suche a solitary lyf was ordeyned: quaue ratione huiusmodi uita ab antiquis uel instituta sit uel usurpata* (1–2).

11–18   *Somme ther wern . . . with longyng desire:* for the thought of this passage, cf. the Carthusian *Consuetudines*, LXXX, 4 (PL 153, cols. 755–6).

12–13   *Ther were also somme to whom, al-though it were not perilous to lyue amonge many, natheles it was ful greuous: Sunt et alii quibus et si non perniciosum, est tamen dispendiosum* (4–5). The MS reading is a striking example of anacolouthon, most probably the result of scribal carelessness, but possibly the translator did not see *quibus* or did not have it in his exemplar. It is also remotely possible that here is an example of ellipsis of the indirect object; ellipsis of subject and object pronouns is well-attested in ME.

15–17 *either thei fledden perel whiche might haue falle, or muche harme whiche might betyde thurgh her presence: antiqui uel ut uitarent periculum, uel ne paterentur dispendium* (7–8).

18 *after the loue of Iesu: ad Christi . . . amplexum* (8–9).

19 *that fledden fro perel and harm whiche might falle:* not in L.

21 *for fredom of spirit: propter solitudinis libertatem et uagandi potestatem* (11–12).

23–4 *the profit of solitary liuyng: rationem huius ordinis* (16).

25–6 *the thoughte rennith aboute besynes of the worlde: mens non solum peruagatione dissoluatur, curis et sollicitudinibus dissipetur, immundis etiam et illicitis desideriis agitetur* (18–20).

26–7 *either aboute tidynges, curiously enquering and sechinge after hem:* the ME here corresponds very vaguely with *per uicos et ciuitates, per fora et nundinas* (20–1).

27–8 *or elles of her neighbores yuel name, by way of bakbityng: per uitas et mores et opera hominum, non solum inutilia, sed etiam turpia curiose discurrat* (21–2).

28–9 *vnnethes now-a-dayes shaltow finde a solitary recluse:* for the following passage, cf. *Ancrene Wisse* f. 23ª/14–18.

30 *an olde womman fedynge hir with tales: anus garrula . . . quae eam fabulis occupet, rumoribus ac detractionibus pascat* (24–6). MS T omits *pascat*, which was clearly present in the translator's exemplar.

30–1 *a new iangeler: rumigerula mulier* (24).

teller of tidynges: formam, uultum moresque describat, illecebrosa quaeque interserat (27–8).

32 *maidens wantownes:* omitting *coniugum in uiris fallendis explendisque uoluptatibus astutiam* (29–30).

34–5 *lust and likynge, bakbitynge, sclaundre and hatrede: uoluptatibus* (33).

37–8 *Alle thes causen gret lettyng to Goddes seruauntes bothe wakyng and slepynge, in meditacion and praier and contemplacion:* a colourless and insipid translation of *Reddita quieti misera, eas quas auditus induxerat, in corde uersat imagines, et ignem premissa confabulatione conceptum uehementius sua cogitatione succendit. Quasi ebria in psalmis titubat, in lectione caligat, fluctuat in oratione* (35–8).

39–40 *suche lusty tales gendren leccherous ymaginatyf thou3tes:* distantly connected with *citantur mulierculae, et addentes noua ueteribus* (39–40).

40–2 *neuere cessynge vnto the tyme she consente to falle, sekynge by*

whom, where and whan she might fulfille in dede that the whiche hath
so longe be vnclenly thoughte: non cessant donec captiuam libidinis
daemonibus illudendam exponant. Nam manifestior sermo, non iam
de accendenda, sed potius de satianda uoluptate procedens, ubi et
quando et per quem possit explere quod cogitat in commune disponunt
(40–4).

43   *This wrecchidnes hath often be seen of hem that han ben enclosed:*
not in L.

44–5   *that euereyther might come in or out to other: aut illa egreditur,*
aut adulter ingreditur (45); possibly the translator read *alter* for
adulter.

50   *Somme also:* the translator has omitted a further reference to the
vice of gossiping (48–50).
   gadrynge of worldly good, in bestaille, in wolle: multiplicandis
pecoribus (52–3).

51   *in multiplieng of peny to peny and shilyng: pecuniae congregan-*
dae (52). MS *multipleng* is clearly an error; in this text the scribe
consistently spells the pr. p. ending as *-eng(e* only when the verb-stem
ends in *y* or *i* (cf. *seieng* (170), *praienge* (292), *tilyenge* (672)).

52   *thei oughten rather to be called housewyues than recluses:* cf.
Ancrene Wisse, f. 112ª/20–3.

52–3   *They ordeyne mete for her bestes:* cf. ibid., f. 112ᵇ/25–113ª/2.

53–4   *atte yeres ende they loke after the nomber or after the price:*
annui fructus uel pretium, uel pondus, uel numerum a custodibus
expetunt (56–7).

58   *her frendes: pro aduenientium parentum uel amicorum caritate*
(60–1).

58–9   *poure religious men or wommen and suche othir:* the L. mentions women only: *religiosarum feminarum* (61–2).

59   *and al this is but a disceyt:* translator's addition.

62   *for hir lyflode: de crastino* (66).

64–6   'First . . . to yow': Matthew 6: 33. The L. quotes only *Primum*
quaerite regnum Dei et omnia adicientur uobis. of him is the equivalent of *his,* the standard form of the neuter possessive pronoun in ME.

69–70   *for that is the moor syker way to parfeccyon-warde: hoc enim*
perfectius (71).

73   *suche frendes where: certas personas . . . a quibus* (72–3). Here
the local, concrete sense of the relative *where* is blurring into the sense
'from whom' (see Mustanoja, p. 338).

73–4   *with othir pore peple: humiliter* (74).

74 *that thou mightist haue noo cause to gadir worldly good: nec causa pauperum uel hospitum quidquam adiciat* (74–5).

76–7 *I say not this for I wolde thou lettist it:* not in L.

80–1 *'If thou haue moor than mete and drinke and vesture, thou art neither good mynchen ne recluse':* si praeter necessarium uictum et uestitum aliquid habes, monacha non es (81–2).

82–3 *I wolde it were deled to pore peple by other menes than thiself: mittat cuilibet fideli, qui pauperibus eroget* (84–5). Cf. *Ancrene Wisse*, f. 112ª/23–4.

84 *waiter of vnclennesse:* insidiatrix pudicitiae uetula (86). *insidiatrix* is the feminine form of *insidiator*, 'one who lies in wait'; *waiter* is first recorded in ME *c.* 1382 with the meaning 'one who is on the look-out'; in 1400 (*Master of the Game*) it means 'one who is set to watch the movements of the intended game', which would be an appropriate meaning here, and it is used by Caxton in 1471 to mean 'an observer in secret, a spy'. The sense, 'one who lies in wait' is not recorded; possibly it is a coinage of this translator, who elsewhere shows a predilection for nouns formed in -*er* (e.g. *former* (221)), *greither* (212). (See *OED* WAITER.)

85 *rowne venym in thyn ere of veyn lust or of likynge: blanda uerba in aure susurret, ne pro accepta eleemosyna osculans manum, uenenum insibilet* (88–9).

86–8 *for thereof . . . honest persone:* not in L.

92 *I wolde thou were war of resceiuynge of yistes:* L. Cauendum praeterea est, ut nec ob susceptionem religiosarum feminarum quodlibet hospitalitatis onus inclusa suscipiat (90–1). Cf. the ME translation of the *Speculum Inclusorum* which parallels the whole paragraph: 'Forsoþe yt apperteneyth nat to ȝoure estat . . . to receyue poure folk and pilgrymes . . . or to bere the charge of helpynge of ȝoure cosyns and frendes' and 'Tho recluses bien ofte vesitid wiþ men and women þat schewen gay and neyce aparail and cloþid in her syȝt and tellen hem þinges of worldly lust as vnclene wordes and vncouenable and tellen hem tydynges and auentures þat fallen in diuerse contrees of þe whiche þinges þo þat remaynen and duellyn in her mynde, þouȝ þei seme outward mortel and deedly synnes, ȝet naþeles inward þei vexen and troublen merueyllously her þouȝtes and dryuen hem in to diuerse fantasies so þat her redynge is þe more vnsavoury, her preier lasse deuout and al her meditacion vicious' (MS Harley 2372 ff. 4 and 4ᵛ).

94–7 *al-though her communicacion atte begynnynge be of sadnes and vertuous lyuynge, er than thei departe worldly daliaunce shal be shewed furthe, and otherwhile wordes of flesshly loue: praemissis ualde paucis de religione sermonibus, ad saecularia deuoluuntur.*

Inde subtexere amatoria, et fere totam noctem insomnem ducere (93–5).

98   *thou woldist not:* L. adds *Forte enim uidebuntur amara cum audiuntur uel cernuntur, quae postea sentiuntur dulcia cum cogitantur* (97–8).

101   *thy naked purpos: tuam nuditatem propositumque* (100).

104   *a mony-maker: pecuniosam* (103). The collocation *money-maker* is recorded by *OED* with the meaning 'one who makes money' for 1400, and 'maker of counterfeit coins' for 1420; but the meaning which it clearly has here of 'one who accumulates money' is not recorded before 1864. (See *OED* MONEY-MAKER.)

109   *witnesse of hir good conuersacyon: testimonium sanctitatis* (106).

110   *to kepe thyn houshold and thy lyflod: Haec quae ad uictum necessaria sunt recipiat uel conseruet* (108–9).

114   *greithynge of mete and drynke: coquat fabas et olera, aut, si hoc infirmitas exegerit, praeparet potiora* (110–11). The translator has misunderstood *potiora* (< comp. of L *potis*, 'stronger', here presumably implying flesh-meat in contrast with 'beans and cabbages'), confusing it with *potiones* < L *potio, n.*, 'drink'.

114–15   *And that she be ouerloked:* ellipsis of main clause (cf. 132); formally, this clause must be dependent on 'I nolde' (l. 104).

   vnder gret awe: sub magna disciplina (112).

116   *thyn holy temple be defouled and sclaundred: tuum sanctum habitaculum polluatur, et ita nomen Domini et tuum propositum blasphemetur* (112–14).

116–17   *Be war also that thou be not occupyed in techynge of children:* cf. *Cistercian Institutes* XLI, *Nullus puerorum doceatur litteras intra monasterium uel in locis monasterii, nisi sit monachus uel receptus in probatione nouicius,* and *Ancrene Wisse,* f. 114^b/20–5.

119   *doo not so:* the translator completely omits ll. 117–25 of the L., which contain a lively description of the anchoress as school-mistress, but would hardly be relevant to a Carthusian audience.

124   *as the prophete saith:* in the L. the 'prophet' is Jeremiah but as the translator has here omitted ll. 130–4 of the L. the ME refers to the psalmist: the quotation that follows is from Psalm 38: 2.

127–8   *as Seint Iame saith:* James 3: 8.

129   *kepe wel thy tunge by silence:* a reference to Psalm 38: 2 again; L. *ponat custodiam ori suo* (137).

129–30   *and sitte alone from worldly noyce and be styl: sola sedeat et taceat ore,* omitting *ut spiritu loquatur, et credat se non esse solam, quando sola est* (138–9).

130–1 *him whiche list not to speke but with suche that ben allone:* cf. *Consuetudines* LXXX, 4 (PL 153 cols. 755–6).

131–2 *yf thou shalt speke, speke selde:* cf. *Spec. Car.*, I, ll. 1836–9. The translator has here omitted ll. 141–4 of the L.

132–3 *and that . . . to soule:* Quid loquatur, id est de necessitate corporis uel animae aedificatione (147–8). The L. which is here being somewhat loosely translated, is strictly speaking dependent on a clause some lines back, *quibus et quomodo loquatur attendat* (143–4); in the ME there is no main verb anywhere in the vicinity on which this subordinate clause can depend, even formally. Clearly such a verb has to be understood; cf. note to l. 114–15.

134 *ne with noon hye chere: nec mixta risu* (152).

134–7 *And sith . . . assigned to the:* this passage is not in the L. The translator has omitted to translate ll. 152–4, *Nam si hoc ad quemlibet uirum honestum pertinet, quanto magis ad feminam, quanto magis ad uirginem, quanto magis ad inclusam?* For the advice in the ME cf. *Ancrene Wisse*, f. 14^b/24–6 and the practice of the Carthusians who, on meeting in the cloister, 'neither looked at each other nor spoke, but drew the hood of their cowls over their faces' (G. H. Cook, *English Monasteries in the Middle Ages* (London, 1961), p. 205).

137 *but if it be suche that ben assigned to the:* although there is no direct equivalent of this clause in the L. it was undoubtedly suggested by *Quibus loquatur, id est certis personis et quales ei fuerint designatae* (149–50). In the ME the referent of *suche* is ambiguous: it should be 'homly communicacyoun' formally, from the point of view of sense 'men' seems preferable, and is supported by the L., but one must then posit the suppression of '(that of)'. The kind of difficulty is typical of this translator's style, which has an easy, informal syntax which would no doubt be perfectly clear in oral delivery. *assigned*, being suggested by *designatae* < L *designatus, adj.*, has the sense 'nominated, ordained, officially appointed'.

138 *a blessed womman and wel sette:* L. simply *felix* (158). *wel sette* is not recorded in *OED* but the collocation is found in Chaucer where it is glossed by both Skeat and Robinson as 'seemly'. It also occurs in *Ancrene Wisse*, f. 19^a/4: 'forte speoke lutel and wel isette wordes', where it would seem to mean 'appropriate, well-chosen'.

139 *Seint Martyn:* this story (the source of which is Sulpicius Severus, *Dialogues* II, 12) is also used in *Ancrene Wisse*, ff. 15^a/25–15^b/2.

139–40 *ne speke with:* omitting ll. 160–63 of the L., where Aelred reflects that modern recluses are content with avoiding pregnancy and the open shame of a wailing baby.

142 *a confessour:* omits *in uicino monasterio uel ecclesia* (166–7).

143 *of gode oppinyon: bonae opinionis* (167–8). The sense of the ME here is clearly 'having a good reputation'; *OED* however does not record the sense of 'what others think of oneself' for 'opinion' earlier than 1577. The phrase here would seem to be a direct borrowing from the L.

145 *as it were for deuocyon:* not in L.

145–6 *for that makith deed folke, be thei neuere so olde, prone and redy to synne:* the L. here is *suscitat et emollit emortuam senectutem* (171–2), i.e. 'arouses and enervates dead old age' literally. The expression is hyperbolic and has caused the translator some trouble; he has tried to render the sense *emortuam* (< L *emortuus, adj.,* 'dead') by 'deed folke' and *senectutem* (< L *senectus, n.,* 'old age') by 'be thei neuere so olde' but the result is really near-nonsense. A possible emendation would be to 'for that makith olde folke, be thei neuere so deed' etc.

146 *Al this:* omitting ll. 173–5 of the L., a caution against passing personal remarks on one's confessor's appearance.

147 *other that in tyme comynge: adolescentiores* (177).

149 *eny worthy persone: aliqua magni nominis uel bonae aestimationis persona* (180).

151 *be not to famulier in suche visitacions: Nullam certe personam te frequentius uisitare uellem, nec cum aliqua te crebrius uisitante familiare te uellem habere secretum.* (182–4).

152–3 *were thei neuere so good:* not in L.

154–5 *and lette the fro many gode meritory occupacions that thou are bounde to:* not in L.

158 *to admitte the voyce of a man: uiri uocem . . . admittere* (190–1). 'admit' in the sense of 'allow (sb.) to enter (a place)' is first recorded by *MED* as used by Trevisa *a.* 1387, but there are no other fourteenth-century examples.

162 *rest in conscience:* the translator here omits ll. 195–209 of the L., which forbid the anchoress to receive letters or presents from men, or to give embroidered belts or purses to young monks or clerks. Let her make only useful objects and, if she cannot use them herself, have them donated to the church or to the poor.

163–4 *Gete by grace the vertu of shamfastnesse, for that arayeth a clene soule in vertuous maners and vertuous speche: Ornet etiam omnes motus omnesque sermones inclusae uerecundia* (210–11).

165–6   *if a chaste soule be a-shamed honestly to speke honest thinges:* of the MSS of the L., only D, H and V read *Nam quam pudere debet honeste honesta loqui* (212), of which the ME is clearly a translation; all others omit *honeste*.

169–70   *alle wronges, bothe pryue and apert: in omnibus quae in occulto uel publico aut obiciuntur aut susurrantur* (215–16).

170   *ne charge it not as for hirself:* not in L., which has *ex conscientiae serenioris arce contemnat* (217): i.e. 'let her despise it from the citadel of a calm conscience'.

171   *Michi autem:* I Corinthians 4:3.

174   *and foryete suche outwarde thynges:* not in L.

174–5   *hauynge hym in mynde that is liuyer euerlastynge:* MS *louyer* is superficially acceptable, but the translator has gone astray here. L. *ut . . . illum sui pectoris aeternum habeat . . . inhabitatorem* (219–21) should mean 'that she may have him as an everlasting inhabitant of her heart'. But the translator has mistranslated *sui pectoris*, taking it with *habeat* and not realizing that it modifies *aeternum . . . inhabitatorem*, which he almost certainly rendered, with desperate literalness, 'liuyer euerlastynge'. Not surprisingly a scribe, either Dodesham or the transcriber of an earlier copy, who did not have the original L. before him, thought the phrase strange and 'emended' it to 'louyer euerlastynge', a more familiar collocation but hardly relevant to the context here. *liuyers* occurs elsewhere (see ll. 644, 667, 668) though in the sense of 'those who live in a specified way' (see *OED* LIVER *sb.* (*b*)) rather than 'one who lives; inhabitant, dweller' (ibid., 1), first recorded in Wycliffe (1382).

175–6   *In pace factus est locus eius:* Psalm 75: 3.

178–9   *Super . . . sermones meos?:* Isaiah 66: 2.

181   *dredynge my wordes:* this phrase, which is clearly in apposition to *the quiet and meke and contrite of spirit* is of course a literal rendering of *timentem sermones meos*, where the L. pr. p. acts as a noun.

181–2   *Al this I saye for that I wolde thou louedist silence and litel speche: Hunc sacratissimum mentis statum, non solum stultiloquia, sed etiam multiloquia euertunt, ut aduertas, nihil tibi magis esse sectandum quam silentium* (225–7).

186–7   *vnto Estern:* until Lent in the L. (*ad quadragesimam*, 230–1).

187–8   *to speke with noon:* for the infinitive used as an imperative, cf. l. 196, 'to speke with thy mynistres'.

190   *tyl thou haue ete: usque ad tertiam* (234).

190–1 *in deuoute praiers and holy meditacions:*translator's addition.

And than vse communicacioun tyl euensonge-tyme: the ME allows speech between the time of the main meal of the day and Vespers (or Evensong). If the main meal is taken at Terce, as the translation of *usque ad tertiam* by 'tyl thou haue ete' at l. 190 suggests, the ME version offers a more relaxed rule than the L. original which here reads *Inter tertiam uero et nonam his quae superuenerint personis si admittendae sint competenter respondeat, et ministris quod placuerit iniungat. Post nonam sumpto cibo omne colloquium . . . caueat . . . .* (235–8). That is, Aelred allows his recluse to speak between Terce and None, when she takes her meal; but she must keep silence between None and Vespers.

192–3 *Sedit . . . ludere:* Exodus 32: 6, also quoted at I Cor. 10: 7.

they rysen and pleyden: et surrexerunt ludere (240). *rysen* is clearly pa. t.; the forms *risen, rysen* as pl. forms of the pa. t. of *rise* are well attested in the fourteenth and fifteenth centuries. See *OED* RISE.

196 *and so kepe silence for al that nyght:* not in L.; Aelred takes it for granted that, like all religious, the recluse will observe silence from Compline onwards.

199 *After tyme pryme is seide:* in the L. during the summer the recluse may speak to her servants after Prime, and with visitors (when necessary) between None and Vespers (ll. 247–52). In the ME, more laxly, she may speak with visitors between Prime and Terce and between noon (that is, the time of the canonical office, i.e. about three in the afternoon) and Vespers as well.

203–4 *But in Lente kepe silence: Tempore uero quadragesimae, inclusa semper tenere silentium deberet* (242–3). For the Lenten rule of silence, except as regards servants and distant visitors, cf. *Ancrene Wisse*, f. 17[b]/6–11 and E. J. Dobson, *The Origins of Ancrene Wisse* (Oxford, 1976), pp. 37–8.

205–6 *from fer contre: ex aliis prouinciis* (246).

209 *ydelnesse is a deedly enemy to mannys soule:* St Benedict's famous statement (Rule XLVIII, 1) became a popular maxim or *sententia*; cf. the opening of the *Second Nun's Tale* (Chaucer, *CT* G, 1–7 and I, 713–15) and Gower, *Confessio Amantis* IV, 1088–9.

210 *wurcher of alle lustes: libidinis artifex* (257).

211 *former of vnclene affeccions: nutrix uitiorum* (ibid.).

211–12 *sturer of vnclene desires, greither of heuynesse:* a condensation of the L: *fomentum acediae, tristitiae incentiuum. Ipsa pessimas cogitationes seminat, affectiones illicitas creat, suscitat desideria. Ipsa quietis fastidium parit, horrorem incutit cellae.* (257–60).

212–13 *I wolde thou were not vnoccupyed:* Nunquam proinde te nequam spiritus inueniat otiosam (260–1). Cf. *Spec. Car.* I, 1841–5, where Aelred prescribes writing, reading and meditation, and *Ancrene Wisse*, f. 11ᵃ/26–8.

213 *with dyuerse honeste occupacions:* the L. (262–5) explains that this diversity is a necessary concession to human weakness.

215 *After tyme thou hast saide diuyne seruice:* the L. says, more specifically, *Itaque a Kalendis nouembris usque ad quadragesimam secundum aestimationem suam plus media nocte repauset, et sic surgens . . . secundum formam Regulae beati Benedicti nocturnas uigilias celebret* (266–9). This is one of the few mentions by name of the Benedictine Rule in Aelred's treatise.

215–16 *thow shalt occupie the with som honest labour of thyn hondes:* not in L., but manual labour is mentioned at l. 281.

217–18 *as for a grete refute and helpe of thyn holy purpos that thou stondist inne:* not in L.

219–20 *be wel war of multitude of psalmes in thy pryuat prayer:* *Caueat autem, ne prolixior oratio fastidium pariat* (272). Cf. the caution against extensive or lengthy use of vocal prayer, particularly psalms, in *Orcherd of Syon*, ed. P. Hodgson and G. Liegey. EETS 258 (1966), p. 147/16–25.

put it in noo certeyn: Caue autem ne de numero psalmorum aliquam tibi legem imponas (277), omitting ll. 272–7. *MED* records the expression *putten in certain* under CERTAIN adj., one of its meanings being 'to establish (sth.) with certainty'. However, it would seem that in this text *certeyn* is either a noun, or an adj. acting as a noun, as it is modified by *no* (cf. 'an vncerteyn' at l. 971). The meaning of the phrase if one takes the L. into account seems to be 'to make subject to a definite pledge'; *MED* records the sense 'a fixed amount or number' for CERTAIN sb., but CERTAINTE sb. can indeed mean 'a binding agreement, pledge' (see *MED* svv). For the idea that an anchoress should not make any definite commitment as to her devotions by vowing obedience to a detailed rule, cf. *Ancrene Wisse*, f. 2ᵃ/5–17.

223 *diuersite of besinesse:* cf. *Speculum Inclusorum*, ed. L. Oliger (*Lateranum*, Nova Series An. 4 no. 1), p. 103: *occupacionis variacio vitet ocium, expellat accidiam, devocionem continuet et naturam recreet fatigatam* and *The Chastising of God's Children*, ed. J. Bazire and E. Colledge (Oxford, 1957), p. 111.

223–4 *thou might putte away slouthe and ydelnesse:* spiritum recrees, et pellas acediam (282).

225–6 *Thus shalt thou be occupied bitwene euery diuyne houre of the nyght and of the day, from the kalendes of Nouembre vnto Lente:* a drastic condensation of the L., ll. 281–93. Aelred here prescribes manual labour and the recitation of psalms after the night office until dawn; reading, prayers and psalms between Prime and Terce; manual labour between Terce and None; a meal at None followed by a similar mixture of devotion and manual labour until Vespers.

227–8 *redynge of holy faders priuely by thiself: aliquam lectionem de Vitis Patrum, uel Institutis, uel miraculis eorum sibi secretius legat* (293–5).

228 *in stede of thy collacyon:* not in L. *in stede of* has here the sense of 'by way of, as for' which is far less common than its sense 'in place of': almost all the examples given by *MED* are from Trevisa, who apparently often uses it to render L *pro*. *collacyon* here has its original sense of 'a reading from Cassian's *Collationes*.'

232–4 *restynge the there vnto the tyme that it be passed mydnyght; here than thou begynne thy matyns, for thou shalt slepe no more of al day:* not here in L., but reverting to ll. 266–9. The translator here omits ll. 298–304, which prescribe a simple rule for illiterate anchoresses.

234 *This same rule:* a condensation of ll. 305–14.

235–6 *saaf that thou shalt slepe after mete afore the houre of noon: Post sextam sumpto cibo pauset in lectulo suo usque ad nonam* (311–12). In the summer the main meal is at Sext, not None, and is followed by a siesta between Sext and None.

237 *Take heed of oo thynge:* cf. Benedict, *Rule*, XLI and Guigo, *Consuetudines*, XLIII, 5 (PL 153 col. 725).

242 *not oonly religiouse peple: non singulis quibusque personis, non illius uel illius ordinis hominibus* (321–2).

243 *is bounde:* L. adds *diuina auctoritate* (321).

245 *Moyses:* L. adds *famulus Domini* (324).

246–7 *Helye the prophete:* L. adds *cum manducasset de pane subcinerico aquamque bibisset quam ei angelus ministrauerat* (326–8), which refers to I Kings 19:6.

247–8 *that he might deserue to here the voyce of God: et tunc uocem Domini audire promeruit* (329); possibly the translator misread *et* as *ut*.

252–3 *and to deuoute praier a souereyn fode: orationibus nostris irrefragabile fulcimentum* (334–5). *fulcimentum* here means 'prop, stay, support'; *fode* could here mean 'food' in a metaphorical sense (i.e. 'that which supports, sustains') – *MED* FODE n. (1) 2 (a) gives 'spiritual sustenance, comfort or support' – or it could be a spelling of ME *fote* which can have the meaning 'the lowest part of something; that upon which something rests or is supported' (*MED* FOT n. 4), specifically 'the leg of a bench, chair, table etc.' (ibid., (e). It is even possible that the text originally read *fote*, which is a more literal translation of the L., but which divorced from its original would look very strange to any scribe, who would be tempted to 'emend' it.

254 *taughte his disciples:* L. adds *interrogantibus . . . cur daemonem qui lunaticum inuaserat, eicere non potuerant* (336–7).

254–5 *he saide that ther was o kynde of deuels might not be caste oute:* Mark 9: 28.

255–6 *al-though fastynge be the duke and the leder of al religion:* Licet autem religionis comes semper debeat esse ieiunium (340). A mistranslation: in Aelred *comes* means 'companion, accompaniment'; however in ML *comes* can also mean 'count' or 'earl' (see *RMLWL* sv) which is clearly how the translator understood it here, rendering it 'duke', which can mean 'hereditary noble ranking above earl, baron or knight' and hence, presumably, is a legitimate equivalent for *comes*. This example of blind literalism, showing little regard for context or sense, would tend to support the arguments in notes to l. 174 and ll. 252–3.

257–8 *mightily passeth al other:* the ME has merely the most tenuous connection here with L. *magnum in se continet sacramentum* (342).

261 *with blessed spirites and aungels: cum angelicis spiritibus* (344). *if we wel do:* not in L.

262 *betokeneth no more than fourty days: betokeneth* here must mean 'denotes, means' (*MED* sv 4(a)) rather than as it does more commonly, 'symbolizes', unless we are to take 'no more than forty days' as the awkwardly inverted subject of the sentence. The L. would in fact support such an interpretation as it reads *Significant autem isti quadraginta dies totum tempus* (345), but a reader had only to miss *isti* and misread *significāt* as *significat* for the meaning of the sentence to become ambiguous.

269–70 *but for we ben freel and mowe not contynuely with-oute cessynge vse this weilynge and wepynge: Sed quia hoc facile non potest humana fragilitas* (352–3).

271–2 *a certayn tyme of contynuel wailynge: certum tempus quo id faciamus* (354).

273 *that we ben putte away out of paradyse: nos pulsos esse et addictos morti propter peccatum* (356–7).

274 *it is saide thus:* L. adds *uerbum ipsum quod dixit Dominus ad Adam, cum eum expelleret de paradiso, cum cinerum aspersione dicitur nobis* (357–9).

274–5 *Memento quod cinis es et in cinerem reuerteris:* the Latin quotation in the ME is different from Aelred's which reads *Puluis es et in puluerem reuerteris* (359–60), a reference to Gen. 3: 19 and the words used at the Imposition of Ashes on Ash Wednesday in the Roman Rite. In the Carthusian Rite *Recognosce homo* is substituted for the Roman *Memento, homo*, so the ME adaptation here cannot be attributed to Carthusian influence. (See A. A. King, *Liturgies of the Religious Orders* (London, 1955), p. 28.) But both the Dominicans and the Carmelites use the formula given in the ME here (see King, pp. 264 and 354). The Dominican Rite was extremely influential in Sweden and at the English Royal Court (*ibid.*, pp. 344–5). Possibly, then, the change in the ME indicates that this translation was intended for the Bridgettines who had, of course, been founded from Vadstena in Sweden, and whose rite may have shown Swedish influences.

277   *letted from heuenly desire: negatur nobis uisio Dei* (360–1).

278–80   *ther is hanged bitwene vs and Crist, his flesshe and his blood, the sacrament of the autere, a veyl: oppanditur uelum inter nos et sancta sanctorum* (361). Aelred is undoubtedly referring to the so-called Lenten Curtain which in the Middle Ages 'was hung during Lent before the sanctuary in many churches, symbolical of the truth that sin excludes from the presence of God' (King, *op. cit.*, p. 152. See also H. Thurston, *Lent and Holy Week* (London, 1904), pp. 99–103). But it is not clear whether the ME translator has this in mind, or whether he is thinking more of the silken canopy enveloping the pyx which, containing the Sacrament, commonly hung above the altar (see D. Rock, *The Church of Our Fathers* (London, 1849–53), 4 vols., III, Pt. 2, 206–7).

280–1   *we leuen vnsongen: intermittimus* (365). *OED* does not record the form *unsungen* but it does record *unsung* in the sense 'not sung' (comparing MHG and G *ungesungen*, Sw *osjungen*) as first used in the fifteenth century.

a songe and a worde of melodye: uerbum laudis (365), i.e. 'expression of praise'. *MED* records the phrase 'worde of melodye' sv *melodie* as meaning 'sung phrase, antiphon', which is an accurate enough description of 'Alleluia'. At l. 729 of this text *melody* is used to refer to the angelic *Gloria in excelsis*. 'songe' and 'worde of melodye' are thus virtually synonyms, the reason for the redundancy perhaps being that the L. suggested 'word of melodye' and 'songe' was added in explanation. On the laying-aside, or 'closure', of the Alleluia (which now takes place on the eve of Septuagesima) see Thurston, *op. cit.*, pp. 26–34. In the twelfth century the Cistercians were much criticized (by, for instance, Rupert of Deutz and Peter Abelard) for retaining the Alleluia after Septuagesima right up till the beginning of Lent: see B. K. Lackner, 'The Liturgy of Early Cîteaux', *Studies in Medieval Cistercian History* (Cistercian Studies Series No. 13; Spenser,

Mass., 1971), pp. 18–19, and King, *op. cit.*, p. 70.) The deviation was not supressed until 1605.

285–6 *shuld euery cristen man adde somwhat moor to his fastynge:* cf. Benedict, *Rule* XLIX, 5, which, however, limits this obligation to monks.

288 *and shuldest passe alle othir in lyuynge: quae temporis huius rationem tanto melius intelligit, quanto eam in propria uita sua expressius recognoscit* (370–2).

289 *vowynge thiself to his seruice:* the MS reading *bowynge* is not obviously wrong but as the L. here reads *totam se Deo uoueat* (373–4) it seems likely that the ME translation originally had *vowynge*.

291–2 *sighynge and sorwyng, wepyng and wailyng, knelyng and praienge: Frequentius solito incumbat orationi, crebrius se pedibus Iesu prosternat, crebra dulcissimi nominis illius repetitione compunctionem excitet, lacrymas prouocet, cor ab omni peruagatione compescat* (377–80).

292–3 *after thy lorde, thy maker, thyn ayenbier, thy loue and thy louyer, thy spouse and thy domesman, Iesu Crist: ad amplexus Christi* (376).

294–5 *The manere of þi slepynge in this tyme a-fore mydnyght shal be lasse than in a-nothir tyme:* the L. here refers to a diminution of the amount of sleep after rather than before midnight: *Finitis itaque sacris uigiliis, interuallum quod a nocturnis laudibus diuidit matutinas orationi et meditationi subseruiat* (381–2).

295–6 *so that thou may night and day for þe moor partie deuoutly be occupied with praier, meditacion and redyng:* this gives the gist of the L. (383–7), which prescribes that Prime should be said after Matins and then that the recluse should be occupied until Terce in reading and psalms. After Terce she should spend the time until 'the tenth hour' (about four in the afternoon) in manual labour interspersed by prayer. After Vespers she may take her only meal (Vespers was sung early during Lent) and then recite psalms until Compline.

301–2 *and also what shal be thyn array and vesture of thy body:* translator's addition.

303 *euir: ab ipsa infantia usque ad senectutem quae nunc tua membra debilitat* (389–90).

304–5 *whiche konnen not rule hem, that outher wiln take to muche, either to litel:* not in L., which has *quibus id utile futurum arbitraris* (391–2).

305–7 *that the semeth shulde enflaume thy compleccyon and make the prone and redy to synne: quod inebriare potest* (397).

307 *but if thou be syke or feble:* not in L.

307–8   *Abstyne the also from mete and drinke, as thou woldist vse a medicyn:* not in L. The construction is elliptical: one must supply a clause such as 'using them . . .'

309–10   *a certeyn weight of brede and a certeyn mesure of drynke: libram panis et eminam potus* (394). The reference is to Benedict, *Rule*, XXXIX–XL.

313   *al the while thou art not syke:* not in L.

313–14   *as venym and poyson, contrary to thy clene and chast purpose: quasi pudicitiae uenenum* (398).

315   *fulfilled:* L. adds a concession to those who cannot aspire so high and who are to be allowed St Benedict's allowance of food and drink.

317   *formente potage:* MS *formage* is not recorded in dictionaries of English. The L. here reads *pulmentum . . . de farinaciis* (403–4). In classical L *pulmentum* means 'anything eaten with bread', but in ML more specifically it means '(dish of) potage'. As *farinaceum* means 'cornmeal, flour' one suspects that Aelred had in mind something similar to porridge. ME *frumente* (see *MED* sv) is defined as '"potage" made of boiled hulled grain mixed with milk and sweetened', which is exactly the meaning of the L. However, *formage* does not seem a possible form for *frumente* (other spellings given are *frumite, furmenty, formenty, firmenty*). But *MED* records the collocation *furmente potage* and it is possible that by eye-skip a scribe might reduce *formente potage* to *formage*. It is less likely that *formage* is a genuine ME formation from ML *formaticus* or *formagius*, recorded in *RMLWL* as meaning 'cheese' (cf. F. *fromage*).

318   *a-voyde the bitternes:* L. adds *et hoc ei si ea die coenatura sufficiat* (405–6).

318–19   *and with o kynde of fysshe, with apples or with herbes: Ad coenam uero parum sibi lactis uel piscis modicum, uel aliquid huiusmodi si praesto fuerit, apponat, uno genere cibi contenta cum pomis et herbis crudis si quas habuerit. Haec ipsa si semel comederit in die praelibato pulmento possunt apponi.* (406–10). The ME blurs the distinction between what may be eaten if one eats only once in the day, and what may be taken if one eats twice. See also previous note.

319–20   *And vpon the Wednesday . . . Lent metes: In uigiliis tamen sanctorum, et quatuor temporum ieiuniis, omni etiam feria quarta uel sexta extra quadragesimam, in cibo quadragesimali ieiunet* (411–13). The ME has added Saturday to Wednesday and Friday; Saturday had long been regarded as a fast day in honour of the Virgin. Cf. William Caxton, *The Book of the Knight of the Tower*, ed. M. Y.

Offord, EETS, ss 2 (1971), pp. 19–20. However, Carthusians fasted on bread, water and salt three times a week (Monday, Wednesday and Friday); see *Consuetudines* XXXIII, 1 (PL 153 cols. 705–6).

321 *In Lente o manere of potage:* again, this sentence shows ellipsis of the main verb, which has to be understood from the preceding sentence.

322–3 *And the tyme . . . euensonge: Ab Exaltatione sanctae Crucis usque ad quadragesimam semel in die hora nona reficiat. In quadragesima dicta uespera ieiunium soluat* (416–18). Cf. Benedict, *Rule* XLI, 6. *hye none*, which translates L. *hora nona* here means 'the hour at which the office of None is sung', that is, about three in the afternoon. Clearly it is to be distinguished from *mydday* (l. 325) which corresponds to *ad sextam*, that is, about twelve noon. See *OED* NOON and SEXT.

324 *Whitsone Eue: uigilia Pentecostes* (419). MS *Withsone* is not intrinsically impossible in ME but this scribe never spells /hw/ as *w*, or /t/ as *th*.

324–5 *thou shalt ete at mydday and sithen at euen: ad sextam prandeat, et ad seram coenet* (419–20); the ME obscures Aelred's distinction between *prandium* (lunch; the main meal of the day, indeed the only meal on the days on which the recluse eats only once) and *coena* (supper).

327–8 *Also thou maist . . . to slepe:* the construction *may* + *to* + inf. is unusual, but is probably due to the lengthy clauses separating the auxiliary from the verb it governs.

328 *meridyan: somno meridiano* (422). *OED* does not record the appearance of *meridian* in the sense of 'siesta, afternoon sleep' before 1798–1801, so this is clearly a direct borrowing from the L.

330 *Thy vesture:* for similar instructions as to clothing, cf. *A Fifteenth-Century Courtesy Book and Two Fransiscan Rules*, ed. R. W. Chambers and W. W. Seton, EETS 148 (1914), p. 84/15–19.

331–2 *a warme pylche for wynter: Grossioribus pelliceis utatur, et pellibus propter hiemem*, omitting *Porro talia ei uestimenta sufficiant, quae frigus repellant* (426).

331–2 *oo kirtel . . . aboue hem: Propter aestatem autem unam habeat tunicam* (427).

333 *of a mene blak: mediocri nigro* (429). *mediocris* has the sense 'ordinary, undistinguished'.

333–5 *lest preciosite . . . with-ynne:* not in L., which has *ne uideatur colore uario affectare decorem* (430).

339 *outwarde lyuinge:* omitting *non pro antiquitatis feruore, sed pro huius nostri temporis tepore, te compellente scripsi, infirmis temper-*

atum quemdam modum uiuendi proponens, fortioribus ad perfectiora progrediendi libertatem relinquens (435–8).

339–41   *Now shal I . . . deuoute prayers:* translator's addition.

344   *First:* omits ll. 439–42 of the L; cf. Vernon ll. 3–6.

345–6   *Virgo . . . spiritu:* cf. I Corinthians 7: 32.

349–50   *a fre oblacyon: oblatio spontanea, ad quam non lex impellit, non necessitas cogit, non urget praeceptum* (446–7).

350   *Qui potest capere, capiat:* Matthew 19: 12.

351–2   *as ho saith, hoo may atteyne to come to the vertu of chastite, take he it and forsake it not:* translator's expansion.

353   *enspirith with good wille: hanc inspirauerit uoluntatem, et praestiterit facultatem* (449–50).

354   *comaunde: commenda* (452). *comaunde* is from ME *commaunden* in the sense 'entrust, command' (see *MED* COMMAUNDEN 6(b)) but the fact that it translates L. *commendare* suggests confusion with ME *commenden*.

356   *Thinke what mede:* omitting *Cogita semper quam pretiosum thesaurum in quam fragili portes uasculo* (455–6).

357   *what ioye: quam gloriam, quam coronam* (456–7).

357–8   *what confusion: quam insuper poenam, quam confusionem, quam damnationem* (457–8).

360   *coueitith to loue and to yeue: ipse cupidus est, quo illicitur ad amandum et prouocatur (om.* NUTM) *ad praestandum* (461–2).

362   *sauoreth mightily in the blys of heuen: in caelestibus dans odorem suum, facit ut concupiscat rex decorem tuum et ipse est Dominus Deus tuus* (464–5).

364–5   *he passith in semlynesse the shap of eny man moor firther than the sonne: Ipse est speciosus forma prae filiis hominum, speciosior etiam sole* (466–7): a reference to Wisdom 7:29.

365–6   *swetter than hony: Spiritus eius super mel dulcis, et haereditas eius super mel et fauum* (Eccli. 24:27).

He it is that desireth thi bewte: translator's addition.

368   *and wil crowne noon but such as ben preued:* see note to Vernon l. 40.

369   *Thy maydenhood is golde:* see note to Vernon l. 42.

thy selle is an ouen: cella fornax, omitting *conflator diabolus* (473).

370   *the vessel that thou berist: Caro uirginis* (474).

372–3   *thy golden maydenhood: aurum* (474).

375   *a mayde:* omitting *cogitans pretiosissimum uirginitatis thesaurum* (477–8).

376 *that so lightly may be lost: tam irrecuperabiliter amittitur* (478–9).

 be kept: omitting *Cogitet sine intermissione ad cuius ornatur thalamum, ad cuius praeparatur amplexum* (480–1).

377 *that blessed lombe:* that is, Christ; cf. Revelation 14: 4.

378 *oure blessed Lady:* cf. Vernon l. 55 ff. and note.

379 *but suche as ben vndefouled: nisi utriusque sexus uirgines,* omitting *de quibus scriptum est: Hi sunt qui cum mulieribus non sunt coinquinati, uirgines enim sunt* (485–7).

381 *yhis certeyn, ful foule and abhomynably:* summarizes ll. 488–93 of the L.; cf. Vernon ll. 61–7 and note to l. 65.

383 *halowed, incorporat to the Holy Gost: sanctificata Deo, incorporata Christo, Spiritui sancto dedicata* (494–5).

384 *youe:* the only occurence of this form of the pp. of *yeuen* in this text; elsewhere we have *youen*.

 fende: omitting *et uirginea eius membra erubescat uel simplici motu maculari* (496–7); cf. Vernon ll. 70–1.

386 *atteyne . . . that thou may holde: cogitationes expendat, ut uirtutis huius perfectionem esuriens . . . putet* (498–500). *attain* usually takes a sb. as object, or is followed by *to* + inf., but *MED* (s.v.) gives some examples of *atteinen* + *that* + subordinate clause.

390–1 *chewe vpon chastite: decorem pudicitiae mente reuoluat* (504).

393–4 *and if thou do thus, than shaltow litel lust haue of mete or of drynke but as nede axith, and vnnethes that: cibos fastidiat, potum exhorreat. Et quod sumendum necessitas iudicauerit, aut ratio dictauerit . . . sumat* (505–7) omitting ll. 508–11; cf. Vernon ll. 82–4.

398 *in-to his hondes that loueth clene and chaste soules:* translator's expansion of *Deo* (512); omits *sic signo crucis armata* (513).

398–9 *remembrynge the hou thou hast mysspended the day: reuolue animo quomodo die illo uixisti, si . . . Domini tui oculos offendisti* (513–15).

401 *dissolucyon of chere: si plusculo cibo crudior, si potu dissolutior* (515–16).

402 *wayle hem and wepe hem:* L. simply *suspira* (517).

403 *by grace: hoc sacrificio uespertino* (518).

403–4 *to thy lord Iesu Crist: tuo . . . sponso* (518–19).

405–6 *thorugh entysynge of the fende: arte tentatoris* (520), omitting ll. 521–4; Vernon ll. 100–3.

407 *as Agnes, Cecile, Lucye and other moo:* translator's addition.

409 *they:* Aelred cites St Agnes only, but elements from her legend are also found in the legends of St Cecilia and St Lucy. On St Agnes,

see Vernon ll. 105–19 and notes; on St Cecilia, see H. Delahaye, S.J., *Etude sur le légendier romain* Les saints de novembre et décembre (*Subsidia Hagiographica*, xxiii, 1936, 77–96). She was a virgin martyr of the second or third century but her true history remains obscure. On St Lucy, see her Latin *passio* (*Sainte Lucie*, ed. A. Beaugrand (Paris, 1882)). She was probably martyred in 303 and her name appears in the Canon of the Mass.

410 *precyous stones:* L. adds *et tota saecularis gloriae pompa* (527–8).

    the foulist fen in the felde: L. simply *stercora* (528). The phrase, which has a lively alliterative ring to it, is not a recorded collocation. Cf. 'chewe vpon chastite' (ll. 390–1).

    They: omitting *Vocata ad tribunal non abfuit* (528–9); defiant scenes before the Roman magistrates occur in all the legends of the early virgin martyrs.

413 *And somme ther were, as Seint Agnes:* St Agnes survived the brothel unscathed (see *South English Legendary*, ed. C. D'Evelyn and A. J. Mills, EETS 235–6 (1951–2), I, 21/51–2). Attempts were made to inflict a similar punishment on St Lucy but were miraculously thwarted when it became physically impossible to move her (see *The Early South-English Legendary*, ed. C. Horstmann, EETS 87 (1887), p. 101ff., and *Bokenham's Lives of Holy Women*, ed. M. S. Serjeantson, EETS 206 (1936), ll. 9248 ff.)

414–15 *the aungel of God:* L. adds *lucem infudit tenebris* (532).

    auenge hir of hir enemy: insectatorem pudicitiae morte multauit (532–3).

416–17 *trust right wel that an aungel, keper of thy chastite, shal be ful nye: non certe angelus tuo casto deerit cubiculo, qui prostibulo non defuit* (535–6).

418 *We rede also of othir maydens:* L. has only *beatam Agnetem* (536), but immunity from fire is a popular motif in other saints' legends. St Lucy remained unharmed by fire (see *Early South English Legendary*, ed. cit., ll. 143–8; *Bokenham's Lives*, ed. cit., ll. 9382–92) and St Cecilia is said to have remained unharmed for some time in a boiling hot bath (see *Early South-English Legendary*, p. 493/217–26, *Bokenham's Lives*, ll. 8210–16); St Agatha's ordeal of being laid on hot coals was interrupted by a miraculous earthquake (ibid., ll. 8779–84).

419 *the fire vanysshed and did hem no harme: ignis iste materialis nequiuit adurere* (536–7).

420 *the leyt of flesshly lust:* see note to Vernon l. 118.

423 *As ofte . . . vnclennes: Quotiescumque tibi uehementior in-*

cubuerit aestus, quoties nequam spiritus illicita quaeque suggesserit (539–40).

424 *oure Lorde:* L. adds *illum qui scrutatur corda et renes* (540–1), a reference to Psalm 7: 10.

425 *the whiche cherisshith the:* no sense can be made of ME *the cherisliche* and this emendation is offered to render *quem tibi assistere non dubites* (543). Possibly the succession of *th*s and the conjunction of two *ch*s confused the scribe as *t* and *c* are virtually indistinguishable in many medieval hands.

426 *'I haue an aungel to my loue':* Angelum Dei habeo amatorem (544) which appears here in Aelred's L., also appears in the legends of St Agnes (see, e.g., *Barbour's Legendensammlung*, ed. C. Horstmann (Heilbronn, 1881), 2 vols., II, 152/151–2 and *Bokenham's Lives*, ed. cit., ll. 4319–21). (A very similar phrase, *Angelum Dei habeo custodem*, is in fact the second antiphon at Lauds for the Feast of St Agnes.) The saying, however, is also recorded of St Cecilia, who spoke these words to her husband on their wedding-night (see Chaucer, *CT* G/151–4, *Barbour's Legendensammlung*, II, 163/45–6 and *Altenglische Legenden*, ed. C. Horstmann (Paderborn, 1875), p. 160/63–6. The source of all three is the *Legenda Aurea* – see W. F. Bryan and G. Dempster, *Sources and Analogues of Chaucer's Canterbury Tales* (Chicago, 1941), p. 672).

427 *day and nyght:* translator's addition.

431–2 *withoute gret affliccion of the body: sine magna cordis contritione et carnis afflictione* (550–1).

434–5 *and may . . . so vertuous: nisi Deus det, nec ullis nostris meritis donum hoc, sed eius gratuitae sit gratiae ascribendum* (554–5).

435–7 *whan . . . vertuouse menes:* loosely rendering the sense of the L., *illos tamen tanto dono indignos iudicat [sc. Deus], qui aliquid laboris pro eo subire detrectant* (555–7).

437 *It is ful harde:* a much abbreviated translation of ll. 557–61; cf. Vernon ll. 138–43.

439 *amongst conuersacion of children: inter puellas conuersari* (558), *pueros et puellas* DHV. Aelred presumably had in mind contact with young girls still in the world. ME *child* can mean 'a boy or girl (usually to the age of puberty)'; see *MED* sv 3a(a).

440 *a man: monachum* (562).

441 *with many vnclene thoughtes: tum naturalibus incentiuis, tum uiolentia uitiosae consuetudinis, tum suggestione callidi tentatoris* (563–4).

441-2   *he dredde hym to falle: pudicitiam suam periclitari timeret*
(564-5).

442-3   *no thinge hatynge so moche as himself: aduersus carnem
suam immanissimum concipiens odium, nihil magis quam quod eam
afflictaret expetebat* (565-7).

444   *that almost he failed for defaute: et quae ei de iure debebantur
subtrahens, etiam motus eius simplices comprimebat* (568-9).

446-7   *the saam temptacyon was as breem* . . . *or moor: ecce caro
rursus caput erigens, acquisitam, ut putabatur, infestabat quietem*
(570-1).

447-8   *he praide, he wepte, he snobbed, he wailed: tremens aliquan-
diu psallebat et orabat* (572-3).

450   *not-withstondynge al this: Et cum haec omnia non sufficerent*
(576).

   the spirit of vnclennes: spiritus fornicationis (577).

452   *besechinge him: orat, plorat, suspirat, rogat, adiurat, obtestatur*
(578-9).

452-3   *to delyuere* . . . *pleased him:* L. simply *occidat* (579).

   of these vnclene thoughtes: translator's addition.

454   *with stedfaste abidynge: crebro* (579).

455-6   *I shal* . . . *I aske:* a mistranslation of *nec te dimittam nisi
benedixeris mihi* (580), a reference to Genesis 32: 26 where the words
'I shall not let thee go until thou blessest me' are spoken by Jacob to
the Angel of the Lord.

457   *gete:* omits ll. 582-6 of the L. Cf. Vernon ll. 171-6.

457-8   *this passion* . . . *fresshe:* a much abbreviated rendering of *Et
tunc quoque recessit ab eo, sed usque ad tempus. Et nunc senectuti
morbus accessit, nec sic tamen sibi de securitate blanditur* (586-8).

459-60   *Sithen* . . . *withstood it:* translator's addition. The ME translator here shows himself well aware that the preceding anecdote
relates to Aelred's own early experiences as a monk. See note to
Vernon l.145.

460-2   *what shulden we* . . . *shold not falle?:* a summary translation
of ll. 589-94; cf. Vernon ll. 179-88.

463-4   *for though* . . . *not so: cum desit sceleris perpetrandi facultas,
adhuc manet in ipsa foeditate voluntas, nec quiescit turpe desiderium, quamuis ei frigiditas neget effectum* (595-8, omitting ll. 598-602
of the L.).

465   *as the culuer doth:* see note to Vernon l. 194.

466   *the ensaute* . . . *enemy: accipitris* . . . *superuolantis effigiem*
(606).

467–8 *So do thou . . . ouercome the: Riui aquarum sententiae sunt Scripturarum, qui de limpidissimo sapientiae fonte profluentes, diabolicarum suggestionum produnt imaginem, et sensum quo caueantur elucidant* (607–9).

468–9 *ouercometh so sone the fende: cogitationes excludit inutiles, uel compescit lascivas* (610–11).

469–70 *redynge . . . passyon:* the L., *meditatio uerbi Dei* (611), is an unequivocal reference to the reading of Holy Scripture; the rather vague ME translation is no doubt quite deliberate and is an interesting example of the late medieval ambivalence towards recommending the reading of the Bible in a vernacular treatise. On this subject, see M. Deanesly, *The Lollard Bible* (Cambridge, 1920), pp. 211–20. After 1408 it was commonly believed (incorrectly) that the reading of the Bible in English was forbidden.

meditacyon of Cristys passyon: as indicated above, this is an addition of the translator's. In 1410 Thomas Arundel licensed a Carthusian translation of the *Meditationes Vitae Christi* for the specific purpose of counteracting Lollard emphasis on the Gospel texts themselves (see Deanesly, *op. cit.*, p. 321) so the translator's changes here are well in line with orthodox policy.

479 *that wil not vse bodily affliccion: a salutaribus exercitiis . . . retrahuntur* (616).

480 *by liggynge, by weryng and such othir:* translator's addition. It is clear that these are pentitential practices of some sort. *liggynge* may have the sense 'lying awake, i.e keeping vigil', though this would merely repeat earlier 'wakynge' (l. 479), which translates L. *uigilias* (617). It is more likely to mean 'lying prostrate', which was a common ascetical exercise. The meaning of *weryng* is not at all clear but possibly it comes from *wear, vb.*, in the sense 'the wearing of penitential garments', though *OED* provides no authority for this sense. It is interesting that the phrase 'of werunge, of liggunge' occurs in *Ancrene Wisse*, f. 2b/3: 'alle oþer swuche þinges, of werunge, of liggunge, of ures', which in the Latin version is rendered *vestimentum et abstinencias consimiles seu orationes* (f. 92b/36–7), but in M. B. Salu's translation the phrase is rendered as 'clothing, rest' (*The Ancrene Riwle* (London, 1955), p. 3). It is possible that the ME translator here remembered the phrase from a reading of *Ancrene Wisse* and was aware that it signified some sort of physical hardship, though perhaps even he was not entirely clear what was intended.

480–1 *for drede of bodily infirmyte: ne . . . incidant in languorem* (617–18).

483 *to chastise her body so:* not in L.

484   *now-a-days:* omitting ll. 622–3 of the L.

485–6   *thei . . . her soule: languorem animae quem praesentem senti-mus, territi negligamus* (624–5).

486–7   *as though . . . the wombe: quasi tolerabilius sit flammam libidinis quam uentris tolerare rugitum* (625–6). In the L. *flammam libidinis* (= *temptacion*) and *uentris . . . rugitum* (= *honger of the wombe*) are parallel, both being the obj. of *tolerare*. It is therefore unlikely that *temptacion* is the subj. of *were moor tolerable*, although in fact the MS pointing suggests this. *and were more tolerable* is probably an impersonal verb-phrase with the formal subject *it* unex-pressed (cf. Mustanoja, p. 143); it clearly translates the impersonal L. construction *tolerabilius sit*.

487–8   *treuly . . . to hemself:* a very feeble substitute for the L., *Quid enim interest utrum abstinentia an languore caro superbiens compri-matur, castitas conseruetur?* (628–30); cf. Vernon ll. 220–5.

488–9   *Be war . . . lustes:* the translator seems to have misunder-stood the L. here (ll. 630–1), which criticizes those who consider that one must avoid excessive asceticism as it leads to sickness which then demands a milder regime which in its turn leads to sensual in-dulgence.

490   *thy stomak waxe drye for abstynence: si torquentur uiscera, si arescit stomachus* (632–3).

494   *custumably vsed to vnclennes in tendir age: in pueritia sua, ui consuetudinis oppressus* (635–6).

495   *and byhelde hou he had mysspended his lyf:* translator's addi-tion.

495–6   *he waxe therby hugely ashamed: supra modum erubuit, et mox concaluit cor eius intra eum, et in meditatione eius exarsit ignis* (636–8).

496–7   *and began . . . abstinence: salubriter irascens sibi, invectione grauissima irruit in seipsum, et bellum indicens corpori* (638–40).

498   *he waxe sad, he spak litel: Successit grauitas leuitati, loquaci-tati silentium* (640–1): DH omit *loquacitati silentium*.

500   *al manere comforte of bodily thinges: temporales consolationes et quidquid carni suaue putabat* (643–4).

502   *so scrupulous in conscience: ita sollicitus et scrupulosus* (646–7); the earliest appearance of *scrupulous* in any sense (in fact in the sense here of 'troubled with scruples of conscience') is dated by *OED* as 1450. All other examples, in any sense, are sixteenth-century or later so it is possible that the form here is a coinage on the part of this translator, taken over directly from the L. Cf. *meridyan*, l. 328, and note.

502–3   *that he had . . . confession:* the corresponding L. here is *ut in hoc solo nimius uideretur* (647), i.e. 'so that in this alone he seemed to be intemperate or excessive'. Aelred is contrasting the man's immoderate indulgence in self-examination and introspection with his exiguous use of food and other physical comforts. The ME bears little if any relation to the L.; possibly the translator found the expression obscure.

505–6   *he was . . . the erthe: demisso uultu oculisque deiectis* (647–8).

507   *Trowist . . . gret eese?:* translator's addition.

509   *an entishynge of his stomak: grauissimum stomachi . . . languorem* (651–2); *entishynge* has two possible explanations; (i) < *entice* < OF *entisier*, ONF *enticher* with its literal sense 'to set on fire' – *entishynge* could then plausibly mean 'inflammation'; (ii) < *enteche* (see *OED* ENTACHE) < OF *entechier*, 'to infect, imbue', therefore meaning 'infection'. The form of the vbl. n. *entysynge* (l. 406) suggests that in this scribal dialect *entice* was adopted from OF rather than from ONF, and as the scribe does not use *s* and *sh* as interchangeable graphies, the second explanation seems the likelier.

510–11   *whan . . . slepe:* a mistranslation of L. which has *cum iam dormitionis eius instaret hora* (652); on the meaning of *dormitio* see n. to Vernon, l. 254.

511   *than wolde he say thus:* there is no justification in the L. for a frequentative verb.

511–12   *Abyde . . . doom:* a considerable expansion of L., which has simply *Sine, inquit, ecce Iesus uenit* (652–3).

513   *for that I wolde destroie thy discrecyon: ut discretioni, quae omnium uirtutum et mater et nutrix est, derogem* (654–5).

513–14   *for I wolde thou fleddist:* L. simply *cohibeamus* (658).
    slouthe: somnum (656).

515   *lechery:* translator's addition.
    familiarite: feminarum et effeminatorum familiaritatem (656–7).
    and suche other: omitting *atque conuictum infra metas necessitatis cohibeamus* (657–8).

516   *vnder colour: falso nomine* (658).

516–18   *If . . . subieccyon:* a considerable expansion of, and hardly an improvement on, the L., *Vera enim discretio est animam carni praeponere* (659–60).

518–19   *and . . . wille:* substituted for *et ubi periclitatur utraque, nec sine huius incommodo illius potest salus consistere, pro illius utilitate istam negligere* (660–2). For a closer translation, cf. Vernon ll. 263–5.

525 *she . . . colour: aret atque marcescit* (665–6). Here *fade* is used transitively in the sense 'cause to fade': see *MED* FADEN *v.*(1), sense 1(c). Possibly *she* could be emended to *he*, though virtues are commonly assigned a feminine gender; the use of *his* may illustrate the tendency of some nouns to become masculine (see Mustanoja, p. 51).

525–6 *Therfor . . . mekenes:* translator's addition.

527–8 *alle gostly begynnynges: quidquid aedificas* (668).

528–9 *Right . . . bifore:* translator's addition.

529–30 *the grounde and the moder:* L. simply *initium* (668), but cf. 654–5.

530 *Lucifer: angelum* (669).

531 *Adam: hominem* (668).

532 *mown be diuyded: diuiduntur* (671).

533–4 *Bodily pride stondith in bostynge and veyn-glory of outwarde bodily thinges: Carnalis superbia est de carnalibus . . . . Carnalis praeterea in duas subdiuiditur species, iactantiam scilicet et uanitatem* (672–5).

536 *Cristys mayde: ancilla Christi* (675); therefore *mayde* here has the sense 'handmaid, servant' rather than 'virgin'.

537 *of eny array:* not in L.

of tyre: there is no obvious authority in L. for this phrase. The manuscript reading *tyme* makes no sense here and the most plausible emendation (though it is really impossible to know what the original translator had in mind) is *tyre* < ME *tire*, 'garments, especially head-coverings.'

537–8 *of beute, of shap of body, of semelyheed:* a very summary translation of ll. 576–9; cf Vernon ll. 281–6.

538 *dyuerse ornamentes of thy selle, of clothes, of peyntures or of ymages and suche othir: in affectata aliqua pulchritudine etiam intra cellulam delectari, parietes uariis picturis uel caelaturis ornare, oratorium pannorum et imaginum uarietate decorare* (680–3); cf. Vernon ll. 287–8.

539–40 *thou offendist thy lorde and thy special louyer in pride of outward thinges:* not in L., which has *Haec omnia, quasi professioni tuae contraria caue* (683).

540–4 *If thou haue . . . inward thinges:* translator's addition; no doubt he felt that Aelred's promised consideration of spiritual and carnal pride had been left incomplete.

544–5   *Oure Lord whom thou louest so specialy:* not in L., and omitting *Qua enim fronte de diuitiis uel natalibus gloriaris quae illius uis sponsa uideri* (684–5).

545–6   *whan he cam in-to this worlde:* translator's addition.

   he made hym poure to make the riche: pauper factus cum esset diues (685), but the translator had in mind II Cor. 8: 9: *quoniam propter uos egenus factus est, cum esset diues, ut illius inopia uos diuites essetis.*

547–8   *in stede of a ryal bedde:* translator's addition.

549–51   *Loue him therfor . . . if thou may:* this passage has a very tenuous connection with the L. (ll. 687–90); cf. Vernon ll. 294–301 for a closer rendering.

551–2   *if thou be ioyful: Si gloriaris* (691); ME *joien* can mean 'to glory in, boast' (*MED* sv 5(a)) as it does here.

   with-in-forthe: omitting ll. 692–6 of L.; cf. Vernon ll. 302–9.

552–3   *for þe prophete saith thus:* not in L.; the 'prophet' is, of course, the psalmist (see next note); cf. l. 124.

   Omnis . . . varietatibus: Psalm 44: 14–15.

556   *and there may she here hir fader speke: Si tu iam filia regis es, utpote Filii Regis sponsa, Patrisque uocem audisti dicentis* (698–9) – a slight mistranslation. Cf. Vernon ll. 311–15 and note to l. 314.

557–8   *et obliuiscere . . . decorem tuum:* not in L. but a continuation of the quotation from Psalm 44: 11–12.

560–3   *To listne . . . for his sone:* this passage has no authority in the L. and is a completely new thought introduced by the translator.

564–5   *this ioye shuld be thy gardeyn, thyn orcharde and thy disport:* translator's addition. Dictionaries of English do not record a metaphorical use of *orchard* to mean 'spiritually fruitful garden' or 'place of recreation', but this is surely the meaning here. The word is used similarly in *The Orcherd of Syon*, ed. cit., e.g. p. 1/12–22: 'Þis book of reuelaciouns as for ʒoure goostly cumfort to ʒou I clepe it a fruytful orchard . . . . In þis orchard, whanne ʒe wolen be conforted, ʒe mowe walke and se boþe fruyt and herbis . . . . in þis goostli orcherd at resonable tyme ordeyned, I wole þat ʒe disporte ʒou. . . .' If the expression were peculiar to Bridgettine circles, this addition would strengthen the case for the Syon connections of this text. See also Intro. p. xxxi and note to l. 274–5.

568   *she that is fair ynowgh in hir owen kynde:* a mistranslation of *qui in sui natura minus lucet* (704), i.e. 'the one that shines less brightly in its own nature'.

571   *lighter: lucidius* (706).

572   *myldenes: modestiam* (708).

573   *thy gostly eye: tuae mentis oculos* (708–9).

575–6   *the whiche thy lord Iesu hath ordeyned for þe:* not in L. which has *in qua te Sponsus cum summa delectatione conspiciat* (710–11).

580   *not in outwarde thinges: non foris, in ueris uirtutibus, non in picturis et imaginibus* (714–15).

585–6   *hou flexe . . . maad white: quo labore, quibus tunsionibus terrenum in quo creuit linum colorem exuerit* (718–19).

586–8   *as with dyuerse . . . fire and water:* this summarizes the description of the preparation of flax which in the L. fills ll. 723–45. See Vernon ll. 344–76 for a close translation, and the note to l. 342 on Aelred's sources here.

589   *that cam oute of the erthe:* L. adds *quoniam in iniquitatibus conceptus sum et in peccatis concepit me mater mea* (721–2).

590   *by baptem: in aquis baptismatis Christo consepelimur* (723–4).

592   *for cause . . . in vs: pro naturali, quae restat, corruptione* (726–7).

596–8   *and so . . . beren aboute:* a condensation of ll. 733–9; cf. Vernon ll. 360–7.

597   *foule rust of synne:* the metaphorical use of *rust* in connection with sin is very common. It seems likely that the original meaning of *rust* in such a context was not 'corroded metal' but referred to a disease in plants which causes their leaves to be marked with rusty spots.

599   *an hyer grace of . . . chastite: refrigerium castitatis* (744–5).

600–1   *Thus . . . thyn oratorye:* not in L., which has *Haec tibi oratorii tui ornamenta repraesentent, non oculos tuos ineptis uarietatibus pascant* (746–7).

602   *an ymage of Cristis passion: Saluatoris in cruce pendentis imago, quae passionem suam tibi repraesentet quam imiteris* (748–9). A crucifix was specifically permitted to Cistercians; see *Cistercian Institutes* XX in I.Turk, *Cistercii Statuta Antiquissima* (Rome, 1949).

603–4   *to resceyue . . . axe it:* tenuously connected with the L., *ad suos te inuitet amplexus, in quibus delecteris, nudatis uberibus lac tibi suauitatis infundat quo consoleris* (750–2). For a closer translation see Vernon ll. 380–3.

606   *for commendacyon of moor chastite: ad commendandam tibi uirginitatis excellentiam* (753–4).

608   *the whiche he halowed in oure Lady and Seint Iohn:* little sense if any can be made of MS *ended*. The L. here reads *quam . . . consecrauit* (756–7), 'which he sanctified'; *halowed* is offered to render this sense (cf. its use at 383 where it translates *sanctificata*). The most

probable explanation for the MS reading is that the translator read
confec^t (*confecit* < L *conficere*) for *confec^at* (*consecrauit*) in his
exemplar, could make no sense of it, and was reduced to the desperate
remedy of translating it literally.

Beholde: omitting ll. 757–9 of L.

609   *helper of mankynde: totius humani generis decus, spes mundi*
(760).

610   *refute of wrecches . . . disperate: miserorum refugium, afflictor-*
um solatium, pauperum consolatio, desperatorum erectio, peccatorum
reconciliatio (761–2); NRTU omit the last two phrases.

612–13   *And than . . . oure Lorde himself:* substituted for ll. 765–9 of
the L.; cf. Vernon ll. 397–401 and note to l. 399.

616–17   *whiche is the hemme and the ende of al the lawe, as I haue*
saide before: quasi spiritalis ornatus finis et fimbria (772).

618   *a motley cote: Vestis . . . ex uirtutum uarietate contexta* (773).

619   *the whiche shuld be a maydens cote:* translator's addition.

619–20   *vmbigoon with diuersitees of vertues, annexed to the whiche*
the hemme of charite: id est caritatis splendoribus ambiatur, quae
omnes uirtutes contineat, et constringat in unum et suam singulis
claritatem impertiens, de multis unum faciat, et cum multis uni
adhaereat, ut iam omnia non sint multa, sed unum (774–8); for a
more literal translation see Vernon ll. 408–13.

622–3   *in good wille and in innocence: in innocentiam et*
beneficentiam (780–1).

625   *doon to the:* omits *quantum ad te duo ista pertineant, diligenter*
aduerte (786).

626   *The first: Secundum illud, non erit difficile* (789), as the translator has reversed Aelred's order (see note to ll. 622–3), and has also
omitted *non*.

626–7   *sith thy profession wolde that thou sholdist noo temperal good*
haue: si propositum attendas tuum, si professam dilexeris nuditatem
(789–90).

nay, is it not so: translator's addition.

627–8   *The seconde the semeth is light ynowgh: Primum illud facile*
tibi (788).

629   *Certeyn the first is as light as thys:* translator's addition.

629–30   *matere . . . of yuel wille:* a literal translation of *malae uolun-*
tatis materia (791).

wher no couetise is: ubi cupiditas nulla, ubi nihil diligitur quod
possit auferri, nihil tollitur quod debeat amari (791–3).

633   *Thou seist wel, good suster:* translator's addition.

634   *Ther wern too sustirs:* see note to Vernon l. 435.

634–5   *as the gospel tellith:* translator's addition.

637–8   *in resceyuynge of pore gestes:* a combination of *suscipiendis hospitibus* (801) and *non pauperum clamoribus intenta* (802).

640   *to the worlde:* omitting ll. 805–7 of L.; cf. Vernon ll. 442–3.

641   *Martha was commended as for good occupacion:* a more positive statement than the L. *Exequatur partem suam Martha, quae licet non negetur bona* (807–8); cf. Vernon ll. 445–6. (MS D reads *exequitur.*)

644–5   *good comoun lyuers of the worlde: optimae . . . in saeculo* (810). Aelred probably means women of high rank in the world (see note to Vernon l. 449), but the ME means 'those who live vertuously in the world, virtuous members of the laity'.

  thei . . . grucchen: all MSS here read *aemulentur* (subj. of L. *aemulare*) except MS D which has the ind. *aemulantur.*

646   *almes that shuld be youen: eleemosynarum largitio* (812); *almes* is clearly still apprehended as a singular noun.

647   *godes* is here used as a singular collective noun.

648   *to holy chirche: sacrosanctis ecclesiis* (814).

648–9   *the mynistres that han it to kepe: episcopi, sacerdotes et clerici* (815).

649   *shulde departe it:* omitting *non recondenda, nec possidenda, sed eroganda. Quidquid habent pauperum est* (816–17).

650–1   *and also to hem that seruen in holy chirche: et eorum qui altario deseruiunt, ut de altario uiuant* (818).

652–3   *it is committed . . . to dispende:* this is probably an impersonal verb phrase translating *dispensari oportet* (820) rather than governed by 'godes'.

  of the saam house: translator's addition.

653   *shuld be shitte in hucches:* the L. says the opposite: *non includatur marsupiis* (821).

654   *to poure folke: hospitibus, peregrinis atque pauperibus* (821–2).

654–5   *Alle this peple representen þe staat of Martha: Et hoc illorum interest, quibus pars est Marthae commissa, non qui salutari otio uacant cum Maria* (822–4). *peple*, plural in sense, is treated as formally singular in *alle this peple* but as plural in governing *representen*. The sense of *representen* here seems to be 'serve as a visible or concrete embodiment' (see *OED* REPRESENT, 6), a meaning first recorded from Wycliffe c. 1380. Another sense (*OED* 8) 'act for another by deputed right', is attractive, but the word was not used to mean this before 1809.

656   *han not to do with this:* a summary of ll. 824–7; cf. Vernon ll. 469–72.

656–7   *þei shulden norisshe her affeccions with blessed idelnes:* not in L., which has *Nutriantur potius in croceis* (827).

657–8   *gostly delytes:* here are omitted ll. 828–38 of L.; cf. Vernon ll. 474–89 for a close translation of the missing passage.

   cloistrers: illis qui in coenobiis sunt, quibus cum Martha non parua communio est (838–9).

659–60   *that vtterly hast forsake al worldly besynesse:* a condensation of *quae totam te saeculo exuisti, cui non solum non possidere, sed nec uidere, nec audire licet quae saeculi sunt* (840–2).

   and art called a recluse: not in L.; omits *Cum enim nihil tibi quisquam det ad erogandum, unde habebis quod eroges?* (842–3).

661   *dele it:* omits *non tua, sed alterius manu. Si aliunde tibi prouenit uictus, unde tibi aliena distribuere, cum nihil supra necessarium tibi liceat usurpare?* (844–6); cf. Vernon ll. 496–500.

662–3   *Yhe . . . sight of God:* not in L., which has *Quid igitur beneficii impendes proximo?* (847).

   a gode wille . . . bodily yifte: Nihil ditius bona uoluntate, ait quidam sanctus (847–8).

666   *in the bosom of loue and charite: uno dilectionis sinu* (850).

666–7   *whiche thou fyndest good lyuers: qui boni sunt* (851).

668–9   *by wailyng . . . for hem: intuere et luge* (852).

   as pore peple: omits *orphanorum gemitus* (854).

670   *destitucion of widowes: uiduarum desolatio* (854). The earliest example given by *MED* of *destitution* in the sense of 'deprivation, loss' is dated *c.* 1425.

   desperat soules: tristium maestitudo (854).

672   *laboures of tilyenge peple:* the L., *labor militantium* (857) can only mean 'the labours of those who fight'. For *tilyenge* see *OED* TIL (<OE *tilian*). The-*i*-element, which is clearly attested here by the *-enge* spelling for the pr. p. (see note to l. 51) is preserved in some forms of the verb in ME; *OED* records *tilly* as a fourteenth-century spelling. The sense here is presumably that of 'labouring, toiling'. Possibly the translator misread the L. phrase as *laborantium*.

673   *charite:* omitting *his tuas impende lacrymas, pro his tuas preces effundas* (858–9).

675   *most spedful and profitable: fructuosior* (861).

676   *purpos:* omitting ll. 862–4; cf. Vernon ll. 521–4.

   as Seynt Gregory seith: a misunderstanding of ll. 867–72, which are also misunderstood in Vernon; see note there to l. 525.

685   *hou thou shalt loue him:* translator's expansion; omits ll. 875–7 of the L.; cf. Vernon ll. 534–9.

686   *desire . . . body: affectus mentis et effectus operis* (878–9); the translator apparently read *operis* as *corporis*.

687–8   *vertuous worchinge of the body: Exercitatio uirtutum* (880).

689   *in silence: in silentio* (882); this phrase is omitted by NUT.

692   *thre thinges the nedeth to haue in mynde: triplici meditatione opus habes* (884–5).

695   *thy soule: mens tua* (888).

696   *than:* omitting *iam oculos defaecatos ad posteriora retorque* (889–90).

697   *praide deuoutly vnto the tyme the aungel grette hir:* translator's addition.

702   *Al-though thow be astonyed of this seconde comynge: et sic repleta stupore et extasi* (893–4).

705–6   *what fulnes of grace this might be, of the whiche al the worlde is fulfilled: quae sit haec gratiae plenitudo, de qua totus mundus gratiam mutuauit quando Verbum caro factum est et habitauit in nobis, plenum gratiae et ueritatis* (896–9); for a closer rendering see Vernon ll. 563–6.

707   *what lord this myght be: Dominum qui terram implet et caelum* (899–900).

707–8   *a maydens wombe:* L. adds *quam Pater santificauit, Filius fecundauit, obumbrauit Spiritus Sanctus* (901–2).

709   *that thou were fulfilled with: inebriabaris* (903).

710–1   *whan a blessed lord chees a bodily substaunce, verray blode and flesshe of thy body: cum de tua carne sibi carnem assumeret, et membra in quibus corporaliter omnis plenitudo diuinitatis habitaret, de tuis sibi membris aptaret* (905–7); cf. Vernon ll. 574–6.

712   *in thy blessed wombe: in mente et in uentre* (904).

713   *This shuld be a maydens meditacion:* not in L., but substituted for ll. 908–9; cf. Vernon ll. 576–9.

714   *the gretynge bitwene hir and Elizabeth: et sterilis et uirginis suauem intuere complexum, et salutationis officium* (911–2).

715–16   *where also the seruaunt knewe his lorde and with passynge ioye dide him reuerence: in quo seruulus dominum, praeco iudicem, uox uerbum . . . agnouit, et indicibili gaudio salutauit* (912–4); cf. Vernon ll. 583–5 and note to l. 583.

718   *wombe:* L. adds ll. 914–6; cf. Vernon ll. 585–8.

718–19   *wurshipe thy lorde and thyn husbonde: tuum Sponsum amplectere* (919).

719–20   *beholde louely thy frende: amicum uero eius . . . uenerare*
(919–20). Aelred has in mind 'his (i.e. Christ's) friend' but this
may be a deliberate change on the part of the ME translator, as Carthusians regarded themselves as particularly under the protection
of St John the Baptist, who was patron saint of hermits. *louely*
presumably = 'lowly' rather than 'lovely' here as it helps render
uenerare.

722   *and whan thou comest there:* not in L., which has *et in hospi-
tium diuertens* (922).

723   *and than:* omitting *locatoque in praesepi paruulo* (923).

725–6   *Leeue not . . . he lay in: Amplectere dulce illud praesepium*
(925).

727   *with loue:* L. adds *ut sacratissimis pedibus figas labia, et oscula
gemines* (926–7).

729   *put the boldely in prees: tuas interpone partes* (929).

733   *but folewe . . . yeue the:* not in L. The translation here omits the
whole story of the encounter with the Good Thief on the Flight into
Egypt (ll. 932–51 of the L.; cf. Vernon ll. 612–36).

734–5   *hou he . . . norisshe Ioseph: puerum inter pueros . . . obsequen-
tem matri . . . operanti nutricio assistentem* (953–4).

736–7   *sittynge . . . questions:* not in L. The translator has substituted a reference to the actual Finding in the Temple for Aelred's
emphasis on Mary's search (ll. 957–8).

739–40   *Fili . . . querebamus te:* Luke 2: 48.

742   *Wilt thov yit se pryuyer thynges: Si autem Virginem sequi
quocumque ierit delectet, altiora eius et secretiora scrutare* (962–3),
a reference to Rev. 14: 4.

742–3   *to the place wher he was baptised: in Iordane flumine* (963).

745   *Folewe yit . . . Architriclyne:* not in L., which refers only to
spirituales . . . nuptias (965); cf. Vernon ll. 656–9. The reference at
l. 746 to the miracle at Cana and its allegorization are the translator's own additions.

749   *Yit:* the translator has here omitted Aelred's reference to the
Temptation in the Wilderness (ll. 968–71 of the L., translated in
Vernon ll. 659–64).

749–50   *what Iesu . . . of auoutrye:* a summary of ll. 972–7, more
literally translated in Vernon ll. 665–71.

752   *whan he had a-shamed hir accusours:* not in L.

753   *Nemo . . . condempnabo:* John 8: 10–11. At this point the
translator omits ll. 982–5; cf. Vernon ll. 675–8.

756–7   *Praye him . . . his blessed voys: Audiatur tamen de caetero uox tua* (985).

though thou be vnworthy: translator's addition.

760   *Mary Magdalen:* translator's addition: on the identification of the Blessed Sinner with Mary Magdalene see note to Vernon l. 686.

761   *wassh Iesus feet:* MS *wasshith* is not impossible but generally this translator (unlike that of the Vernon version) is quite consistent in his use of tenses. He uses the preterite here when he is describing the historical events as given in Holy Scripture, and the present when describing how the recluse is to take her own part in them. So here pr. *wasshith* has been emended to the strong form of the pa.t., which prevailed until the close of the sixteenth century (see *OED* WASH) to bring it into line with *dried* and *kissed* (ll. 761, 762).

762–3   *an holy oynement:* L. adds *Nonne iam sacri illius liquoris odore perfunderis?* (990–1).

764   *go . . . praier: insta, ora* (992).

765   *beholdynge hym . . . weylinge: grauidos lacrymis oculos attolle, imisque suspiriis inenarrabilibusque gemitibus* (992–4).

766   *as Iacob dide:* Gen. 32: 24.

768–9   *praye . . . loue: insta oportune, importune, clama* (997), omitting ll. 998–1001; cf. Vernon ll. 699–702.

775   *and yaf him therto helthe of soule:* L. adds *quam non petebat, quam non praecesserat confessio, non meruerat satisfactio, non exigebat contritio* (1007–8).

777   *ryse and goo:* translator's addition; he here omits ll. 1010–1016; cf. Vernon ll. 738–40.

Now lyfte vp thin hondes: clearly a word has been omitted here and though one cannot say conclusively what was intended, *hondes* aligns the ME with the L. here, *Leuentur purae manus in oratione* (1016–17). The following ll. 1017–20 are omitted.

777–8   *and pray . . . thy synnes:* not in the L.; the translator here omits a considerable passage, ll. 1021–28; for this see Vernon ll. 721–38.

781–2   *were knytte . . . Lazarus: auctoritate Domini consecrantur* (1030–31).

783   *Lazar:* omitting *Quod ob specialis amicitiae priuilegium qua illi familiariori adhaerebant affectu dictum, nemo qui ambigat* (1032–3); cf. Vernon ll. 744–5.

783–4   *that he wepte for hym:* omitting *quas totus populus amoris interpretabatur indicium, 'Vide,' inquiens, 'quomodo amabat eum'* (1035–6).

784–5 *what was doon . . . atte soper: faciunt ei coenam ibi* (1037).

786 *Art thou . . . thys?:* not in L., omits ll. 1037–42; cf. Vernon ll. 751–4.

790–1 *Though the pharise grucche with the: Pharisaeus murmurat* (1050); the translation omits Aelred's reference to Judas' complaint (ll. 1047–50).

791–2 *charge it not, for Iesu will excuse the:* a summary translation of *Sed iudex accusationem non recepit, accusatam absoluit. 'Sine,' inquit, 'illam, bonum enim opus operata est in me.'* (1051–3).

793–4 *Leeue not this blessed idelnes for Marthays besynesse, for treuly thou hast chose the best partye:* not in L.; the ME translator has here omitted ll. 1053–60; cf. Vernon ll. 773–81. *Marthays:* the possessive form has been formed by adding the *-ys* possessive ending (cf. *Cristys, Cristis*) to *Martha.*

794 *the best partye:* a reference to Luke 10: 42: *Maria optimam partem elegit, quae non auferetur ab ea.*

795 *in-to Ierusalem:* translator's addition.

796 *hym:* L. adds *caelique terraeque Dominum* (1062).

towarde hys passyon: not in L; omits ll. 1062–5; cf. Vernon ll. 784–8.

797 *in-to the hous where he made a soper to his disciples:* not in L.; omits *in coenaculum grande stratum, et salutaris coenae interesse delicis gratulare* (1066–7); cf. Vernon ll. 788–91.

798–9 *Be not ashamed, al-though thou be a womman, to come amonge men:* translator's addition.

let loue put away shame: Vincat uerecundiam amor, timorem excludat affectus, ut saltem de micis mensae illius eleemosynam praebeat mendicanti (1067–9); cf. Vernon ll. 791–3.

799–800 *as a pore womman and axe som almes with wepyng teres: quasi pauper intendens in diuitem, ut aliquid accipias extende manum, famem lacrymis prode* (1070–1).

801 *Loke vp now:* the translator has here omitted Aelred's account of Christ's washing his disciples' feet (ll. 1072–77); cf. Vernon ll. 797–801.

801–2 *leieth . . . Cristys lappe: supra pectus eius recumbit, et in sinu eius caput reclinat* (1079–80).

804 *what deuocion: quid luminis et deuotionis* (1082).

809 *worthier than Iames: caeteris omnibus apostolis gratior* (1086–7).

810 *thou art a mayde:* on the virginity of St John, see note to Vernon l. 817.

811–12   *to norisshe with thy deuocion:* not in L., omitting ll. 1091–4;
cf. Vernon ll. 819–24.

816   *that thou be oon of thoo: ut et tu merearis audire* (1097).

816–17   *O here is good abidynge, ho-so myght tarye: Bonum tibi est
hic esse* (1099).

817–19   *bot thou . . . forsake him not: Praecedit ipse ad montem
Oliueti, tu sequere* (1099–1100).

819   *Iohn and Iames: duobus filiis Zebedaei* (1101).

819–20   *to trete wiþ hem of the counceyle of his passyon: ad secretiora secesserit* (1101–2).

820–1   *yit he forbiddith the not, and thou wilt come:* not in L., the
translator here omits ll. 1102–7; cf Vernon ll. 833–9.

824   *gadere vp clene these swete dropes: suauissimas illas guttas
adlambe* but the very corrupt MS B reads *collige.* The translator
omits *et puluerem pedum illius linge* (1109–10).

824–5   *for certeyn they ben ful preciouse:* translator's addition.

   as Petir did: L. adds *ne merearis audire: 'Sic non potuisti una hora
uigilare mecum?'* (1110–1).

826–7   *with a companye of peple: impiorum turba* (1112).

   to take oure Lord: manus iniciunt in Dominum tuum (1113–4).

827–8   *they bynden . . . ful soor:* the whole passage is in the historic
present in L.: *tenent, ligant, et illas dulces manus uinculis stringunt*
(1114–5). The apparent preterite *streyned* may be an isolated example of the phenomenon of *-ed* for the pr. 3sg. and pl. ending *-eth*
which occurs in the Vernon text (see Intro., p. xlvii), although *-eth* is
far less common than *-en* as the 3pl. ending in the Bodley text.

829–30   *with pyte:* omits *omnia uiscera tua zelus inflammat* (1116).

   I holde it no wonder, yit suffir a while and thou shalt se moor: not in
L.; the translator here omits ll. 1116–20; cf. Vernon ll. 854–62.

831–2   *beholde hou vnkyndely they ferden with him:* substituted for
speciosissimam eius faciem, quam illi sputis illiniunt, tu lacrymis laua
(1122–3).

834   *wepynge bitterly for sorwe: quando ille conuersus, et in se
reuersus, fleuit amare* (1124–5).

838–9   *Beholde now and se hou he stondeth as a meke lombe before
the iuge: Sed iam mane facto traditur Pilato. Ibi accusatur et tacet,
quoniam tanquam ouis ad occisionem ducitur, et sicut agnus coram
tondente se, non aperuit os suum* (1129–31).

840   *Se than:* omits *Scio non potes ulterius sustinere, nec dulcissimum dorsum eius flagellis atteri* (1135–6).

841–2 *and his hondes despitously bounden with bondes:* dexteram quae caelum fecit et terram arundine dehonestari (1137–8); for a closer translation of the whole passage see Vernon ll. 877–85.

842–3 *natheles yit loke vp with thyn wepynge eyen:* translator's addition.

843–4 *and beholde hou he berith his cros to his passyon with a clothe of purpure arrayed:* Ecce educitur flagellatus, portans spineam coronam et purpuream uestimentum (1139–40).

844–5 *cleuynge ful sore to his forbeten woundes:* translator's addition. The suffering Christ underwent when stripped of his garments was a popular theme among medieval devotional writers.

846 *Now:* the translator has here omitted a lengthy passage of L. (ll. 1140–56) which is translated in part by Vernon ll. 888–910.

847 *bytwene too theues:* omits Mediator Dei et hominum inter caelum et terram medius pendens, ima superis unit, et caelestibus terrena coniungit (1157–9).

848–9 *I trowe . . . be sory:* Non mirum si sole contristante, tu contristaris, si terra tremiscente, tu contremiscis (1161–2).

850 *beside his passyon:* iuxta crucem (1163).

851–2 *haue mynde . . . for wronge:* considera illud dulcissimum pectus, quam tranquillitatem seruauerit, quam exhibuerit pietatem. Non suam attendit iniuriam, non poenam reputat, non sentit contumelias, sed illis potius a quibus patitur, ille compatitur (1165–8); for a closer translation cf. Vernon ll. 920–6.

856–8 *Falle down . . . trespas:* tenuously connected with the L., ll. 1170–77; cf. Vernon ll. 933–41.

856 *beseche him:* MS before seche him is clearly wrong. Possible emendations are: (i) *and before him seche him;* (ii) *and forebeseche him;* (iii) *and beseche him.* (iii) has been chosen as it is the simplest, but (ii) is in some ways attractive. *forbeseche* is not recorded in dictionaries of English but is a possible formation from beseech preceded by the intensive *for-,* and elsewhere this scribe transposes syllables (*selden* for *sendel,* l. 877).

859 *Seest thou:* translator's addition; omitting ll. 1178–81 of L.; cf. Vernon ll. 942–6.

859–60 *What eyleth . . . wepe?:* Tu sine lacrymis, amantissimae dominae tuae lacrymas uidebis? (1181–2).

862 *wiþ-oute snobbynge:* omits et Iohanni: 'Ecce mater tua', cum discipulo matrem committeret, latroni paradisum promitteret (1184–6); the Vernon version, far from omitting this passage, expands it considerably.

862–3 *An harde . . . now:* translator's addition, omitting ll. 1187–90 (the piercing of Christ's side; cf. Vernon ll. 960–4).

863–4 *Crepe . . . cam forthe:* tenuously connected with *Facta sunt tibi in petra flumina, in membris eius uulnera, et in maceria corporis eius cauerna* (1191–2).

865 *wel likynge . . . blood: deosculans singula* (1193).

865–6 *til that thy lippes be maad like to a reed scarlet hood: ex sanguine eius fiant sicut uitta coccinea labia tua, et eloquium tuum dulce* (1193–4). The reference is to Cant. 4: 3. *hood* is just possible as a translation of L. *uitta*, 'fillet, head-band', but the translator can hardly have made any attempt to conceive the image in visual terms.

867–8 *wher . . . Armathye?: nobilis iste decurio ueniens* (1195). There is no biblical authority for the statement that Joseph was an old man, but this was perhaps deduced from the fact that he had a tomb prepared for himself.

868–9 *Stonde . . . wil do:* translator's addition.

Als sone as he cometh: translator's addition.

870–1 *byclippeth . . . burye it: felicissimis brachiis dulce illud corpus complectitur, ac suo astringit pectori* (1197–8).

he: uir ille sanctissimus (1198).

as I fynde in a boke of loue: translator's addition. *The book of love* is a common ME periphrasis for the Song of Songs.

872 *Fasciculus . . . mihi:* Cant. 1: 12.

874–5 *or elles . . . by the way:* the translator seems to have misunderstood the L., *defluentes minutatim preciosissimi sanguinis stillas curiosius collige* (1202–3), where *minutatim* is an adv. ('dropping one by one') not an adj. (the translator seems to have taken it as *minutas* from L. *minutus*, 'small').

876 *thay:* L. has only *beatissimus Nicodemus* (1204), but the translator has in mind Joseph of Arimathea as well.

877 *sendel:* MS *selden* is not recorded in dictionaries of English. The usual ME translation of *sindon*, the L. here, is *sendel, sendal*; clearly the scribe has transposed the syllables.

878 *Wiltow now do wel:* translator's addition.

879 *ayenst the day of his resurreccyon:* translator's addition, omitting ll. 1208–12 of L.; cf. Vernon ll. 991–7.

880–1 *hou oure Lord . . . hir name: nunc ipsum Iesum Mariam flentem et tristem tam dulci reficientem oculo, tam suaui uoce dicentem* (1212–14).

882 *alle the veynes . . . dissolued: rumpuntur ad hanc uocem omnes capitis cataractae* (1215–16); only MSS DVMB have the indicative

here (and *infra* in ll. 1216–17); the other MSS of the L. read *rumpantur*, etc. See Intro., p. xxxiii. The translator here omits ll. 1217–19; cf. Vernon ll. 1003–6.

886 *thy plenteuous wepynge:* L. simply *lacrymae* (1221).

887 *loue:* L. adds *omnesque animae corporis que sensus nimius amor absorbeat* and ll. 1224–5; cf. Vernon ll. 1010–14.

888 *an harde worde and an vntolerable: O uerbum durum, uerbum intolerabile* (1226).

889 *Certys:* omitting ll. 1226–9 of L.; cf. Vernon ll. 1017–22.

889–91 *yit . . . touched hym:* suggested by *non dimittam te, non recedam a te, non parcam lacrymis, pectus singultibus suspiriisque rumpetur, nisi tangam* (1230–1). A more literal translation may be found at Vernon ll. 1022–4.

891–4 *Gode suster . . . right wel:* translator's addition. It suggests that the recluse should emulate Mary Magdalene rather than completely identify with her, which is the implication of Aelred's description of the events of Easter morning.

895–6 *Here . . . 'Touche me not':* translator's addition and summary.

896–7 *though . . . fro the: non aufertur tibi bonum hoc, sed differtur* (1232–3). The referent of *hem* is far from clear. The nearest pl. n. which is a possible candidate is *feet* in l. 902 and though this would seem to give a plausible meaning to the passage it is strange not to find a possible referent in the preceding lines.

898 *and than come ayen:* MS D here reads *Redi*, all other MSS *Redit* (1234).

899 *Now . . . come ayen: Currit cito, cito uolens redire* (1234).

899–900 *hir erande was sone doo:* translator's addition.

901 *of his curtesy: blanda salutatione* (1235).

902 *Than . . . feet:* not in L., which has simply *Tunc est datum, quod fuit ante dilatum* (1236–7), but 896–7 shows that the translator has absorbed the L. here (see note).

902–3 *Accesserunt et tenuerunt eum:* Matthew 28: 9.

904–5 *and fede thy soule with these delicious meditacions:* not in L., which has *Non has delicias tuas somnus interpolet, nullus exterior tumultus impediat* (1238–9); cf. Vernon ll. 1039–40.

907 *The seconde meditacion:* the translator has omitted ll. 1240–48 of L.; cf. Vernon ll. 1040–50.

909 *forshape or deed in the moder wombe: qui uel abortiui proiecti sunt ab utero, uel qui inter materna uiscera suffocati, poenae uidentur concepti non uitae* (1248–50).

911   *meschefs:* L. adds *ne essemus nostris dolori, opprobrio alienis* (1251–3).

Whethir . . . God?: Magnum certe et hoc (1253).

912–4   *Another . . . holy chirche: Sed quomodo illud quantae bonitatis fuerit aestimabimus, quod eo tempore, et inter tales nos nasci uoluit, per quos ad fidem suam et sacramenta perueniremus?* (1253–6).

918   *he kepith . . . this day:* summarizes ll. 1260–3; for a more literal translation cf. Vernon ll. 1067–71.

919   *feith of holy chirche:* the translator here omits ll. 1265–1353 of L., a long autobiographical passage in which Aelred describes his debauched youth and contrasts it with the story of his sister's soul. None of the extant L. MSS omits the passage, which may be found translated in full in the Vernon version, ll. 1072–1200.

919–20   *And . . . amende vs:* the sentence, the translator's own addition, in fact effectively summarizes the theme of the passage he has just omitted (see preceding note).

921–2   *and than . . . vpon the: Vilescat tibi mundus, omnis amor carnalis sordescat* (1355). The more usual ME idiom is *stinken to* or *in.* The translator here omits ll. 1355–6 of L.; cf. Vernon ll. 1204–5.

923   *and not in a bagge of golde and seluer: cum argenteis simulacris uili marsupio* (1358–9).

925   *or eue:* translator's addition.

926–7   *Be not aferde . . . colde: non te futuri temporis sterilitas terreat, non futurae famis timor tuam mentem deiciat* (1362–3).

928–9   *thy whicche: apotheca* (1364), which probably here actually means 'storeroom'.

thy wurship: at this point in the L., BM add *ipse honor tuus;* V *ipse hort=iuis* (?).

929–30   *and al that thou nedyst: solus sit tibi omnia in omnibus* (1365–6).

932–4   *The thridde . . . dye:* this passage has been provided by the translator, who has omitted ll. 1368–86 of L., translated in Vernon ll. 1224–50.

934   *For a blessed deth is the begynnyng of lyf: mors beatitudinis principium est* (1387); the translator has taken *beatitudinis* with *mors* and has therefore been forced to provide his own modifier for *principium*; cf. however the reading of MS D which here has *mors beatitudinis principium est quietis.*

rest and ende of al trauayl: laborum meta (1387–8).

936–7   *Beati . . . suis:* Revelation 14: 13.

940–1   for . . . ioye of conscience: MS *in deth of conscience* hardly makes sense; it is clear from the L., *Dormiunt quippe in gloria quorum mortem bona commendat conscientia* (1394–5) and from ll. 942–3 of the translation, 'They dyen also in ioye of conscience', that the phrase should be 'in ioye of conscience'. One can only suggest that the scribe was distracted by three appearances of *deth, deeth* in so many lines. As we have two more minor slips (at ll. 946 and 948) and probably one major mistake in the next few lines we may reasonably deduce a temporary loss of concentration.

943–4   Rightwyse . . . prayer: occurrunt sancti, et conciui suo praebentes auxilium et impertientes solatium, hostibus se opponunt, obsistentes repellunt, refellunt accusantes (1397–9); for a more literal translation see Vernon ll. 1262–5.

obsequyous: the earliest example of this word given in *OED* is dated *c.* 1450.

945   þer can no tonge telle: quia experientia non docuit, stilus explicare non poterit (1410–1).

946   chosen soules: felices (1411).

947   fulfilled: the translator here omits ll. 1412–3 of L.; cf. Vernon ll. 1286–9.

Wiche folke dyen not thus: MS *whiche folke* would make some sort of sense only if one deleted 'by the whiche' (949), but it is extremely unlikely that a scribe would insert such a phrase accidentally. The L. here (1402) has *Non sic impii non sic*, and what is needed is clearly some form of *wick,* adj. The form *wiche* is suggested, although not recorded by *OED* sv WICK, because /w/ is never spelt *wh* in this text but /k/ sometimes appears as *ch* (cf. *worchinge* 686, *wurcher* 210). However, as *OED* derives *wick* adj. from the OE *wicca, wicce,* sbs., from which we have NE *witch,* and for which it records as forms in ME *wiche, wicche* among others, it is quite possible that the *ch* spelling is etymologically sound.

947–50   but in foule . . . her mede: tenuously connected with L., ll. 1403–7; see Vernon ll. 1268–81 for a closer translation.

951   the dredful day of doom: diei illius . . . quando uirtutes caelorum mouebuntur, elementa ignis calore soluentur, patebunt inferi (1414–16).

952   in his owne kynd: not in L.; the translator here omits ll. 1416–18; cf. Vernon ll. 1294–7.

952–3   he is . . . God: Beatus qui paratus est occurrere illi (1418–19).

954   Ymagyne: the translator has omitted ll. 1419–22 of L.; cf. Vernon ll. 1299–1303.

954–5   *in the doom: ante Christi tribunal* (1423).

958–9   *gnastyng . . . sight: Stant miseri et infelices stridentes dentibus, nudo latere palpitantes, aspectu horribiles, uultu deformes*, omitting *deiecti prae pudore, prae corporis turpitudine et nuditate confusi* (1427–30). For a more literal translation see Vernon ll. 1308–11.

960   *they seen a dredful iuge: desuper iudicis imminet furor* (1431).

960–1   *thei seen the horrible . . . after hem: infernalis putei eis ingeritur horror* (1432); *gapen after* is a ME idiom meaning 'to be greedy for', and when used of Hell means 'be wide open, open up'; the translator seems to have cleverly combined these two ideas in his translation.

961–2   *the rightwyse domesman mown they neither plete ne accuse: Non suppetit criminum excusatio, nec de iniquo iudicio aliqua poterit esse causatio* (1432–4).

for he is rightwys in his domes: cum quidquid decretum fuerit, iustum esse ipsam eorum conscientiam non latebit (1434–5). For a more literal translation of the whole passage, see Vernon ll. 1313–18.

963   *Now:* the translator has omitted ll. 1436–38 of L.; cf. Vernon ll. 1319–22.

964–5   *to the whiche . . . chosen the to:* not in L., which has simply *sit inserturus* (1440), omitting ll. 1440–41; cf. Vernon ll. 1323–5.

969   *oo bonde of chastite and charite: uno caritatis foedere* (1444).

969–70   *and oure Lorde beholdeth eche of hem ful amyable: Lucet eis uultus Iesu, non terribilis, sed amabilis, non amarus, sed dulcis, non terrens, sed blandiens* (1444–46); cf. Vernon ll. 1330–33.

971   *as it were in an vncerteyn: quasi in medio, nesciens* (1447).

972   *O that . . . abidynge: O dura expectatio! Timor et tremor uenerunt super me, et contexerunt me tenebrae* (1448–9).

973   *what drede shaltow than haue:* not in L., which has *non causabor iniustum* (1449–50).

974   *what ioye shaltow than haue:* not in L., which has *gratiae eius hoc, non meis meritis imputandum* (1450–51). For a closer translation see Vernon ll. 1339–41. The effect of the translator's changes is to play down Aelred's uncompromisingly Augustinian emphasis on the necessity of divine grace for salvation. At this point are omitted ll. 1452–62 of L., translated in Vernon ll. 1341–58.

975–6   *Whan . . . and se:* not in L., which has *Sublatis uero impiis ne uideant gloriam Dei, iustis quoque singulis secundum gradum suum et meritum angelicis ordinibus insertis* (1463–5); cf. Vernon ll. 1359–61.

976–7 *what a fair . . . court of heuen: fiet illa gloriosa processio, Christo praecedente capite nostro, omnibus suis membris sequentibus* (1465–6); cf. Vernon ll. 1361–4.

977–8 *after her meryt resceyuynge her heritage: et tradetur regnum Deo et Patri ut ipse regnet in ipsis, et ipsi regnent cum ipso, illud percipientes regnum* (1466–68); cf. Vernon ll. 1364–6.

979–80 *whiche ioye . . . thenke: Cuius regni status nec cogitari quidem potest a nobis, multo minus dici uel scribi* (1470–71).

982 *absent:* omitting ll. 1472–98 of L., of which a somewhat abbreviated version is given in Vernon, ll. 1370–80.

986 *without besynes: sine sollicitudine* (1500–1).

986–7 *yeuyng . . . neden: impertiens se et quodammodo dispertiens singulis pro sua capacitate* (1501–2).

988 *departyng:* omitting ll. 1503–7 of L.; cf. Vernon ll. 1386–91.

990–1 *Qui . . . meipsum:* John 14: 21.

992–3 *Of this loue . . . knowlache: Ex hac uisione illa procedet cognitio* (1510–1).

994–5 *Hec . . . Iesum Christum:* John 17: 3.

998–9 *suche swetnes and charite: tanta dulcedo caritatis* (1514).

1000–1 *What . . . tonge telle: quod oculus non uidit, nec auris audiuit, nec in cor hominis ascendit, quae praeparauit Deus diligentibus se* (1516–18), a reference to I Corinthians 2: 9.

MS VERNON

3 *Nou let heere here: Sed iam nunc audiat et intelligat uerba mea* (439), probably a deliberate reminiscence of the opening words of the Benedictine Rule, *Ausculta, o fili, praecepta magistri,* which in its turn recalls Proverbs 4: 20, *Fili mi, ausculta sermones meos* and Psalm 44: 11, *Audi, filia, et vide, et inclina aurem tuam.*

heere: almost certainly the oblique form of the feminine pronoun. The usual spelling in this text is *here* but *heere* is recorded elsewhere in *OED* from the fifteenth century. Possibly *heere* = 'hear' (as in ll. 995, 1412); the least likely interpretation is as 'here' which in this text always appears as *hir, hier(e.*

5 *as a deed body: quasi mortua* (441).

9 *Virgo prudens . . . A wys mayden:* the L. (all MSS), following the Vulgate text (I Cor. 7: 34) has simply *uirgo;* the translator was probably influenced by Matt. 25: 4 and the parable of the Wise Virgins to make this addition.

10 *þynges þat beþ to Godward*: L. *quae sunt Dei* (444–5).

11 *hou þat heo may plese God, þat heo be holi in body and in soule:*
cf. I Cor. 7:34 and 32.

11–12 *Þys vertu, þat is to seye of maydenhood or chastite:* translator's addition.

13 *an offryngge to God vre and liberal: oblatio spontanea* (446).

15 *Qui potest capere, capiat:* Matt. 19: 12.

19–20 *wyt most tenty preyere besechyngge:* cf. Benedictine Rule,
Prologue, 41.

22 *hou freel a vessel:* cf. II Cor. 4: 7.

23 *blysse:* here, and frequently elsewhere, *blysse* translates L.
gloria, in the sense 'glory' (cf. *MED*, sv BLISSE *sb.*, 4).

30 *Wherfore . . . swete sauour: Itaque nardus uirginitatis tuae
etiam in caelestibus dans odorem suum* (463–4), which alludes to
Cant. 1:11, *Nardus mea dedit odorem suum.*

30–1 *smytyngge is swete sauour: dans odorem suum* (464). The
sense of *smytyngge* here appears to be 'sending, causing to penetrate
into', which is not recorded elsewhere. However, an intransitive
sense, 'to shoot or move rapidly, dart, rush' is evidenced from the
thirteenth to the fifteenth centuries (cf. *OED*, sv SMITE *v.* 24), and
the example here could plausibly be regarded as the causative version
of this. It is also possible that the translator was still thinking of nard,
which is essentially an ointment, and was using *smite* in the sense 'to
smear (a substance) on something' (cf. *OED*, *loc. cit.*, 2).

34 *he is fair in schap:* cf. Ps. 44: 3.

  before alle þat euere were born: L. *prae filiis hominum* (467).

34–5 *fayrere þen þe sunne . . .:* cf. Wisdom 7: 29.

35 *wit-outen mesure:* translator's addition.

35–6 *His breþ is swettere þan eny hony . . .:* cf. Eccli. 24: 27.

37–8 *Longitudo dierum . . . gloria:* Prov. 3: 16.

40 *he nel not corounne þe er þu be asaid:* cf. James I:12, Eccli. 34: 9
and *Ancrene Wisse* f. 48^b/23–28.

42 *maydenhood is gold:* on the indestructible nature of gold see
Pliny, *Natural History*, XXXIII, xix. This was probably the source
for such medieval encyclopedists as pseudo-Hugh, whose *De Bestiis*
(PL 177) may well be Aelred's direct source here (though it seems
almost certain that the Cistercian knew Pliny: see note to l. 361).
Aelred seems to have made some use of the *De Bestiis* elsewhere (see
note to l. 205), and the (thirteenth century) catalogue of Rievaulx
lists a *liber sermonum et quedam excerpta de libris iustiniani et
bestiarium in uno uolumine* which could be either the *Phisiologus* or

the most recent treatise of Hugh of Folieto (d. 1174). See A. Hoste, *Bibliotheca Aelrediana* (Steenbrugge, 1962), p. 155.

43 *fuyr is temptacioun:* cf. Eccli. 2: 5, Prov. 27: 21 and Wisdom 3: 6. These texts are also utilized in *Ancrene Wisse* f. 64ᵃ/2–4 and f. 77ᵇ/23–7, but the metaphor is admittedly a commonplace.

44 *a vessel off irþe:* cf. II Cor. 4:7 and *Ancrene Wisse* f. 44ᵇ/25–30.

49 *an holy womman:* L. simply *uirgo* (477).

51 *wit-oute recouerer: irrecuperabiliter* (478). There is no need to emend to *recouere* with H., as the phrase is a common ME idiom, < AN infinitive *recoverer*, meaning 'irrecoverably'. Cf., for example, *The Pricke of Conscience*, ed. R. Morris, *TPS* (1863), l. 6095, and *OED*, sv RECOVERER².

53–4 *þe lomb þat heo scholde folwen whydur euere he walke:* Rev. 14:4. *þat heo scholde folwen* translates *quem sequi habet* (481–2).

55 *blessede Marie wit þe tympane of chastete: beatissimam Mariam cum uirginitatis tympano* (482–3); as this is an allusion to Exodus 15: 20 Aelred probably has in mind Miriam, the sister of Moses (regarded by St Ambrose (*De Virginibus* II, ii, 17; PL 16, col. 221) as a type of the Virgin) whose name appears in the Vulgate as *Maria*, rather than the Virgin herself. The impression left by the ME, however, is of a direct reference to the Virgin, the first of a number of changes (possibly misunderstandings) which give the whole translation a decidedly more Marian tinge than its original. Cf. St Jerome, *Ad Eustochium*: *Qualis erit illa dies, cum tibi Maria, mater domini, choris occurret comitata virgineis, cum post Rubrum Mare et submersum cum suo exercitu Pharaonem tympanum tenens praecinet . . .* (*Select Letters of St Jerome*, trans. F. A. Wright (London, 1933), p. 154), who also identifies Miriam with the Virgin Mary.

58–9 *Hii sunt . . . .:* cf. Rev. 14:4. The ME translator supplies the latter half of the quotation, which is absent from Aelred's Latin.

59 *defoyled:* on the complex pedigree of ME *defoilen*, and of *foylede* (l. 1094) see A. Bowman, *Aspects of Semantic Change as Exemplified in some Representative Plays of Shakespeare* (unpubl. MA thesis, University of Durham, 1969), pp. 76–80, and cf. also *OED*, sv DEFILE *v.*, DEFOUL, FILE *v.*, FOIL *v.*¹ and FOUL *v.*¹

63–4 *which schal not be sayd now ne ynemned:* omits *cum detestandum illud scelus quo uir in uirum, uel femina furit in feminam, omnibus flagitiis damnabilius iudicetur* (488–90) – a strong condemnation of both male and female homosexuality. Clearly this is an echo of Aelred's own personal experience in his youth when, at the court of King David of Scotland, he first became aware of the homosexual leanings against which he was later to struggle so strongly; Aelred himself refers obliquely to these in *Spec. Car.* I, Cap. 28. See also Walter Daniel, *The Life of Ailred of Rievaulx*, ed. and trans. F. M. Powicke (London, 1950), p. 76 and A. Squire, O.P., *Aelred of Rievaulx: A Study* (London, 1969), pp. 14–15, and also note to l. 1102.

65   *witowte flehslich doingge:* the ME translator here omits Aelred's allusion to the possibility of loss of virginity through autoeroticism: *et absque alienae carnis consortio uirginitas plerumque corrumpitur* (490–1).

67   *menbres:* the *n* in place of etymological *m* is not to be explained on phonological grounds, but rather by the influence of ML, which frequently spells *membrum* as *menbrum*. No doubt this is to be explained as a hyper-correct spelling: as *n* + labial frequently appears as *m* + labial in L., attempts to restore the original spelling sometimes resulted in an etymologically unjustified change of *m* to *n*. Cf. in this text the hyper-correct spelling *conpilatoris* (l. 932).

70   *vnsemly: indignum* (495).

72–3   *let heore strecche al heore herte:* a literal translation of L. *totum animum tendat* (498).

80   *loke sche turne aboute in here herte:* a literal translation of L. *mente reuoluat* (504). *Revolvare* has, in post-Augustan L, the sense 'to brood, reflect upon', of which the translator appears to have been ignorant. While 'to direct, set' with reference to thoughts is a well-attested ME sense of *turn* (see *OED* T U R N *vb.*, V 26), there are no recorded ME examples of the phrase *turn about* with the sense 'weigh up, ponder'; for the translation of *mente* as 'herte', cf. l. 73.

81   *þe clennesse of here chastete:* L. *decorem pudicitiae* (504).
     inwardliche: translator's addition.

83   *þat þat neode dryfþ forto take:* all MSS except NTU here add *aut ratio dictauerit* (506–7).

92–3   *beþenk þe hertyliche:* L. *reuolue animo* (513): see note to l. 80.

93–4   *ȝif . . . þu hast offended:* cf. *Ancrene Wisse* f. 11^b/12–15.

99   *of to muche slep:* L. *ex quiete soporis* (520); possibly the translator mentally heard the phrase as *excessu soporis?*

101   *þyn cruel enemy:* L. *callidus hostis* (521); the translator seems to have had his doubts about the meaning of *callidus* ('crafty, sly'); at l. 148 he translates it as 'wyckede' and at l. 662 'gostly'.
     wolde drawe þe in-to nyce fantacye: translator's addition.

103–4   *þe blessede vyrgines:* omits *quae in tenera aetate tam crebro reportarunt de impiissimo hoste triumphum* (524–6).

105   *þilke blessede Agnete:* Agnes was an undoubtedly genuine

third-century virgin martyr. Her cult is extremely ancient and her name occurs in the Canon of the Roman Mass. Early references to her include Ambrose, *De Virginibus* Bk I Cap. ii, 5–9 (PL 16, cols. 200–2), Augustine, *Sermo* clxxvi, Cap. 6 (PL 38, cols. 1250–1). The *Acta*, no earlier than the fifth century, and largely apocryphal, provide the details of her fully-developed legend, on which Aelred draws here (see *ASS* Jan. II (1643), 351–4); see also *Gesta sanctae Agnes* in *Bibliotheca Hagiographica Latina* I (Brussels, 1898–99), 156, referred to in *The Old French Lives of St Agnes*, ed. A. J. Denomy (Cambridge, Mass., 1938), p. 25ff.

Only MSS R & T consistently spell the saint *Agnetem* (not *Agnem* or *Agnam*).

closes: this interesting form of the plural, meaning 'clothes', evidently arose as follows: with the reduction of the ME dissyllabic form *cloþes* to one syllable, by change of /-əz/ to /-z/, the /ð/ began to disappear by assimilation to the final /z/ (the spelling of the plural as *close*, *cloes* is abundantly recorded in *OED* from the fourteenth century onwards, and the orphoepist R. Brown records the pronunciation [kloːz] in 1700 (see E. J. Dobson, *English Pronunciation 1500–1700* (2nd. ed.) (Oxford, 1968), vol. II, §401c.); and indeed, this pronunciation remains common to this day; the resulting plural *close* was evidently liable to be apprehended as a singular form, and thus the analogical plural *closes* came to be coined (cf. *dice*, *dices*). This analogical plural is not recorded in the dictionaries of English.

106–7   *despysede as styngynge dunge:* cf. Phil. 3: 8. On the form *styngynge*, 'stinking', see Intro., p. l.

107   *to doom: ad tribunal* (528–9).

110   *for here loues sake:* translator's addition.

111–12   *entryngge in-to prysoun:* not in L. The translator presumably equates a brothel with a (spiritual) prison.

112   *turnede derknesse in-to liȝt: lucem infudit tenebris* (532).

115   *holy angeles: angelus* (535); cf. l. 26.

118   *þe leem of lecherie was iqueynt:* cf. *Orcherd of Syon*, ed. P. Hodgson and G. Liegey, EETS 258 (1966), p. 372/26–33: '. . . Petir & Poul, Steuen & Laurence, & siche oþire, whiche, whanne þei weren put into þe fier for to brenne, þei semeden þat þei stoden in no fier, but raþir on flouris of greet deliit. . . . What was þe cause? Certeyn, for þe fier of dyuyn charite had quenchid in him þe feeling of his litel sensualite.'

121–2   *þat aschercheþ entrayles of þyn herte:* L. *qui scrutatur corda et renes* (540–1), a reference to Ps. 7:10. It might seem that the translator (in defiance of anatomy) has understood the L. as an example of hendiadys, but in fact 'entrails' already had the sense 'the inward parts regarded as the seat of the emotions, thoughts, etc.' (cf. *OED*, ENTRAIL 4), so *entrayles of þyn herte* here means 'your inmost heart'. Cf. also *alle þe veynes of his herte*, l. 631 n.

125–6 *'I haue to my louyere þe angel of God, þat wit gret ielouste kept my body': Angelum dei habeo custodem* is the second antiphon at Lauds for the Feast of St Agnes; the phrase *angelum dei habeo amatorem*, however, occurs in some versions of her legend, e.g. *Barbour's Legendensammlung* II, 152/151–2; *Bokenham's Legendys*, ed. M. Serjeantson, EETS 206 (1938), ll. 4319–21.

127 *þy partye: conatum tuum* (546).

134 *greuously iperisched: periclitatur* (552); see note to l. 148

135 *alþouȝ castete be a special ȝift of God:* cf. *Ancrene Wisse*, f. 99^b/13–28 and see Intro., p. xl.

140 *nyce wommen: puellas* (558).

141–2 *to bere leyt of fuir in here bosum and nouȝt be brend:* this image, which is ultimately scriptural (cf. Prov. 6:27), also occurs in *Ancrene Wisse*, f. 99^b/26–7 and Guigo, *Consuetudines*, XXI, 2. ME *leyt* usually means 'lightning' but has the occasional sense of 'flame, flash of fire' as here, where it translates L. *flammas:* cf. *Ayenbite of Inwyt*, ed. R. Morris, EETS, os 23 (1866) rev. P. Gradon (1965), p. 66, 'efter þe layt' where *layt* translates F *flambe*. Cf. *leytyngge*, l. 1297.

145 *I knew sum-tyme a monke:* Aelred himself. See Walter Daniel, *The Life of Ailred of Rievaulx*, ed. cit., p. 25.

146 *þorouȝ steryngge of naturel complexioun: naturalibus incentiuis* (563).

148 *þe wyckede temptour: callidi tentatoris* (564); see note to l. 101.

persced and spild: periclitari (565). In l. 134 the translator renders *periclitari* (= 'to be endangered', also 'to be ship-wrecked') as *iperisched*, which raises the question of which verb we have here. ME *persced* could be from either 'perish' or 'pierce' as *OED* notes that some forms of *pierse* (*persche, persshe, perisse, perch(e, perish(e, peresche*) were confused with forms of *perish*. In this text *sc* is an acceptable graphy for /ʃ/, so *persced* could well = 'perished'. On the other hand the sense 'pierced, punctured' is more consonant with the metaphorical presentation of chastity as contained in a fragile vessel, the body. It is possible that the translator did not in fact think of 'perish' and 'pierce' as two separate verbs.

149 *conceyuyngge:* MS *coueytyngge* hardly makes sense here; the scribe's eye was no doubt caught by *coueytede* in the next line. The emendation brings the ME into line with the L. at this point, which is

concipiens; it is however possible that the translator's text had *concupiens* and that the MS reading represents a genuine attempt to render the L.

151 *wit mysese: inedia* (567).

152–3 *forto refreyne vnlyfful mociouns of flehs: etiam motus eius simplices comprimebat* (568–9).

153 *lyfful:* cf. *vnlifful* l. 121, *vnlyfful* l. 152 and *vnlyfsum* l. 375. Only two other occurrences of an *i*-graphy are recorded for these words in the dictionaries of English. Both *OED* and *MED* agree that they were based ultimately on ME *lę̄f*, *lę̄ve* n., 'permission', < OE *lēaf*. However, the *i/y*-graphies are scarcely consistent with a development from *ę̄*; the frequent *ff*-graphy suggests that the *i* may have arisen through shortening and partial raising of an antecedent *ę̄*. If this is the case, it may be thought preferable to reject *OED*'s and *MED*'s etymology in favour of one which traces the adjectives back to the OA verb *lēfan* (WS *lȳfan*), 'to allow, permit' (see *OED*, SV LEVE *v*.1), which would also account for some of the other recorded forms of these words, such as *lief(f)ul*, *leif(f)ul*.

155–6 *anoon þe flehs gan wexe proud: ecce caro rursus caput erigens* (570). It is unusual for the translator to eschew a metaphor in his original.

158 *he cryde and preyde: psallebat et orabat* (572–3): possibly the translator read *plorebat*.

164 *þo cowde he noon oþur refut: tunc, quod solum superfuit* (577).

165 *longstreiȝt: prostratus* (578). This word, which also occurs at ll. 840 and 1005, is not recorded in dictionaries of English, but evidently it means 'at full length, prostrate'. The second element represents the ppl. of ME *strecchen* (< OE *streccan*), 'to stretch', which in adjectival use commonly had the sense 'extended at full length'; the first element is intensive.

167–8 *Non te dimittam:* Gen. 32: 26.

171 *soerte was deveyed hym: negatur securitas* (581). It is not necessary to emend to *deneyed* as the verb *deuayen* (of which *deveye* is an acceptable variant) is recorded twice in ME, *Sir Gawain and the Green Knight*, ed. J. R. R. Tolkien and E. V. Gordon, 2nd. ed., rev. N. Davis (Oxford, 1968), ll. 1493, 1497. There the sense is clearly 'to deny, refuse'; it is derived from OF *deve(i)er*, 'to refuse, fail to grant a request'.

178 *many mannes woodschype: quorumdam impudentiae* (589). Evidently the translator read *imprudentiae*.

mannes: context and the L. demand the gen. pl. of 'man' here, which elsewhere in this text is *menne* (< OE *manna* with analogical substitution of the root vowel) and the analogical reformation *mennes*. *Mannes* therefore probably comes from the OE weak n. *manna*, with analogical plural.

whyce: the MS reading here may fairly confidently be said to be *whyte*, for the scribe is always careful to distinguish *t* from *c* (when not conjoint); the cross-bar of the *t* always extends well beyond the main body of the letter, whereas in the *c* it stops abruptly where it joins the bow (but cf. *stenc*, l. 552 n.). *Whyte*, however, is unsatisfactory here; L. *Vnde non parum pudet quorumdam impudentiae*, qui *cum in sordibus senuerint* (589–90) suggests an emendation to *whyce*, in which case *whyce þat* renders L. *qui*. In this text *c* is a fairly well attested spelling for final /tʃ/ (cf. *whic*, ll. 124, 145, 257, 268, 405, 614; *stenc*, l. 552 n.).

181   *seyn þat þey ben siker ynow of hem-self:* a vague and euphemistic translation of *quod . . . ad scelus perficiendum tepescentia membra deficiant* (593–4).

182–3   *þey spare not to taken hym nyȝt and day to occasiones of sunne: eodem lectulo cubantes, inter amplexus et oscula . . .* (591).

183–4   *among alle resonable creatures: prae cunctis mortalibus* (595).
       foles: infelices (594).

188   *here falsnesse lye openly in here face: mentiatur iniquitas sibi*, omitting *et dum nititur uelare unum, duplex in se prodat flagitium* (598–600). The L. makes it almost certain that we must take *lye* in the sense 'tell lies' rather than 'repose, be situated (for all to see)'. *in here face* presumably, in some sense, translates *sibi*: it may be connected with the NE idiom 'to lie in one's teeth', earlier ME variants of which include 'to lie in one's head' – but here it is the 'falsnesse', not the people, that is lying.

190   *half ded and half alyue: fere decrepitos* (600).

191   *fantasies of fowl lust:* MSS NMU *phantasma* (601): DHTUV all read the corrupt *plasma* here, though U has a marginal note, *vel fantasma* (MS R is not running at this point).

192   *bodyly disesed:* as this renders *inquietat*, *disesed* probably has its usual ME sense of 'troubled, discomforted' rather than the later sense 'be affected by a bodily infirmity, be ill', which would otherwise be the more attractive alternative here.

195   *as a dredful douve:* cf. Cant. 5: 12, *Oculi eius sicut columbae super rivulos aquarum . . . et resident iuxta fluenta plenissima* and, more specifically, Bede's comment, *Super Cantice* LV (PL 91, col. 1164): *Columbae siquidem super rivulos aquarum . . . ut venientis umbram accipitris in aquarum perspecuitate praevidere, ac si imminens ab hoste periculum evadere possint. Cujus figura naturae in*

propatulo est, quia jugi divinorum eloquiorum meditatione opus habe-mus, ut vel facta sanctorum vel dicta legentes . . . sollicita mente perscrutemur. Aelred is possibly also drawing on pseudo-Hugh who provides another element in the allegory absent from Bede's inter-pretation – the water as a symbol of Holy Scripture: *Columba super aquas sedere saepissime solet, ut cum viderit umbram supervenien-tis accipitris fugiens delinet. Ecclesia vero scripturis se munit, ut insidiantis diaboli fraudes evitare possit* (PL 177, col. 19). Both authorities are more likely to be Aelred's sources than the Bestiary cited by A. Squire, *op. cit.*, p. 168 (MS C.U.L.Ii. 4. 26, f. 41) where the dove sits beside the waters, not to use them to mirror the hawk, but so that at his approach she may escape by submerging herself. *where þu miȝt isee:* L. adds *quasi in speculo* (605–6).

196 *þat flikt aboue: superuolantis* all MSS except R (*superuolitan-tis*) and H (*superuenientis*).

198 *þat is Crist:* translator's addition.

þe schadue: imaginem (609).

199 *wyt and consayl: sensum* (609).

200 *wyckede and vnclene:* L. merely *inutiles* (610).

200–1 *good ocupacioun in holy scripture: meditatio verbi Dei* (611). The term *meditatio*, in the ancient monastic tradition, meant much more than simply 'meditation'; it was the process of reading and re-reading a text from the Holy Scriptures and learning it by heart, in the fullest sense of the term – that is, with one's whole being. Thereby one arrived at a true and complete understanding of the text, and its sense was woven into the fabric of one's mind by constant reading and thought. This unceasing 'rumination' on the Scriptures, as the anony-mous author of the *Formula honestae vitae* called it (PL 174, col. 1170 C), is one of the most marked characteristics of monastic spirituality. See *La Vie de Recluse*, ed. C. Dumont (Paris, 1961), p. 92, n. 3, and also J. Leclercq, *The Love of Learning and the Desire for God*, trans. C. Misrahi (New York, 1960), p. 90 and the bibliographical references given in Note 8, p. 366.

201–2 *a good womman, and specially a mayde:* L. simply *uirgo* (611); cf. l. 49.

202 *al here herte and wit: animum suum* (611).

203 *Let slep fynden here:* cf. Jerome, *Ad Eustochium*, p. 86 and *Ancrene Wisse*, f. 78ª/19–20.

206 *let cleue to here ribbes: haerens memoriae* (614–5). Probably an example of a ME idiomatic phrase not recorded elsewhere. Else-where, this translator renders *memoria* as *herte* (in the sense, well-attested by *MED*, sv, 4(c) of 'memory, remembrance') and it is

possible, though *OED* does not record it, that 'ribs' could adopt the meaning 'heart' by extension. ME *hert* can in fact mean 'breast, chest, that part of the thorax in front of the heart' (see *MED* HERT 1b(b)) so the reverse might also be possible.

207–8 *þat mowe moor surliche kepe here menbrys, and also boþe body and soule in here slep:* translator's addition.

210 *Bote þe more sorwe is:* translator's addition.
manye: quidam (616).

210–1 *gostly ocupacioun: salutaribus exercitiis* (616): it seems likely that the translator confused *salutaribus* ('healthful, conducive to salvation') with *spirit(u)alibus*.

212 *gret wakyngge in Godes seruise: uigilias immoderatas* (617–18).

214 *þis is oure synful excusacioun: Haec excusatio nostra in peccatis nostris* (620): cf. Ps. 140:4, *ad excusandas excusationes in peccatis*.

215–16 *þat habbeþ þo gret feruour:* L. *quos talis feruor igniuit* (621) suggests a possible emendation of *þo* to *so*. However, *þo* is a not uncommon form of the uninflected definite article in late ME (< OE *þa* pl. and fem. sg. acc. by levelling under a general uninflected form; see *OED* THE I 1 aβ), which occurs twice elsewhere in this text (ll. 667 and 1239), so we have preferred to retain it.

217 *we smelleþ auer a faynt batayle: Procul odoramus bellum* (622–3), a reference to Job 39:25. *faynt*, for which there is no authority in L., must have the sense 'false, deceptive' (see *MED* FEINT l) rather than the more superficially attractive 'scarcely perceptible, as yet only dimly perceived'.

218 *to-comyngge:* cf. l. 678. These two forms are probably the pres. ppl. of *tocomen*, used to denote futurity. The syntax of the first example suggests that it could be a corrupt form of the inflected infinitive (see A. S. Irvine, 'The *To Comynge(e)* construction in Wyclif', *PMLA*, xlv (1930), 468–500, G. von Langenhove, *On the Origin of the Gerund in English* (Gand, 1925) and F.T. Visser, *An Historical Syntax of the English Language*, Part 2 (Leiden, 1966), §1031) but elsewhere in this text the inflected infinitive is *to comen(e* (ll. 1175, 1212, 1223, 1247, 1410).

221–2 *vnclene wildenesse of þe flehs: carnis . . . lasciuiam* (627).

227–8 *chier and delicate kepyngge in syknesse which he my3te fall into of to muche abstinence:* a considerable expansion of *occasione infirmitatis* (630–1). It is not clear whether *chier* is an adjective modifying *kepyngge in syknesse* with the sense 'careful', or a noun, in apposition to *delicate kepyngge* with the sense 'meat and drink, good food'. For the idea, cf. Gregory, PL 76, col. 976.

229   *ȝif þe flesh be mornyngge, syk and feble: si languet, si aegrotat, si torquentur uiscera* (632). It seems quite likely that the translator failed to notice that these are not three parallel verbs with the same subject (*uiscera*) but *languet* and *aegrotat* are singular, their unexpressed subject 'a man'. As for the translation of *languet* as *mornyngge*, there are two possible explanations: (i) *mornyngge* here has the sense 'grieving, by extension, drooping' (a meaning, however, not recorded until the eighteenth century) or of 'pining away' (recorded, of animals, from the late sixteenth century), a sense which may well have been introduced at an earlier stage by ON *morna*, 'pine away'; or: (ii) the translator misread *languet* (possibly abbreviated to *lāg^{ut}*<*langueo*, 'sicken, droop') as *plangent* (which could be abbreviated to *plāg^{nt}*<*plango*, 'lament, mourn'), and assumed *uiscera* (= *flesh*) to be the necessary plural subject.

235   *he took hede of his owne perilous stat:* translator's addition.

237   *his herte gan brenne wyt-ynne hym as eny fuyr: concaluit cor eius intra eum, et in meditatione eius exarsit ignis* (637–8): MSS DR read *exardescit* for *exarsit*, which is possibly closer to the ME . Cf. Ps. 38:4.

238   *beyngge ynlyche wroþ: salubriter irascens sibi* (638).

240–2   *Per þat he hadde be toforhand lyȝt and nyce, he wax sad; þer he hadde ibe blaberynge and chaterynge, he took hym to silence: Successit grauitas leuitati, loquacitati silentium* (640–1).

246   *to refreyne hem:* translator's addition.

248   *wyþ so euy chiere: demisso uultu* (647–8).

250   *his dredful domesman at þe day of dome: diuinis tribunalibus* (649).

252   *his wickede tiraunt, his flehs:* L. simply *tyranno* (650).

254–5   *his laste slep, þat he schulde be deed: dormitionis* (652) all MSS except R, *dormitacionis*. *dormitio* (ante- and post-classical only) has the primary significance of 'sleep', but in Eccl. L. came to mean death (as in the Vulgate, 2 Macc. 12: 45). However, it is clear from *RMLWL* that the meaning 'sleep' continued to be the predominant meaning throughout the medieval period, though *dormitio in Christo* specifically = 'death'. *last sleep*, with the sense 'death', is not recorded in *OED* before 1579, when it is used by Spenser, nor is the collocation recorded in *MED* LAST; but *sleep* alone, meaning 'death' is well-attested from OE onwards. Clearly the ME translator found it necessary to explain his innovative phrase.

258   *we schulde resteyne or elles doon awey: cohibeamus* (658). It is not necessary to emend to *refreyne* with H. (if emendation were needed *restreyne* would be more likely). While dictionaries of English do not record a verb *resteyne*, OF has *resteindre*, used intransitively to mean 'to be extinguished' and transitively to mean 'to extinguish, blot out, quell'. The (figurative) sense of 'quench, quell, do away with' is self-evident from the context, and the form *resteyne*, from the OF present stem *resteign-*, is in accord with other ME verbs derived from the present stem of OF *-eindre* verbs.

260   *nyce men of here body: effeminatorum* (656).

261–2   *we colourep to excuse owre foule lustes: palliamus negotium uoluptatis* (658–9).

268–9   *chastete maydenly, alþou3 it be ornament and flour of vertues, 3it witowte meknesse it wext al faad:* cf. Aelred, *De Spiritali Amicitia* I, 374–7, but the idea is a commonplace: cf. *The Book of Vices and Virtues*, ed. W.N. Francis, EETS 217 (1942), pp. 255/35–256/6.

wext al faad: aret atque marsescit (665–6); *wext* therefore is present tense of *wax*, not a weak preterite form.

274   *proude:* the spelling *proude* for the abstract noun 'pride' (as opposed to its concrete sense, 'a proud person') is recorded only twice elsewhere in English: (i)
    'iche shal swo stronge ferde lede
    þat ower proude [*3* prude] schal aualle'
                                  (*The Owl and the Nightingale*
(MS Cotton Caligula A ix), ed. J. W. H. Atkins (Cambridge, 1922),
                                                      ll. 1684–5);

Atkins, noting that *ou* is a very rare spelling for *u* at such an early date, suggests that the MS Caligula form is a scribal error, and Miss Mabel Day (quoted in *The Owl and the Nightingale*, ed. G. F. H. Sykes and J. H. G. Grattan, EETS, ES 119 (1916)) conjectures that the Caligula scribe took *ower prude* (presumably with an ambiguous *wynn* in *ower*) in his exemplar to mean 'other proud people', and thus wrote *proude*; and: (ii)
    'Alle þat is in þe wordle oþer it is fals couetise of flesch, or fals
                          couetise of yen, or prowde of life.'
(*Gesta Romanorum*, ed. S. J. Herrtage, EETS, ES 33 (1879), i, 4).

Possibly in the present text *proude* is a back-spelling from *prude*, which was a fairly common form of Southern ME /prūdə/.
    More puzzling is the adjectival form *pruyd* (l. 278). In this text the graphy *uy* consistently represents the reflex of OE $\bar{y}$ (see Intro., xliv), but there are no grounds at all for supposing that the vowel /ū/ could be present in the adjective *proud*. The most likely explanation is that the scribe was influenced by the nominal form *pruyde*, which occurs in both the preceding and the succeeding lines in the MS.

273   *Inicium omnis peccati:* Eccli. 10: 15.

275 *cursede: pessimae* (670).

276 *venenous:* not in L.

277 *3ynges:* cf. *3ou3tes* (552), *by3enkeste* (648), *wy3* (992). The 3-graphy for þ probably arose originally due to the difficulty Anglo-Norman scribes had, when copying ME texts, in distinguishing ME /θ/ from the ME voiceless palatal fricative /ç/, for which 3 was a common graphy; it is not uncommon to find the reverse of this phenomenom in ME texts, e.g. *miþte* for *mi3te* (see J.A.W. Bennett and G.V. Smithers, *Early Middle English Verse and Prose*, 2nd. edn. (Oxford, 1968), p. lxi).

280 *haþ a veyn-glorie in here herte: intus in animo suo glorietur* (675–6).

281–2 *and þerwit haþ a fleshsly delytyngge:* translator's addition.

283–4 *þat sche holde here-self wonderliche holy: quasi magnum aliquid admiretur* (679).

288–9 *alle þyse iapes:* L. simply *haec omnia* (683).

290 *Whit what vorheed:* cf. L. *qua enim fronte* (684), of which this phrase is a literal translation, with the sense 'with what audacity'. *MED* records several examples of the use of 'forehead', with various qualifying adjectives, in the figurative sense 'outward appearance, face presented to the world', but the direct, unqualified loan-translation as exemplified here is not recorded elsewhere before 1560.

293 *a pouere mayne:* MS *mayde* is otiose as it merely repeats preceding 'moder'; the text has been emended to render L. *familiam* (686), 'family, household' with an acceptable variant of ME *meyne*.

þe streytnesse of an oxe-stalle: praesepii uilitatem (687).

295–6 *þat þu hast forsake to wedde a monnes sone for þe loue þat þu hast to to be Cristes spouse:* L. simply *quod Dei Filium hominum filiis praetulisti* (688). The ME translator makes several additions such as this which intensify the metaphor of the recluse as Bride of Christ: cf. note to l. 110.

298 *þe swete sauour of maydenhood: uirginitatis decore* (689): possibly there was here a confusion between *decor* (= beauty, fairness) and *odor* (= scent, perfume). Elsewhere, 'swete sauour' renders *odor*, as in l. 31.

299 *of stench and of corupcioun: stercorum* (690).

302 *si gloriaris:* I Cor. 1:31.

304–8 *I nel not . . . babounrye:* this aesthetic puritanism was one of the characteristics of early Cistercianism: see *Cistercian Institutes* XX and also *Spec. Car.* II, 1298–1311 where Aelred stigmatizes delight in physical beauty as *curiositas*, the lust of the eyes. He describes the typical Cistercian abbey church as 'made of unpolished stone, without paintings, sculpture, precious objects; no marble strewn with carpets, no walls decorated with gay tapestries showing the histories of nations or royal battles, let alone scenes from scripture'.

305 *þu:* this form, as written in the MS, appears as *þɑ*, and it is evident that the scribe initially made a mistake in writing the second letter, made an only partially successful attempt to expunge it by scraping, and then wrote *u* on top of it. A thorough examination of the MS, with the help of an ultra-violet lamp, has failed to reveal what the original letter was, but it seems quite likely to have been an *e*.

311 *Omnis gloria fille Regis abintus:* Ps. 44: 15; L. adds *in fimbriis aureis circumamicta uarietatibus* (697–8).

313 *heuene:* in the MS, *heuene* completes one line, and at the beginning of the next, immediately above a hole in the membrane, are written what appear to be three, or possibly four, *x*'s. No writing is visible beneath these marks, and indeed there is scarcely any room between the top of the hole and the line above to write in. It may be that the scribe tried to do so, found the result unsatisfactory and cancelled it; or that *x*'s may be a direction to someone to sew up or otherwise repair the hole, which was never carried out.

314 *loke þu hiere:* this construction (*loke* + subj.) usually translates L. imperative or jussive subjunctive in this text, but here L. *audisti* cannot be anything but perfect indicative. Perhaps the translator was distracted by nearby *audi*. In fact, he has subtly mistranslated the whole passage, the sense of which is: if the recluse is *now* the daughter of a king (in that she is the spouse of the king's son), she has already heard the voice of the father saying, *Audi etc.*

316–17 *Loke þerfore þat al þy gladnesse come of clene wytnesse of a good conscience wit-ynne:* Vide ut gloria tua sit testimonium conscientiae tuae (700–1); cf. II. Cor. 1: 12. *Gloria* is more usually translated *blysse* in this text: see note to l. 23.

317–18 *Let þer be fair peynture and grauyngge of diuerse vertues: Ibi sit pulcherrima uirtutum uarietas* (701–2). The sense of ME *vertues* (as of ML *uirtutum*) could be either 'high moral qualities' or 'efficacious properties', but the juxtaposition with 'good þewes' (l. 318) suggests the former.

318–19 *let þer fressche coloures of good þewes wit curious knottes be knet to-gydere: ibi diuersi colores sibi sic conueniant et sic iungantur sibi* (702–3).

322 *good inward wysdom: prudentiae* (706).

324 *to alle þyse þanne put good temprure and good discrecioun:*

Adde fortitudini modestiam (707–8). *good temprure* and *good dis-crecioun* are apparently synonyms placed in apposition which sug-gests that the translator read *Adde modestiam*: in fact MSS NTU omit *fortitudine*.

326 *In swich curiosite ocupye þyn eȝen of þyn herte: In hac uarietate tuae mentis oculos occupa* (708–9). Although *eȝen of þyn herte* is here a literal translation of the L., it is a well-attested ME idiom meaning 'the understanding' (see *MED* sv HERT, 2a(a)).

326–7 *swich vertuous diuersite fourme in þy soule wit al þy wit: hanc in anima tua omni studio forma* (709).

327–8 *and þerwit let enbroude þy spiritual cloþynge:* translator's addition.

328 *In fimbrijs aureis etcetera:* Ps. 44:14.

329–30 *a garnement wel iweue adoun to þi foot:* the reference is to Joseph's coat, the *uestem polymitam* of Gen. 37:23. There it is described as *tunica talari et polymita*. The translator was clearly conscious of the allusion as he describes the garment as full-length (= *talari*) rather than 'multi-coloured' (= *polymitam*) as does Aelred.

332 *þe ende wherto draweþ al þe parfeccioun of Godes lawe: Finis autem praecepti* (712).

333 *Finis precepti est caritas:* I Tim. 1: 5.

334–5 *Þis charyte most þu nyede haue, louyngge God and þyn euene-cristene of clene herte, wit good conscience, and wit fey not feyned ne fayllynge: caritas . . . de corde puro et conscientia bona et fide non ficta* (712–3), a reference to I Tim. 1: 5.

339 *ȝif þu hast eny:* translator's addition.

342 *lynne or flex:* it is clear from distinct verbal similarities that Aelred's source for this description of the processing of flax was Pliny, *Natural History* XIX, iii, 16–19. Detached from its allegorical exege-sis, Aelred's account runs: *Primum igitur linum aquis immergitur. . . . Post aquas linum siccatur. . . . Deinde linum malleis tunditur. . . . Post haec linum ferreis aculeis discerpitur, ut deponat superflua. . . . Adhibetur post haec lino suauiorum stimulorum leuior purgatio. Iam nunc a nentibus linum in longum producitur. . . . Porro ut ei perfectior accedat pulchritudo, ignis adhibetur et aqua* (723–43). The corres-ponding passages in Pliny's account are: 'virgae ipsae *merguntur in aquam* solibus tepefactam. . . . sole *siccantur*, mox arefactae in saxo *tunduntur* stuppario *malleo*. . . . ipsa (*sc.* stuppa = 'tow') tamen pectitur *ferreis aculeis*, donec omnis membrana decorticetur. . . . iterum deinde in filo politur, inlisum crebro silici ex aqua, textumque rursus tunditur clavis, semper iniuria melius' (XIX, iii, 16–18). (It should however be noted that *aculeis* is apparently a nineteenth-

century emendation of MS (*a*)*enis*, first made by Mayhoff in his edition of 1892; see J. P. Wild, 'The Roman flax-hackle (AENA)', *Museum Helveticum*, 25, Fasc. 2 (1968), 139 ff.) The reference in Aelred to a final processing by fire and water possibly conflates the end of this account of the preparation of common flax with the beginning of Pliny's account of an incombustible fabric (asbestos): *Inventum iam est etiam quod ignibus non absumeretur. vivum id vocant, ardentesque in focis conviviorum ex eo vidimus mappas sordibus exustis splendescentes igni magis quam possent aquis* (XIX, iv, 19). Pliny goes on to say that this fabric is used to shroud the bodies of kings, which might well have pleased Aelred by its appropriateness in drawing together three of the major images of his treatise – the recluse as a king's daughter, the wedding-garment of virtues and the recluse's death to the world and burial in her anchorhold. As Aelred combines in his account features from the preparation of flax proper, tow (or oakum) and asbestos it would seem unlikely that he was drawing on practical experience, nor need we presume that Rievaulx was engaged in the production of linen.

345 *so be we ybrout forþ: nascimur.*

346 *Quoniam ego:* Ps. 50: 7.

348–9 *whan we ben take out of owre oune moder wombe:* translator's addition.

352 *in þe wasschyngge awey of þe vielþe of synne: in peccatorum remissione* (725–6).

353–4 *þe enclinaunce . . . to synne: naturalis corruptio. enclinaunce* (< OF *enclinance*) is not recorded in *MED* or *OED* but clearly has the meaning 'tendency, disposition'.

358 *to be þe mor suple to werk:* translator's addition.

358–9 *ibete and bouyd: fatigatur* (732): *bouyd* is an orthographic variant of *bowed*<ME *bowen*, which, like L *fatigo*, can mean 'wear down, overcome' (see *OLD* FATĪGŌ, 5).

359 *temptacioun many and diuers:* the sense of this phrase is clearly plural (translating *multis temptationibus*) but the construction is singular. The use of *many* and *diuers* with a singular noun is quite idiomatic in ME.

360–1 *is ipurged wit grete yrene kombes: ferreis aculeis discerpitur* (733). A modern translator of Aelred's original renders this phrase 'threshed with iron nails' while the Loeb translation of Pliny (at this point *pectitur aculeis ferreis*) offers 'combed with iron spikes'. *discerpo* has the meaning 'tear, rend to pieces, mangle' and *aculeus* 'barb, pointed implement'.

361–2 *so mote we wit þe scharpe ȝerd of discipline putte awey alle*

superfluites: et nos disciplinae ungulis rasi (734). The modern translation here has 'scraped with the teeth of regular observance' but it
seems more likely that Aelred was referring to the claws (*ungulis*) of
the discipline, the monastic instrument of physical penance. The ME
translator, however, seems to have misread *ungulis* as *uirgulis*
(dimunutive of *uirga*, 'a rod'), possibly influenced by the scriptural
phrase *virga disciplinae* (Prov. 22: 15).

363–4   *a comb of smallere pryckes: suauiorum stimulorum leuior
purgatio* (736–7).

364   *to clense it more curiously:* translator's addition.

368   *flex is ispunne a-long: a nentibus linum in longum producitur*
(740).

371–2   *we mote þorouȝ vier of tribulacioun and water of scharp
contricioun: et nobis transeundum est per ignem tribulationis et
aquam compunctionis* (743–5), a reference to Ps. 65: 12. On the
non-expression of the verb of motion, which is idiomatic in ME, see
Mustanoja, p. 543.

375–6   *not fulfylle þyn eȝen wit vnlyfsum iaperyes and vanites: non
oculos tuos ineptis uarietatibus pascant* (746–7).

378–9   *þe ymage of þe crucifix hangynge on þe cros: Saluatoris in
cruce pendentis imago* (748–9). A crucifix was specifically permitted
to Cistercians; see *Cistercian Institutes* XX.

380–1   *he is ysprad abrood to byklepe þe:* the image of the crucified
Christ, longing to embrace all mankind from the cross, is very popular
in medieval devotional literature. Cf. *Ancrene Wisse*, f. 108[b]/18–20;
Mirk, *Festiall*, p. 112/31–6; *Orcherd of Syon*, ed. cit., p. 294/38ff.:
'He bowiþ þere his heed to salowe þee and greete þee. He sprediþ hise
aarmes abrood þere, þee for to clippe and brace to hym, and strecchiþ
forþ hise feet for to stonden with þee aȝeins þi goostly enemy.'; also
the actual experience of the English visionary Godric who *ex more
crucem adoraret, vidit in spiritu crucis imaginem submisso vultu
adorantem resalutare et protensis brachiis in amplexus excipere* (C.
Horstmann, *Nova Legenda Anglie* (Oxford, 1901), I, 102). The idea
also appears in ME lyrics, e.g. C. Brown, *English Lyrics of the
Thirteenth Century* (Oxford, 1932, repr. 1950), No. 69; see R.
Woolf, *The English Religious Lyric in the Middle Ages* (Oxford,
1968), pp. 32–3.

382–3   *to ȝyue þe melk of spiritual delectacioun and confortacioun:
lac tibi suauitatis infundat quo consoleris* (751–2); for the metaphor,
see *infra*, note to l. 822–3.

392   *a blessed testament was þis to seynt Ihon: testament* (translating L. *testamentum*) has here the meaning of 'legacy' rather than

'testimony'. On the concept of Christ's 'legacy' or 'will' (by which he bequeathed the Blessed Virgin Mary to St John) see Woolf, *op. cit.*, p. 211.

394–5 *cumfort of pouere, and at þe laste, lady of al þe wordle:* omitting *desperatorum erectio, peccatorum reconciliatio* (762), two phrases also omitted by MSS NRTU.

395 *wit so gret auctorite:* the translator apparently read 'tanti auctoritate' for *testamenti auctoritate* (763 – so all MSS).

399–400 *Porro vnum est necessarium:* Luke 10:42. The thought of both the ME and L. at this point is somewhat cryptically expressed. It would seem that the 'one thing necessary' is the contemplation of God (cf. Bede's commentary on Luke 10:42: *Una ergo et sola est theologia, id est, contemplatio Dei*, PL 92, col. 471) which is to be found only in God, the One (cf. Aelred, *De Iesu Puero* II, 1–3: *Dominus Deus noster, Deus unus est. Non potest uariari, non potest mutari, dicente Dauid: Tu semper idem es et anni tui non deficient*, and *Spec. Car.* III, 1).

401 *in whom is noon vnstabilite ne chaungyngge: apud quem non est transmutatio, nec uicissitudinis obumbratio* (668–9), a reference to James 1:17.

401–2 *and þat cleueþ: þat* translates L. *qui*, 'he who'; the ellipsis of the antecedent to the relative pronoun *þat* is fairly common in ME – see Mustanoja, p. 190.

403 *þat is eueremoore oon wit-outen eny mutacioun: quod semper idem est* (771).

404 *Tu semper idem ipse es, et anni non deficient:* Ps. 101:28. The complete quotation is not given in L., but is implicit in the preceding lines.

405–6 *whic, as I seyde, is as it were a goldene hem, finally to make fair þy weddyng-coote: quasi spiritalis ornatus finis et fimbria* (772).

408 *Þis weddyng-garnement:* the *uestis nuptialis* is possibly a remote reference to Matt. 22:11–2 (the parable of the Lord's Wedding Feast).

409–10 *swiche goldene hemmes . . . þe wyche mowen conteyne:* in the L. the subject of *contineat* (= *conteyne*) is *caritas*; either the translator has misunderstood this or else his exemplar had *contineant*. In either case, there is no need to emend *mowen* to *mowe*.

417 *innocence:* in Aelred, *innocentia* refers to that state in which the love of God in man (*diuinus amor*) leads him to a proper love of himself and his fellow man, and causes him to treat himself and his neighbour without harm. 'Indeed, it is necessary that each love – that by which we have regard for our own salvation and that with which we

are united to our neighbours in pure affection, should be animated by a certain portion of divine love . . . the love of God prompts us to that two-fold love . . . in which innocence is achieved, which clearly consists in both types of love. . . . For he is innocent who harms neither himself nor another' (*Spec. Car.* III, 250–8 – our translation).

beneficience: cf. 11. 422, 502, 522. *OED* records this word as an erroneous form of *beneficence*, found passim as a misprint in various books or editions, but gives no examples; it is not recorded at all in *MED*. However, against the theory put forward in *OED* must be noted the following points: *MED* records only one example of the 'correct' form *beneficence* <L *beneficentia* ('Þat he ʒeueþ wormes to bite me, is of goddis beneficence; and alle þese ben his benefetis to me' (R. Pecock, *The Folewer to the Donet* (*c.* 1454), ed. E. V. Hitchcock, EETS 164 (1924), p. 201, l. 5)), and *OED* records none before 1531; against which must be set the four clear examples of *beneficience* in this text, which antedates Pecock by at least fifty years, as against none of *beneficence*. Clearly it is possible that *beneficience* may be an earlier and valid form, which was subsequently ousted in 'correct' usage by *beneficence* because the latter was apprehended to be in closer conformity with L *beneficentia* (and F *bénéficence*). Almost certainly *beneficience* was a ME coinage (it does not occur in OF), and the intrusive *i* infix is probably to be accounted for on the grounds of analogical association with L *beneficium* n. (>ME *benefice*), OF *beneficier* v., etc. However, the form *beneficientia(m)* appears twice as a ML spelling, in MSS M and U.

419　*for þis is lawe of kynde:* translator's addition. 'lawe of kynde' is the standard ME expression for *lex naturalis*, 'natural law' (see *MED* sv KYNDE), which may be defined as 'a rule of conduct that proceeds from human nature as rational' (*New Catholic Encyclopedia* sv NATURAL LAW). According to Gratian, 'this law goes back to the beginning of mankind; its content is to be found in . . . the Gospel which dictates the golden rule of doing to others what one wishes done to oneself.'

Quod tibi non vis: Benedictine Rule 4: 9; cf. Tobit 4: 16.

420–1　*Omnia quecumque:* Matt. 7: 12 and Luke 6: 31.

424–5　Þe *ferste is þat þu schost greue no-man; and certayn, þat howte be liʒt inouʒ to þe: Primum ut nulli noceas, deinde ut nulli uelis nocere. Primum illud facile tibi.* NU omit all but the first three words and are closer to the ME.

425　þey þe *woldest:* þe here is the fairly common reduced-stress form of þu. There is no authority for this phrase in L.

427–8   *ʒif þu . . . loue þe nakede and bare pouerte þat þu hast take þe to: si professam dilexeris nuditatem* (790).

435   *Þer were two sustren:* Luke 10: 38–42. The use of Mary and Martha, the sisters of Lazarus of Bethany, to exemplify the active and contemplative lives is very ancient, going back at least to Augustine, and very popular in the medieval period. For more contemporary treatments of the theme, see *Ancrene Wisse*, f. 112ª/2–17 and Guigo, *Consuetudines*, XIX, 2. For Aelred's own further thoughts on the subject, see PL 195, col. 306.

441   *his word and his lore:* L. simply *uerbum illius* (803).

444–5   *þu schalt not be bysy ne distract aboute wordly ocupaciouns: nec debes distendi sed extendi, impleri non exhauriri* (806–7).

449   *hem þat beþ beste wommen i þe wordle:* the sense of the L. – *quae optimae uidentur in saeculo* (810) – seems to be 'women of the highest social status'; 'beste' renders this literally and does not convey the full force of the original.

449–50   *let hem . . . haue a spiritual enuye to folwe þy lyuyngge: tuam uitam aemulentur* (810) except MS D, *aemulantur*.

458–9   *for þey þat ministreþ þe awter, it is skyleful þat þey lyue of þe awter:* a reference to I Cor. 9: 13, which was a favourite text in justifications of church endowments.

467–8   *hem þat resteþ hem in holynesse of contemplacioun: qui salu- tari otio uacant cum Maria* (823–4).

469   *þoo þat beþ in cloystre: claustralibus* (824). The *claustrales* were technically the choir monks who had no duties other than the obligation to sing the Divine Office to the glory of God; they were distinguished from *obedientiales*, officers such as the porter, cellar- er, and *prelati*, superiors such as abbot and prior. Cf. Aelred's exposi- tion of this in PL 195, 295B-D.

471   *þat schulde make no purvyaunce fro o day to anoþer: quibus nulla debet esse de crastino cura* (826); cf. Matt. 6: 34.

472–3   *þey schulle be okepied in swettere þyngges: nutriantur potius in croceis* (827), a reference to Lam. 4: 5.

474–5   *hem þat beþ more contemptible and rude to spiritualte:* a misunderstanding of *Hi autem qui contemptibiles sunt constituti ad iudicandum* (828–9), which alludes to 1 Cor. 6: 4.

475   *let hem bysie hem wit þe wordle:* translator's addition, presu- mably an attempt to allegorize the following 'let hem clepe to hem carayne and dung' (*amplexentur stercora*, 829).

477   *Quorum piger:* Eccli. 22: 2.

480 *in desert:* translator's addition. The phrase is a calque on OF *en desers, desert*, and is quite widespread in ME. Cf. *infra*, 659.

481 *angeles mete: manna caeleste* (832). Cf. *angeles bred, fode*, which are common ME terms for manna, no doubt under the influence of ML *panis angelorum*, 'the consecrated Host', of which manna was regarded as an OT type.

Anima nostra nauseat: translator's addition; Numbers 21: 5.

482–3 *For swyche nyce foolys, whan þey beþ ydulled in here life:* translator's addition.

485–6 *for a lytul stynkynde vielþe, in þe whiche oþre beþ defoyled in þe wordle: pro stercoribus quibus ipsi foedantur* (833–4).

488 *Qui nutriebantur:* Lam. 4: 5.

491–2 *bote þilke þat beþ assigned þer-to, and to whom is itake Marthes bisynesse:* not in L., but cf. ll. 839–40 of L.

496 *more þan þu dispendist þy-self:* not in L.

a Godes alf: not in L.

498–9 *wherto schalt þu care to ȝyue almesse of oþere menne godes:* cf. *Ancrene Wisse*, f. 111^b/28–112^a/2.

499 *a namely:* the MS reading is somewhat ambiguous; before *namely* appears a symbol which resembles but is not identical to the scribe's capital *A and* his ampersand. It is the opinion of Mr J. E. Fagg, of the Department of Palaeography and Diplomatic in the University of Durham, that on balance it probably represents the former. This reading is linguistically quite acceptable, since *a* is a well-attested ME variant of *and* in reduced stress. The collocation with *namely* tends to confirm this explanation, for once weakly-stressed *and* had lost its final *-d*, the way was open to assimilation to the initial *n-* of the following word. Corroboration of this theory may be found in, for example, J. de Trevisa's translation of Bartholomaeus' *de Rerum Proprietatibus*; of a random sample of nine examples from the BL MS Add. 27944 version of this text where *nameliche* is immediately preceded by *and*, the BM MS Harley 614 version of the same text reads *anamely* in at least five cases (for this information we are indebted to Mr V. E. Watts).

501–2 *What þanne almesse or good schalt þu doo to þyn emcristen, as I sayde byforn, whan I spake of beneficience: Quid igitur beneficii impendes proximo?* (847).

502–3 *an holy seynt seiþ: 'Þer is noþynge rychere þan a good wyl':* St Gregory the Great, PL 76, col. 1094B: *Nihil quippe offertur Deo ditius voluntate bona.*

504 *more ful of manhoode: humanius* (849) all MSS except DN, *utilius.*

511 *let renne þer in þy myende:* a literal translation of *Ibi occurrant animo* (853).

516–7 *oþer in oþer maner ry3tful trauayle:* translator's addition.

517 *to þyse 3if þyn almesse:* translator's addition.

521 *þan eny oþer bodyly 3ifte:* translator's addition.

521–2 *Swych maner 3ifte, þat is to seye gostly almesse, spiritual beneficience: Huius munus beneficii* (861–2).

525 *as seynt Gregory say3t:* in PL 76, col. 1094C: *Sancti ut perfecte possent proximos diligere studuerint in hoc mundo nihil amare, nihil appetare, nihil vel sine appetitu possidere.* Aelred's text has *habere* for *amare.*

527 *þe wolde: þe* is here a weakly-stressed variant of *þey*: see Intro., p. liii.

529–31 *for þey trauayled ny3t and day to haue wordly good; and þey seyn to doo charite and almesse, for þey wolde haue what for-to 3yue: Vt enim caritatis impleant legem, quaerunt ut habeant quod erogent* (868–9).

531–2 *Bote certayn, þyse wel ofte fayled of þe he3e parfeccioun off charite: cum eius perfectionem ipsis adscribat, qui nihil habendum, nihil appetendum, nihil uel sine appetitu possidendum arbitrantur* (870–2); the translator has considerably altered the sense of the original, which is that Gregory ascribed the height of perfection in charity to those who wished to have absolutely nothing.

535 *of þe loue of God: de dilectione Dei* (873). MS *good* is admittedly a recorded ME spelling of *God* but as it does not appear elsewhere in this text it is presumably an error on the part of this, or an earlier, scribe.

alþou3t: the form *(al)þou3t*, with unexplained final *-t*, is strictly Northern and Scottish in distribution.

536 *boþe hem:* i.e., both Mary and Martha.

538–9 *holy affeccioun of þe euerlastyngge welle of loue: ex diuinae uero dilectionis fonte* (877).

541 *in taste of gostly swetnesse: in spiritualis gustus dulcedine* (880).

544 *in pouerte:* omitting *in silentio* (882), also omitted by NUT.

545 *gostly and bodyly:* translator's addition.

551 *þyn herte: mens tua* (888).

552 *vielþe and stenc of foule 3ou3tes: cogitationum sorde* (888). MS *stent* is probably simply a slip of the pen; *c* as a graphy for /tʃ/ is exemplified in *whic* for *which.* For *3ou3tes*, see l. 277 n.

553   *to þyngges þat be þ apassyd, of þe whiche is imaad miende in þe trewe gospel:* L. merely *ad posteriora* (890).

555   *wit oure lady Marie:* L. adds *libros quibus Virginis partus et Christi prophetatur aduentus euolue* (891–2), for which the translator substitutes *wher schee abood þe angel message*. The change of reference from Isaiah's prophecy of the Incarnation and Virgin Birth to the Annunciation itself, seems to be a conscious choice. As a result the recluse is not invited to meditate on any subject from the Old Testament. Cf. l. 55, where the translator also chooses to ignore an OT reference and substitute for it a reference to the Blessed Virgin Mary.

556–7   *þe angel comyngge: aduentum angeli* (892); the endingless genitive *angel* is formed on analogy with the still-surviving OE endingless genitive, preserved in this text in *moder* (349, 583, etc.).

559–60   *whanne þe angel begynþ is salutacioun to þilke blessede mayde and modur: dulcissimam dominam tuam cum angelo salutante* (894).

561   *Aue Maria:* Luke 1: 28.

565–6   *whanne Godys sone was maad man, ful of grace and sooþfastnesse: quando Verbum caro factum est et habitauit in nobis, plenum gratiae et ueritatis* (898–9), a reference to John 1: 14.

570   *fulfelde of grace:* a very free translation of *obumbrauit* (901–2), which refers to Luke 1: 35. The obvious rendering, *overshadow*, is in fact a sixteenth-century formation (see *OED* sv).

571   *wit how muche swetnesse were þu iuisited: quanta inebriabaris* (DMN *inebriaris*) *dulcedine* (903).

574   *whanne of þy clene maydenly blood he made hym blood:* translator's addition.

575–6   *in þe whyche was þe fulle godhede bodyly:* cf. Col. 2:9.

577   *be-cause þat þu schuldest take good heede: ut . . . diligenter attendas* (908–9), except BDMV, *ut . . . diligas*.

580–1   *wher þat Eliȝabeth and blessede Marye wit swete kleppyngge and kissyngge mette to-gydere: et sterilis et uirginis suauem intuere complexum* (911).

583   *Ihon Baptiste in his moder wombe, hoppyngge for ioye: inter anilia uiscera conclusus* (913) accounts for *in his moder wombe* but the only authority for *hoppyngge for ioye* is *indicibili gaudio* (914). Possibly the translator read following *salutauit* (<L *salutare*, 'to greet') as *saltauit* (<L *saltare*, 'to dance', frequentative form of *salire*, 'to hop'). 'To hop for joy' is a common ME idiom which later (around 1775) gave way to NE 'to jump for joy'.

585   *as a kniȝt is verrey kynge:* not in L., but replacing *uox uerbum*

(912–13). Aelred's idea is that John, the Voice crying in the wilderness, here greets Christ, the Word made flesh. There is a play on words, as *uox* can also mean 'sound', which is naturally subordinate to a whole word, and possibly an allusion to the fact that Zachariah's voice was not restored to him until after the birth of his son John (see Luke 1: 64 and the second stanza of *Ut queant laxis*, the Office Hymn for the feast of John the Baptist). The ME translator does not attempt to convey the subtleties of this conceit.

587–8 *aȝens derknesse of wo and sorwe þat long to-fore hadde reygned:* this phrase translates an absolute construction in L., *pulsisque tristitiae tenebris* (915–16). Apparently the translator read *sempiterna* (from the subsequent phrase, *sempiterna laetitia prophetatur*) as *sempiterne*, assumed it must be a feminine adjective in the genitive case modifying *tristitiae*, and did the best he could with it, rendering it as *þat long to-fore hadde reygned*.

591 *honoure þyn husbonde Criste: tuum Sponsum amplectere* (919).

592 *sein Ihon:* translator's addition.

595 *to bern here child:* translator's addition.

597 *Paruulus natus est nobis:* Isaiah 9: 6.

600 *driwe:* a scribal variation of *driue*; the reverse of this phenomenon is seen in *yveue*, 'woven', l. 408.

    and baldely go forþ: not in L.

601 *þilke tendre feet of Crist: sacratissimis pedibus* (926–7).

601–2 *kissyngge hem wit al þyn herte ofte-tyme er þu reste: oscula gemines* (927) <L *geminare*, 'to double'.

603 *taak heede enterly in þy sowle: mente pertracta* (928).

603–4 *þe walkyngge of þe scheperdys: pastorum excubias* (928).

    walkyngge must clearly be a form of 'to wake, keep vigil': the line-division occurs after *wal-* and the first stroke of this scribe's *k* is identical to his *l*, which suggests that this form is an error. But *OED* records *walk* as a fairly common Northern and Scottish form of *wake* from the fourteenth to the eighteenth century, where *l* acts as a diacritic to indicate the extreme back quality of the reflex of lengthened OE *a*. As there are other traces of a northerly dialect in this text (see Intro., p. li), it seems best to accept *walkyngge* as a genuine form.

604–5 *syngynge and wurschepynge:* translator's addition.

606 *Gloria in excelsis:* Luke 2: 14.

609–10 *and also whan vre lady for drede of Herowd fleþ in-to Egypte wit here child in here lappe:* L. simply *fugientem in Aegyptum* (933).

610 *let here not goon alone, bot go forþ wit here: nec . . . incomitatum*

relinque (933). The L. refers to Christ (*incomitatum* is masculine in gender) not the Blessed Virgin; if this is not a mistake, it is in line with the translator's apparently deliberate aggrandisement of her role throughout.

611   *haue on opinion: opinare* (934): either = 'have an opinion' or 'have on opinion', since in this text *an* appears as a variant of *on* prep. in reduced stress. At l. 1133 there is another example of *on*, used in a weakened sense, merging into the indefinite article. There is no support in either ME or (O)F for either idiom but it seems safer to assume that *on* represents the indefinite article; in l. 636 the expression is unambiguously *haue an opinioun*.

613   *Whanne hure lady wente to Egipteward, she was itake of þeues: eum a latronibus deprehensum in uia* (934–5). Again, the reference in the L. is to Christ, not his mother.

612   *Narracio bona*: the editor of Aelred's Latin cites M. R. James, *Apocryphal New Testament* (Oxford, 1924, repr. 1953), p. 81 as the source for this story of the Holy Family's encounter with the Good Thief during the flight into Egypt. This, however, refers to the 'Arabic Gospel of the Infancy', which certainly contains a version of this legend but cannot have been Aelred's source, unless there existed an unrecorded Latin translation. However, according to James, another version of the story is found in the *Vita Rhythmica*, a Latin composition of the thirteenth century (ed. A. Voegtlin (Stuttgart, 1888), I, 2234–68). A version, short but very close to Aelred's, is also found in the Holkham Bible Picture Book, which is probably of English origin and has been dated as 1320–30 (ed. F. P. Pickering, ANTS 23 (1971), f. 14^r/15–26), and in two ME poems printed by C. Horstmann, *Sammlung Altenglischer Legenden* (Heilbronn, 1878), found in MS Harley 2399 f. 47 (fifteenth century) and MS Harley 3954 f. 70 (fourteenth century).

614   *þe maister-þef: principis latronum* (936).

614–5   *whic sterte to vre lady and vndyde here lappe:* not in L., but cf. MS Harley 3954, f. 70:

> He askyd our lady be here lay:
> 'Qwat beryst þou?' she seyde: 'a chylde'
> . . . . . .
> He tok Mary al in hey,
> He helde here stylle be þᵉ lappe.

617–8   *of grettere mageste þan an-oþer pur man: supra hominem esse* (939). *pur* is ambiguous, either 'pure' or 'poor'. In view of the stress Aelred places on the human, as opposed to the divine characteristics of Christ, it may be that the sense of the passage is 'than any (other) completely, unmixedly human man'; thus, in one aspect,

Christ is like any other man in having no trace of superhuman, non-mortal characteristics, although in his divine aspect he is of *grettere mageste.*

620–1 *heraftur whanne þu cumst to þy grete lordschipe:* translator's addition.

622–3 *for I wyl kepe þe and þy moder harmles:* translator's addition.

626 *Neque tu times Deum:* Luke 23: 40–1. *hic vero nichil mali gessit* accurately reflects the Vulgate text; the MSS of Aelred's original all read *hic autem nihil mali fecit* (946).

628–9 *wit gret meknesse and contricioun:* not in L.

631 *wit alle þe veynes of his herte:* not in L. *vein* is frequently used in a figurative sense in ME, but the phrase 'with all the veins of one's heart', meaning 'from the bottom of one's heart, fervently', is not recorded elsewhere before 1587. See *OED* VEIN. Presumably it was formed by analogy with such phrases as *entrayles of þy herte* (ll. 121–2).

632 *Memento mei:* Luke 23: 42. The Vulgate text, and all the L. MSS, read *cum* for *dum.*

634–5 *for he answerede anoon and seyde: Amen dico tibi, hodie mecum eris in paradyso:* a reference to Luke 23: 43 added by the translator.

634 *And for-soþe, Crist forȝat not is couenaunt:* in the L. it is the thief who remembers the pact: *Conuersus ad Dominum . . ., pacti sui non immemor* (946–8).

636 *haue an opinioun þat þis tale is soþ:* the more cautious L. has *haud inutile arbitror hac uti opinione, remota omni affirmandi temeritate* (949–51) ('I do not consider it unprofitable to hold this opinion, as long as any rashness in asserting it positively is laid aside'). Aelred has more to say on the subject of 'pious opinions' (as distinguished from articles of faith) in *De Iesu Puero* I, 157–9: 'Where were you, Lord? It is permissible to guess or conjecture or hazard an opinion on all this; but it is forbidden rashly to state anything for certain.' Nicholas Love, *Mirrour*, gives a similar, fifteenth-century, view: '. . . We may, to stirring of devotion, imagine and think diverse words of Him, and others that we find not written, so that it be not against belief' (quoted in M. Deansley, *The Lollard Bible* (Cambridge, 1920), p. 322).

637–8 *þy ȝunge husbonde Crist:* L. simply *eum* (953).

638 *childly and myryli:* translator's addition.

640–1 *how swete and gracious he was to his nursche: operanti nutricio assistentem* (954). It is clear from the L. that *nutricio* (<L *nutricius,* 'nurse, tutor') refers to St Joseph. ME *nursche* refers

indifferently to a woman or man charged with the upbringing of a child; here it probably has the specific sense of 'foster-father'.

643   *wanne after þat he is twelf ӡer old:* cf. Luke 2: 42 ff. Aelred's fuller treatment of Christ's visit to Jerusalem as a child is, of course, to be found in his treatise *De Iesu Puero Duodenni, ed. cit.,* I, 249–78.

644   *in-to þe temple:* not in L.

   hem unwytyngge: illis redeuntibus et nescientibus (957).

646–7   *what sorwe schalt þu haue?:* not in L.

648–50   *whanne þu byӡenkeste of þe sorwe of his moder Marie, whanne sche hadde iloste so dire a child? And after, whan sche hadde ifounde hym syttyngge among þe doctoures in þe temple:* translator's addition.

   byӡenkeste: MS *byӡenkest'*. The scribe's somewhat cavalier use of abbreviations prompts the doubt as to whether this should be taken at its face value. However, in this text 'bethink' is regularly (though not invariably) a reflexive verb, so *byӡenkeste* may well reflect assimilation of the following reflexive pronoun *þe*. Cf. ll. 1125–6 and note.

651   *wit þis mornful vndernymyngge: dulci quadam increpatione* (959).

   Fili, quid fecisti: Luke 2: 48.

653–4   *ӡif þu folwe þis blessed mayde whider þat euer sche goþ: Si autem Virginem sequi quocumque ierit delectet* (962), a reference to Rev. 14: 4. It is clear from comparison with the passage in Revelation, and from the following sentences in Aelred's original, that *virginem* refers here not to the Blessed Virgin but to Christ, the Lamb and Virgin Spouse. Cf. notes to ll. 55, 610, 613.

657   *vnderfonge:* MS *vnderfounde* could only be either the pp. of *underfinden* 'to perceive, understand', which would be grammatically inappropriate, or the inf. of *underfounden,* a verb whose existence is unrecorded. L *suscipis* (966) suggests that the original verb here was *vnderfonge,* 'receive'. Probably the scribe was distracted by nearby *husbounde.*

659–60   *Aftur þis many day þy spouse Crist goþ in-to desert, ӡyuyngge þe ensaumple to fle blast and bost of þe wordle: Exinde solitudinis tibi secreta dicauit* (968) ('Next he dedicated for your benefit the solitude of the desert'). *many day* = 'for many days'; *blast and bost* are clearly contrasted with the solitude and silence of the wilderness which suggests that *bost* here has the sense 'noise, bustle', rather than 'boasting' (*MED* sv BOST 4).

660   *þer he fastyde fourty dayes:* L., more allusively, *santificauit ieiunium* (968).

662   *vre gostly enemy: callido hoste* (969); see note to l. 101.

663–4 *I prey þe tak good heede, þat þu mowe do þer-after: meditare, et imitare* (970–1) all MSS except BDMV which have *diligenter attendens, dilige a quo facta sunt*. This, which is not adopted by Talbot, seems the better reading. If the archetype read *Haec tibi facta, et pro te facta, et quomodo* facta diligenter attendas, dilige a quo *facta sunt, meditare, et imitare* it is easy to see how the non-italicized phrase could have been omitted through homoioteleuton.

665 *þilke wrecchede wymman:* John 8: 3 ff. MS *wymmen* must be an error as elsewhere the scribe always differentiates between *wym-*, *wom-*, *wumman* sg. and *-men* pl.

667–8 *preyȝid to ȝyue þo doom: rogatus sententiam* (973) all MSS except R, *rogatus dare sententiam*.

669 *irþely: terrenos . . . non caelestes* (974–5).

669–70 *Qui sine peccato:* John 8: 7.

675 *Nemo te condempnauit:* John 8: 10–11.

680 *ho may acuse: quis condemnabit* (984), a reference to Rom. 8: 33–4.

680–1 *þat noman be to bold herfore:* translator's addition.

682 *Vade:* John 8: 11.

686 *Marie Magdeleyn:* translator's addition. The identification of 'the woman who was a sinner', who anointed Christ in the house of Simon the Pharisee, with Mary, the sister of Martha and Lazarus who anointed Christ in their house at Bethany, and of both of these women with Mary of Magdala who first saw the resurrected Christ, was traditional in the Western Church but has no scriptural foundation. Modern biblical scholars distinguish three separate women.

687 *ley to softly þyn eȝen:* the critical text reads *demulce osculis* (989) but RHa have *demulce oculis* which is clearly nonsense but was equally clearly the reading of the translator's exemplar. *Oculis* and *osculis* would be pronounced identically in ML.

689 *gostly smel in þy sowle:* L. simply *odore* (990).

690 *for þyn vnwurþynesse:* translator's addition.

690–1 *trawþ awey his feet, and foucheþ not saaf þat þu kysse hem: negat pedes* (992). *trawþ:* as there are no other examples in this text of devoicing of initial [d], this form is probably an isolated example of assimilation to the preceding final [t].

692 *for-smoteryd: grauidos lacrymis* (992–3; U has *grandes*); cf. l. 948. This word is not recorded elsewhere in English. The context (~ *wit terys*) suggests the sense 'bespattered', and we would therefore posit an ideophonic formation from *smit-*, the preterite pl. root of OE *smītan*, 'to pollute, blemish' or 'to smear' (see G. V. Smithers, 'Some

English Ideophones', *Archivum Linguisticum*, VI (1954), 73–111). The stages in the formation must have been as follows (not necessarily in chronological order): i) the final -*t* of *smĭt*- was geminated, giving *smĭtt*- (recorded in OE *smittian* 'to defile, stain'); ii) the process of apophonic variation operated, giving the series *smĭtt*-/*smătt*-/*smŭtt*-/*smŏtt*- (the *a*-variety is preserved in the verb *smatter*, first recorded in the fourteenth century); iii) the iterative suffix -*r*- was added (whence (besides *smŭttern and *smŏttern) *smăttern*); and iv) the intensive or completive prefix *for*- was added, giving *for-smo(t)ter(n)*. The continuity of sense, in the general area 'stain, spot, blemish', is apparent throughout these stages. Cf. Chaucer's *bismotered*, 'bespattered with dirt' (*Canterbury Tales*, A 76), which shares the foregoing etymology in all its essentials.

693   *pytous cryingge: inenarrabilibusque gemitibus* (993–4), a reference to Rom. 8: 26.

694   *as Iacob dede:* Gen. 32: 24.

697   *and wil not hiere þe:* translator's addition.

697–8   *for þu schuldest not kysse hem:* translator's addition.

699   *Vsquequo auertis:* Ps. 12: 1.

700   *Redde michi:* Ps. 50: 14.

701   *Quesiui faciem tuam:* Ps. 26: 8.

707   *Fili, inquid:* Matt. 9: 2, Mk. 2: 5.

711   *ne duely ne hadde not deseruyd:* the translator here substitutes a vague summary for Aelred's explicit reference to the three essential elements of penance — confession, contrition and satisfaction: *quam non praecesserat confessio, non meruerat satisfactio, non exigebat contritio* (1007–8). Aelred develops the subject further in one of his sermons: see PL 195, 420D.

713   *lyf and deþ is in þy hondes: uita in uoluntate tua* (1010), a reference to Ps. 29: 6.

715–17   *ʒif þe envyous pharyse gruccheþ þat Crist is so merciable to forʒyue a synful man his synnes: Pharisaee, quid murmuras?* (1013).

717   *Crist hym-self smyt hym in þe face:* this extraordinary phrase, for which there is no authority either in the Vulgate or in Aelred, is the translator's own contribution. Cf. 719, *maugre þe pharises face*, and note.

718–19   *Crist wyl haue mercy of whom þat is wille is:* cf. Rom. 9: 18.

719   *maugre þe pharises face:* that is, 'in spite of the Pharisee's opposition, notwithstanding all he can do'. *Face* is one of a large and somewhat bizarre array of nouns (e.g., *teeth, beard, nose*) used with

maugre in this ME idiom, all of them being metaphors for the outward 'front' presented in defiance to the world. The idiom is an adaptation of *maugre* + possessive pn. (a calque on OF *malgré mien* (*tien*, *sien*, etc.)) which meant 'in spite of me (you, him, etc.)', due probably to a gradual misunderstanding of the function of the possessive pronoun (see Mustanoja, pp. 165 and 392).

725–6 *noon auarice haad wit-drawe:* this makes no sense at all. The translator has obviously totally failed to grasp the meaning of his original, but in so doing has opened up the way to some speculation as to which particular original he was working from.

It is self-evident that he is unlikely to have failed to recognize the straightforward form *coinquinavit* ('has sullied'), which is that of Talbot's edited text and MS N, or indeed the variant readings *corrupit* (T) and *exasperauit* (BDMV); there is, however, one further variant reading, *contraxit*, which occurs in U, R and Ha, and it seems certain that the translator must have been working from a MS which contained this form, and that, being entirely unfamiliar with and nonplussed by it, he was forced into the desperate expedient of translating it literally as *haad witdrawe*.

He might be forgiven for being unfamiliar with the construction, for which cf. *Spec. Car.* I, 751 *mentem . . . non avaritia contrahit*. A primary sense of L *contrahere* is 'to draw together, draw in, contract, especially the body and various parts of it', which is often used in various figurative senses (e.g., *frontem contrahere*, 'to frown, scowl'). There appear to be no other recorded examples where, as here (*manus . . ., quas . . . avaritia non [contraxit]*), specific reference is made to the hands, but a very instructive parallel is to be found in the adjectival use of the pp. *contractus* with the sense 'parsimonious' (cf., for example, *parcissimum . . . hominem vocamus pusilli animi et contracti*, Seneca, *de Beneficiis*, ed. K. Hosius, Bibliotheca Teubneriana (1914), 2.34.4); the inference to be drawn from this is that there existed a colloquial Latin phrase *manus contrahere*, meaning 'to draw together, contract the hands', and thus 'to be avaricious' (cf. NE 'tight-fisted'), of which the ppl. adj. *contractus* later came to be used independently, of people or their dispositions, as 'mean, sparing' &c. (cf. NE slang 'tight' with this sense). Cf. also the analogous *manus . . . ad dandum collecta*, Ecclesiasticus 4: 36 and the allegorization of the contrary, 'open-handed', nature of Generosity in Alan of Lille, *De Planctu Naturae*, Prose VIII: 'Her hands which . . . lay open, ample and broad, cared for the offices of giving' (trans. D. M. Moffat (New Haven, 1908), p. 81). The sense of L. here is thus '. . . which no avarice has drawn together, caused to be tight-fisted'. (It may be pertinent to add that Aelred seems to have been familiar with the above work of Seneca's, since he quotes from it in his *de Anima* (ed.

C. H. Talbot, *Mediaeval and Renaissance Studies* (London, 1952), p. 100, l. 6).)

726–7 *wit-oute wraþþe, wit-oute stryf: sine ira et disceptatione* (1019) (D *discepcione*, M *deceptione*), a reference to I Tim. 2: 8.

727 *þees haad imaad fair: pax composuit* (1019–20), except Ha, *compescuit*. L *componere* can, with reference to hair, clothes, etc., mean 'to set in order'.

732 *a woodschipe: stultissimum* (1024).

733 *to haue to gret hope þerof:* emendation of the MS reading is obviously needed and is suggested by L. *praesumere* (1024).

734 *paltyk: paralyticus* (1021). *paltyk*, 'palsied, suffering from paralysis' is not recorded in dictionaries of English, but completes the equation *paralysis: paralytic; palsy:* –. It may probably be traced back to an AF *parletike (=OF *paralitike* >ME *paralitike*; cf. AF *parlesie*, OF *paralisie*) which is probably represented in the form *parlatyk* (*Cleanness*, ed. Sir I. Gollancz (Oxford, 1921), l. 1095). The subsequent development of *parlatyk* to *paltyk* is parallel to that of ME *parlesie, -asie* to *palsie*.

740–1 *to þilke blessyde feste of Ihesu and Marthe, Marie and Laʒar:* not in L.

742 *loue and frendschipe: amicitiae* (1030).

743 *Diligebat:* John 11: 36.

744–5 *a greet priuilegie of special loue: specialis amicitiae priuilegium qua illi familiariori adhaerebant affectu* (1032–3). From the L. it seems that Aelred had in mind the love of Lazarus and his sisters for Christ; the English (*For ywis Ihesu louede hem feruently*) has the opposite implication. The adj. *special* may be an echo of courtly love terminology where it has the sense of 'particularly intimate' (cf. *Lancelot of the Laik*, ed. W. W. Skeat, EETS 6 (1865), l. 906).

746–7 *þat he wepte wit hem for Laʒar, whanne þat he was deed: quibus collacrymatus est lacrymantibus* (1034).

749 *Ecce quomodo:* John 11: 36. Aelred has *Vide:* as so often seems to be the case, he apparently quotes from memory. The ME adopts the reading of the Vulgate.

749–50 *Bote now, forto speke of þis feste þat þyse þre, as þe gospel seiþ, made to Ihesu: Et ecce faciunt ei coenam ibi* (1037).

758 *of eny maner spiritual swetnesse:* translator's addition.

761 *grynte wit his teþ:* cf. l. 1309, *gryntyngge wit teeþ*. The vowel of *grynt-* presumably represents eME *ĕ*, raised to *ĭ* before *n* + consonant. The pair *grent-, grint-*, which are amply recorded in ME, are phonetic variants of *grunt-*, 'to grunt, roar' (<OE *grunnettan*). All

three are cited, from the fourteenth century onwards, with the sense 'to grind, gnash', always with reference to the teeth; this sense development is presumably due to the influence of *grind*, assisted perhaps by the fact that *grynt* was a common form of the pr. ind. 3 sg. of this verb in ME.

762–3   *seye þat þis oynement of spiritual deuocioun is not bote ilost: si perditionem uocat deuotionem* (1047–8).

763   *Vt quid:* Matt. 26: 8.

765   *and þis is þe voys of manye men now-aday:* translator's addition. This gratuitous comment most likely refers to persistent proposals, in the later fourteenth century, for the disendowment of the Church. In his *Determinationes* of 1373 Wycliffe replied to the proposition of Uhtred of Boldon that no one should teach that priests can be deprived of their tithes or oblations with the assertion that laymen may judge if these endowments are being misused and may deprive the clergy of them if they are (see G. Holmes, *The Good Parliament* (Oxford, 1975), pp. 168–9). Holmes suggests that this probably reflects arguments provoked by the secular taxation of the clergy in 1371. In his *De Civili Dominio*, the first book of which (ed. R. L. Poole (London, 1885)) was probably written in 1375–6, Wycliffe went further and argued that the Church had no right to own property at all. These ideas, however, hardly became general until the Peasants' Revolt and the subsequent rise of Lollardy. John Ball is said to have advocated 'the distribution of clerical property among the laity' (R. Hilton, *Bond Men Made Free* (London, 1973), p. 227), and Wat Tyler proposed that 'No churchmen, whether monastic or secular, were to hold property but only to be given their reasonable subsistence. The surplus in the parishes . . . was to be divided among the parishioners. The great property of the possessioners . . . should be redistributed to the commons' (ibid., p. 228). A scheme for disendowment was actually put forward by Lollards in 1395 (see H. Workman, *John Wyclif: A Study in the English Medieval Church* Oxford, 1926, repr. 1966) II, 398). The addition here, of course, could have been interpolated at any stage in the transmission of the text, and can hardly be used as a precise indication of date, but it seems likely that the addition itself, at any rate, dates from the post-1381 period, which would agree with the dating of the Vernon MS as 1382–1400.

768   *he þat was ry3tful and mercyful iugge: iudex* (1051).

769–70   *þat was Marie Magdeleyne:* translator's addition; see note to l. 686.

770   *Sine, inquit:* Mark 14: 6.

775–6   *let Maryes partye suffise to me, and I wil be entendaunt to here: Ego solus Mariae, et illa mihi, mihi totum praestet quod habet, a me quidquid optat expectet* (1055–6). The translator has altered the subject of the sentence from 'Mary' to 'I'.

776–7   *Whoþer eny man woolde conseyle me: Quid enim? Tu ne Mariae consulis* (1057). Only the very corrupt MS B reads *me* for *ne*.

778–9   *þat blessyde face so fair and frehs: illa speciosissima facie* (1058–9).

783   *þy meke husbonde:* translator's addition.

784   *so homly:* translator's addition.

784–5   *beyngge as hit were astonyed of þe grete honour and reuerence þat is idoo to hym:* the L. *tantaque fieri pro te obstupescens* (1062–3) refers to the astonishment the recluse should feel at the great condescension shown to her. Either the translator has deliberately altered the sense or his exemplar omitted *pro te*, as does MS Ha.

786   *in which aray:* an example of what Jespersen (*A Modern English Grammar on Historical Principles*, Heidelberg and London (1922–49), Vol. III, § 6.53) characterizes as the adjunctive use of *which* in a loosely appositional clause, where there is no word to which the apposition can be strictly referred. Thus here, *in which aray* refers to Christ's sitting humbly on an ass (l. 784), and is to be translated 'presenting that appearance, an appearance like that'.

786–7   *children of Ebru:* the sense is evidently, despite L. *puerorum* (1063), 'children of Israel' (there is no biblical authority for supposing that 'children', in the literal sense, are being referred to (see Matthew 21: 9)). 'Members of a certain tribe or race' is of course a well-attested sense of ME *children*, but the phrase *children of Ebru* is not recorded elsewhere in English. Several parallel constructions occur, however, which exemplify the use of the noun *Ebru* with the sense 'the Hebrew nation, race (in relation to its members)' (cf., for example, 'Bede, folowenge the trawthe and the trewe acompte of men of Hebrewe [L. *sequens Hebraicum*]', *Higden's Polychronicon*, 2. 339).

787   *Osanna filio Dauid:* Matt. 21: 9.

789–90   *for Cristes soper a Scherepursday:* translator's addition.

790   *Scherepursday:* it is fairly certainly established that this epithet for the Thursday in Holy Week, which is much earlier in currency than the collocation Maundy Thursday, meant originally 'pure, purified Thursday' (cf. *Shrove Tuesday*, F *jeudi absolu*, also Du *witte Donderdag* (thirteenth century), G *weisser Donnerstag*, 'white Thursday'). *Schere* corresponds to ON *skærr* 'bright, clean, pure', which was possibly adopted into ME in the twelfth century, with the

initial [sk] being modified to [ʃ] under the influence of a native adjective, OE (?) *scǣre. The etymology is clinched by the forms *Skeyr Thurisday* (*Accounts of the Lord High Treasurer of Scotland 1498*, I, 384) and *Skyre thuresday* (*The Life of St. Cuthbert* (*c.* 1450), ed. Surtees Soc. 1891, l. 2277) which latter may be traced immediately to ON *Skíri-Þorsdagr* (ON *skírr*, 'clear, pure'). The epithet appears to have been applied to Maundy Thursday with allusion to the purification of the soul by confession, and possibly also to the practice of washing the altars on that day; the notion that it 'was so named from the ceremonial shaving of the tonsure before Good Friday' (as quoted by M. C. Seymour, *Mandeville's Travels* (Oxford, 1967), p. 233; cf. also Mirk, *Festiall*, p. 125, ll. 3–12) probably has its basis in folk-etymology.

792–3   *preye þat þu mowe sum almese of þoo crummes þat ben o þat blessyde boord:* L. *ut saltem de micis mensae illius eleemosynam praebeat mendicanti* (1068–69). That is, 'pray that you may obtain some alms'; the nonexpression of the infinitive of other than a verb of motion after an auxiliary verb is not common in ME, but it is not unexampled where the sense can be supplied from the context (see Mustanoja, p. 543). Here that context is reinforced later in the same passage: *þat þu mowe sumwhat gete* (794–5).

794–5   *þat þu mowe sumwhat gete: ut aliquid accipias* (1070), omitted by BMV.

795–6   *let biter terys move þilke pytous lord to haue pyte of þyn hungur: famem lacrymis prode* (1071).

806   *so boldely:* translator's addition.

807   *slepþ so sauerly in his lappe: in sinu eius caput reclinat* 1079–80).

808   *Ihon is is name:* the identification of 'the disciple whom Jesus loved' with St John the Evangelist is a very ancient tradition, though it is nowhere explicitly made in the gospels.

810–11   *þat euere-wellyngge welle Criste: ab illo . . . fonte* (1082–3).

812   *alle þe tresores off whit and of wysdom: omnes thesauri sapientiae et scientiae* (1083–4), a reference to Col. 2: 3.

813   *swete and diere disciple: O Ioannes* (1081).

814   *Art þu he33ere þan Petre:* on the pre-eminence of Peter see Aelred's sermon *In sollemnitate apostolorum Petri et Pauli* (*Sermones Inediti*, p. 123); on the complementary nature of John and Peter see *De Spir. Am.*, III, 939–49.

815–16   *þe grete pryuylegie of þy chastete: Speciale hoc uirginitatis priuilegium* (1087).

816–17   *þu were ichose a mayde of God: uirgo es electus a Domino*

(1088), which is Resp. 6 in the Cistercian Breviary for the Feast of St John. St John's virginity was an ancient traditional belief; *Ancrene Wisse*, f. 44ᵇ/21–5 refers to the tradition that the wedding at Cana was John's wedding, after which he left his bride (who, in some other versions of the story, was Mary Magdalene), the marriage of course remaining unconsummated, to follow Christ. Cf. also Mombritius, *Sanctuarium*, ii, 60–1, Aelfric's homily *The Assumption of St John*: '[Crist] hine lufode synderlice; na swa micclum for ðære mæglican sibbe swa for ðære clænnysse his ansundan mægðhades' (*The Homilies of the Anglo-Saxon Church*, ed. B. Thorpe (London, 2 vols., 1844 and 1846), I. 58) and MS Harley 2339, f. 6: 'O Joon euangelist, Cristis owne derlyng, þat of oure Lord Iesu Crist were chosen to be a maiden'.

818 *þu art clene mayde:* L. simply *uirgo* (1090).

819 *And ʒif þu darst auntre þe no furþere, etc.:* the idea contained in this passage is that of the approach to the true knowledge and love of God (the *knowyngge of þe grete godheede*) by way of devotion to the humanity of Christ (*His manhede*); these are what Dumont characterizes as the 'deux degrés dans la connaissance du Christ' (*op. cit.*, p. 132, n.7). The notion of the contemplation of Christ's humanity leading the soul to the love of God is a leading theme of Cistercian spirituality, though not confined to Cîteaux; St Bernard said that 'the principal motive of the Incarnation was God's plan to touch the hearts of men by the humanity of Christ' (*Sermo XX in Cantica*, PL 183, 867 ff.). Imitation of Christ's humanity is the sure path to knowledge and love of His divinity; this is the path the recluse must follow, in the footsteps of John, who has already attained his goal.

Eleventh-century forerunners of the Cistercians in this respect include Peter Damian, John of Fécamp and St Anselm; see L. Bouyer *et al.*, *La Spiritualité du Moyen Age* (Paris, 1961), pp. 146–7, 158 and, on the subject in general, E. Gilson, *The Mystical Theology of St Bernard*, trans. A. H. C. Downes (London, 1940), pp. 78–81.

822–3 *þe pappys of his manhede:* Aelred refers to 'the maternal breasts of Christ' and 'the milk of consolation' which the soul may find there in *Spec. Car.* II, 1090–4. The image, though startling to the modern reader, is not unique in medieval literature: cf. Julian of Norwich, *Revelations of Divine Love*, p. 150, 'The Mother may lay the child tenderly to her breast, but our tender Mother, Jesus, He may homely lead us into his blessed breast, by his sweet open side, and shew therin part of the Godhead and the joys of Heaven, with spiritual sureness of endless bliss' and *Orcherd of Syon*, ed. cit., p. 214/1–16: 'As a child þat is pesid resteþ at his modir breste and takeþ her mylk by meene of þe fleisch, in þe same wyse a soule, aftir tyme it is come to þis last staat [tears of union], it resteþ at þe brest of my

dyuyne charite, hooldynge in her mouþ of holy desier þe flesch of
Crist crucified . . . . By þe which brest sche drawiþ to her mylk of
vertu, in þe which vertu is conteyned liif of grace, þat makeþ her to
taaste my dyuyne nature, þe which ȝeueþ swetnesse to vertues.'

823–4 *þat þu mowe gostly be fed in þenkyngge what he dude for vs in
vre flehs: quo nutriaris* (1094).

825   *by-fore his passioun*: translator's addition.

826   *Pater:* John 17: 11.

827–8 *þat þu mowe hiere þe same oryson yseyd to þe fader for þe:* in
the L. this refers forward to the prayer 'volo ut ubi sum ego, et illi sint
mecum', which the ME omits.

830–1 *in blody anguyssche, to maken his preyere:* not in L.

832   *Iames and Ihon: duobus filiis Zebedaei* (1101).

833   *at þe hardeste:* here with the sense of 'at least' (L. *uel*); cf. *The
Book of the Knight of La Tour-Landry*, ed. T. Wright, EETS 33
(1868), p. 81, l. 28.

835   *after þe manhoode:* translator's addition.

   Tristis est anima mea: Matt. 26: 38.

838   *þat þu louest me so muche, by-comyngge man for me: te ex-
hibens hominem* (1106) which refers to the human weakness of Christ
in the Agony in the Garden; the ME however alludes to the whole of
the Incarnation as a proof of Christ's love.

840   *and preyest for me: oras* (1107).

   for anguyssche: translator's addition.

843   *þat þey be not spild:* translator's addition.

844   *ȝif þu canst do nomore:* translator's addition.

845–6 *þilke mornful vndernymyngge þat Crist putte to Petre:*
translator's addition.

846   *Sic non potuisti:* Matt. 26: 40.

850   *which acursyd compaynye of Iewes: impiorum turba* (1112).

852   *drawyþ hym forþ as a þef:* not in L., but perhaps suggested by
Luke 22: 52; cf. also Rolle, 'Meditation on the Passion', I/20–7 and
II/103–4, in *English Writings of Richard Rolle*, ed. H. E. Allen (Oxford,
1931), pp. 20 and 30.

855   *sorwe and conpassioun: zelus* (1116).

856   *Bote naþeles, suster, ȝit suffre a while:* translator's addition.

860–1 *forto avenge þyn husbonde:* translator's addition.

864   *þat he was ydemed in:* translator's addition.

865   *þe cursede Iewes defoyleþ wit here foule spatelyngge: illi sputis
illiniunt* (1122).

866   *þu whash hit:* on the expression of the subject pn. in the imperative see Mustanoja, pp. 475–6. The preceding of the verb by the pn., as here, he describes as a phenomenon restricted to early and later ME poetry.

867–8   *whanne he hadde forsake hym: tertio negantem* (1124).

868   *and anon turnede aȝen to hym-self: quando ille conuersus, et in se reuersus* (1124–5); that is, *Peter* became pensive, introspective. The non-expression of the subject pronoun in the second of two co-ordinate clauses is common in ME (see Mustanoja, pp. 138–44).

    anon: the MS here reads *anoñ*; the otiose mark of abbreviation for *n, m* is also exemplified in two cases of *noñ* (l. 1373).

875–6   *as a schep þat is ilad to his deþ:* Isaiah 53: 7.

879   *for þi sake:* translator's addition.

880   *betyngge:* this is an outstanding example of the difficulty of interpreting the scribe's final abbreviation (see Intro., p. lix). The formal correspondence to L. *verbera* (1133) suggests reading *betyngges*; however, the plural *verbera* is frequently used collectively, with the sense 'a thrashing, whipping', so we have preferred to adopt the singular form *betyngge*, which has the advantage of corresponding formally with *dispysyngge*.

883   *wit scharpe thornes to þe brayn:* L. simply *spinis* (1137).

884   *be dishonested wit a ryed: arundine dehonestari* (1138). The MS reading, *dishonestly*, is clearly corrupt. It is possible that a pp. may have dropped out, but the more likely explanation is that the text originally read *dishonested*. There is a well-attested ME verb *dishonesten* < OF *deshonester*, with the primary sense 'to bring dishonour, disgrace or discredit on'.

886–7   *al forbled and beten: flagellatus* (1139).

888   *Ecce homo:* John 19: 5.

890   *þe wannesse of þe woundes: liuor uulnerum* RHa; all other MSS read *liuor ulcerum* (1141–2).

891   *he is a man:* the translator then omits *Iam nunc agnosce, Zabule, quia homo est* (1142–3); see note to ll. 896–7.

896–7   *bote whanne he schal come hym-self to ȝyue riȝtful dom ate day of dome, þanne he schal be knowe a verrey myȝtful God:* L. simply *sed cognoscetur Deus iudicium faciens* (1146–7). The ME then omits the following passage found in all MSS of the L.: *Sero animaduertisti, Zabule. Quid tibi per mulierem uisum est agere, ut dimittatur? Tarde locutus es* (1148–9). ('You have noticed it (*sc.* Christ's divinity) too late, Satan. Why think of using the woman (*i.e.*, Pilate's wife) as your agent to have him set free? You have spoken too late.') This omission may be connected with the earlier omission at l.

891 (see preceding note). The L. in both cases refers to a primitive theory of the Redemption, stemming from Origen, which held that Satan, who as a result of Adam's disobedience had certain rights over mankind, failed to realize that Christ was the Son of God, therefore sinless and not within his jurisdiction. When Satan attempted to exercise these presumed rights in the case of Christ (that is, by having him put to death) he abused them, lost them and man was released, or ransomed, from his domination. Satan was therefore 'deceived' by Christ, just as Adam had been deceived by Satan. This theory (sometimes called the 'Ransom' theory) was, even in the twelfth century, somewhat old-fashioned. It was displaced by St Anselm's theory, expounded in his *Cur Deus homo*, which saw Christ's death as a debt paid to the Father rather than a ransome paid to the Devil. In the omitted passage, Aelred alludes to the idea that Satan realized his danger at the last minute and was responsible for the troubling dreams of Pilate's wife, which were his desperate attempt to have Christ released.

899 *Ihesu stant pouerly to-fore hym:* translator's addition.

902 *þyn husbounde Crist:* translator's addition.

903 *Ecce principatus super humerum eius:* Isaiah 9: 6.

905 *virga regni tui:* the L. here has *regni eius* (1152–3), but the ME reproduces the Vulgate reading (Heb. 1: 8 and Ps. 44: 7). But the translator was sufficiently confused by Aelred's alteration of the scriptural quotation to be led into inconsistency ('þy riȝtwisnesse' but 'his kyngdom').

907 *among knytes: inter milites* (1155).

908 *saue his precious cote þat vre lady hadde iwrouȝt wit-oute seem:* translator's addition. The idea that Christ's seamless garment, the *tunica inconsutelis*, was woven by the Blessed Virgin Mary is somewhat unusual. However, Thomas Netter (*c.* 1377–1431), the Carmelite prelate, refers to this tradition, citing Wycliffe, *De Papa*, cap. XII in his *Doctrinale* III, 210E–211A: *de mutatione Sacerdotalium vestium Jesu Christi, qua induit eum benedicta Mater ejus, puta tunica inconsuteli desuper contexta per totum.*

911 *þouȝr:* this form reflects OE unmetathesized *þurh*, with the 'reversed grapheme' *ȝr* probably representing a still-current pronunciation /rχ/.

912 *and manye oþre dispiteȝ doþ hym:* translator's addition.

914–15 *bryngyngge as hit were heuene and irþe to-gydere: ima superis unit, et caelestibus terrena coniungit* (1158–9).

915 *what þu:* a direct translation of L. *quid tu* (1162), which conforms to no recorded ME idiom.

916–17   *sepþe þe sunne þat is vnresonable is sory: si sole contristante* (1161).

920   *for sorwe of so pytous deþ:* not in L.

922   *what pacience, what benignite: quam tranquillitatem* (1166).

923   *alwey in his torment:* not in L.

928   *þat beþ abouȝte to revyn hym þe lyf and putte hym to þe deþ:* L. simply *a quibus occiditur* (1169–70).

929   *Wit how swetnesse: Cum qua mentis dulcedine* (1170). Cf. *wit how delices,* l. 1183. The fact that this dubious construction occurs twice, and that it translates the L. interrogative pn., raises the question whether it can reflect a genuine usage – that is, whether *how* could be used as a determiner with the sense 'what (like) a . . .'. There is no direct evidence for this, but *how* is commonly recorded in direct exclamations in OE and ME (see *OED*, sv *adv.* 7), a usage shared by *what* (see *OED*, sv, B 1, 4). In both cases, the exclamation is one of the earliest recorded usages. *What* subsequently (in the early fourteenth century) came to be used as an exclamatory determiner (see *OED*, sv, B 5 and cf. *wyþ wat mildenesse,* l. 929). Can it be that in the early stages of the conversion of the interjection and exclamatory adverb to the exclamatory determiner, *how* and *what* were in competition for a place that has been won by *what*?

929–30   *wyþ wat mildenesse of alle his spirit: cum qua spiritus deuotione* (1170).

931   *Pater, ignosce illis:* Luke 23: 34.

934   *adorour:* not recorded elsewhere in English before 1602. It is evidently a neologism, formed on the ME verb *adoren* (<(O)F *adourer,* a refashioning, after L *adorare,* of OF *ao(u)rer,* whence earlier ME *aouren*), for it does not occur in OF. Aelred has used *adorator* earlier (*tuae maiestatis adorator,* here rendered *wurschipere*), but *adorour* actually translates *uenerator* (1173).

935   *a stedefast knowlechere of þy grete mercy: tuae misericordiae contemplator* (1174). L. *contemplator* has the sense 'one who studies, observes' of which *knowlechere* seems a strange translation. It is possible that the translator's exemplar had *confessor* for *contemplator*; in the Wycliffe Bible *knowlechere* translates *confitentem* and in the fifteenth century is used as a synonym for ME *confessour*. See *MED* KNOULECHER(E.

936   *þyn infirmite þat þu haste itake of mankynde:* L. simply *infirmitatis* (1174).

939–40   *for me, þat wyþ mek herte wurschipe þy passioun and þy deþ, þat þu seydest for hem þat putte þe to þy deþ:* translator's addition.

946 *þilke face, þat angeles haueþ delyt to loke in:* L. simply *uultum* (1180). It is not clear from the L. whether the reference is to the Virgin's face or Christ's. The ME addition refers to I Pet. 1: 12, *in quem desiderant angeli prospicere.*

947–8 *Cast also þyn eȝe asyde to Maries cher, and loke how here fresche maydenly visage is al to-bollen and forsmoteryd wit terys:* translator's addition. Devotion to the Compassion of the Virgin (that is, Mary's suffering which came from her witnessing of her Son's Passion) was a characteristic of the later middle ages. See Woolf, *op. cit.*, pp. 239–73 and R. Pfaff, *New Liturgical Feasts in Later Medieval England* (Oxford, 1969), pp. 97–103.

950–1 *so manye salte teris lassche adoun so vnmesurably ouer here rodye chekes:* L. simply *lacrymas* (1182).

952 *a swerd of so scharp sorwe renne þorouȝ here tendre herte: eius animam pertransit gladius doloris* (1182–3), a reference to Luke 2: 35.

935 *wit-oute gret pite: sine singultu* (1183).

how straungely: not in L.

954 *Mulier, ecce:* John 19: 26.

955 *as hoo seyt: 'Tak to þe anoþer sone, for I go fro þe':* not in L.

956 *Ecce mater tua:* John 19: 27.

956–7 *Was not þis a mornful þyng to Marie:* translator's addition.

so passauntly: not in L. *Passauntly* seems to mean 'cursorily'; (the translator is commenting on the contrast between Christ's apparently peremptory committal of his mother to St John and his pledge to the thief that he will share with him the bliss of heaven. In this whole passage the ME translator's attitude towards Christ's treatment of his mother is noticeably more strongly-worded and emotional than Aelred's original, no doubt in a deliberate attempt to stir up the recluse's pity for the Blessed Virgin). This sense is not recorded before the second half of the seventeenth century for either *passantly* or adj. *passant* but the only recorded ME sense, 'exceedingly, very greatly' is inappropriate here.

958–9 *þat he schulde be wit hym þryn þe same day:* translator's expansion.

960–1 *persyde his syde to his tendre herte: latus eius aperuit* (1187).

962–3 *foonde forto gete þe sum of þyse precious liquours:* the L. *comede fauum cum melle tuo, bibe uinum tuum cum lacte tuo* refers to Cant. 5: 1. The translation is (perhaps deliberately) feeble and consequently obscures the sense of the following sentence.

964 *to do þe confort: ut inebrieris* (1190).

966–7   *ri3t as in culverhows beþ ymaad holys in þe wal forto warsche*
þe culvren in: in maceria corpore eius cauerna, in quibus instar
columbae latitans et deosculans (1192–3), which refers to Cant. 2:
14. The comparison of Christ's wounds, the refuge of the faithful, to
the holes of a dove-cote, where the doves are safe, is not uncommon in
ME devotional literature: see, for example, *Ancrene Wisse*, f. 79ᵇ/10–
25, which quotes Cant. 2: 14 (*Columba mea, in foraminibus petrae, in
caverna maceriae*), *The Chastising of God's Children*, ed. J. Bazire
and E. Colledge (Oxford, 1957), p. 159 and, most strikingly, Rolle:
'swet Jhesu, þy body is like to a dufhouse. For a dufhouse is ful of
holys, so is þy body ful of woundes. And as a dove pursued of an hauk,
yf she mow cache an hool of hir hous she is siker ynowe, so, swete
Jhesu, in temptacion þy woundes ben best refuyt to us' (*English
Writings of Richard Rolle, ed. cit.*, p. 35).

969   *and bryngge forþ gostly bryddes:* translator's addition, which
may have been inspired by the passage in *Ancrene Wisse* which
compares the sinful recluse to a pelican; her young, whom she often
kills through her sins but then restores to life by her penitent tears, are
her good works (see *Ancrene Wisse*, f. 32ª/19-f. 32ᵇ/9).

970–1   *þy lippen schulde be as blood reed, as hit were a reed liste:*
fiant siccut uitta coccinea labia tua (1193–4), a reference to Cant. 4:
3. L *uitta* = 'band, fillet'; ME *liste*, in OE meaning 'border, hem,
bordering strip (of a cloth)', later came to mean 'ribbon, strip of
cloth'.

973   *Eloquium tuum:* Cant. 4: 3.

974   *þilke nobel kny3t: nobilis iste decurio* (1195), as in Mark 15: 43.
L *decurio* has the primary meaning 'officer commanding a squadron
of ten cavalrymen', and the secondary meaning 'member of a munici-
pal senate, councillor' (see *OLD* sv). In the Vulgate *decurio* translates
βουλευτής and clearly has the second meaning, referring to Joseph of
Arimathaea's membership in the Sanhedrin. However, this was not
always realized in the medieval period and the description of Joseph as
decurio gave rise to some misunderstanding. The Wycliffe Bible of
1389 translates Mark 15: 43 as 'Joseph of Arimathaea, the noble
decurioun, that hadde ten men vndir him'. It was perhaps a similar
misunderstanding of the Vulgate which inspired a tradition that
Joseph was a knight in the service of Pilate. This is definitely stated by
Robert de Boron in his poem, *Joseph d'Arimathie*, ll. 442–3, which
was composed *c.* 1199 (*Le Roman de l'Estoire Dou Graal*, ed. W. A.
Nitze (Paris, 1927)).

Ioseph ab-Arimathie: supplied by the translator. MS *abarimathie*
may indicate that the L phrase *ab Arimathaea* had passed into a ME
idiom (cf. AN *Barimathia*, *Holkham Bible Picture Book, ed. cit.*, p.

54). *Ioseph ab Arimathie*, as opposed to ~ *of Arimathie*, is not infrequently found in ME texts.

978   *Fasciculus mirre:* Cant. 1: 12.

981   *þat þey hange not doun so pitously:* translator's addition.

982–3   *gadere to-gydere wit al suttilte þilke holsum dropys of blood þat droppeþ doun of his wondes:* it is an interesting possibility that Aelred may here be urging the recluse to imitate Joseph of Arimathea who, in medieval tradition, not only buried Christ's body (for which there is scriptural authority) but also, in the process, gathered up the drops of blood which fell from Christ's feet in none other than the Holy Grail. This is recorded in both Robert de Boron (see note to l. 974) and the First Continuation of Chrétien de Troyes' *Perceval*, which has been dated 1199–1212. These two French texts, however, appear to be the earliest references to this tradition and as Aelred's treatise was written no later than 1167 it would be rash to assert that he did know of it; such an assertion would, for instance, raise the question of whether the association of Joseph with the Grail was simply an invention of Robert de Boron, or whether Robert did indeed base his poem on a Latin text which was also somehow or other known to Aelred. See D. D. R. Owen, 'From Grail to Holy Grail', *Romania*, LXXXIX (1968), 30–53, and V. M. Lagorio, 'The Evolving Legend of St Joseph of Glastonbury', *Speculum*, xlvi (1971), 209–31.

990   *to anoynte Cristes menbrys:* not in L.

994–5   *syngyngge and wurschippyngge þe joye and blisse of Cristes resurrexioun: resurrectionis gloriam praedicantes* (1211–2).

996   *lokyngge wit a gladly eȝe:* the L. has *tam dulci reficientem oculo* (1213) except V (*respicientem*). This is not, however, necessarily proof that the translator's exemplar read *respicientem*, as *oculo* could have suggested the idea of 'looking' (rather than 'refreshing') independently.

997   *for Cristes deþ:* not in L.

1001   *let þy water-veynes of þyn heed alto-berste:* as *let* + inf. regularly translates L. subjunctive in this text, the translator must have read *rumpantur* with NUTRHa, not ind. *rumpuntur* with BDMV (1215). *water-veynes* renders L. *cataractae*, which as used in the Vulgate usually means 'showers of water (from the heavens)' but in Classical L can mean 'waterfall; watersluice'; *RMLWL* records the further meaning 'drain, conduit', in ML. The primary meaning of *water-veynes* is probably 'flow of water through a channel' (see *OED* sv VEIN *sb.*, II, 6) thus, figuratively, 'streams of tears'. However, the juxtaposition of *alto-berste* suggests that *veynes* is used here in its more familiar sense, 'vessels which carry bodily fluids', and that *water-veynes* means 'tear-ducts'. The ambiguity is almost certainly a deliberate play on words which is also present in the L., to a certain extent. Possibly Aelred had in mind Jer. 9:1, *Quis dabit capiti meo aquam, et oculis meis fontem lacrymarum?*

1002   *and terys renne a-doun: ab ipsis medullis eliciantur lacrymae* (1216).

1103   *fro þe deppeste ende of þy bowelys: ab imis . . . uisceribus* (1217).

1004   *what herte haddest þu, what spirit, what strenkþe: quid tibi mentis fuit, quid animi* (1218).

1010   *wepyngge:* omits *cum uocem occludat affectus* (1222).

1014   *Noli, inquit, me tangere:* John 20: 17.

1015   *com not neiʒ me:* not in L.

1016   *a word þat wolde to-breke þey it were a stony herte:* translator's addition.

1021   *art þu bycome straunge and mor enemy: An immitior es* (1226, < L *immitis*, 'harsh, savage') all MSS except Ha (*an non mitior*), V (*inimicitior*) and N (*an inimicior*, < L *inimicus*, 'hostile, unfriendly'). The translator was clearly rendering *inimicior* but he could well have misread his exemplar.

1022   *I nel not lete þe:* Gen. 32: 26.

1025   *Noli timere:* Aelred's own phrase, not a scriptural quotation.

1026   *þat þat þu askest: bonum hoc* (1232).

1027–8   *þat I ham ryse fro deþ to lyve: quia surrexi* (1233). *to lyve* preserves the OE dative *lífe* < *líf* (as fossilized in NE *alive*).

1030–1   *And whanne sche comeþ aʒen, sche comþ not alone:* L. simply *Redit* (1234).

1035   *delacioun:* the MS reading here, *þat arst was put in desolacioun*, makes only very strained sense in this context (i.e., if it is taken to refer to *Marie Magdeleyn and here felawes*, in which case the concord of the verb is faulty), and does not accord with L. *quod ante fuit dilatum* (1236–7). Emendation to *put in delay* certainly restores the sense, and has the virtue of being an amply attested ME phrase meaning 'put off temporarily, withheld for a time' (cf. l. 1027); however, on palaeographic grounds the safer course must be to emend to *delacioun*, which presumes only intrusion of an otiose *-so-*. *Delacioun* is an acceptable variant of ME *dilacioun*, 'delay, procrastination, postponement' < OF *dilacion*, ad. L *dīlātiō (nem*, n. of action from *differre*, *dīlāt-*, 'to defer, put off'. There are no other examples of the phrase *put in delacioun* recorded in the dictionaires of

English, but it is safe to assume that it could easily have been formed on analogy with the phrase *put in delay*, with identical meaning.

Accesserunt: Matt. 28: 9.

1038–9   *and of þyse haue studefast meditacioun:* translator's addition.

1039–40   *no sleep ne smyte of noon outward boostes ne ocupacioun lette: Non . . . somnus interpolet, nullus exterior tumultus impediat* (1238–9). Clearly 'smyte of noon outward boostes ne ocupacioun, must translate *exterior tumultus*, *smyte* having the sense of 'stroke, heavy blow' and, by extension, 'the sound made by such a blow, i.e., clamour' (see *OED* SMITE *sb.* 1) and *boostes* that of 'noises, bustle' (see *MED* BOST 4 (a)).

1043–4   *it is nyedful þat oure soule be ved wit a maner diuersyte of chaungyngge:* Aelred had pointed out in the first section of his treatise the necessity of alternating and varying the tasks to which the recluse applied her mind or body, in order to avoid the sin of *acedia* (262–5). This theme is quite frequent amongst early monastic authors (cf. 'Si autem videmus nos superari a cogitationibus et iam non delectamur in oratione iacere, surgendum est; deinde aut legendum aut psallendum aut operandum est', Hildemar, *Expositio Regulae*, quoted in *Dictionnaire de Spiritualité* ed. M. Viller (Paris, 1932–   ), II, col. 1937).

1045–6   *of þe whiche we mowe be steryd þe mor parfytly to louen vre God: ut ex his quoque quantum a nobis sit diligendus Deus intelligere ualeamus* (1244–5).

1048   *I ne halde it not a litel ȝyfte of God: Non paruum aestimo beneficium* (1246).

1048–9   *ȝif . . . tofore vs:* a misunderstanding of *quod bene utens malo parentum nostrorum* (1246–7) which should mean 'in that, making good use of the sin of our parents'. *parentum* probably means 'parents' rather than 'forebears'; it certainly has the former sense in l. 1261 of the L. As the participle *utens* must modify the understood subject of *creauit* (*sc. deus*), Aelred is surely referring to the Augustinian doctrine according to which inordinate lust, concupiscence, always accompanies the act of intercourse. This sin is turned to good account by God in that it is made the occasion of the generation of offspring. Possibly, too, Aelred had in mind not only the sin inevitably attached to all human generation but also the fact that in his own parents' case the sin was particularly heinous because his father was a priest and should therefore have been celibate.

1049–50   *and hou . . . were in:* translator's addition.

1050–1   *how God made vs of þe same matere þat he maade hem: creauit nos de carne illorum et inspirauit in nobis spiraculum uitae*

(1247): again, Aelred has in mind specifically his own parents, not simply the progenitors of the entire human race.

1056–7   *and not ysuffred vs be bore in meselrye or palsye or elles croked or lame:* translator's addition.

1060–1   *to þe knowyngge of God and to vre byleue: ad fidem suam et sacramenta* (1255).

1062–3   *þis ʒifte is frely yʒeue to vs: quod nobis gratulamur esse concessum* (1257). Probably the translator confused *gratulamur* (< L *gratulor*, 'rejoice') with *gratuito* (adv., 'freely, for nothing') or *gratiose* ('freely').

1063   *only of his goodnesse:* not in L.

1064–5   *and of on mankende:* not in L.

1067   *whanne whe cowde no mor good þan a beste:* not in L.

1070   *not ysmyte ne venymed of no foul wurm:* L. *non percussi a bestiis* (1262–3) implies that *wurm* refers to some generalized conception of a harmful animal (see *OED* worm, *sb.*, 2b), or even, more strongly, to a monster (see W. Caxton, *The History of Reynard the Fox*, ed. N. F. Blake, EETS, 263 (1970), 94/25n.), rather than to a snake. (It is also just possible that the translator read *vermiis* for *bestiis*, as in some hands *v* and *b* are susceptible to confusion.)

1071   *broke vre necke: necati* (1263): ME *breken nekke* can mean 'to die of a broken neck' (see *MED* breken 2 c).

1071–2   *in hool fey, and in sacramens of holy churche: in eius fide et bona uoluntate* (1264).

1073   *in alle þis benefys:* there is no authority for this phrase in L., but the construction appears to be plural. The ambiguity arises from the fact that ME had an anomolous plural *benefis* (alternating with the more normal plural *benefices* (cf. l. 1408)) which was formally identical with the singular *benefis*. In construing the forms in this text we have followed the indications of the syntax of the ME (or, where applicable, that of L.); thus *what a benefys* (l. 1073), *þyse benefis* (l. 1075), *alle þe benefis* (l. 1127), *his gret benefys* (l. 1144), *many . . . grete benefys* (l. 1149) and *so gret benefys* (l. 1222) are probably all plural. On the use of the singular form *þis* as a plural see Brunner-Johnston, § 57.

we beþ parteners ilyke: simul cucurrimus (1265).

1074–5   *oon moder wombe cast out in-to þis wordle: eadem uiscera profuderunt* (1267).

1075–6   *and þyse benefis God haþ doo to vs as to þe body:* not in L.; translator's summary.

1078   *in þat partye haþ departyd betwixe þe and me: Diuisit enim inter te et me* (1268–9); probably an example of non-repetition of the subject (God) in pronominal form (see Mustanoja, pp. 138–45), although here the syntactic boundary at *for* is rather stronger than those in any of the examples cited by Mustanoja.

1079   *in clennesse:* not in L.

1083–4   *þat is to seyn, caste myn vnclene loue on irþely þyngges:* translator's addition.

1085   *Et quicumque:* Gen. 4: 14. As so often, the ME reads with the text of the Vulgate; Aelred has *inuenit, occidit.*

1089   *Fera pessima:* Gen. 37: 20. Having compared himself to Cain, Aelred now compares himself to Joseph.

1090   *þe most wickede best of alle þat is þe deuel:* translator's addition.

1098   *many and greuous synnes: turpia quaeque* (1281).

1101   *in helle, nere þe mercy of God:* not in L.

1102   *byþenk þe of þe vielþys for þe whiche þu weptest vppon me sumtyme, etc.:* the MS here reads *vielþys for þe weptest,* but L. *Recole ... illas foeditates meas pro quibus me plangebas* (1284) indicates that the sense of the passage should be 'for which you wept', so the MS is probably corrupt. The line division, which is a not unusual place for a scribe to miss out a word, here occurs at *þe/weptest,* so one is left only with the decision of how to restore the text. Minimal emendation to *for þe þu weptest* is attractive, but prepositions governing the relative pronoun *þe* are placed either at the end of the clause or immediately before the verb in ME (see Mustanoja, p. 189), so we have preferred to emend to *for þe whiche þu weptest.*

The long passage which follows here, dealing with Aelred's sinfulness in his youth, is adapted from St Augustine (*Confessions*, II, 1–2), and indeed the tenor of this whole section, *De presencium meditacione*, is that of Augustine's *Confessions*; M. P. Courcelle has shown how Aelred, 'profondément nourri des Confessions d'Augustin, peut revivre avec lui les épisodes de sa propre existence et les présenter en conformité avec les chapitres augustiniens, ne fût-ce que par un sentiment intime de leur portée largement humaine' ('Ailred de Rievaulx à l'école des *Confessions*', *Revue des Etudes Augustiniennes*, VIII (1957), 174), and thus, evoking for his sister 'le temps de leur adolescence, il décrit ses propres passions à l'aide des deux premiers chapitres du second livre des Confessions' (*ibid.*, 164). The times that Aelred is recording here are doubtless those of his stay at the court of King David of Scotland while an adolescent. He was a man of strong emotional sensibility, and he was at this time grappling with the onset of an adult passion which, as emerges clearly from beneath scarcely veiled references, was of a homosexual nature (cf. ll. 63–4 n.). In the *Speculum Caritatis* he describes how he was held, during these years, by a friendship which was at once 'dearer to me than all the delights of this life', and yet a source of torment. 'For some offence was always to be feared, and a parting . . . was a certainty' (see Squire, *op. cit.*, pp. 14–15). That Aelred's conduct at this time was not entirely blameless is unwittingly revealed by his biographer, Walter; the latter recounts that Aelred *in tantum enim feruebat spiritu in regali triclinio positus ut magis monachus putaretur.* . . . (Powicke, *op. cit.*, p. 4), but this enthusiastic reference to Aelred's monklike purity so aroused the reprehension of two critical prelates that Walter was forced to explain it away as a figure of speech (see Powicke, *op. cit.*, *Epistola ad Mauricium*, p. 76).

1104 *Nemo potest corrigere:* Eccl. 7: 14.

1106–7 *þat is to seye, wit-owte gret repentaunce of man and special grace of God:* translator's addition, to qualify Aelred's apparent rigour here.

1108–9 *a ʒens we were of on fader and moder ybore: cum esset aequa utriusque conditio* (1288).

1110 *whanne þe cloudes of vnclennesse smokede vp in me, etc.:* L. *cum exhalaretur nebula libidinis* (1290–1). The verb *smokede* is presumably being used in its literal sense (L *exhalare*, which normally means 'to breathe out', sometimes = 'to steam'), and may reflect the medieval theory of digestion according to which overeating causes an excess of vapours ('smoke') to rise from the stomach to the brain, producing headaches, disturbance of reason, etc. (cf. 'Also smoke þat is resolued and comeþ of mete & of drynke by strenkþe of hete comeþ vp to þe brayne, and stoppiþ þe senewys of felynge, and brediþ sleep & byndiþ þe vttir wittis of felynge and so gadreþ kynde hete inward and comfortiþ and helpiþ þe vertue in þe inner parties. And if þe smoke is malencolik, oþir to scharp & bytynge, oþir venemous and resolued, & comeþ of mete oþir of drynke oþir of noyful medicyne, hit passiþ vp to þe brayne and greueþ þe vertue of felynge, and brediþ drede & fere as it fareþ [in] malencolyk men, and wakneþ franesie and woodnesse as it fareþ in he þat hauen litargye, slepynge euel', etc. (*On the Properties of Things: John Trevisa's translation of Bartholomaeus Anglicus De Proprietatibus Rerum, a critical text* (Oxford, 1975), pp. 562–3)). Here it is the *cloudes of vnclennesse* that *smokede vp*, and it is interesting that sexual excesses are often associated, in the above medieval theory, with over-indulgence in food and drink. Notable examples of this occur in *The Pardoner's Tale*, where, amongst others, the case of Lot and his daughters is quoted:

'Lo, how that dronken Looth, unkyndely,
Lay by his doghtres two, unwityngly;
So dronke he was, he nyste what he wroghte.'

(VI (C), 485-7).

Chaucer comments (in the mouth of the Pardoner):

'Thise cookes, how they stampe, and streyne, and grynde,
And turnen substaunce into accident,
To fulfille al thy likerous talent.'

(VI (C), 538-40).

1111 *irþi:* this word is recorded only in one other author before the
mid-sixteenth century, John Trevisa's translation of the *de Rerum
Proprietatibus*, where it is consistently (although not exclusively)
used with reference to the earth as one of the four elements: Wynkyn
de Worde's printed version of 1495 frequently substitutes *erthly* (for
this information we are indebted to Mr. V. E. Watts). The word here
renders L. *limosa*, meaning 'muddy' (fig.), thus 'filthy'; but it is
possible, too, in the light of the above, that for the translator *irþi* may
have had overtones of 'having the properties of the "element" earth'
(fig.), thus 'grossly material, coarse', although there is no explicit
authority for this in L.

1112 *owtrage styrynge of childhood: scatebra pubertatis* (1291-2) (L
scatebra = 'bubbling up'). ME *childhood* usually means 'the stage of life
up to (but not including) puberty'; however, as ME *child* can mean
'youth' *childhood* could presumably be an acceptable translation of L.
pubertatis and one need not posit a MS reading *puerilitatis.*

1113-14 *Spekyngge and styryngge of wycked companye hadde hard
ywrout vppon me: Verba enim iniquorum praeualuerunt super me*, a
quotation from Ps. 64: 4.

1116-17 *bitter swetnesse of charnel affeccioun: affectionis suauitas*
(1295).

1117-18 *þey rauysschede me syke and feble age of childhood:* that is,
'my sick and feeble age . . .' (L. *imbecillem adhuc aetatem meam*
(1296)).

1118 *in-to manye foule vices:* the translator has here missed the
point of Aelred's Latin metaphor contained in *rapiebant . . . per
abrupta uiciorum* (1295-6) ('they hurried me over the steep cliffs of
sin').

1122 *I was cast and possyd: iactabar et effundebar, diffluebam*
(1299).

1125-6 *nadde þe mercy of Crist ikepte: si non te Christi misericordia conseruasset* (1303); an example either of non-expression of the object pron. *þe* (see Mustanoja, pp. 144–5), or, perhaps more likely, of its assimilation to *ikept*, giving the unetymological -*e* of the pp. (cf. ll. 648–50 n.)

1126   *grucchynge aȝens God:* translator's addition.

1128   *in commune, as wel to me as to þe:* translator's addition.

1129   *þe pacience and þe benignite of God was wundurfully yschewed to me:* the translator has here misunderstood the Latin (*mira patientia meas sustinuit iniquitates* (1305–6) – 'He bore my sins with wonderful patience').

1130   *whil I was in dedly synne:* translator's addition.

1130–1   *openede not and swolewode me in:* L. simply *non absorbuit* (1306–7).

1131   *bounde:* MS *boundy* is unlikely to be a genuine form; probably the scribe's eye was distracted by the following *hugely*, causing him to substitute final -*y* for -*e*.

1133   *or deede sodeynly on oþer orrible deeþ:* translator's addition.

1139   *grace, mercy and goodnesse:* L. simply *gratiae* (1311).

1140–2   *þer þat I was agast of euere-lastyng dampnacioun, he confortede me and byheet me lyf: timenti blanditus* (1312).

1143   *whanne I was most vnkynde: ingratum* (1313).

1143–4   *he auaunsede me wit his gret benefys to styre me to turne aȝen to hym: suis obruit beneficiis* (1313). *auaunsede* seems an unsatisfactory translation of *obruit* (< L *obruere* 'overwhelm'); possibly the translator read *ob^{ut}* as *ad^{ut}* (= *adiuuit*, 'helped, assisted').

1150–1   *I were yseye take to me-ward:* a literal rendering of *ad me uideatur transire* (1318), *uideri* being a common L idiom for 'to seem'.

1154–5   *not only to hym þat ȝift al is iȝoue blisse and þank:* translator's addition to clarify the preceding clauses, which are so literally translated as to be somewhat obscure.

1155   *and þat is wronge:* not in L.

1157   *he haþ it of Godes ȝifte:* translator's addition. *freoly* translates *gratis* – out of God's kindness, therefore unearned.

1166–7   *in wylde wawes and in greet tempest alto-breket his vessel: passus naufragium* (1329).

1167–8   *vnneþe naked and quakynge asschapeþ to lond alyue: uix nudus mortem euasit* (1329). MS T omits *mortem*.

1169–70   *wyþ-oute tempest of dedly temptacioun:* translator's addition.

1172–3 *forto cloute aȝen þat was in tempest of temptacioun al-to-rend: scissa resarciam* (1332).

1188 *a fugitif and a rebel wrecche:* L. *fugitiuum seruum suum et rebellem* (1342–3) makes it clear that *fugitif* here is adjective rather than noun.

  may I trowe: crediderim (1345).

1193 *whan þu hast be asadded and dul or wery of þy lyfe: prae timore arescenti* (1347–8, < L *aresco*, 'become dry; languish; pine away'). No *asadden* or OE *asadian* is recorded in the dictionaries of English. Clearly it is formed on OE *sadian* (cf. *saade*, l. 82), 'to weary of', with the intensive prefix *a-*.

1194 *ȝif þu were longynge:* the insertion of *were* restores the MS reading, which lacks a finite vb., and brings it into conformity with the other durative constructions in this passage (ll. 1192–1200). It should be noted that L. here as *quotiens aestuanti prae amore ipse se tuis uisceribus infundebat* (1348–9), and it may possibly be that the translator was unconsciously following the L. construction, where the ommission of a finite verb is grammatically permissible.

1195–6 *ȝif þu hast yrad or ystotid on holy scripture:* L. *quotiens psallantem uel legentem* (1349). The form *ystotid* is extremely puzzling. It corresponds formally to *psallantem*, 'singing psalms', but there any correspondence appears to end. It might be taken to be the past participle of 'study'; its use in the phrase *yrad or ~* could be said to support this view, since the linking of two words with similar meanings is a common ME rhetorical device. However, one is at a loss to explain the spelling *ystotid* in this case. A rather more plausible theory is that it is the past participle of the verb *stote* 'to stand still, halt, stop', hence 'to stammer, stutter'. The first record of the word in the latter sense is in the *Gloss. W. de Bibbesworth* (*c.* 1325) in T. Wright's *Volume of Vocabularies* (London, 1857), p. 173: 'Jo vy cy vener mester Hughe, Ke reyn ne parle s'yl ne bue [*glossed* bote he stote]' (see J. Koch, 'Der Anglonormannische Traktat des Walter von Bibbesworth in seiner Bedeutung für die Anglistik', *Anglia*, LVIII (1934), 73, SV STOTE). The etymology of the word is not clear, but *OED* compares ME *stutten* (whence, with the addition of the frequentative suffix, NE *stutter*) and ME *stotayen* (a possible adaptation of OF *estoutoier, estoteier*), both of which convey the notion 'stumble, falter (verbally)', and both of which may be traced back to Germ. **stut-, *staut-*. Clearly the sense 'faltered, stammered', although it has no direct authority in L., is quite appropriate here, since Aelred goes on to describe how God intervenes in the recluse's reading aloud of the Scriptures and illuminates for her their full spiritual meaning (the inference being that she has previously had some difficulty in grasping this, and faltered over her reading).

1198 *in-to so hei3 desir þat þu canst not tell hit: in quoddam ineffabile desiderium* (1351).

1201 *mowe be turned:* the L. here has *resoluatur* (1354, < L *resoluere*, here with the sense 'to pay, render'). The ME misses the force of this; one might hypothetically posit a reading *reuoluatur* < L *reuoluere*, 'turn', which is in fact found in MS M, though the translation was certainly not made from that manuscript.

1205 *þenk as þei3 þu nere not in þe wordle: Nescias te esse in hoc mundo* (1356).

1206 *Vbi est thesaurus:* Matt. 6: 21

1208 *ful of seluer or gold or wordliche rychesse: cum argenteis simulacris* (1358).

1215–16 *and floures in þe feld fayrere þan euere was Salomon in al his blisse:* L. simply *lilia* (1364) but both refer to Matt. 6: 26. *feld* could well be *fold* (= 'on the earth'): here as so often this scribe's *e* and *o* are virtually indistinguishable. Both *in þe feld* and *in (þe) fold* are common ME idioms but as the translator's addition was inspired by the Vulgate phrase *lilia agri, feld* seems the better reading.

1216 *Let hym be þy stoorhous: Ipse sit horreum tuum* (1364). The sequence of thought in Aelred is inspired by an earlier verse, Matt. 6: 26: *respicite uolatilia coeli, quoniam non serunt, neque metunt, neque congregant in horrea.* The whole passage is perhaps illuminated by the comment of Jerome, *Sup. Ps. CXLIII:* 'Those birds are allegorically monks: they do not have upper stories (*solaria* – 'upper storey, sun-deck, ?pent-house'), nor do they have store rooms (*apothecas:* cf. here *tresour-hows*), but they have Jesus Christ, lord of store-rooms and cellars. They do not have barns (*horrea*) but they have the Lord of barns.'

1218–19 *qui sit benedictus in secula seculorum. Amen:* translator's addition.

1224 *Þe principle and þe bykynnyng: principium* (1370).

bykynnyng: this isolated example of devoicing of medial [g] may simply be an error, but it is just possible that it is a reflection of the process whereby the preterite *bigan*, due to the weakening (and ultimate loss) of the prefix, developed through /b̦ gan/ to /kan, kon/ with devoicing of the now exposed initial [g]. This phenomenon is characteristic of the West Midlands, and occurs also in Northern ME poetic texts (see Jordan, p. 167). This is not the case here, of course, as the loss of prefix and consequent devoicing of [g] did not occur in any parts of the verb except the preterite, but it is possible that *bykynnyng* may be an analogical or hyper-correct form (although, n.b., this text has exclusively *gan*, never *can*).

1227 *For bestes and bryddes:* cf. Aelred, *De Anima* I, 269: 'Do not beasts and birds save their lives, as far as possible, by flight, hiding and other methods, do they not have a horror of death and look after their health with food and drink?'

1231 *what þy feyt is bold on:* L. *quid praesumat fides tua* (1374). The sense of the phrase *is bold on* is evidently 'bases its assurance, confidence in' (for the obsolete sense 'confident' see *OED*, sv BOLD *a.*, 6), but although *bold of* (sthg.) is frequently recorded with the sense 'confident in (sthg.)', there is no record elsewhere of the phrase *bold on* (sthg.) with this sense. On the gradual encroachment during the ME period of the preposition *of* into ground formerly held by *on* (perhaps promoted by French influence) see Mustanoja, pp. 350–1.

1233 *and þy lyf be to heuynesse: Si uita tua tibi oneri est* (1376) – cf. 'to sorwe' (l. 1234) as a translation of *dolori*.

1244–6 *is so ileft vp in-to hei3 clennesse of conscience and holy contemplacioun þat he haþ in a maner for3yten al þis wordle: in liberioris conscientiae auras euasit* (1383).

1253 *Beati mortui:* Rev. 14: 13.

1254 *þe prophete:* Isaiah.

1255 *Godes derlyngges: electorum* (1391), *beatorum* V. While this may be merely a free translation, one wonders whether the translator was confused by a memory of the similarity between L *deligere*, pp. *delectus* ('choose') and *diligere*, pp. *dilectus*, 'love', or whether he read *electorum* as *dilectorum*.

1256 *Omnes reges:* Isaiah 14: 19. The ME omits the second half of the quotation which is given here: *uir in domo suo, tu autem proiectus es de sepulchro tuo quasi stirps inutilis, pollutus et obuolutus* (1392–3).

1260 *Preciosa est:* Ps. 115: 15.

1262 *deeþ . . . laste slep: dormitioni* (1396) – see note to ll. 254–5.

1266 *to Abrahames bosum and to þe si3t of God:* L. simply *ad sinum Abrahae* (1399–1400).

1268 *non sic impij:* Ps. 1: 4.

Noþyng so: non sic. On the use of *nothing* in secondary modification with the sense of NE *not (at all)* see B. M. H. Strang, *A History of English* (London, 1970), § 86.

curslynges: a word recorded elsewhere in ME only in *A Talkyng of þe Love of God*, ed. M. S. Westra (The Hague, 1950), p. 14, l. 19, a text contained in MS Vernon. *MED* glosses it there as 'blasphemer', but in this text, where it has a direct counterpart in L. it renders once *impii* (l. 1268) and once *maledicti* (l. 1355), so a more appropriate sense here might therefore be 'godless people, those excommunicated from God' – literally, 'those cursed by God', *Godys curslynges*. Probably a deliberate contrast is intended with *derlyngges* (l. 1255); indeed, *curslynges* may well have been coined on analogy with this word.

1270   *Tu autem:* see note to l. 1256.

1271–2   *þat is þy foule body:* translator's addition.

1273   *þat is not wurþ bote to þe fuyr:* translator's addition.

1274–5   *as out of a stynkynde put: quasi de foetenti sepulchro* (1402–3).

1269   *of ech of hem seiþ þe same prophete in þe same place þat I seyde nekst: place* refers to the earlier quotation from Isaiah at l. 1256; *nekst* refers to the passage following that quotation.

1273–8   *Fur iwis . . . stench:* the translator has taken the unusual course of transposing this whole passage into the passive voice. In L. the subject of the sentence is 'the wicked spirits' and all the subsequent verbs are active.

   fur: although this form of *for* does not occur elsewhere in this text, there is no reason to suppose it is not a genuine form, the *u* representing the weakly-stressed vowel. Cf. *fursake*, l. 4.

1276   *wiþ instrumens of helle:* translator's addition.

1279   *Expectacio iustorum:* Prov. 10: 28.

1284–5   *noon of vre penne or poyntel: stylus* (1410). The sense of *noon of* here is clearly not partitive but is simply an emphatic *not*. Jespersen (*op. cit.*, Vol. II, § 16.682) quotes numerous examples of this usage (the earliest example recorded by *OED* (sv NONE, A 3 c) is from 1571, but the (apparent) interval of nearly two hundred years without supportive material is probably not critical). It is probably to be explained as follows: *none of* is frequently used emphatically in constructions where the partitive sense is still more or less clear (see Jespersen, *op. cit.*, Vol. II, § 16.681); this latter usage should probably be viewed as a halfway stage between the purely partitive construction and the adoption of *none of*, purely with emphatic force, as an adverbial phrase equivalent to *not*.

1287   *at þey day of dome:* translator's addition.

1287–8   *whanne þey beþ cloþed in duble stole: duplicis stolae induti gloria* (1412) – initially a reference to the *stolae albae* of Rev. 6: 11 but cf. also Eccli. 45: 9, *Et induit eum stolam gloriae*. The 'white garments' of Revelations are interpreted as the glorified bodies of the elect. The phrase is also used in *Speculum Inclusorum*, p. 125: *duplicem stolam glorie, corporis videlicet et anime.*

1292–3 *helle-ʒates schulle ben al open: patebunt inferi* (1415–16).

1295–6 *his chaar þat be terrible as eny tempest:* the strained syntax here probably represents an attempt to render the L. *nominativus pendens* construction: *Veniet desuper iudex iratus, ardens furor eius, et ut tempestas currus eius, ut reddat . . .* (1416–17); thus, *chaar* is in apposition to *wraþþe*.

1297 *Beatus qui paratus est occurrere illi:* Aelred's own phrase, not a direct biblical quotation, but based, possibly, on Matt. 24: 46.

1298 *at þat our:* translator's addition.

1306 *þis riʒtful jugge Crist:* L. simply *iudicis* (1425).

1307 *cursed, wrecchid and weepful:* L. simply *miseram* (ibid.). The only other recorded occurrence of *weepful* in ME is in Wycliffe Bible, Wisdom 18: 10, where *wepful weiling* translates L. *flebilis planctus.*

1308 *wat stench is ter þer:* L. *Qualis ibi horror, quis foetor . . .* (1426). MS *tir* makes no sense, and a smooth enough reading would be obtained by omitting it. However, among explanations for its presence, one might posit that: i) it represents ME *þeir(e)*, 'their', which is occasionally used absolutely, meaning 'theirs'; ii) it represents a corrupt form of the pp. of ME *tiren*, 'to prepare, make ready'; iii) *is tir* reflects what was at an earlier stage a form of OE *gestyrian*, with the unrecorded intransitive sense *'to stir, be about'; and iv) *tir* represents a weakly stressed form of cataphoric *þer*, giving the sense 'What an evil smell there is there'. The last seems to us the most likely. Initial /þ/ could have become /t/ by dissimilation from the preceding /s, z/; and it is not impossible that the *i* could legitimately be intended to represent the weakly stressed vowel, although we have preferred to emend to *e* on the grounds that the MS form probably represents a scribe's error caused by meeting a spelling he did not recognize.

1308–9 *A-cursede coniones: miseri et infelices* (1427).

  þat haþ departyd þe: omits *praedestinando* (1437).

1320 *þilke grete vnsauery multitude: hac damnata societate* (1436–7).

1323 *byhold to how blisful a cumpanye he haþ coupled þe: quibus te glorificando sit inserturus aduerte* (1439–40). The translator must have misread *glorificando*, ger., 'by glorifying' as *glorificatis* or *glorificandis* (pp. or gerundive modifying *quibus*). The very corrupt MS B does in fact read *glorificatis.*

1328–9 *þorouʒ holsum doctrine of Godes lawe: doctrina et eruditione* (1443).

1337 *Timor et tremor:* Ps. 54: 6.

1338 *þe:* in L. this whole passage is in the first person.

1339 *3if he ha ordeyneþ þe:* the verb *ha* is a fairly frequent ME development of the pr. ind. 3sg. *haþ* in weakly stressed positions (although its use here is unconvincing as it would result in an uncomfortable hiatus).

1343 *ha:* the original MS *ha* has been corrected to *he* in noticeably darker ink. No other examples of *ha* for *he* occur in this text, but as it is a well-attested (chiefly South-Eastern) form of the 3sg. masculine personal pronoun as developed in weakly stressed positions (see *MED*, sv HE *pron.* 1) we have preferred to retain the original MS reading.

1346 *associe þe to his blisful derlyng: saluandis inserere* (1455).

1347 *a Godes half:* not in L.

1349 *Venite benedicti:* Matt. 25: 34.

1354 *Discedite a me:* Matt. 25: 41.

1356–7 *into blisse wiþ-outen eende: in uitam aeternam* (1461).

1357–8 *a wrecchyd and wiepful condicioun to þilke acursede caytyfs: o miserabilis conditio* (1461–2).

1359–60 *departid otterlyche fro þe blisse of God: ne uideant gloriam Dei* (1463).

1361–2 *let þilke gloriouse processioun go forþ:* all MSS *fiet illa gloriosa processio* (1465) except V which alone has the subjunctive *fiat.*

1362–3 *in-to þe he3e Ierusalem, þe cite euerlastyngge of heuene:* translator's addition.

1364 *Þanne schal þilke glorious kyng regne in hem: et tradetur regnum Deo et Patri ut ipse regnet in ipsis* (1466–7).

1370–1 *no wepynge ne weylyngge, no sorwe:* the original MS *ne* was altered by a later hand to *no,* but it seems likely that the translator's intention was to connect 'weeping' and 'wailing' as a couplet of two words with closely related sense (cf. ll. 1374–5 *noon hungur ne þurste*), so we have retained original *ne.*

1372 *no chaungynge of þe eyr: nulla temporum mutatio uel aeris corruptio* (1482–3). For the ME sense of *eyr* as 'weather, climate', see *MED* AIR, *n.*1, 3 a.

1374 *no siknesse of old age: non aegritudo, non senectus* (1476).

1374–5 *noon hungur ne þurste, no nyede: non bibendi uel dormiendi ulla necessitas* (1477–8).

1376 *parfit ioye, parfit murþe:* should contrast with weeping, wailing and sorrow; *parfit tranquillite* with tribulation, temptation and harsh weather; *parfit surtee* with fear; *most parfit loue and charite* with discord, envy, suspicion, adulation and detraction; *parfit rychesse* with poverty and avarice; *parfit fayrnesse* with deformity; *parfit reste, parfit strencthe* with toil and weariness; *parfit hele* with old age and sickness; *parfit siȝt* of God with darkness and night; *euere-durynge lyf* with death and mortality, but the translator has here condensed Aelred's original, and tightened up its structure. The first section follows Aelred exactly, but in the second section Aelred repeats the components of the first section in turn, comparing and contrasting the absence of some negative, evil quality with the presence of the opposite, positive, good quality; the translator simply gives a list of the good qualities, relying for the effect of contrast only on the preceding section, plus the brief allusion, 'þer þat noon of alle þyse þynges beþ' (1375–6).

1381–2   *whanne oure creatour God schal be clierly yseyen, iknowen and iloued: Certe quod his omnibus excellit, id est uisio, cognitio, dilectio Creatoris* (1498–9). MS *þat be clierly yseyen* is clearly an error; it looks as though a line translating L. *quod his omnibus excellit* may have been left out at some stage in the transmission of the text, resulting in an awkward lacuna. We have emended *þat* to *schal* to provide a smooth reading.

1382   *blisful:* translator's addition.

1385   *after here capacite:* a mistranslation: the L. *pro sua capacitate* (1502) refers to God's capacity, not that of His creatures.

1386   *laskyngge or diuisioun of his godhede: sui diminutione uel diuisione* (1502–3).

1389   *seye:* here and in l. 1391 MS *seye* has been altered by a later hand to *seȳe*, indicating that the anonymous redactor thought the past participle of 'see' should be *seyne*, or possibly *seyen*. However, loss of final *-n* in the past participles of strong verbs is a widespread phenomenon in southerly dialects of ME, and is amply exemplified in this text (see Intro., p. xlv). Moreover, of the six past participles of 'see' in this text, three are with and three without final *-n*; and of the four past participles of the verb derived from OE *geséon* in this text, one is with and three are without final *-n* (see Glossary, sv ISEE). The original MS reading here has therefore been retained.

1391   *in a myrour or in derknesse: per speculum et in aenigmate* only HaMRTU; *al. per speculum in aenigmate* (1507) as in I Cor. 13: 12, to which this passage refers.

1392   *as þe gospel seyþ:* not in L. As the quotation is from St Paul, *gospel* must here have its ME sense of 'the New Testament in general', not just the evangelists.

1394   *Qui diligit:* John 14: 21.

1398   *Hec est vita eterna:* John 17: 3. HaRMT read *uerum, al.*

unum; the Vulgate has *ut cognoscant te, solum Deum verum*.

1401   *so muche plentevousnesse of lykyngge:* the ME seems closer to the reading of BHaT, *tanta feruendi copia* than of the other MSS, *tanta fruendi copia* (1514).

1405   *Quod oculus non vidit:* cf. I Cor. 2: 9.

1408   *moynde:* the MS reading here, which H. gives as *moyn̄de*, is clearly *mop̄nde* (the scribe is always careful to distinguish between *þ* and *y*), which is nonsense as it stands. The word renders L. *memoria* (1520), which elsewhere in this text is translated *mende, miende*, in various senses connoting 'mind, as the faculty of memory'. Here *memoria* means 'a record (*of* sthg.), that which is remembered (*of* sthg.)', which is a well-attested sense of 'mind' in ME (see *OED*, sv MIND *sb.* 1, 4), so clearly what appears as *mop̄nde* was originally a form of 'mind'.

The standard forms of the word in this text are *mende, miende*, representing OK *(ge-)mend >mēnd(e)*, but from the linguistic evidence (see Intro., p. xliv) one would expect the reflex of the standard OE form *(ge-)mynd* to be written *muynde* here (and *muynde* is in fact a fairly common form of the word in ME). Thus an emendation of *mop̄nde* to *muynde* would bring the word into line with the spelling system of the text as a whole.

However, it is hard to see how an original *muynde* could have come to be mistakenly written *mop̄nde*. The scribe is quite at home with the *uy-* graphy elsewhere, and *u* is unlikely to be mistaken for *o*. In attempting to restore the original reading the most promising course is to emend *mop̄nde* to *moynde*; the graphy *oi, oy* was commonly used in northerly dialects for /ǖ/, for there *ō* had become *ǖ*, so the symbols *o* and *u* were interchangeable (and in these dialects *i* and *y* were regularly used as diacritics of length) (cf., for example, the form *moyles*, 'mules', in *Sir Launfal*, and the editor's discussion (*Sir Launfal*, ed. A. J. Bliss (London, 1960), l. 886 and n.)). In view of the other faint traces of a northerly dialect in this text (see Intro., p. li) an emendation of this nature is quite permissible; and further, from the palaeographic point of view *y* was eminently mistakeable in some hands for *þ*, and once this error had been made, and the word rendered totally incomprehensible, the best efforts of a scribe to restore some sense to it, such as taking the *n* as a *u* and adding a mark of abbreviation, could hardly be successful. We have therefore restored what seems likely to have been the original MS reading, *moynde*.

I haue wryte to þe in schorte wordes: substituted for *quaedam meditationum spiritualium semina praeseminare curaui* (1521–2).

1414   *þy desir mowe brynge þe in-to mornyngge:* the reading here of

U, *lacrymas desiderium educat*, is closer to the ME than that of the other MSS, *lacrymas desiderium excitet* (1524).

1417   *to þy singuler loue, þat þu hast ichose byfore alle oþre:* translator's addition.

1418   *þe book of loue in holy wryt: in Canticis* (1526).

 Dilectus meus michi: cf. Cant. 6: 2.

1428–30   *þat he and I mowe come to þat blisse þat I vnworþyly haue spoken of. Quod nobis misericorditer concedat, qui viuit et regnat in secula seculorum. Amen:* translator's addition.

GLOSSARY

MS BODLEY AND MS VERNON

The glossary is intended to explain only obsolete words and words in senses now unfamiliar. Current meanings are therefore not usually recorded, except for the purpose of contrast, but some unfamiliar spellings for familiar words are glossed. Interesting inflectional forms are also included.

References are selective and not exhaustive; numbers refer to the lines of the texts.

The two texts are glossed separately; the principles of alphabetization are as follows:

For both texts, *i* and *y* when representing a vowel are treated as the same letter, and take the order of *i*; when *i* represents a consonant it has a separate place after *i/y* representing a vowel; initial vocalic *v* precedes initial consonantal *v*.

For Bodley 423, the very occasional *þ* is treated as *th*; consonantal *y* has its usual place; medial consonantal *u* is treated as *v* (the scribe never uses *u* in initial position, vocalically or consonantally).

For Vernon, *3* has a separate place after *g* and *þ* a separate place after *t* (*th* is included under the latter); initial consonantal *u* is included under initial consonantal *v*.

MS BODLEY

abidynge *vbl. n.* expectation 454; delay 972; staying, lingering 817.

aboue *prep.* in preference to 344; on top of 331.

aboundith *v. pr. 3sg.* is present in overflowing measure 592.

aboute *prep.* in the area around 75.

a-brood *adv.* wide 603.

abstyne *v. refl. imp. sg.* abstain, refrain 307.

accordyng(e *ppl. adj.* appropriate to, congruent with 5, 673.

accuse *v.* find fault with, blame 962.

admitte *v.* grant admission, allow access 158. (see note)

affeccyon *n.* (spiritual) love 637; **affeccions** *pl.* 657.

a-fer *adv.* at a distance, afar off 466.

aferde *v. pp.* afraid 506.

affliccion, affliccyon *n.* suffering, affliction 431, 429; **affliccyons** *pl.* 594.

afore *prep.* before 677; in front of 156, 378.

afore-saide *v. pp.* mentioned earlier 120.

afore-tymes *adv.* in the past, previously 9.

after *prep.* for 18, 27; to 339; according to 8, 977; according as 218.

alday *adv.* always 26.

almes *n*. charitable gifts 57.
almes-dede *n*.-charitable actions 968.
als *adv*. as 869.
alway *adv*. always 614.
amyable *adv*. kindly, affably 970.
a-morwe *adv*. in the morning 198.
and *conj*. if 327, 821.
anem(p)st *prep*. among, in company with 527; with respect to 90, 93.
ankeras *n*. anchoress, woman recluse 396; **ancresse** *g*. 45.
annexe *v. subj*. add, attach 574; ~ *the to imp. sg*. unite yourself to 717; **annexed** *pp*. attached 969.
anoon *adv*. at once 250.
apayde *v. pp*. satisfied, pleased 786. *holde the* ~ be content 119.
apert *adj*. overt 170.
array *n*. clothing, adornment 537.
arraye *v*. adorn 583; **arayeth** *pr. 3sg*. 163. **arraye** *imp. sg*. 583. **arrayed** *pp*. 575.
Architriclyne *n*. master of the feast (but understood as proper name) 745.
a-shamed *v. pp*. put to shame 752.
assigned *v. pp*. officially appointed, allocated 137. (see note)
assoiled *v. pa.t*. absolved 752.
astonyed *v. pp*. ~ *of* astonished at, amazed by 702.
atteyne *v*. reach 147, 351; *imp. sg*. 386.
attones *adv*. at once, simultaneously 665.
audience *n*. *without* ~ out of earshot 87.
auncyant, auncyent, anxient *adj*. old, elderly 142, 867, 107.
autere, autier, awtier *n*. altar 279, 584, 582; *the sacrament of the* ~ the consecrated elements 279.
auoyde *v*. get rid of 597; **auoidith** *pr. 3 sg*. 165. **auoyded** *pa. t*. avoided 500. **auoided** *pp*. 113.
avowed *v. pp*. having taken religious vows 22.
auoutrye *n*. adultery 750.
awe *n*. *vnder gret* ~ in great fear, under strong discipline 115.
axe *v*. ask, ask for 604. **axith** *pr. 3sg*. 394. **axinge** *pr. p*. 737. **axe** *imp. sg*. 765. **asked** *pa.t*. 636. **axed, axid** *pp*. 5, 7.
ayen *adv*. back 899.

ayen, ayenst *prep*. in preparation for 879; against 442.
ayenbier *n*. redeemer 292.

bakbiter *n*. slanderer, detractor 169.
bakbityng(e *vbl. n*. slanderous statements, defamation 28, 35.
baptem *n*. baptism 590.
bawme *n*. balsam 876.
be *v*. be 68. **art** *pr. 2 sg*. 6. **is** *pr. 3sg*. 1. **ben** *pr. 3pl*. 23. **be** *imp. sg*. 84; *pr. subj*. 24. **was, were,** *pa.t. sg*. 4, 83; **were, wern** *pa.t. pl*. 11, 12 **be, ben** *pp*. 42, 43. **were** *subj. pa.t*. 12.
begynnynges *vbl. n. pl. gostly* ~ spiritual foundations, bases 528.
behighte *v. pa.t*. promised 990.
beholde *v*. observe, contemplate 566; *imp. sg*. 467; **byhelde** *pa.t. sg*. 495.
benys *n. pl*. beans 316.
bere *v*. carry 113. **berist** *pr. 2sg*. 370. **berith** *pr. 3sg*. 843. **beren** *pr. pl*. 598 **bore** *pp*. born 912.
berne *n*. barn 928.
besy, busy *adj*. industrious, occupied 50; careful 286.
besynes(se, besinesse, bysenesse *n*. diligence, care 48, 376; activity 223. ~ *of worldly gode* secular affairs 67; ~ *of thin hondes* manual labour 68.
bestaille *n*. livestock, cattle, sheep 51.
betyde *v*. come about 16.
betokeneth, bitokeneth *v. pr. 3sg*. symbolizes 584; means, signifies 262 (see note).
bi, by *prep*. ~ *than* before 236; ~ *way of* in the way of 28, 92.
byclippeth *v. pr. 3sg*. embraces 870; **biclippe** *imp. sg*. 665.
bihoueth *v. pr. 3pl*. are necessary 195; **behoueth** *pr. 3sg*. 10.
biseche *v. imp. sg*. beg, beseech 355.
blemysshed *v. pp*. impaired 152.
blys *n*. joy, glory 362.
bondes *n. pl.*[1] shackles, bonds 781, 842.
bondes *n. pl.*[2] ~ *of nede* boundaries of necessity 388; ~ *of honest gladnes* limits of respectable happiness 400–1.
bordel *n*. ~ *hous* brothel 46.
bore *v. pp*. see **bere**.
bounde(n *v. pp*. obliged, required to carry out 155; chained, restrained 841.
boundel *n*. bunch, bundle 873.

breem *adj*. savage, fierce 447.

brennynge *v. pr.p.* burning 748; brenned, brent *pa.t.* 421; brent *pp*. 419. brennynge *vbl. n*. 885.

brest *v*. burst 890.

bringer *n*. bearer, carrier 84.

brused *v. pp*. bruised, pummelled 595.

but *prep., conj*. except 156, 321.

can *v. pr. 3sg*. be able, know how 733. konne(n *pr. pl*. 304. coude *pa.t.sg*. 7. konnynge *vbl. n*. knowledge 806.

caste *v. imp sg*. place, repose 927. caste *pa.t*. expelled, exiled 530; cast *pp*. 265; added 66.

catell *n*. cattle, cows 53.

cause *n. for ~* because 493. causes *pl*. reasons 105.

celle *n*. see selle.

certayn, certeyn(e *adj*. definite, fixed (but unspecified) 132, 309, 652.

certeyn *n*. see putte, *v*., and note to l. 220.

certeyn, certes, certys *adv*. certainly, surely 39, 803, 353.

ceson *n*. part of the year, season 328.

charge *n*. duty 110; *it is to me but litel ~* it matters little to me 172; charges *n. pl*. loads, burdens 113.

charge *v*. value, care about 170; *pr. 3 pl*. 23; *imp. sg*. 791; chargeden *pa.t*. 411.

chargeous *adj*. onerous, burdensome 481.

chere *n. hye ~* arrogant behaviour 134; *dissolucyon of ~* excessive indulgence in meat and drink 401.

chese *v*. choose 550; *imp. sg*. 107, 142; chees *pa.t. 3sg*. 546. chosen *pa.t. 3 pl*. 14. chosen, chose *pp*. 22, 363.

chewe *v*. meditate 390.

chider *n*. quarrelsome person, troublemaker 108, 168.

chidynge *vbl. n*. quarrelling, scolding 165.

children *n. pl*. girls 439.

cleer *adj*. guiltless, innocent 953.

clene *adv*. completely, entirely 824.

clene *adj*. chaste 163.

clennes *n*. purity, chastity 391; innocence, purification 591.

clepynge *v. pr. p*. calling, summoning 880; cleped *pp*. called, named 210.

clerke *n*. one in holy orders 31.

clerly *adv*. entirely, completely 695.

cleueth *v. pr. 3sg*. clings, adheres 613. cleuynge *pr. p., vbl. n*. 844, 615.

cloistrers *n. pl*. enclosed religious living in community 656.

closed *v. pp*. enclosed, secluded 21.

coarte *v. pr. 1 pl*. constrain 283.

collacyon, collacioun *n*. collation (evening gathering for devotional reading) 203, 196.

colour *n. vnder ~ of* under the guise, cover of 516.

come *v*. come 821. comest *pr. 2sg*. 722. cometh *pr. 3sg*. 512; arises 543. cometh, comen *pr. 3pl*. 55, 401, come *imp. sg*. 898. comynge *pr. p. tyme ~* time to come 147. cam *pa.t. sg., pl*. 545, 864. comynge *vbl. n. Cristis ~* the Advent of Christ 699.

comende *v*. entrust 396; comaunde, commende *imp. sg*. 354 (see note), 397; commended *pp*. praised 641.

comfort *n*. strength 143.

commendacyon *n*. praise, approval 343, 606.

communicacion, communicacyon *n*. conversation 94–5; association, dealings 119.

comoun *adj. ~ lyuers of the worlde* seculars 644.

compleccion, compleccyon, complexion *n*. constitution 71, 306; *mighty of ~* of a strong, robust constitution 311.

compunccyon *n*. compunction, contrition, repentance 229.

comune *v*. associate, have dealings with 200.

confusion *n*. perdition, damnation 358.

conuersacion, conuersacyon *n*. manner of living 340, 109; association, company 439. *~ of the worlde* worldly, secular living 345.

conuersion *n*. religious life 441.

counceyle *n*. secrets, private matters 820.

couetise, couetyse *n*. avarice, covetousness 55, 1007.

cracche *n*. manger, stall 547, 726.

crye *v. ~ after* beg, demand 75.

culuer *n*. dove 465.

custumably *adv*. customarily, by force of habit *494.

daliaunce *n.* gossip, intimate conversation 96, 290.

dar *v. pr. 1 sg.* dare 361. **dorst** *p.t. 3 sg.* 506.

dede *n. in* ~ in actual fact 42.

deed *adj.* dead 145.

deedly *adj.* deadly, fatal 209.

defaute *n.* weakness, faintness 444. **defautes** *pl.* faults, failings 598.

deferre *v. subj.* put off, delay, postpone 896.

defoule *v. subj.* defile, make foul 334. **defouled** *pp.* 116.

dele *v. imp. sg.* give away, distribute as alms 661. **deled** *pp.* 83.

delectacyon *n.* sensual pleasure 430; **delectacions** *pl.* 491.

delices *n. pl.* delights 387.

delitable *adj.* sensuously pleasing 492.

deliten *v. pr. 3pl.* take pleasure 359.

delytes *n. pl.* pleasures, delights 657-8.

demed *v. pp.* judged 172.

departe *v.* distribute in alms 57; *subj.* go away 96. **departed** *pp.* separated 955. **departyng** *vbl. n.* death 943; division, distinction 988.

derlynge *n.* darling, beloved 136.

desperat, disperate *adj.* desperate 670, 610.

despitously *adv.* contemptuously, mercilessly 841.

destitucion *n.* deprivation, state of bereavement 670. (see note)

deuocyon *n. wommen of* ~ women of devout, pious disposition 93.

dyeted *v. pp.* had one's food regulated 299.

disciplynes *n.* acts of penance 596.

discrecyon, discrecion *n.* moderation 513; exercise of sound judgment 518.

discret *adj.* moderate; possessing discrimination 484.

dispende *v.* pay out, disburse 647.

disport *n.* pastime, recreation 573. source of comfort 565.

disserue *v.* deserve, merit 756; **disseruedist** *p.t. 2sg.* 807.

disseuerynge *v. pr. p.* distinguishing, differentiating 939.

dissese *n.* state of distress 669.

dissolucion, dissolucyon *n.* laxity 32; dissolute behaviour 115; ~ *of chere* excessive indulgence in meat and drink 401.

dissolute *adj.* frivolous, lascivious 192.

dissolued *v. pa.t.* liquefied, turned to water 882.

distrayt *adj.* distressed, perturbed 638.

diuerse, dyuerse *adj.* various 542, 566.

diuersite, dyuersite *n.* variety, diverseness 223, 573. **diuersitees** *n. pl.* 555.

diuyne *adj.* ~ *service, houre* canonical hour 215, 225.

doctrine *n.* learning 968.

do(o *v.* do 503, 632; *have to* ~ have contact with 67; have dealings 90: **dost** *pr. 2 sg.* 716. **doth** *pr. 3 sg. substitute for another verb* 469. **do** *subj.* ~ *wel* live virtuously 261; be successful 878; **do(o** *imp. sg.* act 119, 465; carry out, perform 222, 630. **dide, dyde** *pa.t. 3 sg.* 504, 791. **diden** *pa. t. 3 pl.* 623; **dide** ~ . . . *eese* comforted 507; ~ . . . *reuerence* honoured, venerated 715-16. **do(on** *pp.* 741, 625; completed 900.

domesman *n.* judge 293; magistrate 411.

doom *n.* judgment 505, 966; Last Judgment 951. **domes** *pl.* 962.

doucet *adj.* sweet, delicious 312.

doughter *n.* daughter 554, 559.

drede *n.* fear 375.

drede *v. refl.* feel apprehensive 127. **dredist** *pr. 2sg. trans.* fear 99. **dreden** *pr. 3 pl.* 477. **drede** *imp. sg.* 101. **dredynge** *pr. p.* 412; *ppl. n.* those who fear 181. **dradden** *pa. t. 3pl.* 14.

dredful *adj.* fearful, wary 387; awe-inspiring 505; dangerous, hazardous 158.

dresse *v. imp. sg.* ~ *the vpward* raise yourself, get up 703.

duke *n.* leader 256. (see note)

edwite *v.* reproach, find fault with 169.

eese, ese *n.* comfort 501, 510.

eftesone *adv.* often 446.

eye *n.* eye 835. **eyen** *pl.* 860.

eyleth *v. pr. 3sg. what* ~ *the*? what is the matter with you, what makes you . . .? 859.

eysel *n.* vinegar 846.

elles *adv.* else 615.

encheson *n. for* ~ *of* because of 488.

enclosed *v. pp.* confined, imprisoned 716; enclosed, secluded 6.

encresse *v.* increase 691; **encressith** *pr. 3 sg.* 567.

ende *n.* bottom, lower edge 577; end 934.

enflaume *v.* arouse 306; **enflaumed** *pp.* inspired, filled with love 710.

enpressed *v. pp.* fixed, imprinted 154.

enquering *v. pr. p.* hunting, seeking out 27; **enquered** *pp.* 72.

ensaute *n.* assault, temptation 466.

enspirith *v. pr. 3sg.* inspires 353; **en-spired** *pp.* 355.

entishynge *vbl. n.* ~ *of his stomak* stomach infection 509.

entysynge *vbl. n.* tempting, urging 406.

er, or *conj.*, *prep.* before 72, 925; ~ *than* 95.

esily *adv.* gently, mildly 133.

estat *n.* religious status 6; condition 374.

euery *pron.* everyone, each 977, 567.

euereither, euereyther *adj.*, *pron.* both, each of two 332, 44; *g.* 718.

excusacion *n.* justification, excuse 482.

excuse *v.* justify 792.

fader, fadir *n.* father 556; *gostly* ~ spiritual director 88. **fadirs** *g.* 561. **faders, fadirs** *pl.* Fathers of the Church 4, 228.

fadith *v. pr. 3sg.* cause to fade 525.

faylen *v. pr. pl.* fail 615; **failed** *pa. t.* grew feeble 444.

falle *v.* sin, fall morally 41, 442; befall, happen 19. **fallith** *pr. 3sg.* 358. **falle** *imp. sg.* 856. **fel** *pa.t.* 508; **falle** *pp.* befallen, happened 16.

fame *n.* repute 142.

familiarite *n.* improper intimacy 515.

famulier *adj.* overly friendly, unduly intimate 151.

fastyng(e *vbl. n.* time of fasting 241, 251.

fauorable *adj.* partial, showing undue favour 487.

feblyd *v. pp.* enfeebled, rendered infirm 71.

feden *v. pr. pl.* nourish, feed 657.

felde *n.* field 410.

fele *v.* experience 356. **felist** *pr. 2sg.* 712. **felynge** *vbl. n.* *simple* ~ rudimentary understanding 8. **felynges** *pl. gostly* ~ spiritual insights, mystical awareness 542.

feloushep, feloushlp *n.* companionship with the heavenly community 964; ~ *of man* sexual intercourse 381.

fen *n.* mud, dirt 410.

fende *n.* fiend, devil 384.

fer *adv.* far 280.

ferden *v. pa.t.* ~ *with* acted towards, treated 831.

fettynge *vbl. n.* bringing, conveying 113.

fewe *n.* few things, words 839.

fynde *v. pr. 1sg.* find 994. **fyndest** *pr. 2 sg.* 668. **foundist** *pa.t. 2 sg.* 804. **fonde, founde** *pp.* 456, 953.

fle *v.*[1] fly 923.

fle *v.*[2] flee 136, 159. *pr.p.* **fleynge** 290. **fledde** *pa.t.* 732. **fleddist** *pa.t. 2sg.* 514.

flexe *n.* flax 588.

flour(e *n.* flower 524, 523.

fode *n.* spiritual sustenance, food (*or* form of **fote** *n.* – support, that on which something rests) 253.

fonde *v. pp.* see **fynde**.

forbede *v. subj.* forbid 383.

forbeten *v. pp.* severely beaten, battered 845.

formente *n.* see **potage**.

forme *n.* rule 9, 300; ~ *of lyuyng(e* rule of life 5, manner of living 148.

former *n.* creator, one who makes or shapes 211.

forsake *v. pp.* forsaken, abandoned 835.

forshape *v. pp.* misshapen, malformed 909.

foryete *v. imp. sg.* forget 174, 560.

foryeue *v. imp. sg.* forgive 855; *pp.* forgiven 777.

foule *adv.* foully, disgustingly 381.

foundement *n.* foundation 527.

freel *adj.* weak, unstable 269.

fresshe *adv.* ~ *and* ~ anew, afresh 458.

fro *prep.* from 19.

fruyt *n.* profitableness 124.

ful *adv.* very, exceedingly 11 etc.

fulfille *v.* carry out 42. **fulfilled** *pp.* satisfied 315; ~ *of* filled full of 282.

fulnes *n.* ~ *of grace* perfection 705.

gadre, gadir *v.* gather, collect 56, 74. **gadre** *imp. sg.* 874. **gadert** *pp.* 9. **gadrynge** *vbl. n.* 50.

gapynge *v. pr. p* ~ *after* being greedy for 961. (see note)

gendren *v. pr. pl.* produce, give birth to 39.

gestes, gystes *n. pl.* guests 638, 91. See also **yistes**.

gete *v.* acquire, earn 82; *imp. sg.* 163. **gate** *pa.t.* 853. **gote** *pp.* 434.

gilden *adj.* golden 574.

gystnynge *vbl. n.* entertainment 58.

glosyngly *adv.* flatteringly, deceptively 134.

gnastyng *v. pr. p.* grinding, gnashing 958.

gost *v. pr. 2sg.* ~ *to reste* go to bed 397; **go** *imp. sg.* ~ *to* enter 232. **goo** *subj.* go, move 377. **goynge** *pr. p.* 378.

good, godes *n. pl.* possessions 651; *worldly* ~ secular possessions, things 75.

gostly *adj.* spiritual 534; ~ *fader* spiritual director 87; ~ *eye* eye of the soul, spiritual insight 573; ~ *spouse* mystical spouse 747; ~ *felynges* spiritual insights, mystical awareness 541.

gouernaile, gouernayl *n.* personal authority 112; administration, management 638.

graciouse *adj.* conveying, filled with, grace 725.

greither *n.* one who makes, prepares 212.

greithynge *vbl. n.* preparation 114.

gretith *v. pr. 3sg.* greets 701. **grete** *imp. sg.* 703. **grette** *pa. t.* 697. **gretynge** *vbl. n.* 714.

grucche *v.* ~ *with* oppose, complain, disagree with 167. **grucchen** *pr. 3pl.* ~ *of* envy 645. **grucche** *subj.* 791. **grucched** *pa. t.* 643.

habite *n.* characteristic attire of religious 331.

halowed *v. pp.* made holy, consecrated 383, *608 (see note).

hamours *n. pl.* hammers, mallets 595.

happith *v. pr. 3sg.* happens, comes about 39; **happe** *subj.* 490.

hatte *v. pr. 3sg.* is called 803.

haue *v.* have 72; **hast, hastow** *pr. 2sg.* 22, 741. **hath** *pr. 3sg.* 8. **haue** *pr. pl.* 102, 244. **hauynge** *pr. p.* 174. **haue** *subj.* 67. **haddist** *pa.t. 2sg.* 7. **hadden** *pa.t. pl.* 408. **had** *pp.* 435; ~ *meruaile* be astounded 848.

he *pron. pers.* he 364. **him, hym** *acc., dat.* 756, 795. **his(e, hys** *g.* 366, 361, 796.

heed *n. take* ~ pay attention 344.

heet, hete *n.* passioun 405; heat, stinging 449.

helde *v. imp. sg.* pour 789.

hem *pron.* see **they**.

hens *adv.* hence 794.

her *pron.* see **she, they**.

hers *pron.* see **they**.

herbes *n. pl.* leafy vegetables, roots 319.

herby *adv.* by this means 481.

heritage *n.* spiritual inheritance, allotted place in heaven 978.

herof *adv.* as a result of this 39.

heuy *adj. waxe* ~ grow tired, drowsy 221.

heuynesse *n.* sloth, depression 212.

hyder *adv.* ~ *and tyder* here and there, hither and thither 637.

hye *adj.* ~ *cher* arrogant behaviour 134. ~ *none* time of None (about 3 p.m.) 323. ~ *voice* loud voice 134.

hise *pron.* see **he**.

hokes *n. pl.* hooks, claws (of instrument of penance) 596.

holden *v. pr. pl.* consider 460. **holde(n** *pp.* held 303; considered 644.

holichirche *n.* Holy Church 271.

homly *adj.* close, intimate 136.

homly *adv.* intimately 802.

honest *adj.* honourable 88; chaste 107.

ho *pron.* one who 351.

hoo *pron. inter.* who? 76.

hood *n.* head-covering 866.

hool *adj.* whole, complete 910.

hosen *n. pl.* hose, stockings *336.

hou *adv.* how, in what way 399 etc.

houre *n.* canonical hour, prescribed time of liturgical prayer 225. **houres** *pl.* times 132

hous *n.* abode, dwelling-place 806.

housewyues *n. pl.* women in charge of households 52.

hucches *n. pl.* money chests, coffers 653.

humours *n. pl.* exhalations, vapours 594.

ymage *n.* representation 602; mental image 154. **ymages** *pl.* carvings 539.

ymaginatyf *adj.* ~ *thou3tes* fantasies 40.

incorporat *adj.* ~ *to* contained in 383.

infirmyte *n.* moral weakness 591.

inne *adv.* within 371.

innocence *n.* inoffensiveness, harmlessness 623.

in-to *prep.* until, up to 918.

ynow(gh *pron.* enough 503, 568.

ire *n.* anger 168.

yren *adj.* made of iron 595.

yuel *adj.* bad 28.
iangeler *n.* gossip, chatter-box 31, 108.
iape *v.* speak jokingly 499.
iocunde *adj.* delightful 882.

kalendes *n. pl.* first day (of the month) 226.
kepe *v. trans.* preserve 126; *v. refl.* restrain, preserve 122; observe 243. **kepith** *pr. 3sg.* 427. **kepe** *imp. sg.* guard 129. **kept(e** *pp.* 376, 431. **kepynge** *vbl. n.* 385.
keper *n.* one who keeps, guards 417.
kynder *adj. comp.* more natural, benevolent 665.
kirtel *n.* woman's outer garment worn under mantel, pilch or gown 331.
knoulache, knouleche, knowlache *n.* knowledge 993, 998.
konne(n *v.* see **can.**

lak *v.* be lacking 981.
lappe *n.* bosom 802.
lasse *adj.* less 295.
lawe *n. the* ~ the Mosaic law 244.
lawghe *v.* laugh 499.
leder *n.* leader 256.
leieth *v. pr. 3sg.* lays 801. **leyde** *pp.* 773.
leiser, leyser *n.* time free from other duties 17; opportunity 461.
leyt *n.* flame, fire 420.
lenger *adv. comp.* at greater length 218.
lese *v.* lose, suffer loss of 380. **lesith** *pr. 3 sg.* ruins 1000.
lette *v.* prevent 76. **lettist** *pr. 2sg.* 77. **lette** *imp. sg.* leave off 763. **letted** *pp.* 277. **lettyng** *vbl. n.* hindrance 37.
lye *v.* lie 547. **lyethe** *pr. 3sg.* consists 687. **lyeth** *pr. 3 pl.* exist 123. **lay** *pa.t.* lay 726. **liggynge** *vbl. n.* lying 480.
liflode, lyflod(e *n.* living, means of existence 20, 110, 62.
lift(e, lyfte *adj.* left 957, 367, 973.
lyfte *v. pa.t. sg.* lifted, raised 751.
light *adj.* easy 628. **lighter** *comp.* brighter 571.
lightnes *n.* levity 400.
liggynge *vbl. n.* see **lye.**
likynge *vbl. n. lust and* ~ sexual desire 34. **likinges** *pl. lustes and* ~ 290.
liknes *n.* semblance 744.
lymes *n. pl.* limbs, parts of the body 382.
list *v. pr. 3 sg.* desires 130.
listne *v.* hear 560.
litel *adv.* ~ *and* ~ little by little 446.

liuyer *n.* inhabitant, dweller *175. **lyuers** *pl. comoun* ~ *of the worlde* those leading a secular life, non-religious 644. (see note)
lyuyng(e, liuynge *vbl. n.* way of life 645, 141. *form of* ~ rule of life 5; manner of living 148.
loke *v. pr. 3pl.* ~ *after* seek to obtain 54. **loke** *imp. sg.* take care 161, 236.
lombe *n.* Lamb (of God) 377.
longeth, longith *v. pr. 3sg.* appertains 645, 135. **longeth** *pr. 3 pl.* belong 336.
loue *n.* lover, beloved 426. *a boke of* ~ Song of Songs 871.
louely *adv.*[1] humbly 719.
louely *adv.*[2] lovingly, amiably 751.
lowe *adj. holde thiself* ~ kept yourself weak, poorly nourished 303.
lust *n.* desire 393. **lustes** *pl.* ~ *and liking-es* sexual desires 289.
lustful *adj.* delightful, pleasurable 492.
lusty *adj.* lustful 39.

mayde *n.* virgin 716; (male) virgin 745, 810; handmaid, servant 536.
maieste *n.* majesty 712.
maist *v.* see **mowe.**
maistrie *n.* mastery, upper hand 372.
make *v.* make 587. **makith** *pr. 3sg.* causes 145; creates 162. **maad** *pp.* ~ *white* bleached, whitened 586; purified 590.
man *n.* man 128. **mannys** *g.* 209. **men** *pl.* 799. **mennes** *g. pl.* 22.
matere, matier *n.* ~ *of vices* potential for vice 514; ~ *of yuel wille* grounds for malevolence 629; ~ *to loue God* reason for loving God 911.
mede *n.* reward 356.
medled *v. pp.* mixed, mingled 94.
meyne *n.* establishment 106; household 547.
melody(e *n.* song 729; *worde of* ~ sung phrase, antiphon 281 (see note).
mene *adj.* undistinguished, ordinary 333 (see note).
menes *n. pl.* agents, intermediaries 83; methods 437.
meridyan *n.* midday rest 328 (see note).
meritory *adj.* meritorious 155.
meruaile *v. refl. imp. sg.* wonder, marvel 706; **merueilynge** *pr. p.* 705.
meschefs *n. pl.* misfortunes 911.
messanger *n.* messenger 84.

mete *n.* food 305; **metes** *pl.* 312.
mightily *adv.* powerfully, strongly 362.
myldenes *n.* gentleness 572.
mynchen *n.* nun, female religious 81.
mynde *n.* *haue* ~ remember 275; *hauynge . . . in* ~ remembering 174.
mynistres *n. pl.* servants 188; administrators 648.
myrre *n.* myrrh 873.
mysspended *v. pp.* wasted, mis-spent 399. **mysspendynge** *vbl. n.* 502.
mistrust *n.* lack of faith 62.
moche *adj., pron.* much 429, 684.
moder *n.* mother 546; that which gives rise to something 210, 530. **moder** *g.* 716.
moysted *v. pp.* made wet 770.
mony-maker *n.* moneymaker 104.
moo *pron.* more 407.
moor *adj. comp. maad* ~ enlarged 44.
mosten *v. pr. 3pl.* must 599.
motley, mottely *adj.* multi-coloured 618, 575.
mowe *v. pr. 3sg.* be able to 147. **maist, maistow** *pr. 2 sg.* 140, 861. **mown** *pr. 3pl.* 532. **mowe, may** *subj.* may 756, 130. **mightist** *pa.t. 2 sg.* 74. **myght** *pa.t. 3sg.* 707. **mighten, myghten** *pa.t. pl.* 17, 486.

naked *adj.* bare, unadorned 952; ~ *purpos* intent of poverty 101.
natheles *conj.* nonetheless, however 8.
ne *conj.* nor 145.
nedes, nedys *adv.* necessarily 849, 850.
nedeth, nedith *v. pr. 3sg.* it is necessary 721, 82.
needful *adj.* necessary, essential 133.
needfully *adv.* under compulsion, necessarily 445.
netlys *n. pl.* nettles 449.
nye, nyhe *adv.* near, close 417, 415.
nyeden *v. pa.t. pl.* ~ *nye* approached, drew near 903.
nobleye *n.* nobility, high birth 537.
noyce *n.* noise, bustle 129.
nolde *v. pa.t. 1sg.* would not 104.
noon *adj.* no 134.
noon *pron.* no one 368.
norisshe *n.* foster-father 735.
norisshe *v.* nourish, nurse 656. **norshist** *pr. 2sg.* 389. **norshyng** *pr. p.* 919. **norsshed** *pp.* 690.

norsher *n.* one who fosters, nourishes 211.
note *v. pr. 3pl.* not know 959.

oblacyon *n.* sacrificial offering 350.
obsequyous *adj.* helpful 722, 944
occasyon *n. be amonge* ~ be in the midst of opportunities 438.
occupacions *n. pl.* activities 155, 213.
office *n.* function 787.
ofte-sithes *adv.* often, frequently 94.
oynement *n.* ointment 763; **oynementes** *pl.* 879.
oo *adj.* one 612. See also **tone**.
oppinyon *n. of gode* ~ of a good reputation 143 (see note).
or *conj., prep.* see **er**.
oratory(e *n.* place of prayer 414, 582.
orcharde *n.* fruitful garden 565.
ordeyne *v. pr. pl.* make provision for 53. **ordeyne** *imp. sg.* 879. **ordeyned** *pa. t.* 309; *pp.* prepared 576, established 4.
otherwhile *adv.* sometimes 96.
ouer *prep.* over and above 82.
ouercome *v.* conquer 449; **ouercome** *pa. t. 3 sg.* 249. **ouercomen** *pa. t. pl.* 408.
ouerloked *v. pp.* watched over, supervised 115.
ouer-pluys *n.* surplus, excess 653.
owen, owne *adj.* own 568, 952.

paleys *n.* palace 831.
palseye *n.* paralysis 773.
parfyt *adj.* perfect, complete 392.
partie *n.* part 577; *in* ~ partially 591.
passe *v.* surpass, exceed 288. ~ *by* pass through, cross 600. **passeth, passith** *pr. 3 sg.* 257, 364. **passynge** *pr. p.* 400. **passe** *subj.* 388; *imp. sg.* pass 749. **passed** *pp.* 1024.
passingly, passyngly *adv.* surpassingly, exceedingly 289, 968.
peyntures *n. pl.* pictures, paintings 539.
perauenture *conj.* perhaps 76.
perel *n.* peril, danger 433.
peses *n. pl.* peas and beans 316.
pylche *n.* heavy outer garment 330.
pitously *adv.* pityingly, compassionately 77.
plente *n.* plenty, abundance 999.
plenteuous *adj.* plentiful, abundant 886.
plete *v.* appeal against 962.

potage *n. formente* ~ dish made of boiled hulled grain mixed with milk *317 (see note).

pouert(e *n.* poverty 690, 387.

praienge *v. pr. p.* ~ *after* praying to 292.

preciosite *n.* great value 333.

prees *n. put the . . . in* ~ bear your part 729.

prelates *n. pl.* those in spiritual authority 671.

presented *pp.* ~ *afore* brought before 505.

preseruacions *n. pl.* safe-keeping from destruction 542.

preued *pp.* tested, proved 371.

pryue *adj.* private 696. **pryuyer** *comp.* more intimate, secret 742.

priuely *adv.* privately 228.

procede *v. imp. sg.* ~ *furth* go on, advance 764.

profession, professyon *n.* professed state 626, 674.

profit, profyt *n.* benefit, good 23, 631.

profitabler *adj. comp.* more beneficial 572.

purginges *vbl. n. pl.* cleaning, removal of impurities 587.

purpure *adj.* purple 844.

pursute *n.* pursuit 466.

putte *v.* ~ *away* get rid of 224. **put(te** *imp. sg.* ~ *a-way* lay aside 726; ~ . . . *in noo certeyn* do not make definite 220 (see note). **put(te** *pp.* ~ *away, oute* exiled, banished 273, 263.

queer *n.* choir 378.

quotidyan *adj.* daily 597.

raby *n.* rabbi 885.

recleuse, recluse *n.* recluse, anchoress 681, 660. **recluse, reclusys** *g.* 582, 1022.

reduce *v.* bring back, recall 277.

reed *adj.* red 866.

refuse *v.* avoid, reject, renounce 677.

refute *n.* refuge 217, 610.

reherse *v. imp. sg.* repeat aloud 704.

religion, religyon *n.* the religious life 256. *houses of* ~ religious houses, monastic establishments 652.

religious(e *adj.* under vows 58, 90.

remors *n.* remorse, guilt 472.

renne *v.* ~ *to* have recourse, resort to

216. **rennith** *pr. 3sg.* ~ *aboute* recurs persistently to 25. **renne** *imp. sg.* 612.

rent *v. pp.* torn 596.

reparailed *v. pp.* repaired, restored 373.

replet *adj.* filled, satisfied 231.

representen *v. pr. 3 pl.* stand for 654 (see note).

repreued *v. pp.* damned 955.

repreues *n. pl.* reproaches 840.

reserued *v. pp.* preserved, saved 910.

rest *n.* spiritual peace, tranquillity of mind 162.

ryal *adj.* royal 547.

rialy *adv.* royally 575.

ryches(se *n.* wealth, riches 367, 387.

rightsyde *n.* right-hand side 964.

rightwesnes, rightwisnesse *n.* justice, righteousness 570, 65.

ryghtwys(e *adj.* just, righteous 962, 961.

riseth *v. pr. 3pl.* arise, spring 998. **ryse** *imp. sg.* rise, arise 777. **roos** *pa.t. 3sg.* 442. **rysen** *pa.t. pl.* 194. **rysen** *pp.* 898.

rode *n.* cross 1002.

royler-aboute *n.* one who roams around, vagabond 108.

rote *n.* root 531.

rowne *v. subj.* whisper 85. **rownyng** *vbl. n.* whisperings 87.

ruynous *adj.* decayed, dilapidated 528.

rust *n.* moral corrosion, corruption 597.

saaf *prep.* except 188.

saam *adj.* same 446.

saat, sate *v. pa.t.* sat 638, 785, 504.

sad *adj.* serious 498.

sadnes *n.* serious matters 95.

say *v. pa.t.* see **see**

say(e, seie *v.* say 511, 171, 462. **say(e** *pr. 1sg.* 80, 181. **saist, seist, saistow** *pr. 2sg.* 76, 633, 79. **sei(e)th, saith** *pr. 3sg.* 170, 177, 124. **say** *imp. sg.* recite, declare 723. **sayinge, seyeng(e, seieng** *pr. p.* 776, 739, 857, 170. **saide, seyde** *pp.* 125, 684. **saienge** *vbl. n.* recitation 230.

sauoreth *v. pr. 3sg.* smells sweetly 362.

scarsete *n.* ~ *of liflode* frugality of living 303.

sclaundre *n.* slander, calumny 35.

sclaundred *v. pp.* slandered, calumniated 116.

scornynge *vbl. n.* mockery, derision 33.

scrupulous *adj.* troubled with scruples of conscience 502 (see note).

se *v.* see 566, 139. **seest** *pr. 2sg.* perceive 153. **seeth** *pr. 3sg.* 466. **seen** *pr. 3pl.* 960. **se** *imp. sg.* 563. **say, sawe** *pa.t.* 445, 499. **seen** *pp.* 43.

sekith *v. imp. pl.* seek, look for 64, **sechinge, sekynge** *pr. p.* 27, 41. **soughtist** *pa.t. 2sg.* 736. **sought** *pp.* 741.

selde *adv.* seldom 132.

selle, celle *n.* cell, anchorhold 46, 118.

seluer *n.* silver 923.

semblen *v. refl. pr. pl.* gather 567.

semelyheed *n.* beauty, attractiveness 538.

semlynesse *n.* beauty 364.

sendel *n.* fine silk used for shroud *877. (see note)

sentence *n.* short passage of scripture in liturgical use 474; judgment 975.

seruice *n.* thy ~ the serving of you 120; *diuyne* ~ canonical hours 215.

sethynge *vbl. n.* boiling, stewing 114.

sette *v. pp.* seated 785; *wel* ~ seemly 138.

shal *v. pr. 1sg.* shall 8, 123. **shalt, shaltow** *pr. 2 sg.* 143, 29. **shal** *pr. 3sg.* 29. **shul, shuln** *pl.* 946, 939. **shuldist, sholdist, shuldest** *pa. t. 2 sg.* should, ought to, *subj. aux.* 72, 150, 156. **shuld(e** *pa.t. 3sg.* 166, 122. **shulde(n** *pa.t. pl.* 649, 460.

shame *n.* sense of shame, embarassment 726.

shamfast *adj.* ashamed 166.

shamfastnesse *n.* modesty 163.

shap *n.* excellence of form, beauty 364.

she *pron.* she 112 etc. **hir** *acc.* 30. **hir, hyr** *g.* 62, 382.

shewed *v. pp.* ~ *furthe* manifested, revealed 96.

shilyng *n.* shilling, coin worth twelve pence 51.

shipmen *n. pl.* sailors, seamen 671.

shitte *v. pp.* see **shutte.**

shoon *n. pl.* shoes 336.

shorter *adv. comp.* more briefly 218.

shutte *v.* shut 24. **shitte** *pp.* 653.

syke *adj.* sick, ill 311.

syker, seker *adj.* sure 526; secure 461.

sikerly *adv.* safely, securely 257.

sikernesse *n.* security 456; self-confidence 464.

simple *adj.* ~ *felynge* rudimentary understanding 8.

symplenes(se *n.* simplicity, absence of guile 571, 585.

sith(en *conj.* since 135, 63.

sithen *adv.* then 325.

slowe *v. pa.t. pl.* slew 853.

smyte *v. imp. sg.* strike 402.

snobbe *v.* sob 18; **snobbynge** *pr. p., vbl. n.* 778, 392, 862. **snobbed** *pa.t. 3sg.* 448.

so *conj.* ~ *that* as long as 226.

sodenly *adv.* suddenly 442.

solempne *adj.* ~ *vigils* eves of important liturgical feasts 326.

somme *pron.* some 413.

sondry *adj.* various 458.

sonner *adv.* sooner 403.

soor, sore *adv.* painfully 828, 844.

sory *adj.* sorrowful 849.

sothe *n.* say the ~ tell the truth 430.

souerayne, souereyn *adj.* excellent 253; ~ *remedye* efficacious, potent remedy 475.

space *n.* opportunity, spare time 461.

special, specyal *adj.* ~ *louyer* one-and-only, unique beloved 540; *in* ~ particularly 983.

specialy *adv.* particularly, pre-eminently 545.

spedful *adj.* useful, helpful 675.

spices *n. pl.* species, types 532.

springeth *v. pr. 3sg.* ~ *out* grows 993. **springen** *pr. pl.* 531.

staat *n.* condition, way of life 655.

stamyns *n. pl.* coarse worsted undergarments 332.

stede *n. in* ~ *of* by way of, as for 228 (see note).

sterres *n. pl.* stars 365.

stilled *v. pa.t.* ~ *out* exuded, dropped 882.

stynke *v.* ~ *vpon* disgust, be abhorrent to 922.

stondist, standist *v. pr. 2sg.* ~ *in(ne* persevere, remain steadfast in 218, 633. **stondith, stondeth** *pr. 3sg.* ~ *in* exists, is in state of 432; ~ consists of 533, 829. **stonden** *pr. pl.* 963. **stonde** *imp. sg.* 799. **stondynge** *pr. p.* 957. **stood** *pa.t.* 503.

stoor *n.* haue in ~ have in sufficient or abundant supply 661.

stopped *v. pp.* silenced 887.

straight *adj.* ~ *liuynge* rigorous, strict way of life 140.

strecche *v. imp. sg.* ~ *out . . . wille* direct intention 385.

streyned *v. pa.t. 3pl.* tied tightly 828.

strengthe *v.* strengthen 445.

studieden *v. pa.t. pl.* were studious, eager 677.

stured *v. pp.* inspired 219; moved, aroused 405.

sturer *n.* instigator, arouser 211.

subieccyon *n.* subjection, subject condition 518.

suche *pron.* such ones 379.

suffre *v.* permit 497; *subj.* 519. **suffred** *pa.t.* permitted 459. *pp.* 472.

suspect(e *adj.* dubious, open to suspicion 159; *hauynge thiself* ~ being suspicious, distrustful of yourself 465.

swagith *v. pr. 3sg.* softens, mitigates 165.

swetter *adj. comp.* sweeter 365.

tarye *v.* linger 817.

temperal *adj.* ~ *good* worldly possessions 627.

than *conj., adv.* then 71, 372.

that *pron. rel.* who 353 etc.; that which 497.

they, thei, þei, thai, thay *pron. pl.* they 78, 15, 656, 604, 903. **hem** *prepl.* 27. **her(s** *g.* 20, 645.

therby *adv.* by those means 495.

therof *adv.* from that 86.

therto *adv.* in addition 775.

thilk *adj., pron.* the, that same 359.

tho(o *adj., pron.* those 347, 816.

thorugh *prep.* through, by means of 413.

thou, thow, thov *pron.* you 5, 566, 645. **the, þe** *acc., prepl.* 102, 576. **thin, thyn(e, thi, thy** *g.* 68, 145, 366, 71.

thryes *adv.* thrice 833.

thridde *adj.* third 932.

tyder *adv.* see **hyder**.

tidynges *n. pl.* ~ *-teller, teller of* ~ gossip 108, 31.

tilyenge *v. pr. p.* labouring 672. (see note)

tyre *n.* (head)dress *537.

to *prep.* in regard to, as to 119.

tofore *prep.* in front of 29; before 227.

togiders *adv.* together 828.

token *n.* sign, indication 62; *in* ~ as a sign, to indicate 606.

tone *adj. the* ~ the one 449. See also **oo**.

too *adj.* two 532.

tother, tothir *pron.* other 450, 636.

touchinge *v. pr. p.* dealing with 338.

to. . .warde *prep. phr.* towards 70.

trauaile *v.* toil, labour 71. *imp. sg.* 173 **trauailed** *pa.t.* 451. **traueiled** *pp.* tormented, racked 440.

trepas *n.* sin, offence 858.

trete *v.* ~ *of* discuss, discourse on 820.

trowe *v. pr. 1sg.* believe 828. **trowist** *pr. 2 sg.* 39, 360.

turmentynge *vbl. n.* torturing 429.

turned *v. pp.* returned 276.

tweyne *pron.* two 621.

vmbigon, vmbigoon *v. pp.* surrounded, encircled 555, 619.

vncerteyn *n.* state of uncertainty 971.

vnclene *adj.* impure, unchaste 441.

vnclenly *adv.* impurely, unchastely 42.

vnclennes(se *n.* impurity, unchastity 494, 84.

vndefouled *v. pp.* undefiled 379.

vnder *prep.* ~ *fewe wordes* with few words 189.

vndoth *v. pr. 3sg.* unfastens, removes 869.

vnkyndely *adv.* inhumanely 831.

vnkyndenes *n.* act of inhumanity 79.

vnlauful, vnleeful, vnleful *adj.* unlawful, forbidden 472, 489, 837.

vnnethes *adv.* scarcely 28.

vnpacyent *adj.* impatient, restless 769.

vnshamful *adj.* shameless, immodest 167.

vnsongen *v. pp.* not sung 281 (see note).

vnspecable *adj.* ineffable, inexpressible 774.

vnto *prep.* until 226; ~ *the time (that)* 40, 232 etc.

vse *v.* make use of, practise 479. **vsed** *pp.* accustomed 494.

veyn *adj.* vain, foolish 85.

veynes *n. pl.* ~ *of hir body* tear-ducts 882.

venym *n.* (moral) poison 85.

verray *adj.* true, veritable 711.

vertu *n.* (moral) virtue 352.

vesture *n.* garments 80.

visage *n.* face, countenance 156.

visitacions *n. pl.* visits 151.

voide *v.* go away 79; get rid of, remove 111, 213.

vouchith-saaf *v. pr. 3sg.* vouchsafes, condescends 707. **vouche-saaf** *subj.* 778. **vouch-saaf** *pa.t.* 771.

wacche *n.* see **wake.**
way *n. by ~ of* in the way of 92.
wayke, weyke *adj.* weak 445, 490.
wayle *v. imp. sg.* bewail, lament 402. **wailynge, weilynge** *vbl. n.* 272, 270.
waiter *n.* one who lies in wait 84.
wake *v.* be awake 238. **wakyng** *pr.p. ~ wacche* vigil 728. **wakynge** *vbl.n.* keeping of vigils 479.
wanne *v. pa.t.* won 508.
wantownes *n.* lascivious behaviour 115.
war *adj.* wary 92.
wassh *v. pa.t.* washed *761 (see note).
waxe *v.* grow, become 221.
welbeloued *adj.* dearly beloved 872.
wenynge *v. pr. p.* knowing 388; believing 543.
wente *pa.t. 3sg.* walked 504; passed 861.
weryng *vbl. n.* wearing of penitential garments? 480.
werkes *n. pl.* activities 267; deeds 836.
whan(ne *conj.* when 41, 184.
what *exclamation* 735.
whethir *conj., introducing direct question* 808.
whicche *n.* chest, coffer 929.
whider-so-euere *adv.* wherever 377.
whos, who-so *pron.* whosoever 351, 613.
wiche *adj.* wicked *947 (see note).
wil *v. pr. 1 sg.* wish, desire 815. **wilt, wiltow** *pr. 2sg.* 327, 878. **wil** *pr. 3sg., fut. auxil.* 763. **wil** *subj. pl.* 598. **wolde** *pa.t. 1sg.* 513. **woldist, woldest** *pa.t. 2sg.* 308, 981. **wolden** *pa.t. pl.* 410. **wolt** *pa.t. subj. 2sg.* 780. **wold(e** *pa.t. subj. 3sg.* 6. **wolden** *pa. t. subj. pl.* 79.
wilful *adj.* voluntary 349.
wille *n. good ~* benevolence, kindness 623; *yuel ~* malevolence 630. *be in ~* intend, purpose 755.

wiln *v. pr. pl.* desire 304. **wilne** *imp. sg.* intend 630.
wise *n.* manner, way 348.
withdraweth *v. pr. 3sg.* draws back 892. **withdrowe** *pa. t.* withdrew, removed 498.
with-in *prep. ~ thiself* by yourself, with your own resources 69.
with-in-forthe *adv.* within 555.
wytnes *v. imp. sg. ~ of* take witness of 783.
witnes(se *n.* proof, evidential sign or mark 564, 109; testimony 244.
witty *adj.* sensible, prudent 484.
wode *n.* wood 113.
wolle *n.* wool 51.
wombe *n.* stomach 487.
womman *n.* woman 30. **wommen** *pl.* 93.
woot *v. pr. 1 sg.* know 829. **wote** *pr. 3 sg.* 424. **wyte, witen** *pr. pl.* 855, 462.
worchinge *vbl. n.* work, labour 686; operation 271.
worde *n.* sentence 896.
wortes *n. pl.* vegetables 316.
wower *n.* one who woos 562.
wowith *v. pr. 3sg.* woos, courts 563.
wrastle *v. imp. sg.* wrestle, struggle 766.
wryt *n. holy ~* Holy Scripture 467.
wroughte *v. pa. t. 3 sg.* worked 504.
wurcher *n.* producer, contriver 210.

ye *pron.* you 65. **yow** *prepl.* 66.
yelde *v. imp. sg.* pay 425.
yeue *v.* give 360, 632. **yeuen** *pr. pl.* 648. **yeuyng(e** *pr. p., vbl. n.* 986, 100. **yaf** *pa. t.* cared 409; gave 636. **youen** *pp.* 8.
yhe *part.* yes, yea 80, 100.
yhis *part.* yes 381.
yhit, yit *conj.* yet 161, 189.
yifte *n.* gift 434.
yistes *n. pl.* guests 92. See also **gestes.**
yonger *adj. comp. ~ . . . of age* younger 112–3.

MS VERNON

a, an *prep.* on the occasion of 789. See also **alf, heȝe.**
a *conj.* see **and.**

abake *adv.* away from the present scene of action 553.
abhominable *adj.* disgusting 63, 1174.

abhominacioun *n.* abhorrence 481. *pl.* odious degrading vices *1124.

abyde(n *v. intr.* stand one's ground 698; wait 801, 805, 974; remain 829, 1267, 1285; ~ *in* keep one's attention fixed on 1038; *tr.* await 556, 556; expect 735, 1283; await submissively 1427. *pr. 3sg.* **abyde** 735. *pl.* **abide** 1285. *pa.t.* **abood** 556. *pp.* **abide** 1283.

abydyng(e *n.* expectation 1280; waiting 1336.

abydyngge *adj.* permanent 1042; eternal 1380; enduring 1410.

abou(3)te *adv.* be ~ *to* be engaged in 366; scheme to 928.

abrood *adv.* with the limbs wide spread 380, 910.

acceptede *v. pa.t.* ~ *not* rejected 769. *ppl. adj.* **acceptyd** welcome 519; **accepted** worthy of approval 815.

acresyd *v. pp.* increased 723.

acursed(e, acursyd *ppl. adj.* doomed to perdition 184, 850, 1085, 1255, etc.

acuse *v. tr.* censure 669, 769; indict 875; *intr.* bring an accusation 680. *pp.* **acused, accuse(e)d** 669, 769, 875.

adi3t *v. pp.* decked out 789.

a-drow *v. pa.t.* caused to come 1108.

adulacioun *n.* servile hypocritical flattery 1373.

affeccioun *n.* inner spiritual love 540, 541, 545, 548, etc.; disposition 1117.

after *adv.* subsequently 242, 649, 1147; behind 593, 681, 831, 850; then, next 599; in pursuit 1140.

aftur, -ter *prep.* to obtain 75, 1183, 1195, 1415; in a manner answering to 835; in accordance with 1151, 1360, 1385, 1420.

afuyre, aviere *adv.* on fire (fig.) 119, 572, 856.

agast *v. pp.* terrified 671. *ppl. adj.* fearful 103, 835, 1025, 1141, etc.; horrorstruck, amazed 915.

agreyþeþ *v. pr. 3sg.* makes ready, dresses up 53; prepares 926, 1351. *pp.* **agreyþed** 53, 1351.

a3e(y)n *adv.* back again 1030.

a3ens *prep., conj.* contrary to 88; with respect to 429; in contrast to 587; towards, to meet 1031, 1182; facing 1315. *conj.* even though 1108.

a3enward *adv.* on the other hand 391; in return 422.

akeled *v. pp.* cooled off (fig.), diminished in ardour 182.

al *adv.* all the way 30; altogether, quite 235, 269, 352, 382, etc.

alaba(u)stre *n. attrib.* made of alabaster 752, 756.

alf, half *n.* behalf: *a Godes* ~ in the name of God 496; for God's sake 1347.

almesse *n.* charitable gifts 451, 495, 496, 498, etc.; charitable works 501, 530.

a-long *adv.* out, into threads 368.

alto-berste *v.tr.* shatter 752; *intr.* burst asunder 1001. *pa.t.* **alto-barst** 752.

alto-breke *v. intr.* break utterly 1023. *pr. 3sg. tr.* **alto-breket** wrecks 1167.

alto-cleueþ *v. intr. pr. 3pl.* split asunder 918.

alto-rend *v. pp.* torn in pieces 1173.

al-þey *conj.* if, that 301.

alþou3 *conj.* if 637; **alþou3t** although 535.

alwey *adv.* perpetually 85, 402, 923.

alwhat *conj.* until 172, 1286, 1415.

amenuseþ *v. tr. pr. 3sg.* diminishes 524.

amyable *adj.* lovable 1332, 1387.

among, amang *prep.* as part of 786; in the course of 825.

anaunter *conj.* ~ *þat* lest 77, 227, 845, 1150.

and *conj.* and 3, 4, 5, 5, etc.; if 114, 1233, 1233, 1234; **ant** 67, 83, 182, 541, etc.; **a** 499.

anhungred *ppl. adj.* hungry (fig.), yearning 74, 1183.

ano(o)n *adv.* straightaway 103, 155, 484, 634, etc.

antermete *v. intr.* ~ *of* have to do with, occupy oneself with 488; *refl.* join in 589.

ap *n. vpan* ~ perhaps 225.

apassed, apassyd *ppl. adj.* (in the) past 550, 553, 678, 1044, etc.

apeyrryngge *n.* impairment 77.

appetit *n.* inclination 1403.

aray *n.* outward show 308; *in which* ~ presenting an appearance like that 786.

areyse *v. tr.* incite to take action 149; raise from the dead 861; lift up (fig.) 1142, 1301. *pr. 3sg.* **areyseþ** 1301. *pa.t.* **areysede** 149, 1142.

aryse *v.intr.* stand up 782; get up 797. *pr. 3sg.* **aryst** 797.

arst *adv.* at first 1035.

asadded ‡ *ppl. adj.* bored 1193. [OE **asadod*]

ascherche *v. tr.* thoroughly scrutinize 121; examine 654. *pr. 3sg.* **aschercheþ** 129.

asent *n.* illicit compliance 67.

asoylede *v. tr. pa.t.* absolved 673, 770. *pp.* **asoyled** 677.

aspyed *v.intr. pp.* discerned 808.

asschapeþ *v.intr. pr. 3sg.* escapes 1167. *pp.* **aschaped** run away 1081.

associe *v. tr.* combine 322; bring together in fellowship 1346. *pp.* **associod** 322.

a-steynt *v. pp.* defiled 725.

astonyed *ppl. adj.* amazed 785; filled with consternation 1292.

astrangled *v. pp.* suffocated 1053, 1277.

ate *prep.* (= *at þe*) at the instigation of 873.

auntre *v. refl.* venture 605, 820.

auarously *adv.* avariciously 465.

auaunsede *v. tr. pa.t.* raised by preferment to an advantageous state 1143.

av(i)er *adv.* in the distance 217; a little way away 793; from a distance 833; at a distance 943.

aviere *adv.* see **afuyre.**

auyse *v. refl.* consider 143, 187, 684, 877, etc.

auyse *adj.* prudent 216. [OF *avisé*]

avysily *adv.* with calm consideration 945.

avoutrye *n.* adultery 666, 677.

awter *n.* altar 339, 344, 378, 459, etc.

baad *v. pa.t.* prayed 437.

baaumes *n. pl.* aromatic preparations for embalming the dead 990.

babounrye *n.* grotesque extravagant ornamentation 308.

bagbyteþ *v. pr. 3pl.* slander 484.

baldeliche *adv.* confidently 28, 600, 702, 1368; without fear 806; **baldely** 600; **boldely** 702, 806; **booldely** 1368.

bapteme *n.* baptism 349.

be, ben *v.* be 5, 6, 25, 47, etc. *pr. 1sg.* **am** 880, 892, 1080, 1081, etc.; **ham** 1027. *2sg.* **art** 97, 442, 468, 576, etc. *pl.* **beþ** 10, 26, 59, 60, etc.; **ben** 181, 276, 348, 508, etc.; **be** 345, 353; **bete** 413; **beeþ** 1274. *pr.subj. sg., pl.* **be** 11, 21, 25, 40, etc.; **bee** 808. *pr.p.* **beyngge** 74, 238,

784. *pa.t. 2sg., pl., subj.* **were** 34, 55, 74, 153, etc.; **where** 44, 104, 304, 669, etc. *pp.* **be** 95, 240, 285, 1061, etc.; **ibe** 241, 1049, 1057, 1069.

be, by *prep.* by 20, 27, 191, 193, etc.; **bi** 211.

beforn *prep.* before: (of rank) 7, 34, 1417; (of position) 122, 165, 590, 878; (of time) 825; **before** 34; **biforn** 122; **byfore** 165, 825, 878, 1417; **by-foore** 590.

begete *v. pp.* begotten 1074.

begynnyng(ge, bygynnyngge *n.* start 6, 145, 273, 1251, etc.; **bykynnyng** 1224. *pl.* **begynnynges** first fruits 1247.

be-goon *v. pp.* surrounded 409.

behoolde *v. intr.* consider 32, 1066; see 833, 849, 901, 945, etc.; *tr.* contemplate 54, 507, 508; watch, look at 604, 779, 1307; consider 1180, 1290. *pr. 3sg.* **be-haldeþ** 779. *imp.* **be-, byhold, be-, byhald** 32, 507, 508, 604, etc.

behoueþ, byhoueþ *v. pr. 3sg.* is necessary 68, 356, 409, 1170.

beneficence, benificience *n.* active kindness towards others 417, 422, 502, 522. [corrupt form of *beneficence*, < L *beneficentia*]

benefys *n.* gracious favour 1066. *pl.* **benefys** 1073, 1075, 1127, 1144, etc.; **benefices** 1409.

benefysed *ppl. adj.* holding a church living 459.

bere *v.* carry 22, 141, 900, 902; give birth to 34, 595, 1054, 1056, etc.; wear 887; ~ *vp* support 981; **bern** 595. *pr. 2sg.* **berst** 22. *3sg.* **berþ** 902. *pp.* **born** 34; **ybore** 1054, 1059, 1109; **bore** 1056.

berst *v. imp.* ~ *out into* make (an utterance) suddenly 596.

best *n.* animal (fig.) 1067, 1090, 1093. *pl.* **bestes** 307, 1227.

betyl *n.* mallet 358.

beþenke *v. refl.* ~ . . . *(on, of)* reflect (on), consider 21, 51, 68, 92, etc.; *tr.* bear in mind 49; *intr.* reflect 798. *pr. 2sg.* **byȝenkeste** (with assimilation of refl. pron.) 648.

by-comyngge *v. pr.p.* becoming 838. *pp.* **bycome** 946, 1021; fled 1081.

byforn *adv.* earlier 502, 729, 1128; before 630; in front 849; **byfore** 630, 729; **before** 849; **beforn** 1128.

by-gyle *v. pr. subj. 3sg.* deceive 132.

byheste *n.* promise 1393.

byhoot *v. pr. 3sg.* promises 1232. *pa.t.* **beheet, by-** 958, 1142. *pp.* **be-hoote** 1283.

bykleppe *v.* embrace 381, 598, 976. *pr. 3sg.* **byklippeþ** 976. *imp.* **beklep** 598.

byleue *n.* religious faith 1061.

bynde *v.* lay under obligation 14, *1131; hold fast (fig.) *233, 505; unite together 411; tie up 853. *pr. 3sg.* **bynt** 14. *3pl.* **byndeþ** 853. *pp.* **ibounden** *233; **bounde** *1131.

bynemeþ *v. pr. 3sg.* takes away 87, 1026, 1402; spoils 1176. *3pl.* **benemyþ** 1176. *pp.* **benomen** 87; **bynome** 1026.

by-schad *v. pp.* wetted 1019.

bysye *v. refl.* be assiduously engaged in 469, 475, 1211.

bysyly(che *adv.* with careful attention 8; assiduously 137, 646.

bysynesse *n.* diligence 267; function 492; distress 515; hard work 1170; disturbance of the Divine equanimity 1384.

bytak *v. imp.* entrust 91, 390, 957. *pa.t.* **bytook** 390; **bitooke** 957.

blaberynge *v. pr.p.* chattering 241.

blast *n.* loud noise 660.

blowere *n.* bellows (fig.) 43.

bodyly *adv.* physically 192; in human form 576.

bofattes *n. pl.* blows 882.

bold *adj.* over-confident 681; presumptuous 715; *is ~ on* bases its confidence on 1231.

bonerly *adv.* humbly 878.

bo(o)c, book *n.* the Bible 41, 167, 328, 476 etc.

boord *n.* table 793.

borwede *v. pa.t.* borrowed 564.

bost *n.* bragging 279; noise and bustle 660. *pl.* **boostes** clamour 1040.

bot(e *conj., prep., adv.* see **but**.

bouyd *v. pp.* bowed down to submission 359, 882.

bowelys, -es *n. pl.* womb 568; one's interior as seat of compassion 855, 1003.

breedale *n.* wedding (fig.) 657.

brek *v. imp.* break 756; dislocate the bones of 1071. *pp.* **broke** 1071.

brenne *v. tr.* burn 118, 142, 1068, 1099; *intr.* 237, 1295. *ppl. adj.* **brennyngge** ardent 66, 119, 571, 723, etc.; stinging 160. *pp.* **brend** 142, 1099, 1276; **ybrend** 1068.

brennyngge *n.* infliction of stinging pain 160; vehemence 161, 220, 1007.

brennyngly *adv.* passionately 1013.

bryddes *n. pl.* birds 307, 969, 1214, 1227.

briȝt *adv.* brightly 1326.

brymme *adj.* fierce, harsh 160.

bryng(g)e *v.* cause 25; bring 373, 886, 914, 1165, etc.; incite 1414; *~ out* remove 342; *~ forþ* cause to grow 344; bear (a child) 345; incubate (fig.) 969 *~ wit childe* cause to conceive 569. *pr. 3sg.* **brenkþ** 25; **brynkt** 1165. *pa.t.* **brouȝte** 569. *pp.* **ibrouȝt** 342; **brouȝt** 344, 1415; **ybrout** 345, 886.

brit *adj.* bright (fig.) 320. *comp.* **bryȝtere** 321.

brytnesse, bri(ȝ)tnesse *n.* splendour 86, 410, 616, 630.

buryed *v. pp.* entombed 6; buried (fig.) 350; cut off from society 443; **ibyryed** 350; **ybyried** 443.

busy *adj.* anxious 246; *~ to* preoccupied about 438, 444; **bysy** 438, 444.

but, bot(e *conj., prep., adv.* but 39, 61, 154, 163, etc.; other than 136, 157, 164, 203, etc.; unless 1024, 1135; *~ ȝif* unless 425. *prep.* except 57, 498, 832, 1156, etc. *adv.* merely 499, 763, 1103, 1188, etc.

caas *n. in ~ (þat)* if, in the even that 85, 98, 487, 621, etc.; *par ~* perhaps 892, 1163.

cacche *v. imp.* wrest 693

caytyfs *n. pl.* wretches 1358.

canst *v. pr. 2sg.* are able to 595, 787, 844, 1198. *pa.t.* **cowde** knew 164; *~ no mor good þan* had no more sense than 1067.

carayne *n.* the flesh 225; filth 476.

care *n.* heed 472.

care *v.* trouble oneself (to do sthg.) 498; be anxious 1211.

caste *v.* throw 157, 348, 349, 1122, etc.; turn 553, 672, 947, 1305, etc.; bestow 1132; *~ adoun* avert 248, 879; deject 1142; defeat 1264; *~ out* expel 274, 1052, 1082, 1271, etc.; eject roughly 907; give birth to 1074; *~ awey* avert 696. *pr. 3sg.* cast 696. *3pl* **casteþ** 907, 1264. *pa.t.* **cast(e** 274, 672, 1083, 1124. *pp.* **icast** 248, 348, 349, 879, etc.; **cast** 1074, 1122, 1142.

celle *n.* single chamber inhabited by the anchoress 42, 288, 306.

celures *n. pl.* tapestries 288.

certayn *adv.* without doubt 16, 424, 472, 525, etc.

certes *adv.* assuredly 164, 214, 217, 251, etc.

cesse *v.* ~ *fro* desist 1023.

chaar *n.* chariot 1295.

chalange *v. imp.* assert one's title to 819.

chape *v. refl.* deceive oneself 131; *intr.* jest 242.

charge *n. be in* ~ *to* be a burden to 213.

chargeþ *v. pr. 3sg.* attaches weight to 924.

charnel *adj.* sensual 1116.

chast(e *adj.* undefiled 116, 139, 267; **chaast** 234.

chastite, -ete *n.* sexual purity 12, 23, 55, 64, etc.; **castete** 135.

chaterynge *v. pr.p.* talking incessantly 242.

chees *v. pa.t.* chose 293. *pp.* **ychose** 4, 33, 39, 816, etc.

cheueryngge *v. pr.p.* shivering 158.

chier *adj.* careful 227.

chiere *n.* expression 248; frame of mind 879, 1181; face 947; presence 1082; **cher** 947.

childhood *n.* youth 1112 (see n.), 1118.

childly *adv.* in a manner appropriate to a child 638.

churche *n. holy* ~ the Church Catholic 453, 454, 458, 460, etc.; **chirche** 454.

cyteseyn *n.* citizen 1263.

clennesse *n.* chastity 73, 81, 87, 88, etc.; **clannesse** 157.

clepiþ *v. pr. 3sg.* summons 107, 998, 1321; calls out 1003. *pa.t.* **clepede** 998. *pp.* **cleped** 107; **yclepyd** 1321.

cleppe *v.* embrace 475, 618, 1416; grasp 1036. *pa.t.* **kleppede** 618. *pl.* **klepte** 1036. *pp.* **ilkept** 1416.

cler, clier(e *adj.* (of eyes) keen 553; certain 1241; glorious 1328. *comp.* **clierere** 323.

clerkes *n. pl.* churchmen 455.

clernesse, cliernesse *n.* splendour and brightness 412; splendour combined with beauty 1388.

cleue *v.* become linked 206, 402, 412, 1153. *pr. 3sg.* **cleueþ** 402. *3pl.* **cleueþ** 1153.

cleuyngge *n.* attachment 405.

cloystre *n.* place of religious seclusion 469.

close *v. tr.* ~ *vp* put away 461; enclose 568; stop up (ears) 696. *pr. 3sg.* **closeþ** 696. *pp.* **iclosed** 568.

closes, cloþys *n. pl.* clothes 105, 307.

cloþ *n.* garment 332; a (piece of) cloth 798, 987.

cloute *v.* patch up 1172.

colour *n. vndur* ~ *of* under the pretext of 305.

coloureþ *v. pr. pl.* make a pretext 261.

come *v.* come 256, 895, 1031, 1182, etc.; arrive 254, 974; ~ *after* follow 681, 850; ~ *aʒe(y)n* return 1030, 1030; ~ *in(to* enter 103, 189, 557, 633; ~ *in after* take the place of 1178; ~ *neiʒ* approach 1015; ~ *of* be descended from 281; derive from 316, 498; ~ *out* issue 961; ~ *out of* emanate from 616; ~ *to* achieve 138, 1428; attain, get possession of 372, 620, 1060; attend 790; ~ *vpon* assail 120. *infl. inf.* **to comen(e** to come, in the future 1175, 1212, 1213, 1223, etc. *pr. 2sg.* **cumst** 620; **comest** 633. *3sg.* **comeþ** 120, 256, 498, 557, etc.; **comþ** 1030. *imp. pl.* **comeþ** 1350. *pa.t.* **cam** 254, 961; **come** 616, 1182. *pp.* **ycome(n** 189, 281. See also **to-comyngge**.

communyngge *n.* (sexual) intercourse 260.

competent *adj.* appropriate, proper 520.

complexioun *n.* temperament (as constituted by the natural humours) 146.

conceyuyngge *v. pr.p.* becoming possessed with *149.

confermed *v. pp.* strengthened 1192.

conflit *n.* struggle 662.

confortacioun *n.* solace 383.

coniones *n. pl.* fools 1309.

coniuryngge *v. pr.p.* entreating 166.

conteyne *v. intr.* keep oneself chaste 234; *tr.* enclose 410.

continent *adj.* chaste 135; temperate 139.

conuersacioun *n.* conduct, mode of life 1179.

conuersioun *n.* (entry into) monastic life 145.

coroune *n.* sovereignty (fig.) 23; circlet 887; aureola 1326.

corounne *v.* crown 40, 883.

cor(r)upt *adj.* defiled 65; foul and adulterated 911.

cotidian *adj.* ordinary 367.

coueytyse *n.* great or inordinate desire 31, 429; avarice 1300.

couenable *adj.* proper 1071.

cowde *v. pa.t.* see **canst.**

crafty *adj.* skilful 47.

criour *n.* officer in a law court who makes announcements 584.

croked *adj.* crippled 1057.

culverhows *n.* dovecote 966.

culvren *n. pl.* doves 967.

cumst *v. pr. 2sg.* see **come.**

curiosite *n.* elaborate workmanship 326.

curious *adj.* intent 247; intricately and skilfully made 318.

curiously *adv.* carefully 364.

curslyn(g)ges *n. pl.* people excommunicated from God 1268, 1273, 1331, 1355. [prob. f. n., OE *curs*]

cus *n.* kiss 851.

custummablely *adv.* habitually 1145.

dampnacioun *n.* condemnation to eternal punishment 24, 1136, 1141.

dampne *v.* pass judgment on 679, 680; condemn to eternal punishment 714, 1062, 1256, 1303, etc. *pp.* **(y)dampned** 1062, 1256, 1303, 1321, etc.

d(a)ar *v. pr. 1sg.* venture to 28, 702, 1368. *2sg.* **darst** have the courage to 819.

dedyed *v. pp.* dedicated 69.

d(e)ed *adj.* dead 5, 190, 255, 747, etc.; ~ *to þe wordle* indifferent, insensible to one's surroundings 442; *be* ~ *die* 1100, 1210, 1257.

deed *n.* death 1225, 1225.

deef *adj.* deaf 443.

deel *n.* share 448.

deeþ *n.* see **deþ(e.**

defautes *n. pl.* failings 367.

defoyle *v.* violate (the chastity of) 59, 62, 66, 72; corrupt 141, 486, 1275, 1300; make dirty 725, 865. *pr. 3sg.* **defoyled** 1300. *3pl.* **defoyleþ** 865.

dey(3)e *v.* die 856, 857, 1133, 1258, etc. *pr. 3sg., pl.* **deyeþ** 1258, 1261. *pa.t.* **deed** 1133.

delacioun *n. put in* ~ temporarily withheld **1035. [OF *dilacion*]

delay *n. iput in* ~ deferred 1027.

delauey *adj.* dissolute 139.

delectacioun *n.* delight 129, 381, 383.

delicat *adj.* over-indulgent 227.

delys *n.* source of pleasure 75; luxury 1218. *pl.* **delices** sensual pleasures 139; joys 300, 474, 1199; delicacies (fig.) 1183.

deme *v.* condemn 864; pronounce as a judgment 1317; consider 1318. *pp.* **ydemed, demyd** 864, 1317.

departe *v. tr.* divide 276, 279, 415, 417, etc.; share out 518, 908; sever connections with 1051, 1320; take away 1359; ~ *to* bestow on 411; *intr.* go away 1354. *imp. pl.* **departeþ** 1354.

derewurthe, deoreworthe *adj.* beloved 1012, 1159.

derke *adj. make* ~ darken 86.

derknesse *n.* darkness 112, 1079, 1374; gloom of sorrow 587; *in* ~ obscurely, vaguely 1392.

derlyng *n.* one dearly loved 1346. *pl.* **derlyngges** 1255.

desiderable *adj.* precious 1018, 1387.

destruye *v.* exterminate 1296.

deþ(e, deeþ *n.* death 112, 478, 862, 876, etc.

deveyed *v. pp.* withheld 171. [OF *deveier*]

di(e)re *adj.* worthy 385, 813; beloved 442, 448, 649.

discipline *n.* chastisement 362.

disconforte *v. refl. imp.* be dismayed 1026.

discryvyngge *v. pr.p.* ~ . . . *fro* . . . making a distinction between . . . and . . . 1254.

disese *n.* harm 151.

disese *v.* trouble 1213. *ppl. adj.* **disesed** ill 192.

dishonested *v. pp.* put to shame **884.

dispendist *v. pr. 2sg.* expend to one's own use 496.

dispyt, despyt *n.* contempt 245, 1233; outrage 924; *be to* ~ *to* be in a state deserving the contempt of 1058. *pl.* **dispite3** *do* ~ *(to)* humiliate 912.

distract(e *adj.* having the attention diverted 439, 444, 470.

do *v. tr.* perform, practise, carry out 122, 157, 418, 430, etc.; inflict 128, 151, 912; *as substitute for another verb* 200, 694, 845, 858, etc.; commit 683, 925, 1134, 1161; consign 926; cause to feel 964; ~ *awey* destroy 258; take away

430; *intr.* act 301, 715, 771, 1027;
doon 258; **doo** 501, 530, 683, 771, etc.
pr. 2sg. **dost** 588, 715. *3sg., pl.* **dooþ**
200; **doþ** 529, 912, 926, 1331. *pa.t.*
dude 157, 667, 824; **dede** 422, 694,
845, 858, etc. *pp.* **ido(o** 128, 301, 663,
785, etc.; **doon** 430, 603, 1134; **ydoo**
771; **do(o** 925, 1075, 1092, 1126.
doctoures *n. pl.* learned men 650.
domesman *n.* judge (here, God) 250,
1314, 1336, 1427. *pl.* **domesmen**
1325.
d(o)om *n.* judgment 107, 668, 895, 896,
etc.; **dome** *day of* ~ day of the last
judgment 250, 897, 1287, 1290.
douter *n.* daughter 311, 312.
drawe *v. tr.* entice 27, 101, 1145; move
690; pull 810, 1276; draw (a weapon)
857; remove, take up 1148; ~ *aȝen*
cause to return 1140; ~ *forþ* drag out
852; ~ *out* extract 975; ~ *out of* separate from 1329; ~ *to* attract to 66; ~
out extract 975; ~ *out of* separate from
1329; ~ *to* attract to 66; ~ *vp* cause to
rise up 1002; *intr.* incline 332. *pr. 2sg.*
drawst 810. *3sg.* **draweþ** 66, 332;
trawþ 690. *3pl.* **drawyþ** 852. *imp. sg.*
draw(ȝ 857, 1002. *pa.t.* **drow** 1145.
pp. **idrawe** 27, 1274, 1276; **drawen**
1148.
dredeles *adv. nay* ~ certainly not 447.
dredful *adj.* fearful 195; inspiring awe
250.
dreynte *v. pa.t.* drowned 1119. *pp.*
(i)dreynt 1069, 1132.
driwe *v.* constrain 14; compel 83; ~
awey dispel 600; ~ *out of* cause to
leave 671. *pr. 3sg.* **dryfþ** 14, 83. *pp.*
dryuen 671.
drunkeschipe *n.* drunkenness 140.
dul *adj.* depressed 1193.
dump *adj.* dumb 443.
dure *v.* persist 127, 351, 369; remain
185, 1042; bear (to do sthg.) 885. *pr.
3sg., pl.* **dureþ** 185, 351, 1042.
dwellen *v.* continue 1042; ~ *among*
associate with 139. *pr. 3sg.* **dwelleþ**
1042.

effecte *n.* carrying out 540, 542.
eȝe *n.* eye 871, 947, 991, 996. *pl.* **eȝen** 53,
123, 248, 326, etc.
eyr *n.* air 1215; climate (fig.) 1372.
eke *adv.* also 1171, 1414.

elemens *n. pl.* substances out of which all
material bodies were assumed to be
compounded; thus, the physical uni-
verse 1292.
elles *adv.* in another manner 258, 1056;
or (else) 283, 779, 1166; *or* ~ (or) con-
versely 100, 166, 188, 793, etc.
emcristen(e *n.* fellow-Christian 416,
416, 501, 523, etc.; **euene-cristene**
334. *pl.* **emcristene** 527, 538.
enbroude *v.* embroider 327.
enclinaunce ‡ *n.* tendency 353. [OF *enclinance*]
ende *n.* physical extremity 332 (1st),
1003; goal 332 (2nd); termination
1225, 1252; *makeþ an* ~ *of* ends 1236;
eende *wiþouten* ~ (with adjectival
force) eternal 1357.
enemy *n.* enemy (here, the Devil) 79,
101, 662; (as adj.) ill-disposed 1021.
pl. **enemys** 252, 1264, 1296.
ennys *adv.* see **hennys**.
ensaumple *n.* model of conduct to be
imitated 660.
entendaunt *adj.* attentive 440; *be* ~ *to*
accompany in order to do service
776.
ententyfly *adv.* earnestly 1230.
ententyly *adv.* with close attention 266;
with careful concern 799.
ent(i)erly *adv.* earnestly 603, 666, 779,
1180.
e(o)rþe *n.* see **irþe**.
er *conj., prep.* before 40, 169, 343, 370,
etc. *prep.* 1351.
ere, erys *n.* see **hiere**.
erraunt *adj.* straying 1088.
erris *n. pl.* foretaste 1246.
eschewe(n *v.* abstain from 199, 221;
escape 1228. *pr. 3pl.* **escheweþ** 1228.
esy *adj.* (of weather) calm 1164.
euel(e *adj.* see **vuel**.
euen(e *adv.* (intensive) exactly 529,
1304; fully 1266.
euene *n.* see **heuene**.
euene *adj.* equal in rank 1175.
euene-cristene *n.* see **emcristen(e**.
euen-sacrifise *n.* offering up of prayer in
the evening 98.
euere-durynge *adj.* eternal 1380.
euere-wellyngge *adj.* constantly flow-
ing 810.
euy *adj.* sorrowful 248; heavy 1209;
heuy 1209.

exclude v. prevent the occurrence of 791.

excusacioun n. ground of excuse 214, 1316.

excuse v. seek to remove the blame of 261; absolve 770. *pa.t.* **excusyde** 770.

faad adj. withered 269.

face n. face 188, 617, 631, 717, etc.; presence 1082; *aȝens here* ~ before them, in their sight 1315; ~ *to* ~ directly 1392; **fas** 617. See also **maugre**.

fader, fadur n. God the Father 314, 569, 655, 658, etc.; father 644, 1068, 1074, 1109.

fayle v. come to an end 335, 404; be mistaken 1104; come to nothing 1281; ~ *of* be lacking or wanting in 531, 1403. *pr. 3sg.* **fayleþ** 404, 1104, 1403. *3pl.* **fayled** 531.

fayn adv. willingly 1311.

faynt adj. barely perceivable 217.

falle v. fall 273, 1071; fall by lot 909; be brought to bear on 1120; turn out 1176; ~ *(a)doun* fall down in obeisance 164, 589, 839, 1005; ~ *aȝen to* lapse back to 487; ~ *in(to)* succumb to 211, 253; lapse into 228, 1097, 1125; ~ *on to* set about 238. *pr. 2sg.* **falst** 839. *3sg.* **falleþ** 273, 1176. *imp.* **val** 589. *pa.t. 1sg.* **fil** 1097. *2sg.* **vylle** 1005. *3sg.* **ful** 164, 238, 253; **fel** 909. *pp.* **yfalle** 1071; **falle(n** 1120, 1125.

fedeþ v. *pr. 3sg.* feeds 1214. *pa.t.* **vedde** 1183. *pp.* **ived** 781; **fed** 823; **ved** 1043.

fey n. faith 335, 1072.

feyned *ppl. adj.* pretended 335.

feyt n. faith 1231, 1241, 1248.

feyþfully adj. in truth 695, 1238.

felaschipe n. ~ *of* condition of being in company with 988; **felauschip** company of saved souls 1348.

feld n. field 1215.

feleþ v. *pr. 1pl.* perceive 219. *3pl.* **veleþ** 182. *pa.t. 1sg.* **felyd** 1121. *2sg.* **vieledest** 572.

felþe n. see **fulþe**.

fer adv. far 116, 1121.

fers adj. wild with rage 1294.

fersly adv. savagely 852.

ferst adv. in the first place 344, 555; **furst** 668.

feste n. feast, entertainment 741, 754, 791; *made* ~ *to* entertained 750. *pl.* **festes** 139.

fewe pron. few people 215.

fiewe adj. few 879, 1404.

fiȝte v. fight 156, 1264. *pr. 3pl.* **fiȝteþ** 1264.

fil v. *pa.t.* see **falle**.

fynde v. find 98, 203, 331, 400, etc.; obtain 325, 1315; **fynden** 203. *pa.t.* **fand** 615. *pp.* **yfounde** 400, 649; *be* ~ prove to be 1175; **founden** 676.

flecchyngge n. wavering 1192.

flehslich(e adj. carnal 65, 129, 161, 223; **flehsly** 282, 1115, 1117, 1203.

flem n. river 655.

flen v. *tr.* abstain from 289; avoid 660; *intr.* flee 609, 1121; fly 1209; **fle** 660. *pr. 3sg.* **fleþ** 609. *pp.* **flowe** 1121.

flesche n. flesh, body 44; **flehs** 78, 100, 128, 150, etc.; **flesh** 229.

flex n. flax 342, 344, 347, 355, etc.

flikt v. *pr. 3sg.* is flying 196.

flood n. river (fig.) 1119.

flour n. choicest one 268. *pl.* **floures** flowers 308, 1215.

foylede v. *pa.t.* defiled 1094.

foonde v. *imp.* try 962.

for *conj.* because 62, 87, 127, 132, etc.; in order that 697; (introductory, in answer to a question) because 1021; **vor** 62; **fur** 1273.

forbede v. forbid 714.

forbled *ppl. adj.* covered with blood 886.

forȝite v. forget 608, 634, 705, 839, etc. *pa.t.* **forȝat** 634. *pp.* **forȝyte(n** 839, 1245.

forȝyue v. forgive 708, 716, 735, 738, etc. *imp.* **forȝif** 931. *pp.* **forȝyue** 708, 735, 738.

fors n. *what* ~ *is it?* what difference does it make? 224; *haue þu neuere* ~ do not worry 763; *makþ no* ~ *of* pays no attention to 924.

forsmoteryd ‡ *ppl. adj.* bespattered, stained (with tears) 692, 948. [of ideophonic origin, f. the pt. pl. root of OE *smitan*; cf. ME *bismotered*]

forto prep. (merely introducing inf.) to 28, 71, 83, 138, etc.; in order to 152, 860, 967, 1171, etc.; **forte** 528.

forþere adv. *comp.* further 829.

foucheþ v. *pr. 3sg.* ~ *saaf* permits 691, 871. *imp.* **fowche** 871.

freel *adj.* fragile 22.
freelte *n.* moral weakness 194.
frehsly *adv.* so as to appear fresh or gay *789.
frely *adv.* generously 1063; **freoly** for nothing 1157.
frend *n.* see **vrend**.
fre(s)sche *adj.* bright 318; (of a countenance) fresh 779, 947; (of water) fresh, sweet 965; **frehs** 779.
fro *prep.* from 116, 180, 197, 210, etc.; on the grounds of 1316.
from *prep.* from 1294.
frotede *v. pa.t.* rubbed 159.
fructuous *adj.* producing good results 520; generous 1327.
fuyr *n.* fire 43, 45, 117, 119, etc.; **vier** 371, 572.
ful *v. pa.t.* see **falle**.
fulfylle *v.* fill 375, 473, 568, 570; complete 1286; fulfil 1393. *pr. 3sg.* **fulfelþ** 568. *pa.t.* **fulfelde** 570. *pp.* **fulfeld** 473, 1286, 1393.
fulsumly *adv.* abundantly 781.
fulþe *n.* filth 179, 1122; **vielþe** 352, 485, 552; **felþe** 891. *pl.* **vielþys** disgusting vices 1102; **fulþes** 1124.
fundement *n.* foundation 271, 272.
furnays *n.* furnace 43.
furst *adv.* see **ferst**.
fuul *adj.* evil, foul 67, 186, 191, 228, etc.; dirty, disgusting, despicable 865, 1207, 1272; horrible, evilly disposed 1070; **fowl** 186, 191, 231, 1115, etc.; **foul(e** 228, 236, 261, 552, etc.

gadere *v. tr. imp.* ~ *togydere* collect together into one 982. *pa.t.* **gadryde** accumulated 1098.
galewes *n.* gallows (here, the Cross) 900.
gan *v. pa.t.* began 155, 156, 237.
garnement *n.* garment 329, 888. *pl.* **garnemens** 907.
gastyngge *ppl. adj.* terrifying 1332.
gawe *v.* see **go**.
gendre *v.* engender 1400; give rise to 1413. *pp.* **igendred** 1400.
gentil *adj.* gracious 569; (conventional epithet) noble 985.
gete *v.* acquire 33, 133, 730, 795, etc.; win (a victory) 251; bring about 816; ~ *aȝen* recover 1171. *pa.t.* **gat** 251; **gaat** 730. *pp.* **ygete** 33, 816; **gete** 133; **geten** 814.

geþ *v. pr. 3sg.* see **go**.
gylous *adj.* treacherous 850.
gystes *n. pl.* guests 439, 465, 470.
gladyngge *ppl. adj.* cheering 1333.
gladly *adj.* joyful 996.
glose *v. pr. sub.* wheedle 108; deceive by flattery 131. *pa.t.* **glosede** 108.
gnawe(n *v. pp.* gnawed *1101, 1277.
go *v.* go 168, 555, 593, 610, etc.; be transformed 402; pass 1044; ~ *forþ* advance 600, 610, 684, 979, etc.; **goon** 610, 1356; **gon** 740, 1088, 1301; **goo** 1044. *pr. 3sg.* **goþ** 593, 643, 654, 659, etc.; **geþ** 849, 1032. *pr. sub. 1pl. (hortatory, with suffixed pron.)* **gawe** let us go 740; **gowe** 1066. See **ȝyde, wente**.
gode *adj.* well-intentioned 19, 369, 1192; virtuous 200, 201, 257, 316, etc.; careful 423, 427, 577, 663, etc.; (as conventional epithet) 646, 679, 713, 809, etc.; gentle 879; (as *n.*) virtuous people 1302; **good** 200, 201, 257, 316, etc.; **goode** 318, 369, 507, 809, etc.; **god** 543.
godh(e)ede *n.* the divine nature 576, 822, 1386.
godly *adj.* kindly 672.
Godward(e *n. phr. to* ~ appertaining to God 10; in respect of God 723.
good *n.* property 530; *do(o)* ~ act philanthropically 418, 430, 431, 501; *cowde no* ~ 1067 (see **canst**). *pl.* **godys** property, possessions 432, 453, 456, 456, etc.; **godes** 457, 457, 460, 499; **goodis** 458; **goodes** 461, 493.
g(o)odly *adv.* liberally 465; benignly 685; kindkly 867.
gostly *adv.* in a spiritual sense 272, 823, 964.
graunte *v.* allow 71, 703 (~ *forto* + *inf.* = allow to be + *pp.* 71); bestow 172, 712, 1222; concede 1034. *pr. 3sg.* **graunteþ** 1222. *pa.t.* **grauntede** 703, 712. *pp.* **igraunted** 172, 1034.
grauyngge *n.* sculpture 317. *pl.* **grauyngges** carvings 306.
grede *v.* cry out 560.
gredyly *adv.* eagerly 698.
gret *adj.* great 45, 75, 126, 132, etc.; **greet** 66, 71, 510, 513, etc.; **grete** 284, 360, 361, 365, etc. *comp.* **grettere** 617.
grettest *v. pa.t. 2sg.* greeted 1005. *3sg* **grette** 558.
greuaunce *n. witoute* ~ *of* without inflicting harm on 263.

greue *v. tr.* do harm to 418, 424, 425.

grynte *v. intr. pr. sub. 3sg.* ~ *wit* gnash (the teeth) 761. *pr.p.* **gryntyngge** 1309. [prob. blending of OE *grunnettan* and OE *grymettan*, poss. influenced by OE *grindan*]

gruccheþ *v. pr. 3sg., pl.* grumble enviously 484, 716, 762, 766, etc.

grucchynge *n.* ~ *of stomac* stomachache 220.

gulty *adj.* guilty 97.

ȝe *pron. 2pl.* you 421, 422, 1350, 1355, etc. *prepl.* **ȝouȝ** 422; **ȝow** 1351.

ȝe *interj.* indeed 860.

ȝerd *n.* rod 362, 904. *pl.* **ȝerdes** 890.

ȝeres *n. pl.* period of existence 404; **ȝer** years (in reference to age) 643.

ȝeue *v.* grant 17, 1128, 1426; give 28, 78, 78, 169, etc.; show 659; pronounce 667, 896, 899; inflict 927; impart 1445; **ȝyue** 382, 433, 495, 498, etc.; **ȝyuen** 451. *pr. 2sg.* **ȝifst** *521. *3sg.* **ȝift** 1154. *3pl.* **ȝyuen** 927. *imp.* **ȝif** 496, 503, 504, 517. *pa.t. sg.* **ȝaf** 436, 437, 1185. *pl.* **ȝaue** 1115. *pp.* **yȝyue** 17, 454, 462, 465, etc.; **iȝeue** 169, 1063, 1128; **ȝyue** 899; **iȝoue** 1154.

ȝyde *v. pa.t.* ~ *aȝens* went to meet 1181.

ȝyf *conj.* if 25, 45, 78, 88, etc.; *bote* ~ unless 425.

ȝyft(e *n.* gift 28, 135, 136, 137, etc.; quality 278. *pl.* **ȝyftes** 278, 1164, 1180, 1223, etc.

ȝynges *n. pl.* see **þyng**.

ȝit *adv., conj.* yet 174, 179, 185, 190, etc.; **ȝith** 829.

ȝouȝre *poss. adj.* your 890, 891.

ȝouȝtes *n. pl.* see **þouȝt**.

ȝouþe *n.* youth 234.

ȝung(e *adj.* young 599, 637, 1103; **ȝungge** (as *n.*) young people 134.

ha *v.* see **haue**.

ha *pron.* see **he**.

halde(þ *v.* see **holde**.

halewode *v. pa.t.* consecrated 69, 388; sanctified 569; **halwede** 569. *pp.* **halwed** 69.

half *n.* see **alf**.

halyde *v. pa.t.* drew out 538.

halt *v.* see **holde**.

halwen *n. pl.* saints 263.

ham *v.* see **be**.

hand *n.* hand 38, 39, 497, 794, etc. *pl.* **hondes** 713; **handys** 724, 801; **handes** 851, 854, 910, 975.

handle(n *v.* touch, stroke 800, 1020.

hangen *v. intr.* be suspended 379, 390, 624, 625, etc.; depend (on) 1214; ~ *doun* dangle 981. *pa.t.* **hyng(e** 624, 625, 913.

happyly *adv.* perhaps 695.

hard(e *adj.* severe 103, 1015, 1336, 1353, etc.; difficult 142; cruel 880, 890; not soft 918; oppressive 1147. *comp.* **hardere** 103. *sup.* **hardeste** *at þe* ~ at least 833.

hardely *adv.* assuredly 702.

harmles *adj.* free from harm 623.

haue *v.* have 71, 82, 161, 169, etc.; **han** 285. *pr. 2sg.* **hast** 33, 33, 93, 94, etc. *3sg.* **haþ** 4, 17, 19, 31, etc.; **haad** 725, 725, 726, 728, etc.; **had** 927, 1055; **heþ** 1061; **ha** 1339. *pl.* **haue** 179, 365, 455; **habbeþ** 215, 333; **haueþ** 452, 484, 946, 1049, etc.; **han** 464. *pa.t.* 1, *3sg., pl.* **hadde** 119, 156, 170, 172, etc. *2sg.* **haddest** 1004, 1010. *pp.* **ihad** 51, 386; **had** 156.

he *pron. 3sg. masc.* he 16, 16, *17, 34, etc.; **ha** 343. *acc., dat., prepl.* **hym** 16, 19, 109, 155, etc. *ethic dat.* **hym** 638. *gen.* **his** 29, 1150. *refl.* **hym** himself 242, 251, 293, 629; himself 574, 575.

hede *n.* take ~ (*of, to*) pay attention (to) 8, 155, 219, 226, etc.; (with direct obj.) 603; concern oneself about 509; observe 577, 582, 754, 851; **heede** 267, 423, 427, 509, etc.; **hied** 754.

hediþ *v.* see **huyden**.

heed *n.* head 687, 753, 759, 827, etc.; ruler 1363.

heep *n.* on an ~ all in a mass, together 1098.

heȝe *adj.* exalted 514, 654, 814, 1362; extreme 531, 1198, 1244; *an* ~ aloft (fig.) 1301; into an exalted position (in heaven) 1325; **heiȝ** 1198, 1244, 1301, 1325. *comp* **heyȝere** 654; **heȝȝere** 814.

helde *v. pa.t.* poured out 753.

hele *n.* healing 586, 711, 712, 1379.

helle-ȝates *n. pl.* the entrance to Hell 1292.

hem *pron.* see **þey**.

hem-self *pron. pl.* themselves 181, 214, 486.

hemward *pron. phr. to* ~ in respect of them 451.

hennys *adv.* away from here 168, 740; **ennys** 782.

hens-ward ‡ *adv.* away from here 805.

heo *pron. 3sg. fem* she 4, 11, 11, 51, etc.; **hy** 49. *acc., dat., prepl.* **heere** her 3; **heore** 73, 669; **here** 82, 87, 108, 108, etc.; herself 538. *refl.* **heore** herself 51, 68; **here** 283. See also **sche**.

heore *poss. adj.* her 53, 68, 72, 73, etc.; **here** 74, 79, 80, 81, etc.

here *v. tr.* hear 3, 86, 243, 443, etc.; listen to 314, 441, 655; **hiere** 314, 443, 494, 655, etc.; **heere** 953, 1352. *pa.t.* **herde** 243, 441. *pp.* **herd** 681.

here *poss. adj.* their 179, 179, 182, 189, etc.; **heere** 1273, 1360, 1360.

herfore *adv.* on this account 681.

herys *n. pl.* hairs 687.

hertyliche *adv.* devoutly 93.

hertly *adj.* from the heart, devoted 1264.

heste *n.* decree 14.

h(e)ete *n.* lust 100; heat 1292.

heuen(e *n.* Heaven 26, 30, 274, 300, etc.; sky 1131; **euene** 568, 1205.

heuy *adj.* see **euy**.

heuynesse *n.* burdensomeness 1235; *be to* ~ *(of)* be burdensome (to) 231, 1233.

hy *pron.* see **heo**.

hyder *adv.* ~ *and þyder* to and fro 438.

hydouse *adj.* abominable 1134.

hye *v.* hasten 805, 962, 962, 1263. *pr. 3pl.* **hiȝetþ** 1263.

hied *n.* see **hede**.

hier(e *adv.* here 431, 1367; **hir** 582, 829, 889, 933.

hiere *n.* ear 859; **ere** 860. *pl.* **heren** 697; **erys** 780.

hyng(e *v. pa.t.* see **hangen**.

his *poss. adj.* his 21, 35, 36, 38, etc.; its 31; **is** 31, 559, 585, 634, etc.; **hijs** 844.

hit *pron. 3sg. neut.* it 12, 19, 24, 25, etc.; (with pl. concord) 59; ~ *is* there is 733; **it** 74, 99, 117, 121, etc. *prepl.* **hym** 320.

h(o)o *pron.* see **who**.

holde *v.* consider 137, 194, 216, 283, etc.; retain 362; ~ *adoun* restrain 225; ~ *(one's) pees* remain silent 875, 1149. *pr. 1sg.* **halde** 1048, 1149. *3sg.* **halt** 137, 875. *1pl.* **haldeþ** 216. *pp.* **halde** 225.

homly *adv.* meekly 784.

hondes *n. pl.* see **hand**.

hool *adj.* sound in health 222, 1055; not cut up 909; perfect 1071; *make* ~ repair 1171; **hole** 1055.

hoold *adj.* see **oolde**.

h(o)olsum *adj.* beneficial 546, 982, 1246, 1328.

hoore-hows *n.* brothel 111, 117.

hoot *adj.* intense 571; (of tears) ardent 686; warm 968; **hote** 686.

hope *n.* hope 393, *733, 1143, 1214, etc.; **hoope** 1143.

hoppyngge *v. pr.p.* jumping 583.

horrour *n.* intense fear 1226, 1249, 1290, 1308; **orrour** horribleness 1315.

hou, how *adv.* how 11, 21, 22, 93, etc.; ? (in quasi-adjectival usage) what, how great 929, 1183; **ow** 341, 1133, 1139.

houre *n.* appointed time 254; short space of time 847; **our** moment 1298.

howte *v.* see **owest**.

huyden *v. tr.* conceal 697, 1312. *pr. 3sg.* **hediþ** 697. *pp.* **yhud** out of the public gaze 56; **hud** secret 1293.

hul *n.* hill 580.

humours, humores *n. pl.* morbid bodily fluids 141, (fig.) 357.

hure *poss. adj.* see **vre**.

husbondrye *n.* household duties 439.

i *prep.* see **in**.

ibete *v. pp.* beaten 357, 358, 887; **beten** 887.

ibouȝt *v. pp.* bought 26.

ychaunged *v. pp.* exchanged 299.

idel *adj.* slack 95; frivolous 243.

ydulled *v. pp.* ~ *in* grown weary of 482.

yliȝted *v. pp.* illumined 1196.

ilyke *adv.* equally 1173.

ymedlyd *v. pp.* mixed 912.

in *prep.* in 6, 6, 7, 11, etc.; on behalf of, in the name of 772; on 840; **i** (preceding the def. art.) 449, 1259.

incorporat *adj.* ~ *to* made one with 69.

ynemned *v. pp.* mentioned by name 64.

informaciouns *n. pl.* advice 1420.

ynlyche *adv.* extremely 238.

innocence *n.* the state in which one does no harm to oneself or to one's fellow man 417, 420.

ynow, inouȝ *adv.* fully, as much as well could be 181, 425, 426.

inpossible *adj.* impossible 20, 143.

instrumens *n. pl.* implements 1276.

inward(e *adj.* pertaining to the spirit 322, 438, 1146, 1422.

inwardliche, -ly *adv.* in one's inmost heart 81, 877, 1077, 1200.

iqueynt *v. pp.* extinguished 118.

yquyked *v. pp.* aroused to spiritual life 728.

irnestly *adv.* determinedly 694.

irþe *n.* clay 44; the ground 348, 668, 842, 1130; the world 568, 784, 884, 914, etc.; **erþe** 568; **eorþe** 1130.

irþely *adj.* not heavenly 669, 1084.

irþene *adj.* (of colour) earthy, like soil 342, 345.

irþi *adj.* grossly material 1111.

is *poss. adj.* see **his.**

ysacryd *v. pp.* sanctified 742.

ischad *v. pp.* see **sched.**

isee *v.* see 5, 195, 557, 1382; discern 630. *pp.* **yseye** in the public gaze 5; *be* ~ seem to be 291, 1151; **yseyen** 1382.

ystotid *v. pp.* faltered, stammered 1196. [ME *stoten*, of uncertain origin]

istrowed *v. pp.* strewn (with rushes) 789.

it *pron.* see **hit.**

ivisited *v. pp.* supplied (with some benefit) 571.

yweue *v. pp.* woven 307, 330; **yveue** 408.

iaperyes *n. pl.* fripperies 375.

iapes *n. pl.* deceptive trifles 289.

ielouste *n.* zealous vigilance 126.

jugge-sege *n.* judgment-seat 898, 1305.

iustefyeþ *v. pr. 3sg.* pardons (through divine grace) 680; declares free from the penalty of sin 1322. *pp.* **iustefyed** 1322.

iustyse *n.* judge 584.

kep *n. taak* ~ observe 806.

kepe *v.* preserve 23, 49, 207, 524, etc.; watch over 126; retain 133, 225, 922; *(refl.)* remain 267; look after 391, 396; reserve 1079, 1223; ~ *of* preserve from 1049; ~ *to* preserve for 1169. *pr. 3sg.* **kept** 126, 524; **kepþ** 1223. *pa.t.* **kepte** 922, 1096. *pp.* **ikept(e** 23, 1049, 1068, 1079, etc.; **kept** 133, 225, 1093, 1097, etc.

kepyngge *n.* looking after 227.

kynde *n.* nature 21, 419.

kyndom *n.* spiritual sovereignty (of Christ) 633.

kitte *v.* ~ *of* cut off 858.

kyttyngges *n. pl.* carvings 306.

kleppede, klepte *v.* see **cleppe.**

knet *v. pp.* joined together as if by knotting 319, 1329.

kni3t *n.* knight 585, (fig.) 974. *pl.* **knytes** soldiers 907, 960.

knowlechere *n.* one who acknowledges 935.

lappe *n.* bosom 610, 631, 807; fold of a garment 615.

lappeþ *v. pr. 3sg.* swathes 987. *pp.* **ilappyd** caressingly enfolded in cradle-wrappings 596.

laskyngge *n.* diminution 1386.

lassche *v. intr.* (of tears) pour 950.

laste *adj.* last 189, 235, 254, 331, etc.; *ate* ~ *of alle* after everyone else 802.

lattere *adv. neuere þe* ~ 163, 730 (see **neuere**).

ledyng *v. tr. pr.p.* taking the lead in (a dance) 55. *pp.* **ilad** caused to come 876, 900.

leem *n.* flame (fig.) 118. *pl.* **lemes** gleams (of light) 616.

left *adj.* left 39, 625, 1302, 1306; **lyft** 1338.

lefte *v. tr.* ~ *(vp)* raise 114, 724, 726, 1244, etc. *pr. sub.* **lyfte** 1313. *pp.* **left** 726; **ileft** 1244.

le33e *v. intr.* laugh 243. *tr. pa.t.* **low** ~ *to skorn* derided 109.

leyt *n.* flame 142.

leytyngge *ppl. adj.* incandescent 1297.

leiþ *v. tr. pr. 3sg.* deposits 987. *imp.* **ley** ~ *to* apply 687.

lene *adj.* thin 152.

leneþ *v. refl. pr. 3sg.* reclines 806.

lest *v. impers. pr. sub. hym* ~ he like 734.

let *v. tr. pr. 3sg.* stands in the way of 524. *sub.* **lette** may cause to be distracted from 1040.

lete *v. tr.* let (sb.) go 169, 1022; + inf. = cause to be + pp., have + pp. 327; leave 445, 1080, 1122, 1186; allow 610; ~ *adoun* lower 706; ~ *be* have nothing to do with 863. *imp.* **let** (special uses) = ought to 3, 16, 72, 82, etc.; = may 98, 127, 317, 318, etc.; cause 103, 339, 384, 510, etc. *pa.t.* **lete** 1122. *pp.* **lete** 706; **ylete** 1080, 1186.

leueþ *v. intr. pr. 3sg.* remains 645.

lieue *adj.* beloved 388. *comp.* **leuere** *haþ* ~ *to* chooses rather to 345.

lyf(e *n.* life 4, 7, 103, 179, etc.; **lyve** 1028.
lyfful *adj.* proper, appropriate 153.
lifnoode *n.* livelihood 497.
ligge *v. intr.* be placed 339; lie 599, 615; ~ *doun* lay oneself to rest 91. *pr. 2sg.* **lyst** 91. *3sg.* **lyþ** 599. *pr.p.* **liggynge** 615.
lyȝt *adj.* easy 21, 424, 426; frivolous 241.
liȝt *adv.* easily 1209.
lykynde *ppl. adj.* agreeable 383.
lykyngge *n.* delight 331, 1401; *haue ~ in* take pleasure in 337.
lynne *n.* flax 342, 360.
lynnene *n., adj.* linen 339, 370, 798.
liquour *n.* liquid 689. *pl.* **liquours** the blood and water from Christ's wounds 963.
lysse *n.* peace of mind 170.
liste *n.* ribbon 971.
lyte *adj.* small in amount 128.
lyueþ *v. intr. pr. 3pl.* conduct oneself 93; pass (one's life) (in the stated manner) 1137; (quasi-tr., with cognate obj.) 179; dwell 1205; ~ *of* depend for one's living on 459. *pp.* **ileued** 93; **lyued** 179.
loke *v. intr.* take care, be sure 49, 54, 80, 83, etc.; look 996, 1314; ~ *in* look at 946, 1388; ~ *(vp)on* regard 867, 871; *tr.* see 947; consider 1251. *pr. 3pl.* **lokeþ** 1314. *pa.t.* **lokede** 867.
lomb *n.* lamb (as metaphor for Christ) 53, *876.
lond *n.* dry land 1168.
longeþ *v. pr. 3sg.* ~ *to* is the concern of 451.
longynge *v. pr.p.* ~ *after* yearning for 1194.
longstrei(ȝ)t, -streyt ‡ *adv.* full length, prostrate 165, 840, 1005. [*long* (adv.) + pp. of ME *strecche* (< OE *streccan*)]
l(o)o *v. tr. imp., interj.* see, behold 256, 933, 954; *interj.* 889; ah! 1123, 1123.
lore *n.* teaching 441.
lotye *v. intr.* lurk 969, 1088, 1312.
lotyngge *n.* hiding 1227.
loue *n.* *þe book of* ~ the Song of Solomon 1418.
louyere *n.* lover 126.
low *v. pa.t.* see **leȝȝe.**
lust *n.* sinful sensuous desire 121, 191,

223, 262, etc.; illicit delight 173, 228, 231; relish 185; pleasure 338.

may *v.* see **mowe.**
mayde *n.* female virgin 18, 68, 118, 202, etc.; the Virgin Mary 392, 558, 560, 577 (2nd), etc.; male virgin 385, 945.
mayden *n.* female virgin 10, 44, 110; the Virgin Mary 384, 569, 578, 942. *g.* **maydenes** 44, 578, 942. *pl.* **maydenes** virgins of either sex 57, 60.
mayne *n.* family *293.
maister *n.* master 1009.
maister-þef *n.* leader of a band of thieves 614.
maieste, mageste *n.* sovereign glory and glory of God 573, 618, 799, 934.
make *v. tr.* cause to be or become 21, 52, 86, 103, etc.; bring about 31; construct 47, 291, 411, 574, etc.; furnish 471; perform, say 831; **maken** 831, 1422. *pr. 3sg.* **makþ** 31, 923; **makeþ** 343, 1236. *pa.t.* **made** 152, 574, 575, 750, etc.; **maade** 1051. *pp.* **maad** 21, 47, 565; **ymaad** 52, 353, 356, 554, etc.; **mad** 291; **ymad** 1055.
man *n.* man 47, 61, 62, 64, etc.; *maad* ~ incarnated 565; **mon** 432. *g.* **monnes** 296; **mannes** 754, 859. *pl.* **men** 8, 57, 190, 214, etc. *g.* **mannes** 178, 1151; **mennes** 285, 440, 800; **menne** 456, 499.
maner(e *n.* (quasi-genitival, with ellipsis of *of*, frequently with pl. construction) sort 72, 160, 211, 271, etc.; way 449, 543, 582; *in a* ~ almost entirely 872, 1245. *pl.* **maneres** conduct 1178.
manhoode, -hede *n.* humanity 504; the human nature in Christ 823, 937; *after þe* ~ as if he were human 835.
mankynde *n.* the human race 393; human nature 936; **mankende** *of on* ~ sharing in the common nature of man 1064.
matere *n.* things or something of the stated kind 299, 1098, 1099, 1100; cause 428; substance 1051; *in þis* ~ on this point 1231; **matyre** 1099. *pl.* **matyres** 259, 494.
material *adj.* actual, physical 117.
maugre *prep.* in spite of: ~ *þe pharises face* notwithstanding all the Pharisee can do 719.
me(e)de *n.* reward 22, 1426.

meete *v. intr.* ~ *togydere* meet 581;
become joined or mingled 707, 1116;
~ *wit* encounter 1086; come into the
presence of 1298. *pa.t.* **mette** 581, 707.

melk(e *n.* milk (fig.) 382, 823, 964.

menbres *n. pl.* parts of the body 67, 69,
575, 985, etc.; **menbrys** 207, 966,
990.

mende *n.* mind (as the faculty of memory) 205; thoughts 511; recollection
665; that which is remembered (*of*),
record (*of*) *1408; *brynge to þyn* ~
remind you of 374; *imaad* ~ *of* mentioned 554; *haue* ~ *of* remember 622,
633; **myende** 374, 511, 554, 622, etc.;
moynde *1408.

merciable *adj.* merciful 716, 1120.

merþe, murþe *n.* (religious) joy 587,
1282, 1377; *pl.* **murþes** delights 1200.

merueyl *n. what* ~ *þey* is it to be won-
dered at that 920.

meschyef, myscheef *n.* misfortune 541,
621. *pl.* **myscheues** 1050; evil-doings
1113.

meselrye *n.* leprosy 1056.

mesure *n.* the bounds of normal moderate conduct 248; *witouten* ~ im-
measurably 35.

mete *n.* food 82, 244, 472, 774; *in* ~
when eating 76, 96; *at þe, ate* ~ at
table, to eat 80, 685; *angeles* ~ manna
481; **meete** 774.

me-ward *pron. phr. to* ~ to myself 1151.

my *poss. adj.* my 125, 126, 442, 837, etc.;
myne 3; **myn** 778, 780, 1083, 1396;
me 1118.

myȝt *n.* capacity 185; *of al þy* ~ as much
as you can 1320.

miȝt(e, -est *v.* see **mowe.**

myȝtful *adj.* omnipotent 897.

ministre *v. tr.* impart 23; officiate at 458;
dispense 463, 1264; *intr.* serve at table
755; be of service to 773; ~ *to* attend to
the wants of 470. *pr. 3sg., pl.*
ministreþ 23, 458, 755.

myrie *adj.* pleasant 828; **murye** cheerful
1181.

my-self *pron. 1sg.* myself 1080; **me-self**
1094.

mysese *n.* suffering 151, 511.

mo *pron.* more (people): *no* ~ *bote* only
832.

mocioun *n.* impulse 161. *pl.* **mociouns**
urgings 152.

moder *n.* that which gives rise to and
nurtures 257; mother 293, 385, 388,
390, etc.; **modur** 560. *g.* **moder** 349,
583, 631, 1052, etc.

moynde *n.* see **mende.**

mon(nes *n.* see **man.**

mornyngge *ppl. adj.* listless 229.

morwe(n *n.* the immediate future 1211;
on þe ~ the next day 874.

mot *v.* must, ought to 77, 97, 226, 267,
etc.; (with ellipsis of v. of motion)
must go 371, 829; may, might 871,
937, 938, 1013, etc. *pr. 1sg.* **mot** 1020,
1020. *2sg.* **most** 97, 267, 289, 334, etc.
3sg. **m(o)ot** 77, 226, 541, 542. *pl.*
mote 361, 369, 371, 662. *sub.* **m(o)ote**
871, 937, 938, 1024, etc. *pa.t. 3sg.*
most 1013.

move *v. tr.* excite the emotions of 174;
prompt 795.

mowe *v.* be able to 11, 15, 25, 56, etc.; be
allowed to 16, 419, 431 (2nd), 1312.
inf. **mowe** 1312, 1339. *pr. 1, 3sg.* **may**
11, 15, 16, 25, etc. *2sg.* **myȝt** 195, 230,
290, 419, etc.; **miȝth** 654. *pl.* **mowe**
173, 340, 1045, 1060, etc.; **mowen**
410. *sub.* **mowe** 203, 207, 320, 386,
etc.; *þat þu* ~ to the extent that you
may be able, as far as possible 792.
pa.t. 2sg. **myȝtest** 847, 991, 1009,
1125, etc. *3sg.* **myȝte** 86, 117, 151,
228, etc.; **myte** 234. *pl.* **myȝte** 245.

murþe(s *n.* see **merþe.**

mutacioun *n.* alteration 403.

nadde *v. pa.t. sub.* had not 1125, 1126.

namely *adv.* especially 133, 499.

nat *adv.* see **not.**

naþeles *adv.* nevertheless 137, 175, 234,
257, etc.

ne *conj.* nor 62, 64, 131, 131, etc.

ne *adv.* not 133 (1st), 174, 186, 404
(2nd), etc.

necligent *adj.* remiss 95.

neyȝ *prep.* near 1014, 1015.

neyȝ *adv.* close 1153. *comp.* **nyer** 818.
sup. **nekst** in the immediately preceding passage 1269.

neyȝȝe *v. tr.* approach 1018.

nel *v. pr. 1, 3sg.* will not 40, 115, 168,
168, etc.; refuse to 137; do not wish
193, 304. *pl.* **nole** 115; **nulle** 137;
nulleþ 180.

neody adj. as n. pl. the poor 433.

netlys n. pl. nettles 160.

neþer adv. see **noþer**.

neuere adv. never 46, 168, 169, 169, etc.; not at all 193, 763; ~ þe lattere notwithstanding this 163, 730.

nyce adj. lascivious 101, 140; not serious 241, 243; effeminate 260; stupid 482.

nyede n. necessity 14, 83, 96, 1218; requirements 455, 500; lack 460, 1375; wants 514; (quasi predic. adj.) necessary 363; han ~ to require 464; **neode** 83, 96, 500.

nyede adv. of necessity 334.

nyedful adj. necessary 1043.

nys v. pr. 3sg. is not 42, 893. pa.t. sub. **nere** 221, 1068, 1205; were it not for 1101.

no adj. not any 13, 14, 14, 46, etc.; (predic.) none at all, non-existant 128; any 689; **non** 14, 637, 923, 1376, etc.; **noon** 128, 164, 219, 309; **noo** 398.

no adv. not 163; (with comp.) not any 820, 831.

no conj. nor 1305.

nobleye n. pomp 283.

noon adv. not 143.

not adv. not 5, 40, 42, 42, etc.; **nouȝt** 140, 141, 142, 446, etc.; **nouth** 524; **nat** 1126.

noþer adv. neither 306, 1368, 1403; **neþer** 493, 494, 857.

nouȝt n. nothing 1135.

noumbre n. full total 1286.

nulle(þ v. see **nel**.

nursche n. that which promotes the development of 258; foster-father 641.

nursche v. nourish 79, 546, 964, 1424; cherish in the heart 437; bring up 1067.

occasiones n. pl. opportunities 183.

ocupien v. employ 326, 473, 483, 537; (refl.) busy oneself 491; fill 854. pr. 3sg. **okepyed** 854. pp. **okepied** 473, 537; **y-ocupied** 483.

oynement n. unguent for anointing 688, 752, 753, 762, etc. pl. **oynemens** 986.

on prep. on 10, 203, 204, 205, etc.; (preceding a vbl. n., denoting an action) 876; **o** 508, 792, 1340.

on adj. one 160, 506, 847, 1042, etc.; (opposed to 'other') 319, 385, 471, 994, etc.; in a condition of uniformity 402, 403; (in weakened sense, merging into indef. art.) 611, 1133; **o** 319, 385, 471, 506, etc.; **oon** 402, 403, 994, 1042, etc.

oold(e adj. old 175, 180, 643, 1374; former 1179; (as n.) old people 134; **hoold** 175; **old** 643, 1374.

oon adv. alone 399.

oostes n. pl. multitudes 604.

open adj. exposed to view 122; frank 737; not closed 1293.

openly adv. plainly 188; publicly 1294.

opinio(u)n n. haue on/an ~ be firmly convinced 611, 636.

oratorie n. chapel 111; recluse's small private chapel 375.

ordeynede v. pa.t. appointed 463; predestined 1059; allotted 1339, 1366. pp. **y-)ordeyned** 463, 1366; **ordeyneþ** 1339.

orisoun, oryson n. prayer 826, 828.

orrible adj. hideous 1133, 1310.

orrour n. see **horrour**.

ostage n. inn 694.

oþer conj. or 224, 516 (1st).

oþurwhile, oþerw(h)yle adv. sometimes 82, 84, 154, 159, etc.

our n. see **houre**.

oure adj. see **vre**.

outerly adv. absolutely 1305; **otterlyche** completely 1359.

ouercome v. prevail over 161, 365, 600, 695, etc.; overwhelm 222; influence excessively 234, 513, 1033. pp. **ouercome(n** 161, 222, 234, 365.

ouermor adv. furthermore 360, 367.

ow adv. see **how**.

owest v. pr. 2sg. have an obligation (to) 1319. pa.t. 2sg. **outest** ought to 1107. 3sg. **howte** 424; **ouȝte** 1153, 1173.

owre adj. see **vre**.

owtly adv. in every detail 1285.

owtrage adj. inordinate 1112.

paal adj. pallid 946.

palsye n. paralysis 706, 729, 1056.

paltyk ‡ adj. suffering from paralysis 734. [AN *parletike]

pappys n. pl. nipples 822.

par prep. ~ caas 892, 1163 (see **caas**).

parfeccioun n. perfect state 75, 81, 532; fulfilling 332; holiness 526.

parfit adj. complete 304, 397, 1143, 1232, etc.; clear, pure 1258; unimpaired 1379.

parte v. tr. ~ to share out amongst 456.

parteners n. pl. partakers 1073.

party(e n. duty 127; allotted role 442, 445, 445, 446, etc.; part 535, 598; share 804, 819, 1150; body of people 1305, 1335; in þat ~ in that respect 1078.

partyneþ v. pr. 3sg. ~ to concern 423; is appropriate to 467; belong to as an attribute 540. 3pl. parteyneþ 423, 540.

passauntly adv. cursorily 957.

passyngge v. pr.p. surpassing 35. pp. ipassed exceeded 96, 247.

pees n. freedom from spiritual conflict 727, 1267, 1282; halt/halde (one's) ~ remain(s) silent 875, 1149.

peynture n. painting 317, 325. pl. peyntures 338.

peys n. weight 1209.

penaunt n. person doing penance 767.

persyde v. pa.t. stabbed 960. pp. persced punctured (fig.), broken 148.

pytous adj. merciful 672, 795, 866, 1194; prompted by feelings of pity 693; exciting compassion 920.

pytously adv. in a manner that excites pity 167, 900, 981; kindly 650.

pleyn adj. complete 730.

plentevous adj. abundant 1403, 1411.

plentevousnesse n. abundance 1401.

poeple n. pl. people 480, 748.

poynt n. particular item 1242.

poyntel n. stylus 1285.

poryngge v. pr.p ~ on gazing intently at 794.

possessioun n. property 452.

possyd v. pp. pushed 1122.

pouere adj. poor 292, 292, 293, 293, etc.; hapless 793; (as n.) poor people 394, 456, 511; pore 292, 440, 456, 465, etc.

pouerly adv. humbly 899.

pouerte n. lack of wealth 76, 374; renunciation of material possessions 283, 428, 544.

pryckes n. pl. prongs (of a comb) 364; tormentings 486.

prince n. ~ of prestys chief priest's 863.

principle n. origin 1224.

pryue adj. private 555; intimate 820; secluded 833; kept secret 1293.

pryuely adv. secretly 79; stealthily 685.

priuilegie n. divine dispensation 745; special God-given advantage 816.

priuitees n. pl. secret matters, mysteries 654.

professioun n. fact of being professed in a religious order 289, 520.

profitable adv. to someone's spiritual advantage 50.

proud(e adj. proud 156, 225, 277; pruyd 278.

proude n. pride 274; pruyde 277, 278, 279, 1300.

puysoun n. poison 1115.

pur adj. complete(ly) 618.

purgacioun n. purification of sin 658.

purge v. cleanse of physical impurities 361; purify of sin 1321, 1422. pp. ipurged, -yd 361, 1321.

purpo(o)s n. intention 19, 369, 427, 522, etc.

purpre adj. crimson 887.

pursuour n. persecutor 113.

purvyaunce n. provision 471.

put n. pit 1275, 1315.

putte v. put, place 44, 53, 262, 338, etc.; grant as protector 125; add 324; pour 798; subject 1336; impute 1340; ~ awey get rid of 200, 350, 361, 362, etc.; dismiss 1012; ~ byhynde reject 265; ~ forþ make (an utterance) 88, 605, 787; stretch out 794, 802; (refl.) offer oneself 595; ~ to challenge with 846; ~ vp put away 466; pote 605; put 1336. pr. 3sg. put 200, 798, 1235. pa.t. putte 846, 940. pp. iput 44, 125, 363, 370, etc.; put 265, 350, 727, 1035, etc.; iputte 1305.

queyntyse n. cunning 100.

quite n. serentiy 524. [L quiēt-, stem of quiēs; AN *quiete]

ray n. clothing 337.

ran v. see renne.

raueynous adj. predatory 196.

rauesceþ v. pr. 3sg. draw forcibly 67, 1117, 1198; take away 1010; ~ of deprive of 558. pa.t. rauysschede 1117. pp. irauesched 558; raueschid 1010; yrauyssched 1198.

real adj. royal 1365.

rebel adj. disobedient to God 1188.

rebuked ppl. adj. ashamed 235; irebuked downcast 1310.

receyue v. receive 658, 1148, 1155, 1156, etc.; give hospitality to 774. pr. 3pl. **receyveþ** 1155. imp. pl. **receyueþ** 1351.

recouerer n. witoute ~ irrecoverably 51.

rede v. pr. pl. read 728. pp. **yrad** 1195.

reed(e adj. red 966, 971, 971.

refreyne v. tr. repress 152, 246; hold back 210; restrain 1135.

refut n. refuge 164, 394.

rehersyngge v. pr.p. repeating 563. pa.t. **rehersede** mentioned 1127.

renne v. run 438, 588, 593, 822, etc.; flow 647, 841, 965, 1002; ~ in þy myende pass through your mind 511; ~ to approach hurriedly 842; ~ to . . . m(y)ende occur to the mind 204, 665; ~ þorou3 pierce 952. pr. 3sg. **renþ** 1029, 1029. pa.t. **ran** 438, 1140. pp. **runne** 1082.

resonable adj. endowed with reason 183.

resoun n. hit is ~ it is (only) reasonable 463.

resteyne ‡ v. quell, do away with 258. [OF resteign-, stem of resteindre]

revyn v. forcibly deprive of 928.

reward n. takþ no ~ of pays no heed to 925.

rychesse n. wealth 39, 76, 282, 290, etc.; valuable goods 1166. pl. **rychesses** riches 1169.

ryed n. reed, cane 884.

ryg n. back 881.

ri3twyse adj. sinless 1356, 1360.

ry3twisnesse n. justice 323, 904.

ryse v. pp. returned to life 1028.

ryth adv. very 142, 292, 828, 1073; ~ as just as 357, 363, 369, 967; ~ so in just the same way 348, 358, 364, 371, etc.; **ry3t** 292, 348, 357, 363, etc.

rodye adj. fresh-complexioned 951.

roode n. the Cross of Christ 390.

rote n. source 275.

roted v. pp. implanted 233.

rude adj. ~ to ignorant of 474.

saade v. tr. weary of 82.

sacramens n. pl. solemn ceremonies of the Church 1072.

say v. see **see**.

say, sayd(e, say3t, sayn, sayþ v. see **seye**.

saluede v. pa.t. greeted 584.

satisfaccioun n. performance of deeds of penance 367.

sauery adj. pleasant 780, 972.

sauerly adv. with enjoyment 807.

sauour n. perfume 31; merit 298; taste (fig.) 1146.

schadue n. foreshadowed image 198.

schal v. ought to 7, 53, 63, 71, etc.; (forming future) shall 46, 321, 322, 325, etc.; (forming subj.) 61, 174, 213, 254, etc.; (forming conditional subj.) 85; be going to 611, 1044, 1238; (forming conditional) 1099, 1100, 1100. pr. 1, 3sg. **shal** 46, 63, 321, 322, etc. 2sg. **schalt** 7, 124, 325, 380, etc. pl. **schul** 366, 1292, 1312, 1355; **schulle** 471, 491, 647, 738, etc.; we ~ goo let us go 1044. subj. **schulle** 85, 949. pa.t. 1, 3sg., pl. **scholde** 53, 174, 213, 456, etc.; **schulde** 71, 202, 254, 258, etc. 2sg. **schuldest** 61, 95, 266, 295, etc.; **schost** 424; **scholdest** 578, 970, 1210.

schame n. shame 71, 84, 1311; disgraceful conduct 178; modesty 600, 791; disgrace 1174, 1179; be to ~ to be an object of shame or revulsion to 1058; **schome** 791.

schap n. form, appearance 34.

sche pron. 3sg. fem. she 54, 74, 77, 78, etc.; **schee** 556; **she** 613. See also **heo**.

sched v. imp. ~ (out) spill 46; pour out (fig.) 518, 758; **scheed** 758. pp. **ischad** 46.

Schereþursday n. the day before Christ's crucifixion (Maundy Thursday) 790.

scheryngge n. on ~ being shorn 876.

schette v. subj. confine 1207.

schorte adj. in ~ wordes concisely 1408.

schortly adv. to speak briefly 369; concisely 535.

schost v. see **schal**.

schrewes n. pl. evil people 896.

schryfte n. confession 367.

schuch adj. see **such**.

schurges n. pl. whips 882.

see v. see 233, 242, 243, 483, etc.; observe, catch 621; understand 1342. pr. 2sg. **sykst** 901, 950, 952, 1342. pa.t. **saw** 233, 243; **say** 242; **sey3** 992. pp. **seyen** 1382, 1383; **seyn** 1387; **seye** 1389, 1391, 1392.

seye *v.* say 12, 28, 522, 676, etc.; **seyn** 211, 259, 410, 417, etc.; **sayn** 279, 1369; **say** 525, 1337; **sey** 1238. *pr. 3sg.* **seiþ** 9, 15, 16, 41, etc.; **seyd** 167, 420; **seyt** 302, 888, 903, 955, etc.; **sayȝt** 525; **sayþ** 944, 1393. *pl.* **seyn** 181, 187, 530. *pa.t.* **sayde, seyde** 255, 405, 502, 635, etc. *pp.* **sayd** 63, 488; **yseyd** 446, 624, 735, 744, etc.; **seyd** 1279, 1368.

seynt *n.* saint 389, 392, 502, 525, etc.; **sein** 592.

seluer *n.* silver 105, 1208.

sennes *n. pl.* see **sunne** *n.*[2]

sentence *n.* passage (from the Scriptures) 206; apophthegm 671; judgment 899, 1335, 1344.

seruaunt *n.* servant 584, 873, *pl.* **seruauns** 462, 1222.

seruitute *n.* thraldom 1244.

seþþe *conj.* see **soþþe**.

siȝȝe *v. imp.* sigh 94, 166, 674; ~ *to* aspire to 81. *pr.p.* **siȝȝyngge** 81, 166. *pa.t.* **siȝȝyde** 674.

siker *adj.* feeling secure 181, 193, 678; certain 880, 892.

sikyngge *n.* sighing 1024, 1243.

symple *adj.* humble 933.

simplenesse *n.* innocence 322, 341.

singuler *adj.* one's own personal 1417.

synne(s *n.* (*pl.* see **sunne** *n.*[2]

sister *n.* see **suster**.

syt *v. pr. 3sg.* sits 685, 755, 898. *pa.t.* **saat** 248, 440, 751.

skyl(e)ful *adj.* proper 117, 459; **skilful** reasonable 264.

skorne *v. pr. sub. 3sg.* mock 762. *pp.* **yskorned** taunted 191.

sleere *n.* killer 934; that which destroys 1252.

slekþe *n.* ruse 1228.

slen *v.* kill 110, 167, 861; **sle** 1086. *pa.t.* **slow** struck down 112.

slow *adj.* dilatory 477, 479; **slouȝ** 480.

smal *adj.* slender 568. *comp.* **smallere** of lesser dimensions 364.

smarte *adj.* painful 927.

smelleþ *v. pr. pl.* have an inkling of 217. *pr.p.* **smyllyngge** giving out a perfume 990.

smyte *n.* clamour 1040.

smyte *v.* send 30; strike 94, 650, 717, 1070; lash (fig.) 426; pierce (fig.) 486; afflict 705; impose 1344; ~ *batayl*

aȝens engage in a struggle against 238; ~ *of* cut off 859; ~ *adoun* destroy 1132. *pr. 3sg.* **smyt** 717, 1344. *pa.t.* **smot** 650, 1132. *pp.* **ismyte** 486, 1070; **ysmete** 705.

smokede *v. pa.t.* ~ *vp* billowed up like smoke (fig.) 1111.

sodeyn *adj.* immediate 112.

soerte *n.* peace of mind 171, 1325, 1377; certitude 1241, 1249; **sourtee** 1241; **surtee** 1249, 1325, 1377.

softe *adj.* gentle 673; (of weather) mild 1164.

sollennely *adv.* solemnly 898.

sooþ *n.* the truth 188.

sooþfastnesse *n.* truth 566.

so(o)þly *adv.* indeed 1173; with truth 1279.

sorwe *n.* grief 84, 171, 210, 214, etc.; *be to* ~ *to* be a source of grief to 1234.

soþ *adj.* true 611, 636, 1318.

soþþe *conj.* since 432, 497; **seþþe** 490, 499, 916, 919.

spatelyn(g)ge *n.* spittle 865, 891.

spende *v.* occupy 74.

spice *n.* sort 286. *pl.* **spices** 276.

spild *v. pp.* destroyed 148; allowed to fall to the earth 843.

spiritualte *n.* (attachment to) the things of the spirit 474.

spytous *adj.* cruel 934.

spreed *v. imp.* ~ *aboute* distribute 505. *pp.* **y)sprad** ~ *abrood* (having the arms) stretched out 380, 910.

sprynge *v.* ~ *out of* grow or be born from (fig.), have its origins in 275, 586, 1400, 1411. *pr. 3sg.* **sprynkt** 1400. *pa.t.* **sprang** 586.

stedefast(e *adj.* resolute 791, 935, 1214; **studefast** 1038.

stee *v. pr. sub., imp.* ~ *vp* ascend 398, 580.

steyned *v. pp.* ornamented (with coloured designs, etc.) 307.

stench *n.* foul smell 1278, 1308; (fig.) 185, *552; evil-smelling properties 299, 1099; **stenc** *552.

stened *v. pp.* stoned (to death) 478.

steryngge *n.* incitement 146; **styryn(g)ge** 1112, 1114.

sterres *n. pl.* stars 35.

sterte *v. pa.t.* rushed 614.

styngyn(g)ge *ppl. adj.* foul(-smelling) 107, 297.

stynkynde *ppl. adj.* foul(-smelling) 141, *179, 357, 478, etc.
styre *v.* incite, stimulate 100, 102, 397, 635, etc.; **styrye** 1412. *pp.* **styred** 100; i)**steryd** 723, 1046, 1096.
stonde *v.* stand 249, 249, 793, 842, etc.; ~ *stille* persist 691. *pr. 2sg.* **standest** 842. *3sg.* **stant** 878, 899. *pl.* **stondeþ** 919, 943; **standeþ** 1309. *imp.* **stand** 691; **stond(e** 793, 1334. *pa.t.* **stood** 249, 249.
straunge *adj.* adventitious 919; cold in demeanour 1021.
strecche *v.* exert to the utmost 73.
streyneþ *v. pr. 3sg., pl.* bind 853; clasp tightly 977.
streyt *adj.* strict 363. *comp.* **streytere** 127.
streytnesse *n.* poverty 293.
strengþe *n.* power of action 78; moral fortitude 1004, 1378; **strenkþe** 1004; **strencthe** 1378.
studeþ *v. pr. 3sg.* ~ *on* applies the mind to 10.
such(e *adj.* such 127, 1113, 1123; **schuch** 17; **swych(e** 153, 251, 288, 308, etc.; **swich(e** 190, 677, *1012.
suffre *v.* undergo 171, 220, 1122; submit patiently (to) 255, 255, 856, 895, etc.; allow 771, 881 (2nd), 1056, 1313; tolerate 854, 881(1st), 1134.
suggestioun *n.* tempting 147, 199.
sumdel *adv.* to some extent 182.
sunne *n.*[1] sun 35, 916.
sunne *n.*[2] sin 183, 869; **synne** 185, 259, 274, 346, etc. *pl.* **sennes** 677; **synnes** 708, 710, 717, 730, etc.
superfluites *n. pl.* things that are in excess of what is necessary 361, 362.
surtee *n.* see **soerte.**
suster *n.* sister 142, 193, 266, 302, etc.; **sister** 442. *pl.* **sustren** 435, 536.
suttylly *adv.* ingeniously 408.
suttilte *n.* skilful assiduity 982.
swast *v. pr. 2sg.* sweat 841.
swolewode *v. pa.t.* ~ *in* swallowed up 1131.

take *v.* take 8, 15, 16, 83, etc.; hand over, give up 70, 1277, 1421; regard 75; (*refl.*) betake oneself 182; ~ *to* (*refl.*) adopt as a habit 242; adopt as a way of life 283, 428; **taken** 70, 182. *pr. 3sg.* **takþ** 893, 923, 925. *pa.t.* **took(e** 235,

242, 573, 752, etc. *pp.* **take** 228, 283, 348, 396, etc.; **itake** 347, 453, 455, 467, etc.
teylys *n. pl.* tiles 706.
temprure *n.* moderation 324.
tent *n.* **tak** ~ notice, pay attention 877.
tenty *adj.* assiduous 20.
ter *adv.* see **þer.**
tetys *n. pl.* teats 382.
t(e)eþ *n. pl.* teeth 761, 1309.
tympane *n.* sort of tambourine 55.
to *prep.* for 52, 52; a source of 1058 (2nd).
to-berste *v. intr. pr. sub.* shatter 45; **to-burste** 919. *tr. pa.t.* **to-barst** 1146.
to-bollen *ppl. adj.* exceedingly swollen up (with weeping) 948.
to-breke *v. tr.* utterly break 1016. *pp.* **to-broke** 1171.
to-comyngge *ppl. adj.* future, yet to come 218, 678.
to-fore *adv.* on ahead 830; in front 1363; *longe* ~ long ago 588.
toforhand *adv.* previously 241.
toforn, -fore *prep.* in preference to 18, 262, 585; in front of 53, 250, 706, 899, etc.; before 1049.
to-gydere *adv.* together 319, 389, 506, 581, etc.; simultaneously 1289.
to-kit *v. pp.* cut up in pieces 909.
to-teryþ *v. pr. pl.* lacerate 852. *pp.* **to-torn** 881.
towayles *n. pl.* altar-cloths 339.
to . . . ward(e *prep. phr.* towards 10, 450, 613, 723, etc.
trauayle *v. intr.* work (hard) 138, 436, 529, 773; *tr.* torment 1070. *pr. pl.* **trauayled** 529.
trawþ *v. pr. 3sg.* see **drawe.**
trest *n.* confidence 942; **trust** 1214.
tretiþ *v. pr. 3sg.* handles 985.
tretourusly *adv.* treacherously 875.
trewely *adv.* indeed 132, 189, 768, 815, etc.; correctly 1279; **trywely** 189.
turne *v. tr.* transform 110, 112, 963; direct 629, 778, 780, 992, etc.; ~ *aboute* ponder on 80; (*refl.*) ~ *fro* give up 1137; *intr.* ~ *aȝen* return 1144; ~ *aȝen to hymself* become pensive 868. *pr. 3sg.* **turned** 594.

þank *n.* gratitude 1155.
þanke *v. imp.* give thanks to 507; **þonke** 790.
þat *pron. rel.* who, whom 4, 19, 34, 41,

etc.; that, which 10, 12, 29, 53, etc.;
whoever 401; *who* ~ whoever 15, 735,
1085.

þat *conj.* (in absolute usage, introducing a
command) 85; when 254.

þat *adj., pron. demons.* that 20 (2nd), 32,
54 (1st), 56 (1st), etc. *pl.* **þo** those 189,
394, *513, 1409; **þeo** 454, 507; **þoo**
459, 461, 469, 508, etc.

þat *adv. rel.* to the extent that 792.

þe *def. art.* the 6, 9, 13, 15, etc.; **þo** 215,
667, 1239.

þef *n.* thief 617, 624, 852; **þyef** 958. *pl.*
þeues 613; **þieves** 910.

þey *pron. 3pl.* they 180, 181, 181, 182,
etc.; **þe** 527 (1st), 1355. *oblique cases*
hem them(selves) 137, 154, 180, 182,
etc.

þey *conj.* though 186, 219, 221, 761, etc.;
(even) if 202, 425, 917, 920; **þeiȝ** 202,
1158, 1205; **þeyȝ** 221, 761.

þenke *v. intr.* ~ *on, of* meditate on 10,
203, 204, 970; *tr.* think, consider 105,
122, 386, 1205; conceive of 173, 1367.
pr.p. **þenkynde** 204. *pp.* **þouȝt** 173,
1367.

þens *adv.* thence 1146; **þannys** 1361.

þer(e *adv., conj.* there 172, 199, 210,
215, etc.; then 506, 509, 511; ~ *þat*
where 128, 240, 263, 1206, etc.; **ter**
*1308. *conj.* where 241, 599, 705.

þer-in *adv.* in it 344; **þryn** in that place
959.

þewes *n. pl. goode* ~ virtues 318.

þyder *adv.* see **hyder**.

þyng(e *n.* thing, matter 431, 433, 957,
1238, etc. *pl.* **þyn(g)ges** 10, 153, 266,
303, etc.; **þyng** 18, 239, 1218, 1383,
etc.; **ȝynges** 277.

þirlyd *v. pp.* pierced 911; **iþirled** 1019.

þis *adj., pron. demons.* this 4, 6, 11, 15,
etc.; **þyse** 539. *pl.* **þyse** these 49, 59,
60, 184, etc.; **þeose** 255; **þis** 1073.

þo(o *adv.* then 164, 628, 977, 1034,
etc.

þorou(ȝ *prep., adv.* through 21, 45, 146,
147, etc.; **þoruȝ** 510; **þouȝr** 911;
þorow 1242.

þouȝt *n.* mind 74, 103; thought 94; heed
472. *pl.* **ȝouȝtes** 552.

þrast *v. imp.* press 601.

þrof *adv.* thereof 455, 1226; **þerof** 507,
733, 823.

þu *pron. 2sg.* you 7, 18, 22, 33, etc.;

þe 425. *oblique cases* **þe** 19, 20, *21,
21, etc.

vnderfonge *v.* entertain 439, 469; receive *657, 1365.

vndernam *v. pa.t.* rebuked 625; **vndernome** 1103.

vndernymyngge *n.* reproof 651, 846.

vnderset *v. pp.* strengthened, supported
722.

vnkynde *adj.* ungrateful 1143.

vnlifful *adj.* reprehensible 121, 152.

vnlyfsum *adj.* ridiculous 375.

vnlusty *adj.* lazy 479.

vnneþe *adv.* barely 1167.

vnsyker *adj.* insecure 176.

vnþryfty *adj.* withered *1272.

vpon *prep.* upon 120, 509, 672, 867, etc.;
vp-an 225.

vppon *prep.* upon 339, 720, 1083, 1103,
etc.; **vp** 784, 902.

vre *poss. adj.* our 31, 609, 614, 662, etc.;
oure 214, 356, 358, 369, etc.; **owre**
261, 348; **hure** 613.

vuel *adj.* wicked 67; **euel(e** 428, 1178.

val *v.* see **falle**.

vattere *adj. comp.* more fruitful 722.

ved(de *v. pa.t.* see **fedeþ**.

veynes *n. pl. wit alle þe* ~ *of his herte*
fervently 631.

veleþ *v. pr. pl.* see **feleþ**.

venenous *adj.* pernicious 276.

verrey, **-ay** *adj.* properly so named 31,
584, 585, 839, etc.; real, true 262, 338,
338, 736, etc.; possessing all the essential qualities of that which is named
655, 759, 759, 766.

vieledest *v. pa.t. 2sg.* see **feleþ**.

vielþe *n.* see **fulþe**.

vier *n.* see **fuyr**.

vylle *v. pa.t.* see **falle**.

voydede *v. pa.t.* absconded 107.

voys *n.* voice 605, 655, 673, 681, etc.;
utterance 597; opinion 765; **veys** 314;
uoys 997.

vor *conj.* see **for**.

vorheed *n.* audacity 290.

vre *adj.* spontaneous 13.

vrend *n.* companion 33; **frend** friend 591.

wayte *v. imp.* observe carefully 593.

wakyngge *n.* keeping vigil 212, 544;
walkyngge 603.

warde *n. haue* ~ *of* have in safe-keeping 391.

warsche *v.* protect 967.

water-veynes *n. pl.* flood-gates (of tears) 1001.

wawes *n. pl.* waves 1166.

wax *v. pa.t.* see **wexe**.

we *pron. 1pl.* we 216, 217, 217, 218, etc.; **whe** 1067, 1068. *oblique cases* **vs** 216, 291, 363, 366, etc.

weepful *adj.* mournful 1307; **wyepful** 1352, 1357.

wene *v.* suppose 61; count on 138.

wente *v. pa.t.* walked about 248; went 613, 1036. *pp.* **went** gone 1081.

wepen *v. intr.* weep 165, 674, 721, 747, etc.; ~ *vpon* weep for 509. *imp.* **wyep** 509. *pa.t. 2sg.* **weptest** 1102. *3sg.* **wiep** 674; **wepte** 747, 868.

werk *v. tr.* manipulate 358; make 908; *intr.* ~ *vppon* be brought to bear against 1114. *pp.* **iwrou3t** 908; **ywrout** 1114.

wettyngge *v. pr.p.* see **whot**.

wexe *v.* become 156, 235, 241, 269; increase 549. *pr. 3sg.* **wext** 269. *pa.t.* **wax** 235, 241.

whan(ne *adv.* when 66, 91, 99, 107, etc.; **when** 551; **wan(ne** 643, 703, 1140.

whasch *v. imp.* wash 686, 799, 803, 804, etc.; **whash** 866. *pa.t.* **wyste** 799. *pp.* **i)whasschen** 803, 804.

what *pron.* (indef.) something 531.

what *adv.* (introducing adv. phr. formed with prep.) in consequence of 146, 146, 147; ~ *þu?* what in the case of you?, what about you? 915.

what *conj.* until 974.

whepyngge *n.* lamentation 511, 951; **wepyn(g)ge** 1010, 1023, 1370, 1414.

wher-aboute *adv.* why 842.

wherre *n. in* ~ at war 516.

wherto *adv.* to which 332; why 498.

wheþur, -ur *adv., conj.* whether 99, 143, 187, 224; *conj.* (introducing simple or disjunctive direct question) 294, 447, 688, 776, etc.; **whoþer** 143, 224, 688, 776, etc.; **where** 1164.

whyche *pron. rel., adj.* which 13, 27, 33, 50, etc.; **whuche** 20, 26, 27, 33; **whic** 124, 145, 257, 268, etc.; **whyce** *178; **wych(e** 410, 452, 586, 625, etc.

whydur, whider, -ur *adv.* whither 54, 653, 782, 1081, etc.; **wyder** 1081; **whedur** 1087.

who *pron.* who 15, 16, 735, 889, etc.; **ho** 679, 680, 806, 854; **hoo** 955, 1389. *acc., prepl.* **whom** 17, 57, 392, 401, etc.; **wham** 111, 118. *g.* **whos** 52, 52, 403, 445, etc.

w(h)ot *v. pr. 1sg.* know 854, 884, 1368. *2sg.* **wost** 331, 1181. *imp.* **wite** 121, 1124, 1173. *pr.p.* **wettyngge** 1335. *pa.t.* **wyste** 617.

wyckenesses *n. pl.* sinful deeds 1162.

wydues *n. pl.* widows 512. *g.* **wydue** widows' 457.

wyep *v. imp., pa.t. 3sg.* see **wepen**.

wy3t *n.* whit 495.

wyl *v. auxil.* wish to 5, 138, 272, 527, etc.; (forming conditional) 101, 102, 109, 110, etc.; (forming future) 114, 198, 330, 695, etc.; (forming conditional perfect) 247; intend to 535, 714, 857; *intr.* like to 202, 421, 425, 1334; *tr.* desire 1136, 1381. *pr. 1, 3sg.* **wyl** 198, 330, 535, 622, etc.; **whyle** 1136; **wyle** 1336; **wylle** 1427. *2sg.* **wylt** 272, 328, 646, 714. *pa.t.* **wolde** 101, 102, 109, 110, etc.; **woolde** 421, 777.

wildenesse *n.* licentiousness 222.

wylful *adj.* voluntary 12.

wilfully *adv.* willingly 1097.

wylne *v. imp.* wish 430.

witdrawe *v. tr.* remove 154, 240; make grasping 726; divert 1199; (*refl.*) abstain 180; go away 943. *imp.* **wyþdraw** 943. *pa.t.* **witdrow** 154, 240. *pp.* **witdrawe** 726, 1199.

wite *v. imp.* see **whot**.

wyth *adj.* white 343; **whith** 353; **whit** 370, 1326.

wit-seie *v. tr.* speak against, derogate 257; **wiþ-seyn** 732.

wyþ *prep.* with 6, 18, 26, 248; **wit** 19, 49, 55, 59, etc.; against 694; **whit** 290; **wy3** 992.

wiþstonderes *n. pl.* opponents 1265.

womman *n.* woman 49, 64, 131, 201, etc.; **wymman** 62, *665; **wumman** 62, 676, 954. *pl.* **wymmen** 57, 60, 590; **wommen** 140, 260, 449; **wummen** 919, 943, 1031.

wondur *adv.* exceedingly 149.

wondurliche *adv.* exceedingly 284.

wood *v. pp.* enticed 1069.

woodschype *n.* shamelessness 178; madness 732.

wordle *n.* world 4, 6, 282, 354, etc.; wordl 1182; world 1352.

wordliche *adj.* not spiritual 106, 244, 432, 452, etc.; wordly 444, 488, 527, 530, etc.; worldly 493.

woundes *n. pl.* wounds 890, 927, 966; wondes 983.

woundour *n.* object of admiration 294, 297, 298; fact or matter to cause surprise 916, 917, 918, 1086; wundur, -er 298, 916, 917; woundur 918; wonder 1086.

wrastle *v. imp.* strive earnestly 694.

wrecche *adj.* hapless 1087.

wryten *v.* relate 58; describe, record 626, 978, 1285, 1368, etc; draw 668. *pa.t.* wroot 668. *pp.* iwryte(n 58, 626, 978, 1417; wryte(n 1368, 1408.

wroþ *adj.* angry 238, 893, 1294.

wurm *n.* noxious animal 1070. *pl.* wormes worms, maggots 1100; wurmes 1277.

wurschipe, wor– *n.* rank, dignity 902; reverence 1150, 1160; esteem 1239.

wurschipful *adj.* majestic 882.